P9-APY-539

**Physical Education and the
Physical Educator:
An Introduction**

Physical Education and the Physical Educator

AN INTRODUCTION

JAMES A. BALEY

*Chairman of Physical
Education Department;
Professor of
Physical Education,
Jersey City St. College*

DAVID A. FIELD

*Director of Arnold
College Division,
College of Education,
University of Bridgeport*

ALLYN AND BACON, Inc.
Boston

TO THE
PHYSICAL EDUCATION PROFESSION

Library of Congress Catalog Card Number:
69-17386

Printed in the United States of America.

Second printing . . . August, 1970

Table of Contents

Preface   xiv

PART I: THE PREPARATION AND WORK OF THE PHYSICAL
EDUCATOR   1

1: The Nature of Physical Education   3

Definitions of Physical Education   4
Physical Education As a Part of General Education in the
Schools   6
How Physical Education Contributes to the NEA Objectives   7
Principles of Physical Education   13
Values in Physical Education   14
AAHPER's Platform for Physical Education   15
Common Misconceptions About Physical Education   17
The Objectives of Physical Education   22
    Physical Fitness   22
    The Human Is an Entity   24
    Emotional Needs   25
    Emotional Catharsis   26
    Social Fitness   27
    Intellectual Development   27
    "Carry-over" Sports or Preparing for Future Needs   27
    Development of Motor Skills   28
    Protection of Students' Health   28
Problems and Goals for Physical Education During Coming
Decades   29
Summary   32
Questions   33
Projects and Activities   34
Footnotes   35

2: The Preparation of a Physical Educator   36

Personal Qualities Desired   36
Undergraduate Preparation   38
    Competencies   39

Recommendations of the Professional Preparation Confer-
ence for Teacher Education in Physical Education   42
A Justification for the Recommended Competencies   48
    General Education   48
    Communications   50
    Social Science   50
    Political Science   51
    Economics   51
    Physical Sciences   52
    Humanities   52
    Objectives of Professional Preparation   53
Continuing Professional Growth   55
    Professional Organizations   55
    Clinics   58
    Research   59
    Publishing   59
    Graduate Preparation (Master's Degree)   60
    Graduate Preparation (Doctorate Degree)   61
Summary   62
Questions   64
Footnotes   65

3: The Physical Educator at Work in the Schools   67

Physical Education Activity Classes   67
Intramural Programs   69
Coaching   70
Camping and Outdoor Education   73
Dance   73
Adapted Physical Education   74
Research   75
Various Physical Education Environments   76
    Physical Education in the Elementary Schools   76
    Physical Education in the Junior High Schools   77
    Physical Education in the Senior High Schools   78
    Physical Education in Colleges and Universities   80
Teaching in the Teacher Education Program   82
Teaching in the Graduate Program   83
Administration of Athletics and Physical Education   83
Directing Physical Education   84
Directing Athletics   84
Summary   85
Questions   85
Bibliography   86

4: Duties of Physical Educators Who Teach Outside the Schools   87

Young Men's and Young Women's Christian Associations   87
Young Men's and Young Women's Hebrew Association or
Jewish Community Centers   90

Boys' Clubs   91
Community Recreational Service Programs   92
Industrial Recreational Programs   93
Athletic Clubs   94
Summer Camps   95
Armed Services   97
Summary   98
Questions   98
Footnote   99

5: **Organizations to Which Physical Educators May Belong**   **100**

National Education Association   101
American Association for Health, Physical Education, and
Recreation   102
National Girls' Athletic Association   105
Athletic and Recreation Federation of College Women   105
International Council on Health, Physical Education, and
Recreation   106
National College Physical Education Association for Men   107
American College of Sports Medicine   108
American Academy of Physical Education   109
Amateur Athletic Union   109
National Collegiate Athletic Association   110
National Association of Intercollegiate Athletics   110
National Parks and Recreation Association   111
Civic Organizations   112
    American Red Cross   112
    Boy and Girl Scouts of America   113
    Young Men's and Young Women's Christian Association   113
Summary   114
Questions   115
Footnotes   115

6: **Relationships of Physical Education with Other Aspects of
School and Community Life**   **117**

Relationships Between Physical Education and Athletics   118
Relations Between Physical Education and Health   122
    Activity and Weight   122
    Activity and the Circulatory System   124
Relationships Between Physical Education and Recreation   126
Relationships Between Physical Education and General
Education   130
Influences of Social Forces upon Physical Education   133
Summary   137
Questions   138
Footnotes   139

PART II: THE ROLE OF PHYSICAL EDUCATION IN
SOCIETY   143

7: Physical Education in Ancient Societies   145

    Java, Neanderthal, and Cro-Magnon Man   145
    Egypt — Birthplace of Civilization   148
    China   149
    India   150
    Persia   151
    Summary   152
    Questions   152

8: Physical Education in Early Greece and Rome   153

    Homeric Greeks   154
    Spartan Greeks   155
    Athenian Greeks   156
    The Romans   159
    Summary   163
    Questions   164

9: Physical Education in Europe from the Dark Ages to Modern
    Times   165

    Monasticism, Feudalism, Manorialism, and Chivalry   166
    The Growth of Guilds   168
    Scholasticism   170
    Humanism, Moralism, and Realism   170
        Individual Humanism   171
        Social Humanism   171
        Moralism   172
        The Counter-Reformation   174
        Realism   175
    Disciplinarian Education   177
    Naturalism   177
    Nationalism   179
    Summary   185
    Questions   186

10: Physical Education in the United States   188

    Early Settlers   188
    Introduction of Foreign Physical Education Programs   189
    Early Efforts of American Physical Educators   190
    Period of Rapid Growth   192
    New Forces and New Emphases   193

Summary   198
Questions   199
Bibliography (Chapters 7−10)   199

PART III: PHILOSOPHY AND PHYSICAL EDUCATION   201

11: Philosophies Influencing Education   203

What Philosophy Is   203
Major Concerns of Philosophy   206
    The Nature of the Universe   207
    Man's Place in the Universe   207
    Determination of Good and Evil   208
    The Nature of God   208
    The Soul and Immortality   209
    Man's Relationship to the State   209
    The Role of Education   210
    Relationships Between Mind and Matter   210
    Implications for Health, Physical Education, and Recreation   211
Idealism   213
    The Nature of the Universe   213
    Man's Place in the Universe   214
    Determination of Good and Evil   214
    The Nature of God   214
    The Soul and Immortality   214
    Man's Relationship to the State   215
    The Role of Education   215
    Relationships Between Mind and Matter   216
    Implications for Health, Physical Education, and Recreation   216
Pragmatism   218
    The Nature of the Universe   218
    Man's Place in the Universe   218
    Determination of Good and Evil   218
    The Nature of God   219
    The Soul and Immortality   219
    Man and the State   219
    Man and Education   220
    Mind and Matter   220
    Implications for Health, Physical Education, and Recreation   221
Realism   223
    The Nature of the Universe   223
    Man's Place in the Universe   224
    Determination of Good and Evil   224
    The Nature of God   224
    The Soul and Immortality   225
    Man and the State   225
    Man and Education   225
    Mind and Matter   226
    Implications for Health, Physical Education, and Recreation   226

Developing a Philosophic Point of View   228
Summary   229
Questions   230
Bibliography   231

PART IV: THE SCIENTIFIC BASES OF PHYSICAL
EDUCATION   233

12: The Physiologic and Anatomic Bases of Physical Education   235

The Unity of Man   235
Adaptability of Man   237
The Skeletal System and Effects of Activity upon It   241
    The Skull and Concussion   245
    The Vertebral Column   248
    Back Injuries   249
    The Thorax   251
    The Pelvic Girdle   251
    Formation of Erythrocytes   254
The Muscular System and the Effects of Muscular Activity   254
    Influence of Muscular Activity upon Venous Return   255
    Influence of Muscular Activity upon the Heart Rate and
    Volume   256
    Influence of Muscular Activity upon the Capillary Bed   256
    Influence of Muscular Activity upon Red Blood Cells   256
    Influence of Muscular Activity upon the Respiratory
    System   257
    Influence of Muscular Activity upon Muscle Tissue   257
    Muscle Fiber   257
    Muscular Endurance   259
    Development of Maximal Strength   260
    Strength and Age   261
    Physical Properties of Muscle   261
    Types of Muscular Contraction   262
    Qualities of Muscle Tissue   262
    Muscular Fatigue   262
The Nervous System   263
    Divisions of the Nervous System   264
    Central Nervous System   264
    The Spinal Cord   265
    Reflex Arc   265
    Effects of Oxygen Deprivation   266
    Autonomic Nervous System   266
    Voluntary Movement   267
    Grading Mechanism of Muscles   267
    Aids to Effort   268
The Cardiovascular System and Effects of Activity upon It   268
    Heart   269

Heart Rate   270
Heart Chambers   271
Heart Valves   271
Murmurs   271
Muscle Fibers of the Heart   273
Arterial Circulation   273
Blood Pressure   274
Effects of Exercise upon Blood Pressure and Pulse Rate   276
Venous Circulation   277
Capillaries   277
Deep Breathing Exercises   278
Venous Return   278
The Respiratory System and Effects of Activity upon It   279
Respiratory Mechanism   279
Vital Capacity   281
Hemoglobin   282
Nervous Control of Respiration   282
Respiratory Rate   283
Effects of Exercise upon Respiration   283
Inhalation of Pure Oxygen   284
Summary   284
Questions   285
Footnotes   287

13: Physical Fitness   289

What Physical Fitness Is   289
Why Physical Fitness Is Important   294
Fitness of American Children, Compared to Fitness of
Children in Other Countries   296
Activity and the Aging Process   298
Differences Between Males and Females   300
Individual Differences   301
Some Contributions of Intercollegiate Athletics   302
Summary   303
Questions   304
Footnotes   305

14: The Psychologic Bases of Physical Education   306

Physical Education Teachers Strongly Influence Personality
Development   306
Organic Bases of Personality   307
Nervous System   308
Autonomic System   310
Endocrine System   311
The Relationships Between the Organic Base and Environment   314
Influence of Environment upon the Intelligence Quotient   316

Socially Induced Modification of Fundamental Drives   316
Booing as a Catharsis   319
Differences in What Is Accepted Social Behavior   319
Developing Skill in Democratic Procedures   320
Psychologic Needs   321
Self-Acceptance   321
Freedom   323
Belonging   324
New Experiences   324
Achievement and Recognition   326
The Learning Process   328
Conditioned Learning   329
Optimum Learning or Practice Periods   330
Suggestions for Improving Teaching Efficiency   330
Physical Education as an Integrating Force upon Human
Personality   332
Summary   334
Questions   334
Footnotes   336

15: The Sociologic Bases of Physical Education   337

Interrelationships Between the Individual and Society   338
Socialization of the Child   338
Achieving Self-Realization   341
Adolescent Needs   341
Teacher Values vs. Student Values   343
Social Influences upon Behavior   343
Ambivalence of Aggressive Drives   343
Frustration and Aggression   344
Substitution   344
Individualized Interpretations of Frustrating Experiences   345
Physical Education and Democracy   346
Democracy and Diversity   346
Anarchy-Totalitarianism   347
Qualities Desired in People Living in a Democracy   348
Cooperation   350
The Present Status of Sportsmanlike Attitudes in Athletics   351
Values Held by Society and Sports   353
Implementation of the Teaching of Social Behaviors   353
Physical Education's Contributions to Individual Qualities
Needed in a Democracy   355
Character   356
Application of the Laws of Learning   357
Evaluation of Sportsmanship   358
Summary   359
Questions and Exercises   360
Footnotes   361

Epilogue   **363**

Appendix A   367

Appendix B   369

Appendix C   372

Index   377

Preface

THIS BOOK PROVIDES a broad, comprehensive view of health, physical education, and recreation for the student majoring in this area. The authors have attempted a new and different approach, in that selected background information from basic disciplines is presented to make more obvious the rationale behind commonly accepted objectives, principles, and methods. The authors have thereby attempted to integrate these various disciplines.

There has been a tremendous acceleration in the rate of growth of knowledge in all areas in recent years. This is likely to continue for some time, since each new item of knowledge makes more obvious the need for still further knowledge and also facilitates the gathering of additional knowledge.

This knowledge explosion has occurred in the disciplines which provide the bases for physical education, such as physiology, psychology, sociology, physics, and medicine — and it has also occurred in physical education. Because there is such a vast amount of knowledge to be acquired, there is a great temptation to become increasingly specialized. This has happened in medicine, and it is in the process of happening in many other areas.

The professions of physical education and physical educators cannot permit themselves to succumb to a narrow specialization, because: (1) they must concern themselves with the whole man — his biologic and psychologic nature, and his society, and (2) these professions are dependent, and always will be, upon many other disciplines from which they draw meanings and suggestions. For these reasons, periodically during the years of his preparation as a teacher and also during his teaching career, at conventions and through the professional literature, the physical educator must make efforts to integrate, relate, and synthesize knowledge from other areas and apply it in his teaching.

The student majoring in health, physical education, or recreation will take courses in sociology, psychology, biology, zoology, physiology, physics, human anatomy, history, and philosophy. These courses are seldom taught by a faculty with a background in physical education. The classes are heterogeneous, with students who are majoring in many diverse areas. It is not likely that the implications of these knowledges for the content and conduct of physical education and sports programs will be made obvious in these courses. These implications are left to the students, who may or may not have adequate experience or knowledge in their fields to realize them. This is often a difficult task even for well-qualified physical educators with many years of experience.

If it could be pointed out to the student, early in his preparation, that the knowledges gained in these courses do have implications for physical education, and if a few of these implications could be pointed out to him, he would be more likely to view these courses as an important part of his preparation for the teaching of physical education. He would then be more likely to search for the meanings for physical education as he studied these other disciplines.

Throughout the typical undergraduate preparation, there are seldom any efforts made to unify and to integrate. In a few cases in physical education, however, efforts are being made to integrate courses. In activity classes, students learn the movement skills. In methods classes, they learn many different teaching methods. In organization and administration classes, they learn proper procedures. Each course is usually taught as a separate entity, with little or no effort made to explain how movement skills, teaching methods, and organizational and administrative procedures arise from the nature of man (his biologic and psychologic nature) and the nature of society (sociology, history, anthropology, and philosophy). Even in principles courses, background knowledge is seldom presented. The authors believe that the objectives, principles, and methods of physical education will be better understood, and consequently more enthusiastically accepted, if the sociologic, historic, psychologic, and biologic facts upon which physical education rests are presented at the same time as the objectives, principles, and methods.

Therefore, the authors have selected information from other disciplines and pointed out its relevance to physical education. We believe that an introduction to physical education cannot be complete without some understanding of the basic disciplines which serve as its foundation. This foundational information is by no means complete — it is merely introductory. Nevertheless, there is much information presented in this book. Students need not be required to commit all of it to memory; however, it is important that they understand the reasons for certain objectives, principles, methods, selection of content, and that they be able to verbalize these concepts.

It is hoped that through reading the early chapters the student will be aided in reaching a decision as to whether or not he would like to teach physical education. Through reading the chapter on philosophy, he will begin to see how man's beliefs have influenced physical education, and through reading the history of physical education he will see the influence of geography, climate, economy, religion, and politics upon physical education and sports.

The prospective physical educator should begin to realize that physical education does not operate in a vacuum, but is influenced by many factors and forces. This will encourage him to become a better all-around scholar.

James A. Baley
David A. Field

Part I
THE PREPARATION AND WORK OF THE PHYSICAL EDUCATOR

1

The Nature of
Physical Education

PHYSICAL EDUCATION IS defined in Webster's New Collegiate Dictionary
in the following manner: "Education in its application to the development
and care of the body, especially with reference to instruction in hygiene and
systematic exercises." This definition is grossly inadequate principally
because it views physical education as being concerned only with biologic
outcomes and it totally disregards the contributions to the social, cultural,
intellectual, emotional, and esthetic outcomes of experiences in physical
education. Furthermore, it places emphasis upon instruction in "hygiene"
(now more appropriately called "personal health"). While some learnings in
the area of health education do occur in physical education classes, these
learnings are only concomitant learnings. Concomitant learnings in other
areas also hopefully occur. Imparting health knowledge is the primary
responsibility of health educators — not of physical educators. This confusion
may have come about because many of the leaders and administrators of the
first college and university physical education programs in this country were
physicians and also because in many public schools until the 1930's the
school physical educator taught his students physical activities for two
meetings each week and "hygiene" during the third meeting. The goals of
physical education and also those of health education are so ambitious today
that it is difficult enough to make progress toward their achievement when
three meetings per week are assigned to each subject.

Objection can also be raised to the use of the words "systematic exercises"
because they imply use of calisthenic exercises and body building with
weights. While these activities are included among school physical education
offerings, they are only a very small part of the total offerings. The majority
of the offerings are not designed primarily as exercises although they usually
are more vigorous than routine daily activities. Modern physical educators

3

strive to conduct their programs so that outcomes are consistent with those of education in a democratic society. They realize that excessive use of "systematic exercise," which implies highly formalized and even ritualized procedures, will leave little time for achieving those goals most desired in a democratic society. Early physical education programs in this country were patterned after those of European countries, notably Germany and Sweden. These programs gave to systematic exercises a prominent role. Today's physical education programs utilize principally athletics and sports as modalities, not only to develop the body, but also to teach social behaviors, to inculcate cultural and esthetic appreciations, and to improve mental-emotional health.

DEFINITIONS OF PHYSICAL EDUCATION

Many definitions of physical education have been offered. Following are those presented by several of this profession's leaders:

J. B. Nash defines physical education as an aspect of the total educational process which utilizes inherent activity drives to develop organic fitness, neuromuscular control, intellectual powers, and emotional control.

Williams, Brownell, and Vernier indicate that in physical education, selected physical activities are conducted in such a manner that they will be beneficial to the participants.

Nixon and Cozens define physical education as that part of the total educational process which utilizes vigorous activities involving the muscular system to bring about the learnings which result from participation in these activities.

While they do not wish to clutter the literature with numerous definitions, the authors offer the following definition of physical education: "Physical education is a process through which favorable adaptations and learnings — organic, neuromuscular, intellectual, social, cultural, emotional, and esthetic — result from and proceed through selected and fairly vigorous physical activities." This definition will be most consistent with the point of view taken throughout this text.

Since contributions to a child's physical education can be made by many people not affiliated with schools, by institutions other than the schools, and through informal as well as planned and formalized activities, this definition is preferred to the preceding definitions. While the physical education programs of the schools may be the most effective media for giving children a physical education, it cannot be denied that parents, childhood friends, and such agencies as the YMCA, YWCA, Boy and Girl Scouts, Cub Scouts, community recreation programs, and others make their contributions. The mother who transmits her fear of water to the child or who constantly screams admonishments at him whenever he attempts any physical skill, is giving her child a physical education. It is a negative type of education which will lead the child to fear attempting new physical skills and to a lack of confidence in his ability to control his body, but it is education, nevertheless. The child is becoming physically educated when he is encouraged to learn to walk, when his father plays "catch" with him, when his friends show him how to hold a bat, and when his playmates tease him for crying because he does not want to share the swing or the slide with others.

Certainly the physical director at the YM or YWCA, the swimming instructor working in the community recreation program, and the athletic director working for a private camp are providing children with a physical education. Physical education takes place in many places other than educational institutions.

Physical education is concerned with the beneficial *adaptations* to physical stress which occur as a result of participation in fairly vigorous physical activities selected as to individual needs, capacities, and interests. Physical educators strive to produce improvements [adaptations] in organic qualities such as cardiovascular-respiratory fitness, strength, power, agility, and speed. They measure improvement affected in these qualities, and they refine old methods and devise new methods for more effectively bringing about this improvement.

Physical educators control and direct the emotional stress inherent in athletics to enable their students to learn emotional control. Students are aided in adapting to emotional stress. Physical educators endeavor to transmit the prevailing social, cultural, and esthetic values of their culture to their students by setting examples of socially acceptable conduct by direct comment, and by reward and punishment. These learnings result from and proceed through the selected and fairly vigorous physical activities which make up the physical education program.

Physical education has an intellectual content and can provide for esthetic appreciations. There are rules, strategies, techniques, kinesiologic principles, history of the sports, cultural significance of the sports, and training rules to be learned.

Sports present to millions of people throughout the world the esthetic appreciations provided by highly skilled performers. The esthetic appreciation in watching a fancy skater doing an arabesque, a diver doing a full twisting forward one-and-a-half somersault, a gymnast executing a layout front flyaway from the horizontal bar, a soccer player leaping high to head the ball into the goal, a football player timing his movements perfectly to evade would-be tacklers, or a baseball player synchronizing his movements flawlessly to leap upward to catch a line drive are similar to the esthetic appreciation of watching the ballet, looking at artistic works, or listening to a concert. While the beauty and artistry of a physical movement in athletics and other physical activities usually occupies only a fraction of a second, the visual memory may remain for many years, and it brings pleasure to many people – just as does art, music, or literature.

PHYSICAL EDUCATION AS A PART OF GENERAL EDUCATION IN THE SCHOOLS

While physical education proceeds throughout a person's lifetime and in many different settings, we are concerned here primarily with that portion of it which occurs in the planned and organized programs of the schools. The area with which we are concerned here is school and college physical education. Physical educators, like all other educators, cannot conduct their programs without regard for the institutions, activities, values, knowledges, and other aspects of the larger society of which education is a part. This means that physical educators must possess an understanding of society – its history, its politics, its philosophies, its economy – if they are to relate successfully that segment of its activities with which they are concerned to the larger whole. Some of the relationships among man's philosophies, history, politics, and economics will be discussed in later chapters of this text. Students majoring in physical education will also be helped to gain a more thorough understanding of these relations through courses in philosophy, sociology, history, political science, and economics which they will take during their undergraduate and graduate years.

Physical educators in the schools must also relate their programs to those of the total educational program. The objectives of physical education must be consistent with those of general education. Objectives of general education are to make the individual an effective and happy individual, family member, member of society, producer, and consumer in a democratic society. In 1938 the Educational Policies Commission of the National Education Association (NEA) surveyed the life needs of youth. They listed the conclusions which they had reached in a book titled: *The Purposes of Education in American Democracy.*[1] They concluded that the following should be the objectives of education:

I. *The Objectives of Self-Realization:* development of the inquiring mind; skill in the fundamental processes such as speech, reading, writing, and numbers; sight and hearing; acquiring of health knowledge; development of health habits; concern for public health; the development of recreational, intellectual, and esthetic interests; development of good character.

II. *The Objectives of Human Relationship:* respect for humanity, friendships, cooperation, courtesy, appreciation and conservation of the home; homemaking; democracy in the home.

III. *The Objectives of Economic Efficiency:* respect for work, occupational information and choice, occupational efficiency, occupational adjustment and appreciation, personal economics, consumer judgment, efficiency in buying, consumer protection.

IV. *The Objectives of Civic Responsibility:* social justice and activity, social understanding, critical judgment, tolerance, conservation, social application of science, world citizenship, law observance, economic literacy, political citizenship, devotion to democracy.

While these objectives were listed over thirty years ago, they have stood the test of time better than any others proposed. They have served as guides to teachers in all subject areas and to educators at all levels. Some subjects make greater contributions to some of the objectives while other subjects make greater contributions to other objectives. School physical education programs, properly conducted, can make substantial contributions to the achievement of many of these objectives. They *must* do so if their existence is to be justified.

HOW PHYSICAL EDUCATION CONTRIBUTES
TO THE *NEA* OBJECTIVES

Physical education when well taught can contribute to the objectives of *self-realization.* A person with good organic health and a vigorous body developed through physical activities will be more likely to possess an *inquiring mind* because of his greater zest for living and his high energy levels. Energy beyond that expended in routine activities and on the job is essential to the night-time study and effort necessary to appease the inquiring mind. Physical educators can stimulate students in their classes to desire the answers to such questions as the effects of exercise, the values of sport, the influence of individual differences upon performance in various sports, the relationship between health habits and performance in sports, and to many other questions.

Physical education can make some contributions to the development of ability in the *fundamental processes of speech, reading, writing, and use of numbers* by assigning written and oral reports and holding examinations on sport and health topics; by aiding students to develop the ability to judge distance, speed, and spatial relationships; by aiding students to estimate impact, force, and weight; and by sufficiently stimulating students' interest in sport to cause them to read about sport.

There is some evidence to indicate that limited movement patterns during infancy have a detrimental effect upon later learned speech patterns although this evidence is inconclusive at this time.

Physical education can make substantial contributions to *health knowledge* by helping the student to know something of the capacities and limitations of his own body, by giving the student knowledge as to how he can improve his physical fitness level and his general health, and by giving him knowledge in the many sports activities which he can utilize throughout his lifetime to sustain his health and physical fitness at a high level.

Physical education makes contributions to the development of *health habits* principally by giving the student the satisfying subjective experience of developing a higher level of fitness which is likely to lead to a desire to sustain this level of fitness, increase it, or recapture it if it has been lost. Participation in sports can help the student learn to control his emotions. Sports and other forms of physical activity can serve as a socially acceptable form of release for feelings of aggression. They can satisfy emotional needs such as the need to belong, to be accepted, to receive recognition, and to follow and lead.

Physical education, when well taught, can make contributions to the *public health* objective by leading students to a realization of the need for adequate athletic and other recreational facilities in the community and by teaching them why sanitary conditions should be maintained in swimming pools, public showers, on tumbling and wrestling mats, and in other recreational facilities. Primary objectives of health education are to increase health knowledge, to develop habits of healthful living, and to induce students actively to support public and private agencies that seek to improve the health of all people.

Physical education makes as great or greater contributions to the *recreational* objective than does any other curricular subject. With increased mechanization, computerization, and cybernation, resulting in greater national productivity and a shorter work week, the wise use of leisure has become imperative not only to the individual but also to society in general. Men, women, and children in the late 1800's worked twelve to fourteen hours per day, six days each week, for a total of seventy to eighty hours per week. Today, many people work only thirty hours each week and it may not be long until all do. In physical education classes, students learn to appreciate and to enjoy both the participating and watching of sports, dance, swimming, gymnastics, outdoor activities, and other fairly vigorous activities. In physical education classes students should learn about the availability of recreational facilities in their community and should be led to a desire to increase the number and to improve the quality of these recreational facilities.

In physical education classes students can be led to develop *esthetic interests* by being taught to appreciate the beauty of the highly skilled human body in movement and the grace and efficiency of the human body in the daily activities of walking, working, and moving about; and by being led to appreciate symmetrical body proportions. In outdoor education, which may be a part of the total physical education program, the student can be led to an appreciation of the beauty, rhythm, and patterns of nature.

Physical education can make great contributions to the development of desirable qualities of *character,* not in spite of, but because of, the highly emotional situations which so frequently occur in athletic contests and not in spite of, but because of, the many pressures from fans, alumni, and other sometimes misdirected, ignorant, or crooked groups which endeavor to influence sports. It is easy to talk about sportsmanship or to behave in a sportsmanlike manner when the goal is not greatly desired. It is much more difficult to behave in a sportsmanlike manner when the goal is greatly desired as it almost invariably is in athletic contests. This feature gives school athletics a tremendous potential for inculcating socially desirable qualities of character — if athletics are viewed as an educational experience for the participants rather than as a media to bring glory and prestige to the school, the coach, or the community; to make money; or to entertain the adults. If physical educators and others who coach athletic teams, athletic directors, school principals and superintendents, and college and university administrators possess sufficiently moral character and moral courage, interscholastic and intercollegiate athletics can become a most effective media for improving qualities of character.

Physical education can make contributions to the objectives of *human relationships.* Sports and athletics can serve as media to teach *respect for humanity* when students of varying national, racial, and economic backgrounds play as teammates or as opponents. As teammates, teaching and coaching one another; working toward common goals; and suffering the same feelings of physical fatigue, joy in victory, and satisfaction in the knowledge of a job well done, team members soon begin to feel a degree of empathy and of unity with one another. When the more skilled in physical education classes help the less skilled to learn, they will begin to identify with one another.

Many lifelong *friendships* have had their beginnings and their nurturing through participation in sports. There is probably no situation, exclusive of war, catastrophe or disaster, which reveals the true nature and character of an individual better than the highly emotionalized situations which occur in sports. It is relatively simple to behave in a gentlemanly or ladylike manner in the routine activities of life. It is exceedingly more difficult to behave in a sportsmanlike manner during a game in which victory is greatly desired — particularly if the opponents have taken unfair advantage. But it is *because* of this difficulty that sports and athletics provide a superior tool for educators to use in inculcating in students those qualities which make them attractive to others.

Physical education programs can be so planned and conducted that they contribute to the development of a *cooperative attitude.* This can be done by giving students both leadership and followership experiences, by having them work cooperatively on an assigned task, and by having them coach, instruct, and spot or guard one another. The following illustration is one of many thousands possible of the process of teaching children cooperation through physical activities on the playground, in the gymnasium, on the playing fields, or in the natatorium:

Children are arguing or fighting about who shall use the swing. The playground director points out that no one is using the swing and that during the time spent arguing all might have had a turn. Then he uses some method, such as the youngest first, or oldest first, or girls first, etc., to determine the order of turns. Analogies to the cooperative efforts demonstrated in the adult world in the home, in the community, in industry, or between nations could then be made. The number of teachable moments which present themselves to the creative and imaginative teacher is almost limitless.

Physical education can contribute to the development of *courtesy* which is merely the surface manifestation of the practice of good sportsmanship in routine daily social relationships. These amenities are relatively easily learned and taught.

Physical education can contribute to the development of an *appreciation and conservation of home and family life* by teaching students recreation activities in which they will be able to participate with their future children

Flying over the snow *(Courtesy: Vermont Development Dept.)*

and wives or husbands. These activities include swimming, camping, fishing, skiing, badminton, tennis, softball, bowling, and many others. Because of the increasingly specialized roles which the several members of a family must play, the divisive forces acting upon family unity have been increasing since the industrial revolution. For example, today in only a few families operating small farms or businesses does the family spend a major portion of its time engaged in a common endeavor. In most families, each family member has his own individual interests, activities, and friends. Sports and other recreational activities provide family members with a common interest by providing activities which have appeal and interest to all members.

In courses related to physical education, such as health education and first aid and safety education, which are often taught by physical educators, students can become better homemakers. In health education they will learn about nutrition, sanitation, rest and exercise, and prevention and care of chronic and infectious illnesses, while in first aid and safety education courses they will learn how to take care of injuries and how to avoid them.

Physical education can contribute to the development of attitudes conducive to the practice of *democracy in the home* by including coeducational activities in the program and by conducting these activities in such a manner as to lead to mutual respect of the sexes. In developing desirable qualities of character, respect for humanity, cooperative attitudes, courtesy, and appreciation and conservation of the home and family life, physical education will make it more likely that democracy in the home will be practiced.

Physical education can make contributions to the *objectives of economic efficiency* by helping to develop the physical and organic vigor necessary for work and also by helping to discover wholesome and enjoyable leisure activities which are inexpensive. In health education classes, students will learn how to evaluate the worth of health services, health insurance policies, drugs, and medicines. This will enable them to become more intelligent consumers.

Physical education, properly conducted, has potential to contribute to many of the objectives of *civic responsibility*. It can contribute to a sense of social justice and *social understanding*. One who has had good friends among members of a minority group is more likely to seek justice and equality for that group. Friendships with people of diverse backgrounds should also result in greater *tolerance*.

Camping, hunting, fishing, hiking, skiing, skating, swimming, boating, mountain climbing (all of which can be a part of the physical education curriculum) can lead to a desire to *conserve* our woods, waters, wild life, fish, scenic beauty, and other recreational resources. People who enjoy these activities are more likely to support legislation designed to establish conservation programs.

Sailing! *(Courtesy: Maine Dept. of Economic Development)*

When physical educators teach their students about the ideals of the Olympic Games, show movies of foreign athletes, sponsor touring groups of foreign athletes, and tell their students about foreign athletic programs, they are helping to achieve the objective of *world citizenship.* Movement is a language common to the people of all countries. In sports, people of all nations can come together in a spirit of friendly rivalry.

Physical education can make contributions to the development of the disposition to *observe and to obey the laws* because in physical education classes and as members of interscholastic teams students must obey the rules of the game, observe the training and conditioning procedures, and conform to those procedures established by the physical educator to conserve and maintain equipment. A successful athlete must have the courage for independent action when it is called for and must also have the disposition to control his impulses and to subjugate his desires in order to become a better performer or for the benefit of his team.

Physical education can contribute to a *devotion to democracy* when its programs are conducted with a view to achievement of this end. This implies that physical education classes and interscholastic sports should be so planned and conducted that dispositions, attitudes, appreciations, and skills conducive to life in a democracy will be developed. These include respect for personality, rights, and liberty of others, a feeling of responsibility for the welfare of others; provision of opportunities for each to become all he is capable of becoming; participation in reaching group decisions; resolving of disputes through reason and majority opinion; and freedom of expression.

Physical education can serve as a laboratory for developing the qualities desirable in a democracy when students are given as many opportunities as feasible to participate in the reaching of decisions which will have influence upon them; when they are given leadership and followership experiences; and when they are taught respect for the dignity and worth of the individual. The imaginative and creative physical educator who has the courage to implement his ideas and who has a democratic and intelligent administrator will come forth with many ideas which will help to achieve this goal.

It can be seen that physical educators, whether they are working with the required physical education program, the intramural program, or the interscholastic athletic program, are concerned primarily with educating the whole child — his emotional and social as well as his physical aspects. From this point of view, it is difficult to give priority to any one aspect of the physical education program. The worth of any portion of the program is to be judged not by the gate receipts or the amount of publicity received but by its educational worth. The student can begin to understand that physical education is not only athletic teams, physical fitness, championships, or fun. It is all of these but it is much more.

PRINCIPLES OF PHYSICAL EDUCATION

We can learn more about the meaning of physical education in the schools by taking a look at what prominent leaders believe should be the guiding principles. A principle is a fundamental truth or basic law. It provides a guide to the attainment of objectives. Dr. Delbert Oberteuffer[2] of Ohio State University has presented ten principles which should guide physical education:

First: That American physical education must be in the image of the American Democracy, must be rooted in the culture of American people, and must have no values different from those conducive to life in the republic.

Second: That the practice of physical education must forever acknowledge the known and proven facts about the human organism.

Third: That in all of physical education there is but one set of purposes, one standard of values, and one criterion for measuring the worth of practice — the good of the individual.

Fourth: That physical education contains within it a great potential for learning, for the cultivation of reflective thinking and for the intellectualization of our choices.

Fifth: That the teaching of values on the ethical-moral plane must assuredly be as definite and planned for as those of skill.

Sixth: That physical education is as much a social science as a biological one because its outcomes are measurable in terms of group behaviors as well as organic enrichment.

Seventh: That the activities and methods producing an objective extroverted flow of consciousness are more to be desired than those which turn the individual upon himself toward an introverted development.

Eighth: That physical education, far from being an isolated and quite foreign element within the curriculum of American education, contains within it elements quite identical with the other expressive arts.

Ninth: That physical education stands upon its own feet as a profession, solidly within the scientific and social culture of the race, beholden to no other group, but ready to work cooperatively with other professions for human betterment.

Tenth: That the high quality of leadership is the primary desideratum of this as of other professions, and that the American university must keep its standards high and its efforts unremitting for the selection and preparation of intelligent, well equipped, and cultured men and women teachers of physical education.

VALUES IN PHYSICAL EDUCATION

Another eminent physical educator, Dr. David K. Brace,[3] has listed the following as values which can accrue to participants in a well- conducted physical education program:

1. Knowledge of one's health status.

2. Knowledge of one's physical abilities and limitations and how to adjust to them.

3. Confidence in the performance of motor skills and the body mechanics of life activities.

4. A personality adjusted to group endeavor and willing to accept assignments selected by the group.

5. Concepts of fair play and respect and consideration for the shortcomings or achievements of opponents.

6. Respect for authority as embodied in the team captain, game official, coach, or school principal.

7. Skill, knowledge, and a real interest in several recreational sports that can be participated in as an adult.

8. Understanding of the purpose and educational and physical values of physical education.

9. An optimum condition of physical fitness in terms of strength, speed, agility, and endurance.

10. An appreciation of community resources and programs essential to preserve the health and fitness of our people.

11. Experience in coeducational recreation activities of an active or semi-active nature.

12. Knowledge and skill in forms of physical exercise, such as home calisthenics, which can be used to keep in condition when circumstances do not permit vigorous recreation participation.

13. Knowledge of the mechanics of sport skills, how to learn new skills, and how to improve performance.

14. An understanding of our heritage in sports and the place of sports in American culture.

15. Experience in leadership of fellow students in such capacities as team captain, scorekeeper, equipment manager, or official.

It can be seen that there are organic, intellectual, neuromuscular, social, cultural, emotional, and esthetic values and that these adaptations and learnings proceed through fairly vigorous physical activities.

AAHPER's PLATFORM FOR PHYSICAL EDUCATION

We can learn what physical education stands for by taking a look at what groups of leaders in the professional organizations believe to be the responsibilities and potential of this profession. Such an opportunity is presented by the statement of the American Association for Health, Physical Education, and Recreation titled: "A Platform for Physical Education":[4]

For every person there should be opportunity to gain the values of physical education by taking part in activities selected according to his interests and according to his needs, as shown by a medical examination and in other ways.

Everyone should be encouraged to take part regularly in a variety of activities appropriate to his age, physical condition, abilities, and social interests. . . .

A thorough medical examination should be one of the main bases for the selection of physical activities for all persons.

In every community all possibilities for physical education should be developed. In making the most of the educational opportunities in physical education, good schools provide guidance, a well-balanced varied program, indoor and outdoor facilities, equipment, and other "teaching tools" adequate for full participation.

Through the elementary schools, every child in this formative period of his development should have the advantage of a well-planned, well-conducted physical activity program. Teachers who understand the place of physical education in child development, and who are competent in guiding the learning, provide ample time and individualized instruction in skills and techniques for a variety of activities.

No boy or girl in junior and senior high school should be deprived of the physical and social development to which physical education contributes so much. Every high school student has a right to a daily period of *instruction* in activities.

Length of periods, credit, methods of grading, and other qualities should be comparable to those of other phases of the curriculum. Maximum values in the time devoted to physical education are achieved when there is selected grade placement of activities and groupings for efficiency and learning. There should be, also, adaptation of instruction to activity needs and interests at various age levels, and student participation in planning and carrying out the program.

Effectiveness and efficiency of college students should be developed and maintained through a coordinated campus-wide program which includes physical education experiences for all students.

Supplementing instruction in physical activity, there should be ample opportunities for all boys and girls to participate in intramural and other recreational activities.

So that all the educational values of interscholastic athletics may be secured for youth, athletics should be administered and conducted by school officials and teachers who are primarily concerned about the welfare of participants.

United through professional associations on national, district, state, and local levels, leadership in physical education should represent the finest in professional preparation, personal integrity, and social consciousness.

State and local communities, assisted where necessary by the federal government, should provide sufficient support for a quality program of physical education.

America must remain strong; all those who live beneath her flag — all agencies concerned with the health, physical, and social well-being of her people — must work together for national security and international goodwill through citizens who possess total *fitness*. National security and international goodwill can be achieved by citizens who "live most and serve best." The role of physical education in their development is not insignificant. The principles outlined in this platform, integrated with those of the platforms of health education and recreation, if applied, will contribute much to the development of total fitness of the people of the United States of America.

Again we note throughout the above platform that physical education is concerned with the welfare of all boys and girls — not only the physically skilled — and that it uses physical activities to enhance the welfare of youth.

COMMON MISCONCEPTIONS ABOUT PHYSICAL EDUCATION

Many lay people hold misconceptions about the nature and objectives of physical education. Unfortunately, a few school administrators also hold some of these misconceptions. These misconceptions have come about because of: (1) lack of adequate information, (2) misinformation, (3) the persistence of puritanical beliefs that play is sinful, (4) the current emphasis upon acquiring material possessions which is promoted through vigorous advertising and other media, (5) the failure of people to realize that a good and full life demands more than material possessions, and (6) the inherent difficulty of bringing people to understand the value of something which is a means to an end.

The last point may require further explanation. Skills learned in an English class are of value in and of themselves since, in this country, the English language is used to communicate ideas. The value of skills learned in a driver training course is immediately obvious since they are useful. The value of skill in soccer is not so obvious because ability to head the ball into the goal has no real personal or social value (unless one becomes a professional soccer player). The values are indirect. A boy who can play soccer with a high degree of skill has gained a measure of self-confidence and self-respect, and in the process of playing the game has improved his organic condition, has learned cooperation, teamwork, followership, and leadership. These concomitant learnings are the qualities physical educators strive to develop. They are the important outcomes even though physical educators rarely lecture their students about these values. If they did say a great deal about these concomitant values, they would become more difficult to achieve. Players do not usually think about these objectives or are they motivated by them. Player objectives are fun, pleasure, fellowship, and recognition.

One misconception is that the interscholastic athletic program *is* the physical education program rather than only a part of it. This misconception arises because the interscholastic athletic program is the part of the total program which is seen by the public. When the interscholastic athletic program is used only to entertain the public, the great potential of interscholastic athletics for enlarging the educational arena, for educating the general public, is not developed. The general public can be educated during athletic programs through comments on the printed program, through half-time demonstrations, through the announcers' comments, and via the news and editorial releases in all publicity media. This misconception arises in part because of the innate appeal of sports contests between highly skilled opponents and also because some physical educators fail to seize opportunities to educate the general public via physical education demonstrations, "open house" programs, talks before civic groups, and articles in newspapers and popular journals.

Another popular misconception is that physical education classes are free play periods. This misconception has arisen because some physical educators conduct their classes as though they *were* free play periods. They establish no specific or general objectives for their activity courses, prepare no lesson plans, give no tests, establish no progressions, prepare no syllabi or course outlines, and base grades on effort or attitude, attendance, showers, and the wearing of a prescribed uniform rather than the degree to which students have achieved stated objectives. Recipients of this kind of physical education, if they have any intelligence, are not likely to develop a high regard for physical education or for physical educators. Physical educators who conduct this type of program should be mercilessly "weeded out" of the profession.

Some people believe that the only purpose of physical education is to relieve tensions and anxieties produced in the "academic" classes. This misconception is related to the preceding one and arises in part for the same reasons. It could be avoided if all physical educators would follow the suggestions presented in the preceding paragraph and in addition spend a few meetings in a classroom with each activity class discussing the values, objectives, and principles of physical education in general and of the specific activity being taught in particular. Participation in physical activities will relieve tensions but this is only one of many purposes of physical education.

A fourth misconception is that the only objective of physical education is the development of muscles. This misconception has come about because early physical educators in this country were primarily concerned with anthropometry — the development of a symmetrical and well-muscled body. This concept was perpetuated by the physical culturists of the 1920's and 1930's who were interested in selling their products. Physical educators should not, on the other hand, feel apologetic or inferior because one of their concerns is that of improving physical fitness. A considerable knowledge of human anatomy and physiology, teaching methods, group dynamics, and psychology (motivational techniques) is needed to improve physical fitness most effectively. The improvement and maintenance of physical fitness has become an important objective in a time when few people obtain adequate physical activity in their occupation or in other areas of living. Physical educators should prepare themselves to prove that one who possesses no leisure skills which involve fairly vigorous activity is not a truly liberally educated person. They should prepare themselves to prove to those who themselves have inferiority feelings because of a puny body that a healthy and efficient body will make even intellectual workers more effective. They should be prepared to illustrate that genetically, phylogenetically, and biologically, man needs large amounts of physical activity and will continue to need physical activity for many generations to come.

There are some people who believe that being a member of the marching band or taking walks can substitute for physical education, that since children play outside of school there is no need for physical education programs, or that a principal value of physical education is that it produces fatigue and enables one to sleep soundly. Those who hold these views have a narrow view of physical education and its objectives. While participation in sports, like walking and marching, will produce fatigue and reasonable physical fatigue will enable most people to sleep more soundly, physical education offers many other benefits such as improvement in emotional and social fitness, improved health habits, and the learning of leisure skills which can be enjoyed for many years after graduation from school.

The misconceptions that physical education exists to serve the strong and healthy students but is detrimental to the weak, that members of inter-scholastic or intercollegiate teams should be excused from physical education, and that the purpose of physical education is to develop highly skilled performers or to discover potential members for varsity teams arise for several reasons. One of the reasons for the holding of these views is failure to understand that *all* people need physical activity in order to achieve optimum health and that those who are weak and underdeveloped need physical activity more than do others. Furthermore, they will continue to need physical activity throughout their lifetimes in order to maintain physical fitness at a satisfactory level. Another reason is that many people think that the purpose of education is only to provide preparation for a profession or some sort of employment. Those who hold this point of view hold little regard for those subjects which will not enhance the student's earning power. In their eyes, subjects which make the student a more effective citizen or a happier and better adjusted person have less value than do the professional courses. Those who believe that members of varsity teams should be excused from physical education classes do not understand that while participation in team sports will satisfy some of the needs and desires of young people while they are of high school or college age, they will not satisfy the needs and desires of these students when they become adults.

After students have left the educational institutions, they will have neither opportunity nor desire to participate in team sports such as football, basketball, or baseball. They will, however, have opportunities to participate in the individual and dual sports and will enjoy them — if they had developed a modicum of skill in these activities while they were in school. Many varsity athletes have been denied the opportunity to learn the individual and dual sports. The result has been that after they had graduated from school, they stopped participating in sports. This happened because there was no longer any team with which they could participate and because they did not engage in the individual or dual sports since they had not learned how to do them. Adults dislike appearing to be beginners (especially if they were formerly superior athletes).

Another misconception which physical educators should strive to eradicate is that when a girl becomes more proficient in sports, she becomes less feminine. Since this point will be discussed in greater detail in another chapter, it will be adequate here to say that all people of both sexes inherit both feminine and masculine characteristics. The proportion between the masculine and feminine characteristics varies in different individuals. Participation in vigorous physical activities has no influence upon these inherited physical characteristics. Feminine behaviors, values, and attitudes are learned. Girls and women who participate in sports learn these behaviors, values, and attitudes just as those who do not. There have been many champion women athletes who have been very attractive and feminine.

A misconception related to the preceding one is that girls and women do not need to participate in physical activity because they do not need to develop muscles. This concept is a vestige of the Victorian era when women were expected to swoon when under any degree of emotional stress, to scream at the sight of a mouse, and to generally portray helplessness. These same women helped their husbands to build log cabins, to till the fields, and to protect their homes. They endured the hardships of the wagon trains to the West where they helped to wrest a living from the harsh land. They did (and still do) move heavy furniture. These tasks require strength.

There are some who believe that students should not be graded in physical education activities. We have presented evidence that the liberally educated person in today's society possesses leisure skills including skills in sports. We have shown that the purpose of general education is to produce liberally educated people. We have also indicated that widely accepted statements of the objectives of general education, which were formulated by the leading organizations of professional educators, have assigned to physical education a prominent place in general education. Physical education is as important as academic subjects. If grades are deemed advisable in these subjects, they are advisable in physical education. The awarding of grades facilitates achievement of the objectives of the course. Since the objectives of physical education are those of general education, they are worthy objectives. The degree to which students achieve these objectives should be evaluated. Grades will guide and motivate the students, the teachers, and the parents to seek fuller achievement of the objectives.

There are some who believe that interscholastic and intercollegiate athletics are not an essential part of the total educational program. While it may be true that in some schools and universities the harm done by the inter-scholastic or intercollegiate athletic program outweighs the educational benefits, this is not because of faults inherent in these programs but is the result of the way in which they are conducted. Interscholastic and intercollegiate athletics can serve the total physical education program by giving some students a reason to seek excellence and in so doing enable them to improve their fitness status and to learn respect for effort, perseverance, self-discipline, teamwork, and leadership and to gain in self-respect and self-acceptance. Interscholastic and intercollegiate athletic programs can be so conducted that they educate the student body and the general public in the values of sports and physical activities and thereby develop a desire within the spectators to participate in sports and to become physically fit themselves.

The greatest amount of participation is in those sports which receive most publicity. These sports, in this country, are football, basketball, and baseball. In many other countries soccer receives most publicity and the largest numbers of participants are to be found in this sport. The most logical solution to the problem of increasing the number of participants in the lesser known sports is not to limit the publicity, recognition, and prestige given the more popular sports but to give greater status to the lesser known sports by giving them more publicity. However, it is to be hoped the sportswriters will ultimately grasp the educational and social significance of their task and will join hands with physical educators in a conspiracy to educate the public through sports. It is already late. Perhaps it is still not too late to return to sports their educational function. If sports can be used as an educational tool in physical education classes, they can be used as an educational tool in interscholastic and intercollegiate athletic programs.

Coaches are educators and as such have a professional obligation to do what is best for the student, for the educational institution, and for society. To best serve the individual, the educational institution, and society, the coach needs to be a highly principled and courageous person because he is subjected to many pressures – both internal and external. The external pressures come from business interests, gamblers, fans, and alumni. The internal pressures arise as a result of the coach's ego involvement with his win-loss record. Ideally the coach should become ego involved with the growth of his players and obtain self-satisfaction from his unswerving dedication to principles.

There are many people who believe there is no scientific basis for the field of physical education. In later chapters the scientific bases of physical education drawn from psychology, sociology, and biology will be presented. Physical education draws pertinent information from a number of other disciplines. Physical educators execute research studies in psychology, physiology, and sociology which are concerned with physical activity or sports. These are occasionally cited by workers in other disciplines. Physical educators should know the scientific bases of their profession. They should keep abreast of research in physical education by reading the *Research Quarterly of the American Association for Health, Physical Education, and Recreation* and the *Journal of Sports Medicine and Physical Fitness* of the Federation Internationale de Medicine Sportive. They should also familiarize themselves with the research publications in related disciplines such as physical therapy, medicine, physiology, psychology, and sociology. If physical educators do these things, they will become qualified to present the scientific bases of physical education to others.

These are only some of the misconceptions held by people concerning physical education. Many more could be discussed. Misconceptions in any field can be minimized through an effective, vigorous, and continuous program of education. No one will do this job for physical educators. They must do it themselves. It is probably both more effective and more economical of time to discuss what physical education is than to refute misconceptions. People are judged not so much by how they look as they are by what they stand for, what they are attempting to accomplish, and what they actually do accomplish. In the same way we can judge physical education (and know it better) by looking at its objectives. These tell us what it stands for and what it is attempting to accomplish.

THE OBJECTIVES OF PHYSICAL EDUCATION

A number of statements concerning the objectives of physical education have been made by leaders and textbook writers in this field. In many statements objectives listed are similar but have been stated in different ways with slightly different emphases. Some statements have included objectives omitted or only implied by others. Those which we will discuss here have been included in one or more of the lists and are generally accepted as objectives toward which this profession should strive.

Physical Fitness

Improvement in the physical fitness status of students is a prime objective of physical education. This is so because the improvement of physical fitness is a unique responsibility of physical education shared by no other subject in the curriculum. Furthermore, a mass of research evidence indicates the importance of physical fitness to total health. On the one hand, a large amount of research evidence proves that physical fitness can be improved. On the other hand, some physical educators question that the social and psychologic objectives can be achieved because they feel that research evidence proving that they can be achieved is still inadequate. For these reasons, physical fitness is usually given priority.

Physical fitness is a measure of the ability of one's body to function under the stress of physical effort. This ability reflects the condition of the body organs and systems. Everyone has some degree of physical fitness. Some people have so little that they become winded in climbing a flight of stairs while some have so much they can run a mile in less than four minutes. Some have so little that they feel exhausted by noon on a working day while others have so much that they can work hard for sixteen hours every day or after an eight-hour work day have enough energy left to enjoy their leisure in vigorous activity.

A number of tests have been devised to measure the various aspects of physical fitness. The three aspects of physical fitness are physique, organic fitness, and motor fitness. Physique refers to physical appearance — body dimensions, proportions, etc. It is measured by assessment of body type, anthropometric measurements of girth, thickness or width, height and weight, and by measurements of fat by means of skinfold calipers.

Organic fitness is usually assessed through measurements of the cardiovascular system by means of blood pressure measurements, pulse rate, and blood counts. These measurements when made by physical educators are an evaluation of response to physical stress. Respiratory efficiency has been evaluated in the past by measurements of expiratory force, breath holding, and lung or vital capacity. These tests are now seldom used because functional respiratory efficiency can be measured more effectively through cardiovascular tests due to the close relationship between the cardiovascular and respiratory systems. Analyses of expired air are, however, being made in physiology of exercise laboratories. Tests of organic fitness are impractical for use in physical education classes.

Motor fitness, which consists of strength, power, agility, flexibility, endurance and balance[5] is the aspect of physical fitness most commonly measured in physical education classes. Strength is measured by means of dynamometers, chin-ups, pull-ups, sit-ups, or dips. Power is measured by means of standing vertical or horizontal jumps or medicine ball putts. Agility is determined by the time taken to run around obstacles or by the number of times a specified movement can be done in a unit of time. Flexibility refers to the range of motion possible in body joints. Endurance is measured by the time taken to run a distance of 380 yards or more and is highly related to organic fitness. Balance may be measured by having the student do specified stunts on a balance beam or on a line on the floor, by having the student stand on one foot blindfolded, or by similar means.

A person's level of physical fitness may decrease or it may be improved. The question: "How much physical fitness does a person need?" is often asked. Some physical educators believe that people should possess only enough physical fitness to see them through their work plus a little extra. It is our belief that no one can have too much of a good thing and since physical fitness is desirable, as much as possible should be desired. No one ever feels he is earning too much money. However, people have needs and desires in addition to the desire to be physically fit. No two people will ascribe the same relative importance to other activities. This is the way it should be in a democracy. Consequently, in a democracy, no individual or organization can prescribe a specified level of physical fitness which must be possessed by every individual. Physical educators should urge all people to develop as high a level of physical fitness as possible. Each person then must make his own decision as to how he shall apportion his time.

The Human Is an Entity

Optimum physical fitness cannot be developed without giving consideration to emotional, mental, and social fitness as well as to the development of healthful habits of living.

The influence of *emotions* upon performance is illustrated by the true story of four combat soldiers in the Vietnam war who were driving their jeep down a narrow road in the combat zone when they were ambushed. All four dove in opposite directions to take cover in the ditch. When they realized that they would be pinned down in the ditch, they all came out, each grabbed a corner of the jeep and they lifted it around to face it in the opposite direction, hopped in, and made a hasty retreat. When they were asked to duplicate the feat upon their return to their home base, they were unable to do so. This phenomenon has been illustrated many times when a highly motivated "underdog" team has defeated an overconfident favored team. Motivation has also been shown to have an influence upon performance in tests of physical fitness.

Mental ability has also been shown to have an influence upon performance in tests of physical fitness. Dr. Hollis Fait of the University of Connecticut, in attempting to appraise the physical fitness status of the mentally retarded, found it necessary to modify existing tests so that the tests were less complex. He was then enabled to obtain valid measures of the retardates' physical fitness status.

Physical fitness must be developed in order to facilitate the accomplishment of socially desirable goals. Physical educators have an obligation to teach ethical behavior and sportsmanship at the same time that they teach the skills of the game and work toward improvement of players' physical fitness status.

A high level of physical fitness cannot be developed without giving attention to habits of *healthful living.* A cold, tuberculosis, foci of infection or many other health problems will obviously exert a detrimental influence upon performance in tests of physical fitness. Consequently, physical educators must concern themselves with improving students' health habits. Physical educators should spend some class time and some of the time devoted to individual counseling in discussing habits of healthful living and in motivating students to practice these habits.

The conclusion which physical educators have been forced to reach as a result of scientific evidence is that physical fitness cannot be developed without regard for the other aspects of man's being. This evidence has led physical educators to conclude that they must be concerned with total fitness — emotional, mental, and social, as well as physical fitness.

The American Association for Health, Physical Education, and Recreation went on record as supporting the total fitness point of view when in one of its reports it indicated that the fit person possesses the following characteristics:[6]

Optimum organic health consistent with heredity and the application of present medical knowledge.

Sufficient coordination, strength and vitality to meet emergencies as well as the requirements of daily living.

Attitudes, values and skills which stimulate satisfactory participation in a full range of daily activities.

Emotional stability to meet the tensions of modern life and an understanding of the value of physical activity in the reduction of stress.

Social consciousness and adaptability with respect to the requirements of individual and group living.

Sufficient knowledge and insight to make suitable decisions and arrive at feasible solutions to problems of fitness.

Spiritual and moral qualities which contribute the fullest measure of living in a democratic society.

Emotional Needs

Participation in athletic contests can serve as an excellent modality for satisfying many emotional needs and as a catharsis for feelings of irritation and anger. Because contestants in athletics are highly motivated to accomplish a goal which, for the moment, is greatly valued and because they are often highly emotionalized as well, athletic contests provide a superlative tool for teaching emotional control.

Sports and physical education activities take so many different forms — from archery to yachting — that everyone can find some activity in which he can excel and in doing so satisfy the need present in all people (in varying degrees) for *ego satisfaction, self-realization, or prestige.* One important criteria, incidentally, for evaluating the quality of a physical education program is the diversity of its offerings. The greater the number of activities, everything else being equal, the better the program since a greater number of students and a greater variety of students can be served. If students are to be aided in achieving self-realization through physical education, physical educators should never unnecessarily demean a student or his efforts but should instead endeavor to enhance his self-concept. One way by which they can do this is to help the student to find an activity in which he can excel.

All people have a need for *self-expression.* Participation in physical education activities can satisfy the need for self-expression by giving students an opportunity to create their own movement patterns, stunts, and routines. The selection of a sports activity is in itself a form of self-expression.[7] The aggressive boys will select some "body contact" sport. Those who enjoy testing themselves to the point of exhaustion will select cross-country running, swimming, or mountain climbing.

In all sports there is always the *challenge* of performing better than others, of improving one's own performance, or of attempting to accomplish something which has never before been accomplished. Acceptance of these challenges provides relief from the routine of school work or a repetitious job. There is also the challenge of overcoming one's own fear and this contributes greatly to personal growth. We suspect that one who has developed physical courage will possess the courage often necessary to behave in a principled and honest manner which, obviously, is of far greater importance than is physical courage in modern society.

Emotional Catharsis

Recent discoveries by archaeologists indicate that man has been on this earth for over two million years. For the major portion of this time man has solved his problems, frustrations, irritations, and angers by bashing in the head of the animal or person who was the source of his problems. If he was incapable of doing this, he ran away. In either case, he reacted with physical activity. Civilized man cannot react in this manner without being regarded as emotionally unstable or being incarcerated. Furthermore, while primitive man could see his tormentor, modern man usually cannot see the cause of his torment and may not even know who or what is the cause of his problems. Primitive man's physical response gave release to his feelings of anger or fear and he burned up the adrenaline which was poured into his bloodstream. Consequently, after his escapade, primitive man felt at peace with the world. When modern man is angered, even though adrenaline is poured into his bloodstream to prepare him for physical activity he must restrain himself — often even to the extent of masking his true feelings. The result is that he suffers hypertension, ulcers, cardiac malfunctions, hives, asthma, and other diseases. Physical education activities, particularly the combative sports, provide a socially acceptable form of release for these feelings of anger and in so doing help to preserve both emotional and physical health.

Social Fitness

Physical educators are also concerned with the social fitness objectives. They realize that because of constant social interaction in sports, sports are an excellent modality for achieving the social objectives. They wish to develop the qualities of character, values, and social skills which are conducive to a satisfying and useful life in a democracy. These qualities, skills, and values include the ability to lead and to follow, respect for the individual, a sense of justice, and a desire to behave in ethical or sportsmanlike manners. The social objectives and the processes and means by which they are achieved will be discussed in Chapter XV.

Intellectual Development

Physical education activities aid in mental development by enabling the student to learn to judge distance, speed, weight, force, direction, and spatial relationships. Recent research indicates a relationship in small children and babies between learning to walk and talking. During children's school years, physical educators aid in the intellectual development of children by requiring them to learn something about the history of sports. The social interactions of physical education activities enable students to learn something about other people — how they react to stress, their values, and their degree of emotional control.

Carry-over Sports or Preparing for Future Needs

Physical educators are concerned not only with the present needs of students but also with their future needs. They are aware that while sports such as football, basketball, baseball, and lacrosse will meet the needs of teenage boys, sports such as golf, tennis, bowling, badminton, swimming, squash, and handball meet the needs of adults more effectively. The latter are called "carry-over" sports because participation in them can be carried over into adult life after the boy or girl leaves the educational institution. The "carry-over" sports are used during adult life to sustain or to improve physical fitness status, for satisfaction of emotional needs, for socially acceptable forms of release for feelings of aggression, and for pure enjoyment and pleasure. Most adults do not have opportunities to participate in team sports because there are neither facilities available to them nor enough other adults who would like and are able or free to play at the same time. Furthermore, most adults do not care to participate in team sports. Most prefer the individual and dual sports. Studies show that as people grow older this preference becomes more pronounced.[8] For these reasons, effective physical education programs provide a generous amount of instruction in both individual and dual sports areas.

Development of Motor Skills

C. O. Jackson[9] writes: "In physical education we are apt to think of skill in terms of sports skills, dance skills, tumbling skills, and so on. This is a valid emphasis but we need to comprehend skill to act in larger terms. There should be understandings about basic body movements – the way the body is structured to act. There needs to be awareness of movement fundamentals involved in everyday activities such as walking, sitting, pushing, lifting, as well as specific skills used at work, in leisure, homemaking, or any other area of living you wish to name." Physical educators may select and manipulate physical education activities in such a way as to improve skill and efficiency in fundamental movements which are as old as man himself. This area has been investigated with greater intensity in recent years from the standpoint of both contributions of physical education to the area and methods for achieving this goal more effectively.

Protection of Students' Health

Finally, physical education has as one of its objectives that of improving and protecting students' health. Obviously, in teaching physical education activities, physical educators cannot devote a large amount of time to direct teaching of health but they can provide health learnings whenever the opportunity presents itself. These opportunities are presented quite often. Comments can be made regarding posture, cleanliness, adequate rest, the importance of exercise, nutrition, smoking, and use of alcoholic beverages.

PROBLEMS AND GOALS FOR PHYSICAL
EDUCATION DURING COMING DECADES

What will life be like in the United States in the year 2000 when students now in college will be forty or fifty years old? What will be the principal concerns of physical education and of physical educators? Is it possible to make predictions based on recent trends? Marion Clawson,[10] in an article in the *National Parks* magazine, made some predictions. She wrote:

There will be many more people. There are now about 200 million people in the United States. By the year 2000 it has been estimated that there will be between 300 and 325 million people. Income in terms of purchasing power will double. The work week will decrease from the present forty hours to twenty-eight hours or less. There will be an increase in the number of variety of labor-saving devices used both in industry and the home. There will be more roads, highways, and superhighways, more cars, more space taken up for parking lots, and greater difficulty in finding a place to park the car. There will be more airports, industrial buildings, office buildings, and houses leaving fewer open spaces for picnicing, hunting, fishing, and other recreational areas such as sports. Building lots will become smaller. Areas which are now woods or fields will contain buildings. Cities will have grown toward one another until they become a megapolis.

These changes will have an influence upon physical education in that they will intensify the urgency of solution of problems which physical education now faces. They will, however, not change the problems. Most men in the United States today do not get enough physical activity on their jobs or at home. With the spread of more labor- saving devices there will be a greater need for people to obtain physical activity through means other than work. Sports provide enjoyable and beneficial physical activity for all. People will not discard their labor-saving devices. They will seek more of them in order to possess more hours of enjoyable leisure. It will be the job of physical educators and others to convince people that they should spend their increased leisure and their greater purchasing power in ways which enhance their well-being.

Many people spend the bulk of their leisure in activities which do not meet this criteria. They spend an excessive amount of time spectating. Millions of people jam football stadia around the country on Saturday afternoons. Millions pack themselves into gymnasia to watch basketball games. Millions spend hours each day watching television. Millions read pulp magazines and watch movies. Millions spend hours sitting in smoke-filled bars or nightclubs consuming alcohol and inhaling smoke. Physical educators and others

Sports have spectator appeal!

interested in elevating the quality and meaning of peoples' lives have to compete for the free time of people against private interests with a profit motive.

The President's Fitness Council and the AAHPER have demonstrated that through a vigorous publicity program progress can be made. It will be necessary to enlist the efforts of the various publicity media to educate large numbers of people to a realization that their increased leisure and greater buying power may be dangerous if not properly used. In later chapters we shall see how these problems contributed to the downfall of two earlier great civilizations – those of the Greeks and the Romans.

With space at a premium, athletic facilities will become more expensive. The public will demand that only those facilities be constructed whose use will justify the expenditure of money and use of land space. Football stadia which are used only five or six afternoons each year may become difficult to justify. School gymnasia, playing fields, and swimming pools will be open evenings and during school vacations.

Community, state, and federal governments will purchase more land to be set aside for recreational facilities. Business interests will present a vigorous fight to possess this land and will endeavor to make encroachments upon it. It will be necessary to oppose these moves vigorously or this country may find itself with no open space remaining.

Physical educators will place an increasing reliance upon research. As a result of greater affluence and a universal increase in respect for the scientific method, departments and schools of physical education will develop a greater

An archer awaits his quarry *(Courtesy: New England Council, Inc.)*

number and more completely equipped research laboratories. The results of these research efforts will be more completely disseminated and will be used by practicing physical educators. Physical educators will overcome their fear of research as a result of learning more about research methods and interpretation of research during their undergraduate and graduate years and at conferences and conventions during their teaching years. As a result, they will do more research studies of their own in addition to utilizing the results of studies coming out of research laboratories.

Interscholastic and intercollegiate athletics will be conducted in an increasingly educationally sound manner and in conformity with total educational objectives. This will result because of greater understanding by school administrators and greater enlightenment by the general public. Greater enlightenment by the general public will result because people with increased leisure will have more time to study the issues which concern them. Public understanding which results in dissatisfaction with current practices ultimately leads to the institution of corrective measures. When the educational potential of interscholastic and intercollegiate athletic programs is recognized, these programs may be financed through the same channels as are other educational offerings. This would result in the elimination of gate receipts which would lead to less concern with the win-loss record. Coaches would then be hired on the basis of their educational qualifications. A major in physical education would likely be mandatory for certification as a coach. Coaches would become regarded as bona fide members of the faculty and would enjoy tenure, rank, and other benefits of membership on the faculty.

SUMMARY

Man is an entity. He cannot be compartmentalized into physical, intellectual, social, and emotional facets. The physical educator must concern himself with the whole child — his physical welfare, physical skills, attitudes, understandings and feelings. The physical educator must also concern himself with the role of physical education in general education and in society at large.

The child learns physical activities and learns about his environment (both physical and human) and also about himself through movement everywhere and he learns physical activities from many people including his physical education teacher.

Physical education endeavors to bring about adaptations in organic and neuromuscular function; to bring about intellectual, social, and cultural learnings; to develop emotional control; and to develop esthetic appreciations. Its modality is fairly vigorous physical activity. For these reasons physical education has been defined as a process through which favorable adaptations and learnings — organic, neuromuscular, intellectual, social, cultural, emotional, and esthetic — result from and proceed through fairly vigorous activities.

If physical education is to continue to be awarded a prominent place in the school curriculum it must continue to make every effort to relate its objectives to those of general education. Several statements of the National Education Association concerning the objectives of education have been presented. The manners in which physical education contributes to the attainment of these objectives have been discussed. Principles and values of physical education and the AAHPER "Platform for Physical Education" have been presented to show how the profession endeavors to meet the objectives of general education.

Common misconceptions concerning the nature and objectives of physical education have been presented. These have been discussed from the point of view of preventing these misconceptions from arising as well as rectifying them.

The objectives of physical education are both diverse and comprehensive. They fall under four major headings: *physical fitness, social fitness, emotional fitness,* and *mental fitness.* Physical fitness has three aspects: physique, organic fitness, and motor fitness. Physique includes relative body proportions, relationships between bone, fat and muscle, height, weight, width, and girth. Organic fitness refers to the efficiency of the vital organs such as the heart, lungs, kidneys, digestive tract, etc. Motor fitness is appraised through measurements of strength, power, agility, endurance, balance, and flexibility.

Emotional fitness is improved through wisely directed physical education activities by providing satisfaction for emotional needs such as self-realization, belonging, rivalry, creativity, and self-expression. Sports can provide a *socially acceptable* form of release for feelings of aggression and thereby prevent the onset of the predominantly psychosomatic ailments such as ulcers, high blood pressure, hypertension, and hives which first manifest themselves during middle age.

When sport facilities are regarded as laboratories and sports themselves as catalysts for human behavior, physical educators can give direction to participation in sports so that socially desirable outcomes result. Leadership, followership, a sense of justice, consideration for others, respect for the individual, cooperative attitudes, ethical behavior, self-discipline, and self-sacrifice are qualities which can be developed through physical education activities when they are wisely directed.

There is intellectual content in school physical education. The activities can be taught in such a manner as to stimulate in students a desire to learn about the history, values, and strategy of sports. The influences of the laws of physics and the application of the principles of healthful living, of psychology, and of sociology have application to the learning of sports skills and can be taught in school physical education classes.

Physical educators are concerned not only with the immediate needs of students such as proving their manhood, which is satisfied through vigorous contact sports such as football, lacrosse, and wrestling. They are also concerned with the future needs of students which can be best satisfied through the "carry-over" sports which can be used in the adult years. For this reason they teach their students tennis, swimming, golf, handball, and squash in addition to basketball, baseball, water polo, and soccer.

Finally, we gazed into a crystal ball in an endeavor to see what the world will be like after those presently being educated to become physical educators will have been teaching for a number of years. On the basis of the available evidence we concluded that the role of physical educators will be increasingly important and increasingly difficult.

QUESTIONS

1. Write a definition of physical education.

2. Why do the authors believe Webster's definition of physical education is inadequate?

3. Where and when does a child receive education in physical activities?

4. Discuss the role of physical education in general education.

5. List the four categories of objectives of education presented by the Educational Policies Commission of the NEA in 1938.

6. How can physical education contribute to each of the above objectives?

7. How should physical education be conducted in order that students will acquire greater appreciation for and skill in democratic procedures?

8. List the NEA's seven "Cardinal Principles of Secondary Education."

9. List Oberteuffer's ten principles of physical education.

10. Explain the difference between an objective and a principle.

11. List ten of the fifteen values which Brace believes accrue to participants in physical education.

12. Discuss ten current misconceptions about the nature and objectives of physical education, how or why these misconceptions arise, and what physical educators can do to prevent their occurrence or to rectify them.

13. Present your own definition of physical fitness. Name the three aspects of physical fitness. List the six aspects of motor fitness. How are these measured?

14. Present your ideas on the amount of physical fitness a person should develop.

15. How is physical fitness related to emotional fitness? Social fitness? Mental fitness?

16. How can physical education contribute to emotional fitness?

PROJECTS AND ACTIVITIES

1. Write a 600-800 word paper in which you defend physical education as a requirement for graduation from college.

2. Debate the potential of interscholastic sports to modify social and ethical behaviors.

3. Discuss and debate unfair or unsportsmanlike procedures which you have seen utilized to win games.

4. Write a 300-500 word paper in which you analyze how your understanding of the role of physical education has been modified.

5. Study the syllabi or course outlines for physical education activity classes from several different schools, rate these, and then explain why you have rated them in the way you have.

6. Observe several physical education classes or practice sessions of

interscholastic athletic teams and report on the extent to which and the methods used to accomplish the objectives of general education.

7. Debate the relative importance of the several objectives of physical education.

8. Discuss the possibility that physical education will play an increasingly important role in society.

FOOTNOTES

1. Educational Policies Commission, *The Purposes of Education in American Democracy.* Washington, D.C., NEA, 1938.

2. Oberteuffer, Delbert, "A Decalogue of Principles," *Journal of the American Association for Health, Physical Education, and Recreation,* January, 1947.

3. Brace, David K., "Physical Education Experience in Relation to Cultural and Educational Values in a Dynamic Society," *Professional Contributions No. 6,* American Academy of Physical Education, November, 1958.

4. Street, W. K., and McNeely, Simon, "A Platform for Physical Education," *Journal of the American Association for Health, Physical Education, and Recreation,* March, 1950.

5. Cureton, Thomas K., *Physical Fitness Appraisal and Guidance.* St. Louis: C. V. Mosby Co., 1947, p. 22.

6. "Fitness for Youth," *Journal of Health, Physical Education, and Recreation,* Sept., 1968.

7. Beisser, Arnold R., M.D., *The Madness in Sports.* New York: Appleton-Century-Crofts, 1967.

8. Baley, James A., *Recreational Habits and Interests of Adult Men,* Unpublished Ph.D. Thesis, Ohio State University, 1952.

9. Kozman, Hilda C., Rosalind Cassidy, and Chester O. Jackson, *Methods in Physical Education* (Fourth Edition). Dubuque, Iowa: Wm. C. Brown Company Publishers, 1967, p. 27.

10. Clawson, Marion, "Our National Parks in the Year 2000," *National Parks Magazine,* July, 1959.

2
The Preparation of
a Physical Educator

IT HAS BEEN pointed out that physical education is a part of general education and that as such it has objectives common to those of general education. In addition, physical education has objectives that are uniquely its own such as improving physical fitness and motor skills. Objectives which physical education shares with other subject areas are the ethical, social, cultural, health, esthetic appreciations, and mental health objectives. These objectives are achieved through activities taught by physical educators when they utilize various physical properties. The physical educator is more important than the activities or the physical properties since it is he who selects and purchases the equipment and oversees the activities. The physical educator is the principal determinant of the amount of progress which will be made toward the objectives. It is vital, then, that the people who will teach physical education be carefully selected and well educated. It is the profession of physical education (through its representatives who are involved in certification, accreditation, and teacher education) that ultimately exerts control over the quality of the people who will become physical educators. Physical educators exercise this control through selective admission by participating in the establishment of undergraduate and graduate curricula in physical education, through participation in the establishment of requirements for certification, and through participation in the establishment of accreditation standards for teacher education institutions.

The first step in insuring that men and women well qualified to teach physical education be employed is that of selection for teacher training.

PERSONAL QUALITIES DESIRED

The physical educator should possess the same qualities which are desirable in all people; however, there are certain qualities which he must possess in abundance if he is to become a highly effective teacher. One of these qualities is a high level of *health*. The physical educator must expend a considerable amount of physical and nervous energy. Because his task is an interesting and challenging one, he often is not aware of how much energy he does expend. Often his first class begins at 8:00 AM and he is not finished coaching until 5:30 PM or later. In the evening there may be scheduled games, evening practice sessions, scouting assignments, reviewing of game films, "skull" sessions with the coaches and players, and the multifarious teaching chores indigenous to the teaching profession.

The physical educator must possess *competency in a variety of sports* gained through practice and participation. These experiences will enable him to feel empathy for his students as they undergo the various trials in sports. He will better understand the monotony of routine training; the agony and joy of the complete physical exhaustion after strenuous competition, the elation of victory and the despair of defeat; and the feeling of achievement following the learning of a new stunt or of overcoming fear. The greater the amount of personal skill in athletics he possesses, the more effective he will be as a teacher. If he can demonstrate skill in an activity, it is more probable that his students will listen attentively to his instructions and endeavor to emulate his techniques and movement patterns.

The physical educator should possess *a desire to serve others*. He should not utilize his physical education classes to nourish his own ego by endeavoring to place the students in awe of his physical prowess. To a young and highly skilled physical educator the temptation to impress his students is great but he must remember that his purpose in leading the students is to teach them — not to impress them. He must be able to obtain as much or more satisfaction from helping his students to improve their skills and to grow in wisdom and maturity as he does from a display of his own skills.

Some young men and women who enjoy participation and are skilled in sports learn, to their own dismay and particularly to the dismay of their supervisors, that they do not enjoy teaching. Basically, they are too self-centered to be able to identify with the progress of their students. Often, one who learns physical skills easily and quickly lacks the patience necessary to be an effective teacher because he expects others to learn as easily and quickly as he did and because it has not been necessary for him to make detailed mechanical analyses of sports skills. The successful physical educator is a person who derives satisfaction and pleasure in seeing the joy and pride in the student's face when he increases his chin-ups from ten to twelve, learns a front handspring, or swims the length of the pool for the first time. He derives as much satisfaction from these evidences of a job well done as he does from the applause of spectators, the plaudits of sportswriters, and the hero-worship of fans.

The physical educator must want to bring ego-satisfaction to all students regardless of their level of motor skill and regardless of the strength of their interest in sports. He must seek, develop, and set up opportunities for the obese, the frail, and the poorly coordinated to secure ego-satisfaction through sports. If his greatest interest is basketball or gymnastics or some other activity, he must not endeavor to make all boys or girls over into his own image by teaching only this activity. All sports have worth. The sports having greatest value for a particular boy or girl are those which he or she enjoys most and in which he or she is most proficient. This is true because these are the sports in which they spend the most time and consequently from which they derive most fitness benefits and also because these sports satisfy their psychologic and social needs. This is why they choose them.

The promulgation of a diversified program is a manifestation of the physical educator's maturity and concern for others. He recognizes that the cross-country runner, the hockey player, the wrestler, the dancer, the golfer, and the volleyball player need recognition as much as does the football, basketball, or baseball player.

The physical educator must possess qualities of *self-discipline, an attractive personality, and an ethical character.* The teacher teaches by example as well as by precept and concept. His admonitions concerning the hazards of smoking are likely to be disregarded if he lacks the self-discipline necessary to abstain. This is particularly true for those teaching elementary or high school students. It will be more difficult for the teacher to help his students to develop warm, friendly, extroverted personalities if he is cold, aloof, and introverted. If the teacher does not practice honesty, integrity, and unselfishness and does not demonstrate the courage to behave in a principled manner in his own relationships with others, all his sermons on sportsmanship and fair play will have little meaning for his students.

The effective physical educator must possess a *concern for his appearance.* He should keep himself physically fit. He should dress neatly and appropriately to the situation and circumstances. He should keep himself and his possessions clean. He should realize that he is contributing to or detracting from the image people have, not only of him, but also of the professional group of which he is a member.

UNDERGRADUATE PREPARATION

One of the purposes of this text is to help students to decide whether or not to select physical education as a career. A study of the competencies required of physical educators can serve as a first step toward reaching this decision. Competencies required determine what courses will be required in the curricula of schools educating future teachers of health, physical education, and recreation.

Competencies

Institutions charged with the education of physical education teachers have a most important role to play in assuring that physical education is conducted according to accepted principles and that it makes progress toward the achievement of its established goals and also toward those of general education. Teacher education institutions accomplish this through developing in future teachers those attitudes, skills, values, and knowledges which will enable them as teachers to move their future students toward the established objectives according to the accepted principles. Schools of physical education and others involved in teacher education have given considerable thought to selection of competencies which should be possessed by physical educators. These competencies are developed through the curriculum — the required and elective courses — and also through the extracurricular activities sponsored by the educational institution. Several nationwide conferences have been convened in order to enable members of the profession to exchange ideas to determine more effectively what competencies should be developed.

One of the earliest and most significant of these conferences was the Jackson's Mill National Conference on Undergraduate Professional Preparation in Physical Education, Health Education, and Recreation held at Jackson's Mill, West Virginia in 1948.[1] The participants concluded that the following personal qualifications are essential to leadership in these three professions:

1. Faith in the worth of teaching and leadership.

2. Personal concern for the welfare of all people.

3. Respect for personality.

4. Understanding children, youth, and adults, and appreciating their worth as citizens.

5. Social understanding and behavior.

6. Community-mindedness.

7. Interest in and aptitude for teaching and leading.

8. Above average mental ability and common sense.

9. Above average health status.

10. Voice of good quality and power, intelligently used.

11. Effective use of language.

12. Sense of humor.

13. Energy and enthusiasm sufficient to the requirements of effective leadership.

A more recent conference was the Professional Preparation Conference sponsored by the American Association for Health, Physical Education, and Recreation. The work of this conference was initiated in April, 1960, and was not concluded until January, 1962. Conference membership included most of the current leaders in physical education. The monumental efforts of these conferees will greatly strengthen professional education in physical education for many years. The recommendations of the Professional Preparation Conference of the American Association for Health, Physical Education, and Recreation have had — and will continue to have — a powerful influence upon the design of teacher education programs in health, physical education, and recreation. These recommendations will influence what courses students will take; the content of the courses; the laboratory courses and field experiences; and administration of teacher education programs. Even though these recommendations are directed primarily at people involved in teacher preparation, a review of some of them will enable the student to understand better why he is required to take certain courses and to have certain laboratory or field experiences. Following are some of the *highlights of the recommendations of the conference which are of concern to students majoring in physical education:*[2]

1. Students majoring in physical education should receive a strong background in general education. It was recommended that 50 per cent of the four-year undergraduate program be devoted to general education.

2. Because of the expansion of knowledge, it was felt that five years of professional preparation are essential for basic preparation for the teaching of health, physical education, and recreation.

3. Professional preparation should not be regarded as having been completed with the attainment of a bachelor's degree but should be a continuous process throughout one's professional career.

4. The physical education profession should determine the content of professional education.

5. The planning and conduct of professional education should be shared by the profession with educational institutions and employing agencies.

6. The curriculum must be responsive to change in a rapidly changing society.

7. Programs of professional preparation should be evaluated frequently in the light of stated objectives.

8. Master's degree candidates must possess the competencies required of the undergraduate major.

9. The program must include emphasis upon the professional obligations and responsibilities of a professional person.

10. Men with coaching responsibilities should be certified if they have not been prepared as physical education majors.*

Further on in its report the National Conference on Professional Preparation listed *general objectives for professional preparation in health education, physical education, and recreation education.*[3] These objectives were formulated on the basis of the duties and responsibilities of practicing physical educators and serve to determine the courses that will be required of students majoring in health, physical education, and recreation. These recommended general objectives were as follows:

1. Teachers, leaders, specialists, and administrators in health education, physical education, and recreation should possess a broad base of knowledge that characterizes an educated person. To this end, the programs for the professional preparation of such personnel should provide for:

   The acquisition of communications and computational skills;

   An understanding of natural laws and phenomena and their significance for man and for society;

   An understanding of social and organizational relationships in modern civilization;

   An understanding of the humanities and their contributions to culture.

2. Professional personnel in health education, physical education, and recreation should possess the knowledge required to direct learning experiences effectively. The programs for the professional preparation of such personnel should provide for:

   An understanding of the psychological nature of the individual, his basic needs, his potentialities, and his problems;

   An understanding of human growth and development and the implications for educational procedures;

   An understanding of the nature of learning and the conditions under which learning takes place most effectively.

*paraphrased.

3. Professional personnel in health education, physical education, and recreation should acquire a mastery of the knowledges and skills unique to their respective fields. The programs for the professional preparation of such personnel should provide for:

An understanding of the history, the philosophy, and the basic purposes of the specialized area; and the relationships among the three areas;

An understanding of the relationship of the structure and the function of the human body to effective living;

An understanding of the nature of the curriculums and the programs that are suitable for various maturity and ability levels and a mastery of the specific activities and concepts that comprise such curricula and programs;

An understanding of, together with experiences in, a variety of methods and techniques suitable for teaching, developing, and implementing programs and services;

An understanding of appropriate evaluative techniques; and the utilization of these techniques for motivation and for the determination of progress and outcomes;

An understanding of the value of research and its implications for the improvement of the profession, and the development of skill in the use of the scientific method and in the reporting of research;

An understanding of the obligations of professional preparation personnel to their profession.

The conference report pointed out that professional laboratory experiences play an important role in the preparation of teachers. Five types of laboratory experiences were described. These included "systematic observation," "initial limited participation," "full participation," "student teaching," and "field work" Each of these types presents the student with increasing responsibility in order that by the time he has completed his professional laboratory experiences he has experienced most aspects of a teacher's work. At the present time, few curricula in teacher education provide all five types of laboratory experiences for their students; however, efforts in this direction are beginning to be made.

Recommendations of the Professional Preparation Conference for Teacher Education in Physical Education

Some of the more important conclusions listed by the conferees which are of concern to students majoring in physical education are listed below. These tell students what is expected of them. The competencies required of a physical educator are obviously somewhat different from those required of a health educator, consequently there are differences in the curricula followed.

1. Highly skilled men and women performers should be encouraged to become physical educators.

2. To be admitted as a major in physical education a student should have an adequate background in science and the humanities; possess good health, above average physical development, a high level of sports skills, and an attractive personality; and demonstrate potential for developing skill in speaking and writing.

3. Only those students should be retained in the program who maintain a satisfactory academic record, demonstrate a satisfactory level of athletic skill, show evidence of good health practices, possess a high level of emotional stability, and show unimpeachable character and integrity.

4. The freshman and sophomore years should be devoted primarily to general education, the junior and senior years to an exploration of the body of knowledge of human movement and physical education activities, and the fifth year should be used to apply the principles of human movement to the problems of organizing, planning, and teaching physical education activities in such a manner as to satisfy both individual and group needs. The Master's program should be devoted to concentration in acquiring knowledge of physical education and in applying research techniques in creative studies.

5. The program should be so designed that it serves not only individual students but also the needs of society.

A student who is contemplating majoring in physical education can make an appraisal of his fitness for this area by checking himself against the first three items of the above list. Students who have already made a positive decision can secure an overview of what will be expected of them and what they will be doing during their undergraduate years.

The conference group recommended that the content of *general professional education* for physical education majors include courses which would develop the following knowledges and understandings:

1. Nature and purposes of education and of educational institutions in their historical and social context.

2. Principles of learning and of teaching, including classroom learning, guidance and counseling, and measurement and research methodology in educational psychology (more specifically, the essential elements are an understanding of the school as a social institution, the sociological structure of the school in its community, the theories of learning and child

development, the management of a classroom or laboratory as a learning situation, curriculum development, and methods of teaching).

3. The major tasks of determining what and how to teach — determining instructional objectives, selecting best learning experiences, organizing experiences into effective learning sequences, managing classroom and laboratory situations, and evaluating the effectiveness of instruction.

4. The various general problems of school administration and supervision.

In *specialized professional education* for majors in physical education, the following are some of the recommendations made:

1. The undergraduate preparation should emphasize preparation as a generalist.

2. The student should be aided in developing a consistent philosophy of physical education through a study of philosophy and educational philosophy in order that as a teacher he be better able to understand some of the problems facing physical education.

3. Students should be aided in developing — and required to develop — skill in performance and in teaching a variety of physical education activities and should know progressions in teaching these activities.

4. The teaching of coeducational activities is strongly recommended and should develop a mutual understanding and appreciation of the differences in program emphases and of those sports which are unique to the opposite sex.

5. Students should develop competencies essential to teaching physical education activities in elementary schools.

In order that physical educators will be reasonably well prepared to assume responsibility for health education where it is still the pattern to require one person to *assume responsibility for health education* as well as physical education and also in order that physical educators will better *understand the relationships between physical education, health education, and recreation,* the following recommendations were made:

1. Physical education students should take courses in personal and community health, the school health program, child growth and development, methods and materials of health education, and in school-community relationships.

2. Physical education students should take a course in safety education where they will become familiar with accident prevention in the home, community, school and in traffic; develop a philosophy of accident

prevention; and become thoroughly familiar with safety practices and legal implications pertinent to physical education.

3. Physical education students should develop understanding of and skill in the use of group processes, in the use of the tools of human relations and in training, using, and supervising volunteers.

4. Physical education students should develop an understanding of the philosophy of recreation and of the role of the recreation leader in contributing to the welfare of both the individual and society.

5. Physical education students should acquire knowledge of the principles which guide recreation programs as well as of various recreation activities.

The conferees listed a number of courses through which the listed competencies are developed and which are offered or required at institutions throughout this country. They then indicated which of these courses they strongly recommended, moderately recommended, recommended on an elective basis, or did not recommend. Listed below are those courses which were strongly recommended:

English Composition	Human Physiology
General Chemistry	History
General Physics	General Psychology
General Biology	General Sociology
General Zoology	Literature (English, American, or Foreign)
General Human Anatomy	Philosophy

The Arts (music, art, theater arts)

Social and Philosophical Foundations of Education

Educational Psychology (growth and development)

Educational Curriculum and Instruction

Directed Teaching

Introduction and Orientation to Physical Education

Administration and Supervision of Physical Education

Curriculum and Instruction in Physical Education

History, Philosophy and Principles of Physical Education

Measurement and Evaluation in Physical Education

Skills Courses (to develop abilities in teaching,
    coaching and officiating)

Specialized Foundation Science Courses (such as
    kinesiology and physiology of exercise)

Adapted Physical Education

Health Education and Safety Education

Recreation Education

Field Work

Electives

   The conference group also rated a number of physical education activities. Those which were strongly recommended for both men and women included:

1. All forms of aquatics — diving, life saving, swimming, water safety, canoeing, scuba, and small craft.

2. Team Sports — basketball, softball, speedball, and volleyball.

3. Individual and Dual Sports — archery, badminton, golf, gymnastics, swimming, tennis, and track and field.

4. Mass or Group Games — games of low organization, lead-up games, and recreational games such as shuffleboard, table tennis, and skish.

5. Individual and group contests.

6. Relays.

7. Rhythms and dance activities — social and square dance.

Activities strongly recommended for men only included:

1. Team Sports — baseball, football, and touch football.

2. Combatives — wrestling.

Activities strongly recommended for women but not strongly recommended for men included:

1. Team sports — soccer.

2. Individual and dual sports — bowling.

3. Rhythms and dance activities — folk dance, fundamental rhythms, and modern dance.

The conferees concluded that people employed as either *part time or full time athletic coaches* should be certified as teachers and should have a minimum of preparation in the following areas:[4]

1. Basic biological science
2. Growth and development
3. Anatomy and physiology
4. Personal health and nutrition
5. Safety and accident prevention specific to activity areas
6. First aid, athletic training, and conditioning
7. Theory and practice in coaching various sports
8. Principles and administration of physical education and athletics.

A number of general qualities and competencies required of a person assuming coaching or training responsibilities were listed. Some of the knowledges and understandings which this person should possess include:

1. The relationship of physical education, including athletics, to the purposes and objectives of education.
2. The relationships between the physical education, intramural, and interscholastic athletic programs.
3. The responsibility of interscholastic athletics in contributing to the objectives of the school-community health program.
4. Legal responsibilities peculiar to athletics.
5. The responsibilities of interscholastic athletics to contribute to the development of social values.
6. The relationships of the coach and the athletic trainer to the physician.

In addition, coaches and athletic trainers need to learn to speak and to write effectively and to maintain emotional control under the stressful conditions peculiar to athletics.

Professional laboratory experiences are a most important part of the professional preparation of a physical educator. Physical education students should be introduced gradually, but early, to directed laboratory experiences of various kinds, requiring assumption of increasing responsibility. Provision should be made for laboratory experiences as a portion of specialized professional courses. Students should be provided with both on-campus and off-campus laboratory experiences. Students should have a full-time off-campus teaching experience at both the elementary and secondary school levels. Students should not receive their student teaching experiences at a school which they formerly attended. The student teacher should receive a variety of experiences including:

1. Teaching different types of activities

2. Coaching athletic teams

3. Supervising intramural or extramural activities

4. Officiating contests

5. Working with clubs or demonstration groups

6. Assisting with administrative functions

7. Attending such functions as staff meetings, athletic banquets, and parent-teacher meetings.

A JUSTIFICATION FOR THE RECOMMENDED COMPETENCIES

The experiences he has had while in high school and the qualities listed earlier help to determine whether the student has the desire, skills, abilities, and personality traits to continue his education in physical education. The formal courses taken in college help to establish the background for the professional work ahead. Some of the curricular experiences apply directly to the tasks to be performed. Others are required or encouraged because they lay a foundation that should prepare the future teacher to better face those situations faced by every responsible member of a community. A kinesiology course enables the future physical education teacher to understand and to analyze physical movement. In the evaluation course, the student learns how to plan, organize, administer, and interpret testing programs. In the methods courses, the student learns the administrative procedures for conducting physical education classes. In the general education courses, the student acquires those skills, knowledges, attitudes, and appreciations which will make him a happier person and a more effective citizen and family member. Courses in this category include English, composition, literature, mathematics, political science, and psychology.

General Education

Many universities provide liberal education experiences during the student's first two years before he begins his professional preparation. This not only provides the student with the time and knowledge to become more certain of his vocational goals but it also helps the institution to eliminate those students who have not shown the ability or desire to enter the professional curriculum.

As stated earlier, the responsibilities of being a teacher should have priority over those of being a physical educator. This makes it necessary that the student see how the general field of education fits into the total social scene. He must also learn about the characteristics of youth. Normally, courses in the history, principles, or philosophy of education lay such groundwork. When one has an understanding of the approaches made to educating people of other societies, he may have a better idea as to what will work in his society.

Although much has been written and said of a five-year program of professional preparation in the teaching profession, four years is the current pattern in most institutions. However, most state certification laws require that the teacher complete a master's degree within ten years of teaching.

There probably are no two identical curricula in the nation; however, many reveal the same characteristics. If one were to examine college catalogs he would find comparatively few major differences in the curricular requirements for a major in physical education. Most institutions require four years of work or about 120—130 semester hours, and of these about forty are in the major field, thirty in education, and the remaining in general education. It is through the curricular requirements that the competencies discussed earlier are developed.

One finds it difficult to find much agreement on a definition of general education (liberal education). Experts are not in agreement on the areas which comprise this field. Generally speaking, the following categories are included: communications, history, social science, physical sciences, and humanities. When one has explored each of these areas, he has begun to lay a foundation for the liberal education which is necessary for social leaders of today. Charles W. Eliot gave expression to this thought back in 1898 when he said about liberal education: "Without it there can be no such thing as an intelligent public opinion; and in the modern world, the intelligence of public opinion is the one indispensable condition of social progress."[5] The statement is as true today as it was in 1898. In even more forceful words, the late University of Chicago president, William Rainey Harper said: "If a student does work in one subject after another, in one department after another, without discovering the interrelationship of the other subjects or departments as distinct entities without relationship, he loses more than one half of the value of his work — for it is the relationship of thought, and of life that man ought to know, if he is to know anything."[6]

The young men or women preparing for physical education have difficulty comprehending the reason for being required to take what seems to be an undue number of liberal education courses. They often remember their athletic participation of high school days and think that the teaching of physical education involves only blowing a whistle, leading calisthenics, leading drills, commanding children to take showers, and maintaining discipline. They did not understand that the techniques followed and duties required of them were based on other disciplines.

Robert Theobald explains the relationship between a liberal education and one's profession very well when he says: "A specialized knowledge of one subject can be fulfilling for the individual and useful to society only if it is used in conjunction with knowledge of other subjects, for specialized knowledge can only be communicated in the context of general knowledge."[7]

Each of the liberal arts or general education areas makes important contributions to development of the future physical educator's effectiveness as a teacher. Let's look at some of these.

Communications

A teacher is always communicating — with students, parents, colleagues, and the general public. Communications implies transmitting thoughts as well as receiving them. In sending, the teacher must have a vocabulary which will permit him to express his thoughts in lucid terms — both in written and in oral form. He will be expected to write reports, articles, and manuscripts. In order to do so, he must know how to spell and use good grammar. He must know how to use the library and where he can find reference books and periodicals. He must know how to use the tools of the library as well as how to use the ball and the bat.

If he is to attain recognition within his profession, he must become an effective speaker. He must often convey his thoughts to sports writers, the objectives of his coaching program to parents, the reasons for needing an additional staff member to a board of education, and the need for increased play space to the community. His English must be correct and his delivery must be effective. The man who haltingly delivers a disorganized, ill-prepared speech expressed in poor grammar would be better off if he had not appeared.

Social Science

The teacher is involved in a professional endeavor which must be geared to the objectives of society. Although the implementation of society's wishes are frequently years behind their inception, the teacher must be a student of society if this time lag is to be shortened. Courses in sociology help him to understand the structure of society, the characteristics of the suburbs, the seemingly insurmountable problems of the city; and the trends that one can see in his own community. Trends in the dislocation of populations, changing traffic patterns, delinquency rates in certain areas, and family disintegration are all of importance to the individual who wants to be a responsible citizen – and to a physical educator.

The physical educator is always dealing with people. True, he is involved with balls, bats, clubs, mats, etc. – but only as they are used by people. His job is to use physical activities as media to satisfy the needs of individuals and society.

There is no easy answer to sociologic problems because each individual and social forces and interactions are quite complex. There has been abundant research in sociology and in psychology which offers suggestions or answers to many social questions making it unnecessary to solve all social problems entirely by means of trial and error methods. The physical educator who is familiar with some of this research will be more effective.

Political Science

One could hardly be expected to cast his vote intelligently in local and national elections if he did not have an understanding of political science and history. History is the foreshadow of things to come, and only from its study can one properly predict the future. Within this century we have seen a proud Germany, England, and Japan rise, fall, and rise again. There is no reason the United States would be exempt from such a fate. Constant vigilance from its citizens and study of the government and its problems will do much to help citizens intelligently assess the various solutions offered. Furthermore, political ideologies influence physical education in many ways.

Economics

We have been called a nation of economic illiterates. This is not surprising since less than twenty-five per cent of the population will take an economics course in high school or college. People need a better understanding of economics since it is important to every family in the country. About six million people owned stock in the New York Stock Exchange in 1950. This jumped to twenty-one million in 1965, and it is estimated that thirty million will hold stock by 1975. With the terms "unemployment rates," "gross national product," and "discretionary income" being a part of the language found in newspapers and in popular magazines, the college student should acquire an understanding of these phrases.

The economic welfare of a nation determines the expenditures that will be made for physical education, athletics, recreation, and health. Expenditures are made in these areas only after basic survival needs have been met.

Physical Sciences

As mentioned earlier, the physical educator is dealing with humans, and therefore, it is essential that he learn as much as he can about them. The psychological aspect was previously discussed. Physical educators need to be able to answer a variety of questions in all fields and need a wide background.

There are many practical questions, the answers to which can be obtained from the biological and physical sciences. The practitioner may know the rote answers but the professional with good scientific background is not only familiar with the research in such areas but he also is familiar with principles from the physical sciences which bear upon these questions.

Humanities

The humanities represent an area concerned with man's relationship with his fellow man — literature, religion, philosophy, and the fine arts. These subjects in the liberal arts or general education curriculum have been struggling to maintain or improve their position because the scientific subjects have received more attention owing to man's concern for vocational preparation and his desire for materialistic improvement. Dean George C. Branam evaluates the situation as follows: "It is not uncommon for educated men, after expressing their overwhelming belief in liberal education, to advocate sacrificing the meager portion found in most curricula to get in more subjects related to the technical job training which is now the principal goal. The respect they profess, however honestly they proclaim it, is in the final analysis superficial and false. They must squeeze in one more math course for the engineer, one more course in comparative anatomy for the premedical student, one more accounting course for the business major. The businessman does not have to know anything about a Beethoven symphony; the doctor does not have to comprehend a line of Shakespeare; the engineer will perform his job well enough without ever having heard of Machiavelli. The unspoken assumption is that the proper function of education is job training and that alone."[8]

The humanities hold values for all human beings regardless of their abilities, interests, or means of livelihood. They hold such values for all men precisely because they are focused not upon specialized need but upon universal needs.

All people should recognize that there is much more to life than bread and work. Shakespeare knew it a long time ago when he had Hamlet say: "What is a man if his chief goal and market of his time be that to sleep and feed? A beast, no more." With the increased leisure which is within our grasp, we can now use it to embellish our lives with appreciation of the beauty of nature and of literature. The difference between existence and life is the intelligent use of leisure.

Not only should the physical educator understand some of the basic tenets of the arts and the sciences, but he should also understand the interrelationships between physical education and the arts and sciences. The interrelationship between sport and economics, health, art, music, literature, and marketing is becoming more obvious. If the reader questions this, he should consider these questions:

What would a football game be like without music?

If a major league football or baseball star did not endorse any products commercially, what effect would this have on his income?

What is the effect of the socializing factor on the personality of a shy youngster?

How important is it to recapture a thrilling moment of sport on canvas, in sculpture, or on film?

Does an international sporting event, such as the Olympics, do anything for world understanding?

What is the effect on a community when a thruway or a shopping center makes it necessary to eliminate the city park or playground?

What part does physical education play in military preparation?

Objectives of Professional Preparation

It is in the professional preparation courses that the student gains his first experiences in education. During the professional laboratory experiences he visits schools to observe and evaluate the methods of experienced teachers. He has the opportunity to put into practice the theories and knowledge which he has learned throughout his previous three years. He actually teaches youngsters, interprets the responses which the students give him to help him understand just how successful he has been. He is placed in a position where he participates in real life teaching situations. He checks in at the main office in the morning, takes charge of a class completely when the teacher is absent, checks his preparedness when emergency circumstances cause his previous plans to be discarded, and works alongside a competent and experienced teacher.

Early in his preparation he took activity courses in basic sports, activities which he had experienced while in high school. These are sports which play an important part in nearly all junior and senior high school programs. They are usually enjoyable to him because he usually has reasonably good skill in them.

Later he will be exposed to the rudiments of archery, handball, golf, and tennis — sports that are far less common in the background of most physical education majors. Nevertheless, they represent areas which should be learned well by prospective teachers because these are the sports which will be played by adults for many years after their interscholastic and intercollegiate athletic careers have been forgotten. In the role of the beginner, the physical education student experiences once again the feeling of being awkward in a sport and yet he feels the satisfaction of learning.

He will take courses in aquatics, gymnastics, and wrestling. He may sense fear — of drowning, of dismounting from a horizontal bar or of somersaulting on a trampoline. In wrestling, he engages in a combative contest with no outside help and he feels the focus of attention on himself with no one to lend a hand and no place to hide.

He takes courses in kinesiology and physiology of exercise which deal with the more scientific aspects of this profession. Through such experiences the student learns more about the effects of sports upon the body. In methods courses, he learns both the art and the science of teaching and the foremost techniques for making activity exciting to young people. In the tests and measurement course he learns to evaluate his own teaching success and his students' successes in acquiring knowledge, skill, and improved physical fitness. The evaluations made in physical education classes are not dissimilar to those experienced in marketing when a company wants to ascertain the effectiveness of an advertising campaign or to the evaluations made by

Judy Wills, at age 9, doing a back somersault

industry when it wants to know how strong a certain piece of steel is and whether or not it will do the task assigned to it. This is why automobile companies road test their cars before they finally go into production. A football coach also wants to know what play is most effective and on what downs and in which part of the field it is most effective.

Health courses are included in the curriculum because sport goes hand-in-hand with mental, social, and physical health. The physical education teacher should know how to evaluate health reports made by the nurse or physician. He should know the symptoms and the aftereffects of a cold, mononucleosis, hernia, or an appendectomy. He must have knowledge about sleeping, smoking, drugs, weight reduction, and methods of countering infectious diseases and tension.

CONTINUING PROFESSIONAL GROWTH

One's professional preparation cannot be measured solely on the number of professional courses he has successfully completed, the number of semester hours on his transcript, or that he has a certain degree. The explosion of knowledge in recent years has made it imperative to keep up with one's profession in a number of ways besides those considered to be "formal education." While they may not show on an academic record, the quality of the work of the individual in the gymnasium, as rated by outside observers and in the teacher's own evaluation of himself, can be changed because of efforts expended in allied learning adventures. Some school systems are beginning to recognize the worth of such activities and give them consideration, along with formal preparation, when it comes to advancing a person on the salary schedule. These allied learning adventures include membership in professional organizations; attendance at clinics, workshops, and conventions; research and publication of articles, textbooks, and monograms.

Professional Organizations

It is natural for people with similar interests to band together to discuss mutual problems and suggested solutions, for fellowship, and to work toward common goals which will improve their profession. Physicians have the American Medical Association. Attorneys have the American Bar Association. Teachers have the National Education Association. Physical educators have the American Association for Health, Physical Education, and Recreation which is a department of the National Education Association. It is a voluntary professional organization which brings together teachers, administrators, leaders, and students in the related fields of health, physical education, and recreation. Its membership has grown from 49 in 1885 to 763 in 1905, to 2879 in 1925, to 6470 in 1935, to 18,912 in 1955, and now stands at over 49,000 members. This rapid growth has occurred because the organization has served its members well by helping them to become more effective teachers. Members are aided in becoming more effective through conferences, clinics, projects, placement services, and the publications of the organization. Many schools of physical education sponsor student physical education clubs which involve membership in this organization. This outstanding organization's aims are as follows:

1. To support, encourage, and provide guidance for personnel as they seek to develop and conduct programs in health, physical education, and recreation education.

2. To facilitate cooperation among the three fields.

3. To increase public understanding and appreciation of the value of the fields as they contribute to human welfare.

4. To encourage research which will enrich the depth and scope of each of the fields.

5. To evaluate continuously professional standards for personnel and programs.

6. To hold national conventions and to sponsor conferences, institutes and meetings which will make the organization more effective; and to support state and regional organizations in similar ventures.

7. To produce and distribute such publications as will be of assistance to professional personnel in their work.

8. To cooperate with other professional groups of similar interests for the ultimate development of these allied fields.

9. To improve the effectiveness of health education, physical education, and recreation in the promotion of human welfare.

10. To conduct such other activities as shall be approved by the Board of Directors and Representative Assembly of the Association.[9]

The organization is comprised of eight divisions, each representing a special interest area of members. These divisions are: Dance, General, Physical Education, Recreation, Girls' and Women's Sports, Men's Athletics, Safety Education and School Health. Geographically, AAHPER is divided into six district associations: Central, Eastern, Midwest, Northwest, Southern, and Southwest. Each district elects its own officers. All fifty states, plus the District of Columbia, Puerto Rico and Guam, have state associations which elect their own officers.

AAHPER has, through its multi-million dollar budget and increased personnel, offered its membership many services during recent years. Most prominent have been the following:

1. Fitness Test Project of 1957-58 and the re-test in 1964-65 to determine norms for school children in grades 5–12 as well as for college age men and women.

2. The Sports Skill Test Project in which norms will be published for twenty sports.

3. The Project on Recreation and Fitness for the Mentally Retarded (ended May, 1969).

4. The National Girls' Athletic Association Project to initiate and expand intramural and extramural programs for high school girls and college women.

5. The Educational Leadership Project on Smoking and Health which has been funded by the National Clearing House on Smoking and Health in the US Public Health Service and which has been established to provide leadership training for school health personnel and other educators who are concerned with smoking education at the national, state, and local levels.

6. The Lifetime Sports Education Project which sponsors many clinics for teachers and recreation leaders in tennis, golf, and bowling.

7. The Knowledge and Understandings Test Project established to develop achievement tests of knowledge and understandings of physical education in cooperation with the Educational Testing Service of Princeton. These tests, with national norms for elementary, junior high, and senior high school levels, will be used by many school systems.

8. The Outdoor Education Project which has sponsored many workshops and clinics on outdoor activities (notably archery).

9. The K-4 Skills Progress Project established to analyze locomotor, nonlocomotor, and manipulator skills according to growth and development patterns of young children and to present appropriate movement experiences for the improvement of these skills.

10. The Athletic and Recreation Federation of College Women which publishes *Sportlight* four times each year and which endeavors to provide guidelines and recommendations for women's athletic programs.

11. Continued publication of books such as *Physical Education for High School Students* and *Research Methods in Health, Physical Education, and Recreation* and pamphlets such as the *Varsity Lettermen's Clubs, Girls Sports Organization Handbook, Youth Fitness Test Manual, Sports*

Library for Girls and Women, How We Do It Game Book, Goals for American Recreation, Suggested School Safety Policies, Accident Prevention in Physical Education, Athletics, and Rhythmic Activities.

12. Publication of the periodicals *Journal of Health, Physical Education, and Recreation* nine times a year and the *Research Quarterly* which keep the members abreast of all developments in their fields. The journal presents national, district, and state news of professional activities and projects and articles of diversified nature from how-to-do-it to philosophical discussions of current problems. The *Research Quarterly* presents research reports on all aspects of health, physical education, recreation education, and safety.

All of the standard professional organizations have annual conventions. AAHPER holds national, district, state, and local conferences. Other professional associations such as the National College Physical Education Association, The American College of Sports Medicine, and the various coaches associations also hold conventions. These afford the members the opportunity to learn more advanced techniques for doing things as well as help them to keep abreast of the developments in their particular fields.

There are also opportunities to renew and to extend acquaintances. Many administrators at conventions are seeking people to fill positions. They will always find men and women who are anxious to move from present positions to other positions which seem to their advantage. While there are numerous values to be derived from attending the scheduled meetings, no one should overlook the values to be realized from informal encounters with other professionals when they can exchange ideas concerning mutual problems.

The majority of public school districts share in the expenses incurred by the teacher who attends conventions providing the school administrators think attendance at the meetings will benefit the school system. The *National Education Association Research Bulletin* reported: "The cost of hiring a substitute is not included in conference funds in most districts although almost all of those surveyed indicated that the substitute teacher is supplied at board expense with no loss of salary to the regular teacher. . .Some values to be derived from attending professional meetings are considered to be the improvement of instruction in the classroom, bringing the best educational thinking and facts to bear on the school program, encouragement of continual professional growth and evaluation, and the promotion of efficiency in spending the school tax dollar."[10]

Clinics

Teacher education institutions, sporting goods dealers, and professional organizations often sponsor clinics in order to improve the knowledge of teachers and coaches in specific areas. Usually, the clinic is centered around a specific sport and outstanding authorities lecture on a subject for which they are noted. The information presented at clinics is often very practical, and question and answer periods are usually conducted after the addresses. These provide "down to earth" answers which teachers can apply to the solution of problems in their own specific situations.

Research

Everyone possesses some degree of curiosity; however, some people are so curious that they are willing to extend themselves to find answers to their questions. Perhaps the reader has wondered how long it would take to improve the performance of a class in pull-ups. He may wonder if it would be done faster if the students did isometric exercises or if it would be done faster by having them do more pull-ups. Perhaps dips on the parallel bars would do as well — or the use of wall pulleys would accomplish the goal more quickly. The physical educator may wonder whether once a person has attained a certain number of pull-ups and is then inactive for six months or a year, how much he will retrogress — or will he? Similar questions are asked by all teachers sooner or later and some are interested enough to try to discover the answers.

Such questions stimulate some instructors so much that they set up experiments in their schools and arrive at answers. Others might read a great deal on the subject, ask questions of their friends, and then construct several experiments to solve the problem. In so doing, they become more expert in this special area. They may also publish their findings and thus contribute to their profession.

Departments, schools, or colleges of physical education in the large universities establish a research laboratory with sophisticated and expensive equipment including heartometers, electromyographs, and heartographs to analyze cardiac response to measured amounts of exercise; gas analyzers to analyze expired air; treadmills; measuring devices of great variety; dynamometers; physiographs; telemetry equipment; and other equally advanced equipment. They also employ one or more research specialists who devote their entire time, or most of it, to research projects of their own or to guiding graduate students in research.

Publishing

When one publishes, his name and knowledge is disseminated farther than is possible in the classroom. He helps to contribute to his profession, and when he does, his efforts may reward him financially. Obviously, publishing is a means of self-improvement because it is not done without much library research, nor could it be done without thoroughly organizing one's experiences.

Some large universities have a "publish or perish" policy which means they place such an emphasis on writing books and manuscripts for professional periodicals that a teacher's career is influenced more by this ability than it is by his ability to teach. Many colleges, while they encourage publishing and are proud of the efforts of its faculty in this area, do not place undue influence upon it.

A recent survey[11] indicates the reaction of faculty members of four-year institutions toward the priority of publishing in reference to promotions. A little less than one in four believe that publishing is the primary factor in promotion of faculty in their institutions. Almost the same proportion think that teaching ability is the primary consideration at their institutions. The tables below indicate that their chances for promotion depend on other factors as well as on their publishing and teaching ability:

IMPORTANCE OF PUBLISHING

Great Weight:	Publishing is definitely the primary factor in promotion and advancement.	22.9%
Some Weight:	Publishing is important, but other factors are equally important.	55.5%
Little or No Weight:	Publishing is definitely less important than other factors.	21.6%

IMPORTANCE OF TEACHING ABILITY

Great Weight:	Teaching is definitely the primary factor in promotion and advancement.	24.9%
Some Weight:	Teaching is important, but other factors are equally important.	61.4%
Little or No Weight:	Teaching is definitely less important than other factors.	13.7%

Graduate Preparation (Master's Degree)

While most states do not require teachers to have five years of preparation, many do. Eventually, however, teachers will spend five years in preparing themselves to teach. At the present time, a few state certification laws require a fifth year but most school systems make graduate study so financially rewarding that most teachers ultimately earn the master's degree. While it is difficult for a student just starting his preparation to project himself to the time when he will be ready to begin graduate work, he should give it some attention.

Regardless of the graduate major he selects, he must first meet the entrance requirements of the institution. As the years go by these will become more arduous. For instance, some graduate schools will not admit a student to their program unless he has earned at least a 2.6 (3=B) cumulative undergraduate average. Others expect a 3.0 (B) average during his last two years or in his major subjects. Still others will admit any recipient of a bachelor's degree to a 30-semester hour program to help him meet certain local or state certification requirements. These programs entail about 24—34 semester hours of specified courses in the major and elective areas. The undergraduate student should recognize the importance of scholastic achievement to his professional advancement and progress.

What the student's major is depends upon his vocational goals. If he is firmly convinced that physical education teaching has been a sound choice for him, he probably should continue in that field. If he is beginning to question this and has thoughts of becoming a director of physical education or a principal, he should prepare for administration and supervision. There are many physical educators who have become principals. Others who are interested in research may select a graduate school and courses which will best prepare them to do research. A discernible trend among graduate schools of physical education is the development of several distinct programs which will permit a variety of specialization pathways.

There are several ways to work toward the master's degree. One, which is becoming increasingly popular, is that of receiving a graduate assistantship. Graduate assistantships are usually awarded to the most qualified students. The candidate is often expected to possess a 3.0 academic average and relatively high graduate record examination scores. He should also have satisfactory recommendations from his major professors.

The graduate assistant does part-time work at a rate that permits him to complete his studies within a calendar year. Simultaneously, he gains experience working in college programs, sometimes as a teacher of basic instruction classes, at other times in coaching, and still other times working in the intramural, recreation, or research areas.

Graduate Preparation (Doctorate Degree)

A student beginning his undergraduate preparation is not likely to give serious consideration to working for a doctorate, because he is too concerned about completing this year's work, or even tomorrow's assignment. However, there are a few students who know their ultimate professional goals require possession of a doctoral degree and who want to begin working toward them as soon as possible. All students preparing to teach should have an understanding of the requirements for the doctorate degree.

At the turn of the 20th century it was recommended that all teachers have some college preparation. Previous to this time any high school graduate could teach. Soon it was required that a teacher complete a two-year program in a "normal school" before becoming certified. In the 1920's this was increased to three years and shortly after the four-year baccalaureate degree became mandatory. It is almost certain that five years of preparation will be required before the end of this century. This country, and particularly the education profession, places a premium on formal education. Doors open and higher salaries are offered to those with a master's degree and still other doors open and still higher salaries are offered those who have a doctoral degree. There are many other criteria that should be and are used before a person is selected for a certain position, but in most instances, the type of degree is the first prerequisite.

The doctorate is rapidly becoming the required degree for positions of administrative responsibility in the public schools as well as for teaching in the colleges. The person who hopes to become a supervisor of physical education in the public schools, to teach at a university or college, or to serve as a chairman of a department in a university, should begin work toward the doctorate. The degree might be a Doctor of Philosophy, a Doctor of Education, a Doctor of Physical Education, or a Doctor of Health, Physical Education, and Safety. There are several categories, and the institution determines the specific requirements. There are two differences between the Doctor of Philosophy and the Doctor of Education degrees. One of these is that for the Doctor of Philosophy degree the candidate must show a proficiency in reading and translating professional literature in one or two foreign languages. The other is that Ed.D. work is directed primarily toward developing teaching and administrative ability while the Ph.D. is directed primarily toward research and teaching.

Almost all doctoral programs require a preliminary examination before entrance; about two years of full-time course work (approximately 60 semester hours beyond the master's degree); satisfactory completion of a comprehensive written examination based on the course work taken, a scholarly research dissertation, and an oral defense of the dissertation.

SUMMARY

A physical educator needs to possess certain personal qualities in greater abundance than do people in most other endeavors. These qualities are a high level of health, competency in a variety of sports, desire to serve others, self-discipline, an attractive personality, ethical character, and a concern for appearance.

Two major conferences have been convened in order to study and to make recommendations concerning undergraduate professional preparation in health, physical education, and recreation. The first of these was the Jackson's Mill National Conference. The second was the Professional Preparation Conference which was sponsored by the American Association for Health, Physical Education, and Recreation between 1960 and 1962. The recommendations of this conference have been cited in the following categories:

I. Highlights of the recommendations

II. General Objectives for Professional Preparation in Health Education, Physical Education, and Recreation Education.

III. Recommendations for Professional Preparation in Physical Education

A. General recommendations concerning selection, retention, and education of students majoring in physical education.

B. Knowledges and understandings to be developed through general professional education courses.

C. Recommendations in the area of specialized professional education.

D. Recommendations to insure that physical educators will be prepared to assume responsibility for health education and also that they will better understand the relationships between physical education, health education, and recreation education.

E. Courses recommended

F. Activities recommended

G. Areas of understanding recommended for athletic coaches

H. Qualities and competencies recommended for athletic coaches and trainers.

I. Recommendations regarding professional laboratory experiences.

General education courses are required of all college and university students in order that they will enjoy life more fully and become more useful and effective family and community members. General education courses will also aid the student in becoming a more effective physical educator through teaching him to communicate more effectively, by developing an understanding of social groups and social processes, functioning of the human body, and man's relationships with his fellow man through literature, religion, philosophy, and the fine arts.

Professional education courses develop in the student those skills, knowledges, and understandings which are necessary to the teaching process. These are developed through courses in kinesiology, physiology, anatomy, tests and measurement, evaluation, health, adapted physical education, and activity and coaching courses.

Increasingly, the possession of the master's degree is becoming required to teach. Admission standards to graduate schools are being raised. At the present time, many graduate schools require a cumulative undergraduate average of 2.6 (3—B). The doctoral degree is rapidly becoming the required degree for administrative positions and college teaching.

Continued professional growth throughout a teacher's lifetime is mandatory if he is to be most effective. He can be aided in keeping abreast of new knowledge and techniques by being a member of professional organizations, reading professional literature, doing research, publishing, and attending clinics, conferences, and conventions.

QUESTIONS

1. Discuss five personal qualities highly desired in physical educators.

2. List some of the personal qualifications essential to leadership in health, physical education, and recreation as stated at the Jackson's Mill National Conference.

3. Discuss the AAHPER National Conference on Professional Preparation.

4. What skills and understandings did the National Conference on Professional Preparation recommend be possessed by a physical educator in order that he possess the "broad base of knowledge which characterizes an educated person"?

5. What understandings did the above group recommend be possessed by physical educators in order that they be enabled to direct learning experiences effectively?

6. What understandings did the NCPP recommend be developed by health educators and teachers of safety education in order that they understand the differences and the relationships between their own area and those of physical education, recreation, and athletics?

7. What recommendations did the NCPP make regarding the content of general professional education for students majoring in physical education?

8. List the recommendations made by the NCPP with regard to specialized professional education for students majoring in physical education.

9. List the recommendations by the NCPP which would help physical education majors to assume responsibility for health education and also enable them to better understand the relationships between physical education, health education, and recreation education.

10. Discuss the recommendations made by the NCPP concerning knowledge and understandings to be possessed by athletic coaches and trainers.

11. Discuss the differences and the relationships between general education and professional education.

12. Why is skill in communications important to a teacher of health, physical education, or recreation education?

13. Why is an understanding of the social sciences important to a teacher of health, physical education, or recreation education?

14. Why is an understanding of the physical sciences important to a teacher of health, physical education, or recreation education?

15. Why is an understanding of the humanities important to a teacher of health, physical education, or recreation education?

16. What are some of the purposes and activities of the American Association for Health, Physical Education, and Recreation?

17. Explain how you could continue to grow in knowledge, skill, and understanding after you have graduated and are teaching.

FOOTNOTES

1. The Athletic Institute, "A Report on the National Conference on Undergraduate Professional Preparation in Health Education, Physical Education, and Recreation," 1948.

2. American Association for Health, Physical Education, and Recreation, *Professional Preparation in Health Education, Physical Education, and Recreation Education,* Washington, D.C., 1962.

3. *Op. cit.,* pp. 24–25.

4. *Op. cit.,* p. 71.

5. Eliot, Charles W., Inaugural Address as president of Harvard College, In Education Reform: *Essays and Addresses.* New York: Century Co., 1898, pp. 3–4.

6. Harper, William Rainey, "Waste in Higher Education," *Trends of Higher Education.* Chicago: University of Chicago Press, 1905, pp. 98–99.

7. Theobald, Robert, "Higher Education and Cybernation," *NEA Journal* *55*:3:27, March, 1966.

8. Editorial Projects for Education, *The Plight of the Humanities,* 1965.

9. *Annual Report of the American Association for Health, Physical Education, and Recreation,* 1966–67, American Association for Health, Physical Education, and Recreation, Washington, D.C.

10. "Attendance at Professional Meetings," *NEA Research Bulletin* *40*:2:46-57, May, 1962.

11. "What the College Faculty Thinks," *NEA Journal, 55*:4:48, April, 1966.

3

The Physical Educator at Work in the Schools

A PERSON WHO aspires to wealth, who covets power or social status, who enjoys working with things more than with people, or who dislikes physical activity would lead an unhappy life as a physical educator. However, one who enjoys sports and the process of teaching sports skills to others, who enjoys working with people of various ages, and who would gain greater satisfaction from performing a worthwhile social service than from accumulating wealth and material possessions will find in physical education a profession which will bring him a lifetime of satisfaction and pleasure and many moments of joy.

PHYSICAL EDUCATION ACTIVITY CLASSES

Physical educators may be called upon to teach any of a great number of activities. A list of activities and the level at which they are usually taught follows:

	Elementary (Grades 1–6)	Jr. High (7–9)	Sr. High (10–12)	College
Acrobatics	x	x		
Adaptive Physical Education	x	x	x	x
Apparatus Stunts				
Parallel Bars		x	x	x
Horizontal Bar		x	x	x
Side Horse			x	x
Still Rings		x	x	x
Long Horse Vaulting		x	x	x
Balance Beam	x	x	x	x
Side Horse Vaulting	x	x	x	x

	Elementary (Grades 1–6)	Jr. High (7–9)	Sr. High (10–12)	College
Apparatus Stunts *(Cont.)*				
Uneven Parallel Bars		x	x	x
Climbing Ropes	x	x	x	x
Springboard and Mini-tramp Stunts	x	x	x	x
Badminton		x	x	x
Bait and Fly Casting			x	x
Ballet	x	x	x	x
Baseball		x	x	x
Basketball	x	x	x	x
Bowling		x	x	x
Calisthenics	x	x	x	x
Camping and Outdoor Education	x	x	x	x
Canoeing		x	x	x
Combatives		x	x	
Darts	x			
Deck Tennis	x	x		
Diving		x	x	x
Fencing		x	x	x
Field Hockey		x	x	x
Figure Skating	x	x	x	x
Fishing	x	x	x	x
Flag and Touch Football	x	x	x	x
Floor Exercise	x	x	x	x
Fly Tieing			x	x
Folk Dancing	x	x	x	x
Football			x	x
Games of Low Organization	x			
Golf		x	x	x
Gymnastic Dancing	x	x	x	x
Handball			x	x
Horseback Riding		x	x	x
Horseshoes		x	x	x
Ice Hockey		x	x	x
Ice Skating		x	x	x
Isometric Exercises			x	x
Leadup Games	x	x		
Lifesaving		x	x	x
Marching		x	x	
Modern Dancing	x	x	x	x
Obstacle Course	x	x	x	
Paddle Tennis	x	x	x	x
Pyramid Building	x	x	x	x
Rebound Tumbling	x	x	x	x
Relays	x	x		
Rhythms	x	x	x	x
Riflery		x	x	x
Roller Skating	x	x	x	x
Rope Skipping	x	x	x	x
Rowing		x	x	
Sailing		x	x	x
Self-testing Activities	x	x	x	x
Shuffleboard	x	x	x	x

	Elementary (Grades 1–6)	Jr. High (7–9)	Sr. High (10–12)	College
Skating	x	x	x	x
Skiing		x	x	x
Snowshoeing	x	x	x	x
Soccer	x	x	x	x
Social Dancing		x	x	x
Softball		x	x	x
Speedball		x	x	x
Square Dancing	x	x	x	x
Squash			x	x
Swimming	x	x	x	x
Table Tennis	x	x	x	x
Tap Dancing	x	x	x	x
Tennis		x	x	x
Tether Ball	x	x		
Toboganning	x	x	x	x
Track and Field	x	x	x	x
Tumbling	x	x	x	x
Volleyball		x	x	x
Weight Lifting		x	x	x
Wrestling		x	x	x

In teaching these activities physical educators explain and demonstrate the techniques of the activity; present the history, values, rules, and strategies of the game; and utilize various visual aids such as film strips, movies, blackboards, charts, and diagrams. They take roll, organize the class for instruction and games, evaluate, and give individual counseling. Through these processes they endeavor to develop sportsmanlike attitudes, to inculcate habits of healthful living, and to achieve the other objectives of physical education discussed in this text.

INTRAMURAL PROGRAMS

Physical educators are often called upon to organize and to administer intramural programs. A great number of activities may be included in the intramural program. This responsibility entails the scheduling of facilities, players, and teams in such a manner that facilities are used maximally but with no conflicts for their use, and in such a manner that all players or teams entered play one another in equalized competition. It includes the promotion and publicizing of the many facets of the program; purchase, maintenance and supervision of equipment and awards; supervision of the games and contests; securing of game officials; planning and administering a scoring system; and arbitration of disagreements. The position may also involve the writing of an intramural handbook and arranging an intramural awards banquet.

At most universities and colleges at this time, intramural activities must be conducted when available facilities are not being used by physical education classes or interscholastic or intercollegiate teams. Consequently, in these colleges and universities intramural activities are conducted principally in the evening. A few very large universities which have adequate facilities can conduct intramural activities in the afternoon and a few, such as the University of Illinois, have a separate intramural building. In the junior and senior high schools they are conducted during the lunch hour and immediately after school hours.

COACHING

Many physical educators are assigned coaching responsibilities which enable them to teach the highly skilled and highly motivated students. In physical education classes, the teacher must teach many students whose athletic skills and strength of interest range from very low to very high. Because, in coaching, the teacher works with the most highly skilled and interested students, he experiences the pleasure of noting comparatively rapid improvements in skill. He is also subjected to many pressures by some students, fans, and sportswriters, and his own ego needs to compromise his principles and to reject the objectives of education and of physical education in order to produce an impressive win-loss record. He must be a highly moral, principled, and dedicated educator in order to resist these pressures. Because of the great popular appeal of some interscholastic and intercollegiate sports and because of the great attention they attract, the coach is in a position of strength either to favorably or unfavorably influence the achievement of important educational objectives.

The person assigned coaching responsibilities must plan, organize, and direct practice sessions; make and study scouting reports; design strategies; view films; plan game strategy; schedule games; cooperate with and educate sportswriters; select, purchase, and maintain sports equipment; attend coaching clinics; evaluate players; deliver speeches at athletic banquets and before various civic groups; counsel players; obtain and evaluate game officials; plan and supervise team trips; obtain ticket takers, timers, scorers, police and concessionaires for games; and assume responsibility for the behavior of spectators and players at games.

Interscholastic and intercollegiate teams have been fielded in a great variety of sports. These have included the following:

Men	Women
Archery	Archery
Baseball	Baseball
Basketball	Basketball
Bowling	Bowling
Crew	Dance
Cross Country	Ballet
Fencing	Folk and tap
Flag Football	Modern
Football	Fencing
Golf	Field Hockey
Gymnastics	Golf
Ice Hockey	Gymnastics
Lacrosse	Hockey
Polo	Riflery
Riflery	Skiing
Skiing	Skish
Skish	Soccer
Soccer	Softball
Softball	Speedball
Speedball	Swimming
Squash Racquets	Competitive
Swimming	Synchronized swimming
Tennis	Tennis
Touch Football	Track and Field
Track and Field	Volleyball
Tumbling	
Volleyball	
Weight Lifting	
Wrestling	

Physical educators in elementary schools seldom are assigned coaching responsibilities although occasionally they may be assigned such responsibilities at the high school which serves the same school district. Physical educators who teach in junior high schools are often assigned coaching responsibilities in the high school and, in a few communities, in their own junior high school. Physical educators who teach in the high schools almost invariably have some coaching responsibility. This is also true of those who teach in small- and medium-sized colleges and universities. In the large universities, specialization by faculty is made possible as a result of a larger staff. Consequently, the duties of physical educators are not as diversified.

While a high degree of skill and a national reputation as a performer in the sport which he coaches is an asset to the coach, these are by no means mandatory to achievement of great success. A coach is not evaluated on the basis of his skill in the sport. His knowledge of the sport; his ability to teach, to motivate, to inspire and to guide; and his vitality, perseverance, effort, and qualities of character are the major determinants of his success. According to a most successful coach, the late Robert Kiputh, the coach should play the role of a strict but understanding father who discourages excessive familiarity by his players while encouraging them to seek his aid in solving their problems. He must insist on the loyalty and respect of the players, have no favorites, and give no special privileges.

Obviously, the success of a team in terms of the number of contests won is dependent upon many factors other than the ability and efforts of the coach. The abilities of the players, luck, and the schedule are a few of the other factors. Yet, when a team does not win enough games to satisfy the students, alumni, fans, and sportswriters, the coach (in some communities) may lose his position. No other member of the faculty is evaluated on the basis of the number of champions which he produces. Pressures to provide vicarious satisfaction for the ego needs of some students, alumni, faculty, townspeople, and sometimes even school administrators, through the winning of games may cause some coaches to compromise their principles. When they note that able and well qualified colleagues in coaching are discharged when they lose games in spite of having done a good job, a few coaches are tempted to overemphasize winning to the detriment of society and particularly to the detriment of the players.

The responsible, highly principled coach may sometimes be forced to make unpopular decisions but which are, nevertheless, in the best interests of the individual player, team, school, or society. Most coaches make such decisions on the basis of sound educational principles. Because of his prominent position in the community, the athletic coach can be the most influential and useful educator in the entire school.

Women physical educators for the past ten years have been increasingly involved in coaching interscholastic and intercollegiate teams. Thanks to the vigorous and studied efforts of the Division of Girls' and Women's Sports of AAHPER, athletic programs for girls have avoided some of the errors committed by men's and boys' athletic programs. Women physical educators are increasingly being called upon to coach interscholastic or intercollegiate teams; however, more often they assume responsibility for clubs in gymnastics, fencing, modern dance, square dance, synchronized swimming, and other activities. These clubs meet once each week or more often and may present demonstrations of their work. Women physical educators also sponsor play days when students from several schools get together to compete in the various sports activities. Each team is made up of students from the several schools. During sports days school teams compete against teams representing other schools. That is, teams maintain their identity.

CAMPING AND OUTDOOR EDUCATION

Many physical educators spend their summers as camp counselors or directors. Some serve as waterfront directors or as sports or athletic directors in camps. A few own and operate their own camps. An increasing number of public schools provide a camping experience for their students. The physical educator is often placed in charge of this program or plays a key role in its conduct. Other schools provide outdoor education experiences for their students. In these programs nature provides the subject, the classroom, and the visual aids. While the program may be conducted in a camp, it may also be conducted at a museum or zoo, during a hike through the woods and fields, during an overnight trip, or at a marine laboratory. Botany, zoology, art, social science, or other subjects may be studied in these settings. Teachers of the various subject areas participate in this program in a team approach. Often the physical education teacher plays a key coordinating role.

In camps, children learn not only outdoor living skills and athletic skills, but also, more importantly, learn to live with other children in a democratic environment. In addition, they live in a healthful setting away from the tensions and anxieties of the city.

Summer camp positions provide the physical educator with a small supplement to his income while providing his wife and children with an enjoyable and healthful summer.

DANCE

A greater number of employment opportunities are presented to the woman physical educator who is prepared to teach dance in addition to other physical education activities. In the large universities, a teacher specializing in dance may teach no other activities; however, there are few such positions. The dance program has become increasingly popular. This has led to greater emphasis upon this facet of the total physical education program, creating more job opportunities for women physical educators skilled in this area.

Dance should play an important role in all programs of physical education. It is one of the oldest of art forms having provided primitive men with a media for transmitting their tribal history, for giving expression to their emotions, or for preparing themselves emotionally for combat or the hunt. Dancing was a part of almost all of primitive man's religious festivals, rites, celebrations, and initiations. Today it is still useful as a media for emotional release, for self-expression, for translating feelings into action, for beneficial physiologic effects, and for developing balance, poise, and graceful movement patterns.

There are a number of forms of the dance which are taught in the schools. These include *fundamental rhythms* such as running, walking, skipping, jumping, hopping, and portrayal of various personalities; *folk dances* and *singing games; athletic* or *gymnastic dancing* which includes cartwheels, rolls, somersaults, handsprings, running and skipping; *tap* and *clog dancing; square dancing, social* or *ballroom dancing;* and *modern* and *creative dancing* which allow much freedom in movement for expressing oneself creatively and esthetically through movement. Fundamental rhythms are usually taught exclusively in the elementary schools. Modern dance is usually taught exclusively at the senior high school and college level. Folk, tap, and clog dancing are taught at all levels. Athletic or gymnastic dancing are usually taught in the elementary and junior high schools and social dancing is taught in the junior and senior high schools and college.

Dance teachers teach the many dance forms in required physical education classes and in the professional classes, plan and present dance recitals, and serve as advisors to dance clubs.

ADAPTED PHYSICAL EDUCATION

Often a physical educator will be placed in charge of an adapted physical education class in which he will conduct an exercise and sports program, under a physician's guidance, for handicapped students. These programs have also been known by the terms corrective, reconstructive, special, individual, rehabilitative, remedial, or therapeutic physical education. However, the term *adapted physical education* is preferred today. Regardless of the term used, the objectives of the program are to ameliorate or to correct, to whatever extent possible, deviations from normal and to help the individual to adjust to his handicap by teaching him to utilize his physical abilities to the fullest. Some conditions may be amenable to correction through physical activity. These the teacher of adapted physical education will endeavor to correct to whatever extent possible.

Other conditions such as cardiac insufficiency, cerebral palsy, poliomyelitis, paraplegia, multiple sclerosis, epilepsy, congenital anomalies, birth injuries, speech defects, sight defects, hearing defects, mental retardation, psychopathology, and missing limbs cannot be corrected through physical activity. The physical educator in charge of the adapted physical education program will attempt to adapt and to select sports and other big muscle activities which will help students with these conditions to receive the same benefits from their physical education program received by students in regular physical education classes. These are improvement in organic and neuromuscular function, self-realization, socialization, release of tensions, and enjoyment. The handicapped often have a greater need for these benefits than do normal students.

The worker in this field must possess a thorough knowledge of anatomy, physiology, kinesiology, exercise physiology, psychology, teaching methods, and medical terms. He must be patient, possess a strong desire to help the handicapped, and be able to accept the guidance of the physician. Evidences of improvement in the handicapped are seldom dramatic. Progress is usually made slowly. Consequently, the physical educator must possess patience when working with the handicapped. Physical educators simply do not have sufficient training in orthopedics and pediatrics to carry on an extensive corrective program. For these reasons, they must work under the direction of a qualified physician.

There are few practicing physical educators who work exclusively in the adapted program; therefore, the student who is interested in working in this area should qualify himself to teach other physical education activities as well.

RESEARCH

Research is essential to improvement and progress. This is as true for physical education as it is in electronics, aviation, the space program, medicine, or any other area. A large amount of research has been done in physical education by research specialists and their graduate students in the physical fitness or exercise laboratories at large state universities. Many master's and doctoral students elect to do a research project (thesis) under the guidance of a faculty member who is often a specialist in research methods and in tests and measurement and who has mastered the techniques for use of the various and often complex machinery found in the laboratory. The research person must have a good mind, imagination, creativity, dogged perseverance and persistence, and a determination to learn the answers to questions. Many research specialists have served an apprenticeship as research assistant to a more experienced man for several years before being placed in charge of a research program.

All physical educators should have an interest in research, keep abreast of current research, and know how to interpret and evaluate research studies. All physical educators should do research at some time during their professional career. Expensive research equipment is not necessary to do worthwhile research. Many outstanding studies have been reported which were done by public school teachers. Research has been made considerably easier as a result of computers which save many hours of tedious computation and also as a result of greater availability of research grants.

VARIOUS PHYSICAL EDUCATION ENVIRONMENTS.

Physical educators teach groups of various age levels in public and private schools; in institutions such as prisons, churches, and hospitals; in organizations such as YMCA's, YWCA's, YMHA's, YWHA's, athletic clubs, youth hostels, the American Red Cross, playgrounds, and in settlement and neighborhood houses; in community and industrial recreation programs; and in the armed services. The activities, methods, and objectives of the physical education programs in these various settings are basically the same but they do differ in certain respects. For this reason it would be advisable that prospective physical educators be aware of the differences in the physical education programs of the different school levels, institutions, and organizations.

Physical Education in the Elementary Schools

Few students majoring in physical education express a desire to teach at the elementary level. However, a number change their mind after undergoing a student teaching experience at this level when they discover, often to their surprise, that it has been an enjoyable experience. Elementary school children enjoy physical activity for the sheer joy of movement. The physical education period for them is a period for fun, action, and relief from the concentration of sedentary study. Elementary school children are coachable and teachable because they accept the suggestions and advice of their physical education teacher. The ages from 6–12 years are most productive times for teaching sports skills. The skills and interests developed at this age are usually retained. Physical educators are friends, confidants, and heroes to many elementary school children. The trust, enthusiasm, and love of physical activity of elementary school children makes the job of the physical educator in the elementary school a most enjoyable one.

During this period, children should be aided in acquiring orderly habits of work and play, in assuming increasing responsibility and self-reliance, in adjusting to frustration and conflict, and in bouncing back after an emotional upset. They like to win recognition. They are developing perseverance in completing tasks. They are learning to accept rules and regulations and endeavor to conform to the social and moral requirements of their group.

Children of elementary school age do not, and should not, specialize in one sport. During this age, physical fitness and skill in a large variety of fundamental movements should be developed. This makes it mandatory that the physical educator be well-rounded from the point of view of skills in and knowledge of sports and other physical activities. She must know a large number of lead-up games, contests, relays, self-testing activities, swimming, tumbling, floor exercise, dance in its many forms, and rebound tumbling. She should understand the importance of these activities in the maturation of the child. She should understand how they promote the child's physical growth and contribute to his success in living as a useful member of society.

The majority of elementary school administrators and teachers feel that since the elementary school teacher instructs in many different subjects, she should also be responsible for physical education. The result has been that physical educators in most elementary school systems serve principally as consultants and supervisors leaving the classroom teachers to do a major portion of the teaching of activities. Where this pattern is followed, the physical educator may visit as many as fifteen different schools each week. At each school she will conduct a model lesson, answer the teacher's questions, and leave instructional materials and pamphlets. Many elementary school teachers regard the physical education period as a free play or recreational period for the students and as a needed rest period for themselves. This is unfortunate in view of the potential productivity of a well-conducted elementary school physical education program.

When the elementary school physical educator is responsible for the programs of three or more schools, she must spend the major portion of her time in improving the ability of the teachers to teach physical education rather than in teaching the children. She confers with the teachers about their teaching problems, offers suggestions for introducing forthcoming units, indicates methods for stimulating interest through intraschool and interschool competition, explains methods for equating teams, demonstrates how to set up tournaments of various kinds, and informs teachers how to conduct competition in various events. There appears to be a trend among institutions preparing teachers of physical education to offer specialized programs for those who plan to teach physical education in the elementary schools.

A supervisory position of this type requires a highly experienced, well qualified, and mature person. This person should be one who is firm yet diplomatic. She must understand physical education's principles, objectives, and scientific and philosophic bases well enough to enable her to convince teachers of other subjects of its worth. The physical educator should possess a thorough understanding of the role physical education plays in the total educational process of the elementary school. This entails, in part, an understanding and an appreciation of the role other subjects play in the total program.

Physical Education in the Junior High Schools

Children in junior high school are usually in early adolescence. This is the time of appearance of the secondary sex characteristics and is also a time of rapid growth which contributes to awkwardness and to early fatigue. These physical manifestations serve as fairly reliable indexes of physiologic age and are useful for classification purposes since children do not reach either puberty or adolescence at the same chronological age. Boys at this time are beginning to realize that girls are interesting but they do not know what to do about their confused feelings toward them. Girls, and some boys, become very sensitive about their appearance. It becomes very important to both boys and girls that they be socially acceptable to their peers, consequently they dress alike, enjoy the same music, hold the same values, and seek certification of their acceptability to their peers by moving about in gangs. Patterns of emotional adjustment acquired at this age often persist throughout life.

The physical educator can help the early adolescent to understand how the physical changes in his body affect both his emotions and his social relationships. The physical educator can derive much satisfaction from helping boys and girls develop from awkward, skinny, underdeveloped, or obese children into well-coordinated, well-built, self-assured young men and women.

If the students have participated in a good elementary school physical education program, they have been well grounded in a variety of sports skills and are ready in junior high school to refine these skills and to begin learning the basic strategy of games. The team games of softball, volleyball, touch football, basketball, and soccer are most common and popular in junior high school physical education programs for boys. Track and gymnastics give both boys and girls an opportunity to objectively measure their own performance. All forms of dancing are popular among the girls.

Intramural programs play a vital role in the total junior high school physical education program. These are usually conducted during the lunch hour and immediately after school. They should include as great a variety of activities as facilities will permit. Some junior high schools sponsor interscholastic teams. Junior high school interscholastic athletic programs, when conducted according to sound educational, psychological, and physiological principles, are greatly beneficial to both the participants and the community. Participants will improve in physical fitness, acquire sound health habits, develop self-confidence, and learn to value perseverance, cooperation, and determination.

Physical Education in the Senior High Schools

While the most rapid rate of growth occurs during the time boys and girls are in junior high school, the rate of growth is still relatively rapid when they are students in senior high school. Puberty, the process through which an organism becomes capable of reproducing, is usually almost completed. Adolescence, which refers to the social aspects of the maturation process, has usually not been completed. Puberty is completed between fourteen and nineteen years of age, the majority of children completing the process at about sixteen years of age. At puberty the boy feels a need to prove himself masculine and strong in order to obtain the recognition of his peers. His status depends greatly upon his ability in sports and games. Boys of this age have a strong biologic need for vigorous physical activity. The innate need for physical activity is not as pronounced in girls but it is present.

The adolescent strives to achieve independence from his parents in order to develop the feeling that he is a mature person. Because his progress toward maturity occurs in stops and starts, he seems to regress to child-like behavior from time to time. The adolescent's desire to achieve and to demonstrate maturity by assuming self-responsibility for making decisions and by becoming self-sufficient can serve as an aid to teachers and other adult leaders of youth if this desire is properly guided.

High school students, particularly boys, enjoy competitive activities. Boys enjoy the rough-and-tumble body contact types of activities because these help them to prove their masculinity. Participation in sports can help them to develop courage, self-discipline, and interest in people. Consequently, a greater emphasis is placed upon these types of activities in the senior high school physical education program than in the junior high school physical education program. Team games of higher organization and dual and individual games play a more important role. During their junior high school years, boys and girls are usually introduced to the fundamentals of these activities. In their high school physical education program students usually work toward perfection of the skills of the games. For example, in basketball they could learn to shoot with either hand. In volleyball they could learn to spike the ball with accuracy and to drive it downward with maximum force. In gymnastics, tumbling, and diving, they could learn more difficult stunts, to put stunts together into routines, and to execute stunts with greater force and precision. In team sports they could learn the strategies of offensive and defensive play. In short, the senior high school physical education program should not become merely a supervised free play period with attendance taken and the class organized into teams for play. Nor should there be merely a repetition of the instructional content and materials presented in the junior high school program. There is adequate skill and intellectual content as well as need for modifying or changing attitudes and values to challenge the most energetic, intelligent, able, and creative physical educator. Certainly, with the superior facilities and with the smaller classes found in most high schools, physical education programs in high schools should be well-conducted.

Almost all high school physical educators have coaching responsibilities. These responsibilities will present the physical educator an opportunity to enlarge the educational arena to encompass the townspeople and faculty. As a coach he will have easier access to the several publicity media which he can utilize to educate the general public concerning the values and objectives of the physical education and intramural as well as the interscholastic program. He can do this, however, only if he does not become obsessed with the desire to win a greater number of games each succeeding year regardless of the sacrifice of other objectives. He must maintain a clear head, a kind heart, and a stable nervous and endocrine system regardless of the hysteria which might surge around him. He must remember that high school athletics do not serve the same purpose as did the Roman gladiatorial contests or as do professional athletics but that high school athletics are a tool with which to achieve educational and social objectives.

Coaches can accept this challenge. They have been leaders in many areas of education. They were the first to give attention to the gifted student, to use audio-visual aids, and to use team teaching.

Women physical educators in the high schools serve as advisors to hockey, modern dance, gymnastic, synchronized swimming, and other clubs. They also direct sport and play days. Interscholastic and intercollegiate athletic programs for girls and women are beginning to be developed in some quarters. For example, in California women coaching interscholastic girls' teams are being given consideration at this time, to affiliating with the California Interscholastic Federation.

The total physical education program in the senior high school is usually very broad and diversified including, in addition to the required physical education classes, a number of interscholastic teams and a diversified intramural program which is conducted during the lunch hour and after school. There are also usually a number of clubs which may or may not achieve varsity standing.

Physical Education in Colleges and Universities

The emphasis in college and university physical education programs should be upon the "carry-over" activities; that is, those sports and recreational activities which can be participated in throughout a person's lifetime. These are principally the dual and individual activities, but instruction is also given in team sports. The major objectives of this program are to provide a release for tensions and to improve physical skills and the physical fitness level of students.

Most colleges and universities provide an extensive intramural program.

Teamwork in track *(Courtesy: U. S. Marine Corps)*

Various incentives are provided to encourage participation. These include certificates, medals, trophies, homogeneous grouping, and encouraging rivalry between the various living units. At many institutions a large number of students participate in the intramural program.

Intercollegiate sports are offered for the most highly skilled men. In some institutions, in sports with great spectator appeal, highly skilled players are attracted to the school by means of generous scholarship aid. This practice serves to discourage regular students from trying out for the sport since most player positions will be taken up by the players with athletic scholarships. The National Collegiate Athletic Association and similar groups have been established to govern, regulate, and establish standards for intercollegiate competition. One of the concerns of these associations is that of insuring equitable recruiting practices among the schools which are members.

Women physical educators in colleges and universities are often asked to serve as advisors to various sports clubs. They may also serve as directors of girls' intramural programs or women's athletic clubs. Intercollegiate athletic teams for college women are increasing in number and particularly in the "less masculine" sports such as swimming, gymnastics, golf, and tennis.

Most physical educators who teach full time at the college or university level are assigned additional responsibilities to that of teaching the required physical education classes. These include the coaching of one to three sports, intramural direction, or the teaching of courses in the teacher education program. The greatest number of opportunities for teaching at this level are found in the community junior colleges which are increasing in number very rapidly.

TEACHING IN THE TEACHER EDUCATION PROGRAM

The physical educator who has responsibilities in the area of teacher education plays a most important role in the profession. He helps to insure that the profession will continue to be conducted on the basis of sound principles and that teachers of the future will strive toward achievement of socially acceptable and intelligent objectives. His effectiveness in teaching will have an influence upon the effectiveness of many future teachers for many years.

A large majority of those in teacher education have had at least a few years of experience in teaching at the elementary or high school level and most have earned the doctorate degree. An increasing number of institutions are requiring possession of the doctorate degree as qualification for employment in teacher education. For those teaching such courses as principles of physical education, professional orientation, methods in physical education, administration of physical education, and student teaching, public school experience is highly desired. For the more technical and scientific courses such as physiology of exercise, kinesiology, personal and community health, corrective or adapted physical education, and tests and measurement, previous public school experience is not demanded as frequently as it was in former years. Because of the time required to prepare well in these subjects and because the demand for personnel qualified to teach these subjects exceeds the supply, the public school experience requirement is sometimes waived.

Those in teacher education have a diversity of duties. They select textbooks and supplementary readings; prepare course syllabi, outlines, lesson plans and lectures; make and evaluate assignments; prepare and evaluate examinations; and serve on departmental, school, and university committees which study curricula, campus safety, housing, recreational life, and other aspects of student and faculty life. They counsel students; sponsor clubs; coach; teach required physical education classes; attend college functions; serve as consultants to civic groups; attend, participate in, and direct clinics, conferences, and conventions; write textbooks; write for professional journals; present speeches to civic and professional groups; and are often asked to lead groups such as Boy or Girl Scouts, the Red Cross, church groups, and others.

People in teacher education must devote a lifetime to learning through attendance at clinics, conferences, and conventions, through discussion, and through reading of the professional literature in their own discipline and of that in the related disciplines.

TEACHING IN THE GRADUATE PROGRAM

Graduate teaching attracts the most learned and scholarly men and women in physical education. Possession of the doctorate degree plus publication of research studies, articles in professional journals, and textbooks have virtually become mandatory for assignment to this responsibility. Members of the graduate faculty in physical education teach such courses as Mechanical-Anatomical Analysis of Activity; Techniques of Research; Tests and Measurement; Seminar in Physical Education, Health, Athletics or Recreation; Problems in Recreation; Foundations and Trends in Physical Education; Problems of Curriculum in Health and Physical Education; and Administration of Health, Physical Education, and Recreation. They counsel graduate students in the selection of courses and in research projects. They guide the student in his work on his thesis, prepare comprehensive examinations, and serve on oral examination committees.

Graduate teachers should be creative people who enjoy searching for answers to unsolved problems and who are able to stimulate others to do the same. They must have an understanding of many research sources and procedures, have a breadth of interest in many disciplines and a depth of knowledge in their own discipline, be meticulous in applying research procedures, be objective at all times, and exercise caution in reaching conclusions.

The graduate faculty in charge of the research laboratories in the larger universities of the country will have thousands of dollars of delicate instruments in their charge. These will include telemetry systems, gas analysis devices, treadmills, heartometers, and devices for measuring force, speed, and weight.

ADMINISTRATION OF ATHLETICS
AND PHYSICAL EDUCATION

As soon as a physical education or athletic program becomes of a size that the school officers determine to be unmanageable without more centralized direction, an administrative head is named. This person must first plan the program with other teachers in the unit and then he must implement the plans. Administrative titles and responsibilities vary according to the level and type of duties assigned.

A chairman of a department is the individual assigned to bring together the faculty of one department in a school to insure that it functions as a unit. The chairman has diverse administrative duties in addition to supervising the administration of his department and coordinating his discipline with other disciplines in the learning establishment.

DIRECTING PHYSICAL EDUCATION

Sometimes the work of the City Director of Physical Education overlaps that of a Chairman of Physical Education in a local school. Whether it does or not depends upon the structure of the school. In larger cities, the director of physical education in a central office would work closely with chairmen of various departments in individual schools. His responsibilities are similar to those of a chairman, except that he must insure that the programs of all of the schools are in line with the educational philosophy of the city school system. He determines the budgetary needs of each school, puts the orders on bid, and selects the company with which he wishes to do business. He helps decide which teacher should be transferred and to which school when there is a vacancy or when a teacher's presence causes personnel problems within the school. Working with others, he employs teachers and helps to determine which should not be retained. He helps to determine policies for safety and insurance, establishes a basic philosophy, and coordinates curricula between the several educational levels for the total school system.

DIRECTING ATHLETICS

Practically anything relating to the conduct of interscholastic or inter-collegiate athletics is under the direction of the director of athletics. This includes: scheduling of games, officials and facilities; representing his institution at league committee meetings; the purchasing of and caring for equipment; arranging for medical examinations; insuring of athletes; preparing of forms to expedite business matters; establishing relationships with the press; "selling" the program to the faculty, students, parents, and community; assuming responsibility for the safety of the players and fans at contests; formulating policies for awards; determining eligibility standards; and formulating scholarship policies.

The interscholastic and intercollegiate programs normally have more attention called to them through the sport pages than do any other segments of the educational program. As the person in charge, the director of athletics must shoulder the responsibility for the success of the total athletic program.

SUMMARY

The physical educator in the school may be called upon to teach a wide variety of activities, including the intramural program, coaching, teaching health or safety, coordinating the total school health program, teaching camping and outdoor education, dance, and adapted physical education classes. He should also spend some time in doing or reviewing research. He endeavors to conduct all the programs and to teach all the activities or academic courses assigned to him according to sound educational principles in order to achieve generally accepted educational objectives. His selection of materials and methods of teaching should always be based on an understanding of the individual human and of his society.

Physical education programs from the elementary schools through the senior high schools should progress from basic fundamental skills toward the more complex ones and involve a continually higher degree of team play. At all levels, the activities should be selected and conducted according to the unique characteristics and needs of the particular age group. The duties of physical educators at all educational levels, from elementary school through the college and university level, are basically the same. There are, however, some differences in the activities selected, teaching methods utilized, the scope of the activities, and in the intensity of participation.

Teaching in the teacher education program at the undergraduate level calls for considerable classroom teaching. Teaching at the graduate level, which almost always requires possession of the doctoral degree, involves classroom teaching exclusively.

The duties of directors of physical education and of directors of athletics involve principally the coordinating of people and facilities, of establishing objectives, of insuring that progress is made toward the selection of people who will work effectively toward achievement of the objectives, and of motivating these people to work toward the objectives.

QUESTIONS

1. List 25 activities which might be taught in physical education classes.

2. Compare and contrast the methods and objectives of the person teaching required physical education classes and one coaching an interscholastic sport.

3. List 25 activities in which high schools or universities have fielded varsity teams.

4. What are the various forms of dance and when are they usually taught?

5. What is the difference between adapted and corrective physical education?

6. Who can do research in physical education?

7. Describe the characteristics of elementary school children. Of junior high school children. Of high school children.

8. Describe the duties of physical educators in elementary schools. In junior high schools. In senior high schools.

9. How do the programs in physical education differ in the three school levels?

10. Discuss the duties of the physical educator in the college or university.

11. Discuss the duties of the physical educator who works in teacher education at the undergraduate level. At the graduate level.

12. Discuss the duties of the Director of Physical Education. Of the Athletic Director.

BIBLIOGRAPHY

1. "Class Size in Secondary Schools," *NEA Research Bulletin, 43:*1:21-22, February, 1965.

2. "Sampling Study of the Teaching Faculty in Higher Education," *NEA Research Bulletin, 44:*1:7, February, 1966.

4

Duties of Physical Educators Who Teach Outside the Schools

THE MAN WHO prepares himself to be a physical education teacher in the schools often does so with great enthusiasm. He remembers the exciting and meaningful experiences he enjoyed while participating in sports and he anticipates the day when he will be able to bring similar pleasures to others. The majority of physical education students can think of no position other than the schools to realize this dream.

Ultimately, students learn that there are many ways of earning a livelihood through teaching physical education in which one can find satisfactions similar to those found in teaching in the schools. To some, this may be the first time they become aware of many other vocational areas. Others learn of related areas through the remarks of a convocation speaker, a visit to the counseling office, a summer or part-time job experience, a volunteer job while in college, or perhaps through an interview by a representative in another field.

The student should not shut his eyes to teaching opportunities outside the schools regardless of how strong his desire to teach in the schools may be. He should keep an open mind because there are many ways in which he may receive the satisfactions he is anticipating. The preparation of a school physical educator lends itself well to numerous positions in allied fields.

YOUNG MEN'S AND YOUNG WOMEN'S CHRISTIAN ASSOCIATIONS

Thousands of boys and girls have received athletic instruction in the pools or gymnasia of the YMCA and YWCA. Thousands of adults continue to use these facilities in order to keep themselves physically fit. Such associations probably come as close as any American organization to duplicating the ancient Grecian palaestra, where the Greeks congregated to exercise, to listen to poetry and music, to philosophize, and to discuss matters of state. While the athletic program probably remains at the core of any contemporary YMCA program, the ancillary programs are receiving increasing emphasis.

YM and YWCA's are always seeking men and women who enjoy teaching a variety of indoor sport skills to youth and who are interested in the ways in which sport can be used as an instrument for improving character. Football, soccer, tennis, lacrosse, baseball, and track and field seldom play a role in physical education in most Y programs. While these sports are found sometimes in Y camp programs, seldom are they found in typical indoor programs. Rather, the emphasis is placed upon aquatics, basketball, gymnastics, volleyball, weight training, handball, wrestling, dance, and conditioning programs.

In earlier years the Y's employed instructors who did not have specialized preparation in college. As employment practices improved, not only did it become necessary for an instructor to have a college degree, but if he expected to advance in the profession, it became desirable for him to have had specific courses in religion and in the philosophy of the YMCA movement. In small Y's the physical education instructor is given the entire responsibility for the sports program for the total membership. In large ones, he may be given primary responsibility for the aquatic phase or the youths', boys', girls', or adults' programs. As he gains experience in any of these areas, he may want to develop his abilities in a different area. As he begins to take

Acrobatic artistry

on a wider range of duties, he becomes more an administrator and less a teacher. He must then provide in-service training for those in his charge to insure that his procedures are learned and followed.

Often, the physical education position is the entree to larger positions with greater status, salary, and responsibility. In such a position, the physical educator learns how to increase membership, analyze defects in the program, determine interests of the membership, and deal with finances. Such a program affords him an excellent background for assuming the position of General or Executive Secretary. The Executive Secretary supervises the work of other employees such as the Boys' or Girls' Director, Physical Education Director, Adult Secretary, Membership Secretary, and Residence Secretary. He is responsible to a board of directors comprised of leading businessmen of the town. Consequently, it is necessary for the General Secretary to become personally acquainted with men from all walks of life, but especially the influential men in a community. He must be ready to join community, social, and service organizations in order to be enabled to learn of the interests and desires of the community. He must also be active in his church if he is to serve as an appropriate image of his organization.

There are some individuals who begin their work as physical directors who wish to remain in that field throughout their lifetime. This is possible and continuing advancement is probable as the person moves to larger Y's in larger cities. In metropolitan centers there is a physical director who supervises the work of all of the directors in the city. He organizes curricula, stimulates city-wide competition in all sports, hires staff, plans buildings, and coordinates activities with other building directors. An increasing number of Y's are working with school systems in using the latter's facilities and teachers for their after- school programs.

The Y offers many of the same advantages found in school teaching. It provides the opportunity to work with not only young people but also with adults. From some points of view, it is a more difficult job than that of the school teacher, because the participants do not attend classes unless they are vital and meaningful. Children are required to attend school. Since attendance at the Y is solely on a voluntary basis, a large attendance is indicative of a successful program. Because it is a private organization, perhaps fewer restrictions are placed upon the director; although good judgment is as necessary as it is in any establishment. While the association receives a portion of its total income from membership dues, it depends to a great extent upon income from its restaurant, room accommodations, and especially contributions and participation in Red Feather programs.

The salaries of the secretaries are similar to those found in education, although usually the working year is eleven months rather than nine or ten months. Night work is expected of the director, but the same is true of most physical educators who have coaching responsibilities.

Because it has branches all over the country, it is quite easy for Y secretaries to move to any state. There is a national clearing house for vacancies so that personnel can be kept abreast of the employment situation in all regions. The Y secretaries have great prestige in their communities, not only because of the lofty goals toward which they work with children and adults, but because they work closely with key men in the community.

YOUNG MEN'S AND YOUNG WOMEN'S HEBREW ASSOCIATIONS OR JEWISH COMMUNITY CENTERS

The loyalty of a Jew to his cultural history is constantly being upset by the modern aspects of the contemporary world. Therefore, Jewish leaders are seeking to combat this trend by increasing the Jews' understanding of their cultural heritage and also by bringing members of the religion together more often. The Jewish Community Centers and Young Men's and Young Women's Hebrew Associations scattered around the nation are focal points, along with the synagogues, for such endeavors.

Scholarships are provided for qualified individuals to attend the Baerwald School of Social Work of Hebrew University in Israel. Scholarships are also awarded to enable persons to attend seminars at other institutions. This is done for the purpose of giving the student a deeper knowledge of the history, culture, and contemporary issues of the Jews. Unlike the Boys' Clubs, which are nondenominational in character, the JCC, YMHA, or YWHA is administered primarily by members of the Jewish faith and, while part-time workers and the membership may include gentiles, this is the exception.

The structure of a typical club is similar to that of a YMCA or Boys' Club. There is an executive director, program supervisor, physical director, and various assistants according to the size of the membership. A Jewish Community Center offers a physical director opportunities to work with both sexes and all ages. The principal objectives of a Health and Physical Education Department were recently outlined by the National Jewish Board as follows:[1]

1. To encourage and help membership use the physical education and recreation program experiences as a means of achieving personal and social growth as well as Jewish identification.

2. To encourage members of all ages, male and female, to attain a greater measure of fitness through healthful participation in sports and related activities.

3. To help the membership develop positive attitudes toward healthier living.

4. To provide programs that help develop members' personal skills with emphasis on the needs of the less skilled.

5. To increase Board and members' understanding and appreciation of the importance and value of Center Health and Physical Education programs and to help staff in related fields such as social group work, nursery school education, and adult education, to develop better understanding of the methods and goals of health and physical education.

6. To help set standards and provide adequate health and physical education facilities.

7. To help membership gain enriched experiences through inter-Center activities with a view to increasing kinship among Jews and to help Jewish members deepen their identification with Jewish life.

8. To help prepare youth physically and mentally for the armed forces.

9. To cooperate with other professional groups of similar interest.

10. To develop more interest and focus more attention on girls' and women's health and physical education programs.

11. To train and prepare membership for democratic participation and leadership roles in the Jewish as well as in the broader American Community.

BOYS' CLUBS

The preparation of a physical education teacher prepares him for any number of positions in the Boys' Clubs of America. This is a national organization comprised of nearly 700 clubs scattered throughout all of the states and has a total membership of nearly a million boys. Most of the clubs are partially supported by the Community Chest and depend upon small membership fees and the philanthropic interests of dedicated townspeople for the balance of their income. Boys' Clubs are nonsectarian in both management and membership.

By and large, most of the efforts of the Boys' Clubs are directed toward underprivileged youth and therefore Boys' Clubs are most likely to be found in the blighted areas of the community. As a result of increasing attention being given to the economically deprived in recent years, it seems likely that increased support will be given to such organizations.

As in the YMCA, there are positions other than that of physical director which can be filled by people prepared in physical education. For example, the Program Director works with club activities — athletic, social, and educational. In a small club, this man seeks volunteer leaders from the community to help with special interest groups. He coordinates some of his programs with the schools and works with industry to locate material that can be of use in the club craft or shop program. He seeks the help of college students in teaching physical education classes or in coaching teams. He looks for adults who can teach boys to paint, to build bird houses, to collect stamps, or to develop film. In larger clubs these responsibilities are shared by the Group Club Supervisor, the Educational Director, and the Social Director.

The highest position in the organization on the local level is that of Executive Director. This person is the administrative head of the organization. He works directly with the Board of Directors as well as the staff. He formulates budgets, makes plans for expansion, hires personnel, and coordinates the Club's operation.

Salaries paid by Boys' Clubs may be somewhat lower than those of other youth-serving agencies but the fringe benefits of sick leave, paid vacations, hours of work, and insurance are comparable.

COMMUNITY RECREATIONAL
SERVICE PROGRAMS

Community recreational programs today endeavor to provide a diversified program which includes a great variety of activities of interest to all age groups. Provision of athletic programs for children should be an objective of community recreational programs but it should be remembered that this is only one part of the program. There is much more to a good recreational program that is worthy of adequate community financial support. Both children and adults may be helped by the farsighted recreation supervisor who recognizes the limitless ways in which people of all ages can grow, once they begin to take a serious interest in a recreational activity. Art, music, crafts, literature, games, trips, needlework, and many other kinds of activities are offered in the best recreational program.

The essential objectives of recreation leadership are to guide and serve the leisure interests of all people, to enlarge and deepen interests so that they will be more satisfying, to provide organization and instruction when they are desired, and to furnish opportunities for self-expression, so that the hours of leisure will become joyous living.

The working day and week are shorter; people have longer vacations and more of them. Because of efforts toward increased efficiency, many formerly personal tasks are now performed by machines. Although a person still has the same needs for identification and belonging as did his predecessors, he has a more difficult time to find avenues to attain such objectives.

Community recreation leaders can influence what will be done when the time arrives for even more increased leisure. The superintendent of recreation must improve his preparation in sports, education, and the biological sciences if he is to function well in a community. He should take electives in sociology such as: community organization, minority problems, delinquency, social control, and public opinion. Electives in business such as general accounting or advertising, a journalism course in public relations or feature article writing, and political science courses in public administration can all be of inestimable value to the recreation superintendent as well as to all of his workers.

The recreational supervisor does not often teach a child how to shoot an arrow, play marbles, whittle a soap form, or do a somersault on a trampoline. Instead, he either employs a part-time worker or enlists the help of a volunteer to do this work. He works with the board of education to determine when the school gymnasium and athletic fields may be used by the recreation department. He watches the growth of the city and attends civic meetings to learn of the thinking of its leaders relative to the re-development of the city so that he will know where playgrounds should be located. He works through the police department in helping to provide worthwhile recreation for all neighborhoods and especially in those areas that present problems. He is aware of the needs of senior citizens and tries to develop programs which will alleviate these problems.

An excellent experience for the undergraduate is to work on a playground for several summers to enable him to see the importance of recreation during the free time of youngsters. To see the excitement a league softball or basketball game provokes in a participating child or adult is gratifying.

Sometimes communities consider recreation to be a frill. This attitude is fast disappearing. Other communities think that recreation is only for youngsters, and this attitude too is disappearing. When one attempts to visualize his community with no golf course (private or public), no swimming pool, no unpolluted stream in which to fish, no park to sit in or walk through, no ball diamonds to play on, no leadership to give incentives for all ages to use their leisure in a constructive manner, and no areas of picnicing, then he understands the *necessity* for a good recreational program and facilities. One of the most important functions of the superintendent of recreation is to interpret constantly his program to the public and to lead the public to desire to improve and to expand the program.

INDUSTRIAL RECREATIONAL PROGRAMS

Labor and management have been arbitrating their differences for the major part of this century and, while wages have always been an issue, the matter of fringe benefits seems to be of concern also. The working man wants a shorter work day and he wants to celebrate more holidays. He wants a coffee break on company time. He would like the company to support a team in a bowling league and to provide uniforms and entry fees for a softball or basketball team in an urban league. These involve money and morale. They also involve management. Office as well as factory workers have similar needs.

Many companies are sensitive to these desires and try to satisfy them in order to retain their workers. It is expensive to train new people. There is too much wasted motion in the process. Also, the reputation of a firm is not enhanced when it has a large turnover of employees.

Outstanding examples of company support for athletic teams are found in the Raybestos Brake Lining Company of Stratford, Connecticut (softball teams for men and women), Anheuser-Busch Brewing Company of St. Louis (bowling), and Phillips 66 of Bartlesville, Oklahoma (basketball). These companies field varsity teams which provide not only good entertainment for the employees but also bring much publicity to the company.

The programs that do most for the morale of a company are usually intramural in nature. Examples of these programs are those of a company supporting two teams in a community recreation or YMCA basketball league, the defraying of greens fees for a company team in a local golf league, sponsoring of a company family outing, or having a Christmas party for the children of the workers.

It is only the largest and most recreational minded of companies that employ full-time recreation directors. Some companies spend three or four cents per hour per employee on such programs while others have their own golf courses, gymnasia, and camps. However, the vast majority of companies look at recreation as a minor adjunct of their services. Consequently, this responsibility becomes only one of the duties of the personnel or industrial relations director who must concern himself with all aspects of employer-employee relations.

ATHLETIC CLUBS

Metropolitan centers often have athletic clubs built principally for and used by businessmen who desire to continue their fitness activities throughout the entire span of their life and who see the value of private surroundings to which they can take their business associates. Ivy League universities have their chapters throughout the country and some cities such as New York, Los Angeles, Chicago, Detroit, Philadelphia, and San Francisco have their own clubs.

Athletic clubs often sponsor track, swimming, and basketball teams and help to subsidize the membership of young competitors. However, most of the effort in athletics is used to provide instruction and to direct tournaments

A gymnastics clinic

in which the membership participates. Handball, swimming, calisthenics, and squash are probably the most popular. The capable physical director not only uses these media to keep the membership happy but he also augments such sports with the associated services of sauna baths, steam baths, whirlpool treatments, massage, and other mild forms of therapy.

The metropolitan athletic club is a business club and its dues and services make it possible for it to continue operations. One responsibility of the physical director is to see that his phase of the enterprise does its share in keeping the budget balanced.

SUMMER CAMPS

Camping and physical education go "hand-in-hand." Probably the majority of physical education students have had camping experience either in private or in organizational camps such as the Scouts or the Y. Here they learned how close friendships can become when one lives with boys or girls of similar age for a short period of time. Here many learn to swim, to shoot a gun or bow, to build a campfire and to be orderly around the bunk and the dining table. It is an experience in community living which will be remembered for a lifetime.

Many collegians, majoring in physical education, later return to camping to serve as specialists or general counselors. Professors frequently advise students who have not had camping experiences to participate in them because they give a prospective teacher experience in working with children. The counselor develops a better understanding of children. He becomes familiar with their fears, their wishes, and their motivations.

Some college students prefer not to accept camping jobs because the first year counselor often earns less money during an eight-week camping season than he could by working in industry. Nevertheless, the man or woman preparing for a career in physical education ideally should obtain some camp counseling experience. Not only will the salary rise when additional experience is acquired, but he may also be permitted to bring his wife and children to the camp. The wife may have a summer free from cooking and domestic chores and the children share in the many benefits available at the camp.

The individual with foresight who thoroughly enjoys camping projects himself years ahead and begins preparing himself to direct the waterfront or other activities. He will want to learn such things as how to install the raft and diving board and the kinds of water skis and life preservers to buy for the sake of economy, safety, and dependability. He learns the safety precautions to institute throughout the entire waterfront, with regard to diving, swimming, sailing, scuba diving, canoe trips, motor boating, and moonlight dips.

If one is a general counselor, he learns how to supervise not only campers, but those counselors in training who are responsible to him. He learns the advantages of certain kinds of cabins. On his days off or when he visits another camp with his boys, he inspects similar structures to improve his present ideas about camp construction. He listens to other counselors talk about their programs. He observes the successes and failures of those with whom he works, and he stores this information so that he can later put it into action.

The person who is considering owning his own camp some day will want to learn how to recruit new members and how to retain former members. He will learn how to advertise in newspapers and magazines, and how to use camp movies or slides during a personal interview with parents of prospective campers. He will learn to employ counselors. In short, camping becomes a business and the physical educator becomes a businessman. He soon learns that there is more to camping than reveille, clean-up detail, an athletic program, campfire, and taps. The responsibility for the educational, recreational, eating and sleeping activities of a group of growing children and counselors of varied experiences is tremendous.

If one has the initiative, the financial backing, business acumen and knowledge of the total camping operation, he may contribute considerably to a child's life and can earn a comfortable living. Advertisements in the newspapers and real estate agents often give leads about camps which are available. A new camp owner often begins with a partner and operates the camp while continuing to teach. Eventually, if the venture looks sufficiently promising, he may devote his full time to it.

In recent years, the day camp has found great popularity. Obviously, it is less expensive to send a child to a day camp and yet it gives the child a worthwhile recreational experience while permitting the parent to continue employment or to enjoy added time without the responsibilities of a child around the house. Day camp operators make things convenient for the parent by providing transportation to and from home, a lunch, and many of the typical athletic and social activities that normally are associated with the resident camp. Owners of day camps do not have the problem of homesickness, overnight accommodations, or of large inventories to carry from year to year.

The residence camps call for a bigger capital outlay in most instances. They require permanent living accommodations, year-round maintenance of buildings, and constant recruitment procedures for the retention of old campers and the enrollment of new ones.

ARMED SERVICES

In wartime, the Physical Training Division plays a vital part in the life of a serviceman. Its physical training experts get raw recruits into physical condition in a short time to prepare them for the rigors of war. Pre-breakfast calisthenic drills, mid-morning physical fitness classes, and evening athletic recreation make a neophyte civilian soldier physically tougher and help him to adjust to a new environment.

The Special Service officer, who may be a physical educator, makes arrangements for the entertainment of the troops by procuring professional entertainers, renting movies for the camp theater, planning bus trips to nearby attractions, working with the townspeople to form committees of young ladies who will attend company dances and swim parties, hiring craft instructors, and buying books for the post library.

Some of the physical training staff coach the post football or baseball team. Other physical educators organize the company or battalion leagues. At other times, these men supervise the pool, weight room, outdoor fields and indoor courts. In short, activity in a gymnasium, pool, or on the field is an important element in the total life of a soldier.

In peacetime, varsity post athletics are conducted on a lesser scale than in wartime. The physical training and intrapost athletics are still very much in evidence. There is one principal difference, though, that being the shift of responsibility for conducting the program from the military to the civilian personnel. This is because it is difficult to meet military needs on a voluntary basis; therefore, it is considered advisable to use civilian manpower for as many jobs as possible.

SUMMARY

There are many job opportunities for the physical educator other than those in the schools. There are opportunities in YM and YWCA's, in YM and YWHA's, in Boys' Clubs, in Community Recreation programs, in industrial recreation programs, in athletic clubs, in summer camps and in the armed services. In all of these athletics play an important role but in most the major role of the physical educator is administrative in that he facilitates participation in sports through securing of volunteer aides, arranging for facilities, and organizing and administering tournaments and other forms of competition. Physical educators in these settings do not provide as much instruction as they do when teaching in the schools.

Often they are responsible for satisfying recreational interests such as music, art, social affairs, crafts, trips, quiet games, etc.

The salary schedules offered physical educators and the fringe benefits are comparable to those offered physical educators in the schools. The working year in these positions is usually eleven months rather than nine months.

In all of these settings the objectives of the program are similar to those in school physical education. These are to improve physical, social, and emotional fitness, to provide opportunities to develop and to improve leisure skills, to provide opportunities for wholesome and healthful use of leisure and to make life more joyous.

In some of the settings there are additional objectives. The YM and YWHA's try to increase the Jew's understanding of his cultural heritage. The Boys' Clubs endeavor to give boys things to do which are needed, useful, and significant. Community recreation directors develop programs which will serve all members of the community — from children in nursery schools to the retired people — in all their diversity of recreational interests. Industrial recreation programs help to retain employees. Athletic clubs provide businessmen with an attractive setting in which to meet business associates. Camping provides an experience in democratic living in the out-of-doors. The physical training programs of the armed services aim primarily to improve the serviceman's physical fitness status.

QUESTIONS

1. List ten settings in which the physical educator might be employed other than in the schools.

2. Compare and contrast the work of the physical educator in the schools with that of the physical director in a YM or YWCA.

3. Compare and contrast the programs of the YM and YWCA with those of the schools.

4. List some of the principal objectives of the Health and Physical Education Department of the YM and YWHA as listed by the National Jewish Board.

5. List some of the activities of Boys' Clubs.

6. Describe some of the duties and responsibilities of the community recreational director.

7. Why should an industry concern itself with the recreational activities of its employees?

8. How can a hospital recreation program be helpful to patients?

9. How would a summer as a camp counselor help to prepare a student to become a more effective physical educator?

FOOTNOTE

1. *Program Goals for the Jewish Community Center Health and Physical Education Departments,* National Jewish Board, December, 1965.

5

Organizations
to Which
Physical Educators
May Belong

TEACHING IS PRIMARILY a venture of service to mankind. Within this framework the professional receives his primary sources of satisfaction. When a teacher, regardless of the activity he teaches or the age of the group taught, observes some improvement in one of his pupils in some skill or personality trait, his sense of accomplishment is immeasurable. Although the rate of progress is slow in many instances, each degree of growth brings a measure of satisfaction to the teacher that can be likened to the satisfaction experienced in hitting a home run, making a touchdown, sinking a basket, or winning a race.

Regardless of the time and effort a man puts forth on the job, he should endeavor to serve his professional organizations. Theodore Roosevelt expressed this attitude well when he said: "Every man owes some of his time to the upbuilding of the profession to which he belongs." There are many organizations which offer countless opportunities in which a person may serve his profession in areas commensurate with his interests. Just a few of those will be briefly described here.

The professional organizations serve the physical educator by assisting in elevating teachers' salaries, by providing assistance in locating job opportunities, and by enabling the physical educator to become a more effective teacher through publication of professional journals; sponsorship of clinics, conferences, conventions, study groups, and research.

The professional and service organizations are a very important part of the total picture of physical education, health, and recreation. A knowledge of them is essential to a comprehension of this profession. It has been largely through his professional organizations that the physical educator has increased his effectiveness as a productive force in society.

NATIONAL EDUCATION ASSOCIATION

In 1857 in Philadelphia, forty-three educators met for the purpose of unifying their efforts to improve the dignity and effectiveness of education. This organization ultimately became the National Education Association.[1]

Since that time the National Education Association has spread its influence throughout the country and has exerted tremendous influence on the educational patterns of American school children. Although it is strictly voluntary and independent, it nevertheless works closely with allied groups and the U.S. Office of Education. Any certified teacher or person who has a bachelor's degree and is active in teaching may apply for membership. Presently there are approximately one million members. One of its principal projects in recent years has been to encourage undergraduate students to begin identifying with the parent body by forming their own campus chapters. As a result, there are over one hundred thousand undergraduate members in the NEA.

Not only is it the largest professional teaching association in the nation, but it is also the largest professional organization in the world. Some teachers and prospective teachers ask how the NEA can be useful to them. It is easy to understand that only when there is union is there strength in any organization. When people of similar interests and goals unite they are more likely to attain their objectives. Never will individuals working independently be able to have as far-reaching an influence as they can when they work with others in a cooperative fashion. The national organization's influence filters down into the states and eventually into local offices so that it reaches to the grass roots of the community. In affiliated state and local organizations the teacher may work with a number of special interest committees.

At present there are seven commissions and a council in the NEA which seek solutions to problems which are of major concern to the profession. They conduct investigations, make recommendations, and disseminate information to the profession, and thereby endeavor to improve education. These commissions are: Educational Policies, Legislative, Professional Rights and Responsibilities, Safety, Teacher Education and Professional Standards, Future Teachers of America, and the Student National Education Association. The NEA's council is concerned with teacher retirement.

Members also receive a copy of the NEA *Journal* nine times each year. This publication keeps its readers up to date on trends throughout the nation, offers challenging editorials, lists free and inexpensive materials, and condenses much research relative to the problems confronting the classroom teacher. Some of its columns provide topics for stimulating conversations in the teachers' lunchroom or methods class.

Thanks to the efforts of its committees and national staff, NEA members are now eligible to receive life, death, accident, and disability insurance policies at a much lower rate than they would otherwise. Over 60,000 members have taken advantage of these insurance programs.

The NEA's research staff makes efforts to improve schools and to improve the professional status of the profession. Sometimes this research staff can assist individual members but more often its efforts are directed toward solution of the problems faced by superintendents or school boards.

The organization recognizes that it must have both public understanding and support if it is to make progress. Consequently, it works with lay groups such as the National School Board Association and the National Congress of Parents and Teachers. Members of all the groups serve on joint committees and pool their efforts for the betterment of the teaching profession.

A member can both extend his professional acquaintances and enhance his status in the profession by working with committees in departments affiliated with NEA. These departments have titles such as: Elementary School Principals, Foreign Languages, Exceptional Children, Higher Education, Home Economics, Industrial Arts, Mathematics, Music Educators, School Administrators, Librarians, Speech, Social Studies, Vocational Education, and Health, Physical Education, and Recreation.

AMERICAN ASSOCIATION FOR HEALTH, PHYSICAL EDUCATION, AND RECREATION

The AAHPER is to the physical educator what the American Bar Association and the American Medical Association are to the lawyer and physician. It was formed in 1885 with 49 members. In 1967 there were over 49,000 members on its rolls, 14,000 of whom were students. It has been a department of the NEA since 1937 and is now the largest of its departments. When one reads of the progress made by this department throughout the years, he feels extremely proud of the dedication literally thousands of his fellow members have put forth in upgrading the profession.

No matter what one uses for criteria — number of members, budget, projects, publications, or committees, everything points to progress. Anyone who has been close to this organization for a number of years realizes this and becomes anxious to recommend membership to others.

This association had an income of $2,227,300 in 1967–68. In 1965–66 about 33% of the Association's income was derived from special projects (briefly described later); 30% from publications such as the *Journal of Health, Physical Education, and Recreation* which is published nine times a year, the *Research Quarterly,* the *Fitness Manual,* numerous books, *Sport Guides for Women,* and athletic booklets; 5% from advertising, 8% from miscellaneous sources, and 24% from membership fees. In 1968 a student was assessed $5.00 annually for student dues. This entitled him to the *Journal of Health, Physical Education, and Recreation.* The fee of $8.00 for an Associate Membership entitled him to receive the *Research Quarterly* as well. Teachers in the field paid $15.00 and $20.00 respectively for similar memberships. The lower fee entitled the member to receive the *Journal of Health, Physical Education, and Recreation* only, while the higher fee entitled him to receive the *Research Quarterly* as well.

Of the budget, about 11% was spent for publications, 22% for staff services, 33% for special projects, 6% for *JOHPER* and *Research Quarterly* expenses, 6% for general operating expenses, 3% for travel, 9% for the professional program, and 2% for miscellaneous expenditures.[2]

The income received from outside projects prior to 1955 was very small, but from that time until 1966 nearly $1,600,700 has been received from outside organizations which have recognized its ability to handle some of their assignments. For instance, sports equipment companies which are primarily interested in the promotion of such outdoor sports as hunting, fishing, and archery have been principal sponsors of the Outdoor Education

Nature, science, and skill combine to make the adventurous life *(Courtesy: Michigan Tourist Council)*

project. These companies acknowledge the fact that the more knowledge teachers and students have about such sports, the more equipment will be bought, and the more revenue will eventually accrue to the companies. The Department of State Project for Foreign Specialists and the Peace Corps have sought this association's help in recruiting men and women to serve the federal government in foreign countries working in physical education and recreational projects. AAHPER has helped to promote these ventures by recruiting personnel, by locating universities to assist in their training, and by helping in the evaluation and supervision of their work overseas.

Increased support has been received from athletic equipment companies in providing scholarships for high school students who have chosen physical education as a career and additional monies have been received from the U.S. Public Health Service for health education projects. Two of the most interesting and most recent projects have been those sponsored by the Lifetime Sports Foundation, and Recreation for Fitness for the Mentally Retarded. Companies dealing principally with bowling, billiards, tennis, and golf equipment (Lifetime Sports) have helped to finance clinics throughout the nation for teachers who could then return to their institutions to pass on their new knowledge to students. Largely because of the efforts of the Kennedy family, money has been made available for research and clinics designed to aid in the rehabilitation of the mentally retarded. The profession hopes to make a contribution to progress in this area.

Although much of the direction of the Association comes from national headquarters in Washington and from its national officers, there is much work accomplished through district association officers and committees. The country is divided into the following districts: Central, Eastern, Midwest, Northwest, Southern, and Southwest. Each district holds an annual convention and each district serves as the host for the annual national convention in its turn. The states within each district are assisted in their annual conventions and in solving their professional problems.

It is easily seen that with so much decentralization there are abundant opportunities for professionally minded people to contribute appreciably to the Association. Both the National and the District Associations have the following special interest divisions: Health, Physical Education, Recreation, Girls' and Women's Sports, Men's Athletics, Safety, Dance, and General. In addition, there are standing committees and President's Committees on all levels of professional endeavor.

The Association has been a leading force in recent years in calling attention to the "softness" of American youth, in experimenting with ways of improving fitness in minimal time, and in creating a desire in people to participate in sports. Its committees are constantly endeavoring to raise the standards of competition from both ethical and safety viewpoints.

Some fringe benefits which might be pointed out are: reduced prices for hotel accommodation where conventions are held, reduced prices for group insurance premiums, free printed materials, free placement services, and reduced registration fees at conventions. Of course, the major benefits of membership in any such organization are the growth in knowledge and understanding of one's profession and the pleasure of being able to deal intimately with colleagues on a high level of professional work.

It may seem paradoxical that the primary value is to find more work for members. Walter Campbell explained this spirit of service when he wrote: "The average man, in his lifetime, is torn between two great opposite forces. On the one hand something within him bids him to shun and even escape the world and its trials. It bids him to live in peace and solitude and the confinement of self-service and self-interest directing everything in life toward the focus of self. Another and more engulfing force bids him to get into the world and make its trials and tribulations, its joys, and its sorrows his own. This stronger force bids him to spend his life in service to mankind. History is precise in its pronouncements on this method. All its religious, political, and worthy economic theories are born in this area of man's idealism. The wise men of old were all of one mind on this; we are called out of this world only to be sent back into the services of others."[3]

NATIONAL GIRLS' ATHLETIC ASSOCIATION

This association is a special project of the American Association for Health, Physical Education, and Recreation, established in 1962 to focus attention on the athletic and recreational needs of high school students. It now represents more than 60,000 high school girls through its 2000 member schools across the nation. An AAHPER consultant coordinates the efforts of local, state, and national groups.

The NGAA publishes its *Bulletin,* a 32-page magazine, five times a year. This magazine contains ideas on programs, activities, and service projects as well as book reviews and news items. The association is dedicated to strengthening and to enlivening girls' athletic associations in high schools across the nation.

ATHLETIC AND RECREATION FEDERATION OF COLLEGE WOMEN

This association, like the NGAA, was established as a service arm of AAHPER which provides a consultant who represents the ARFCW at state and national meetings and within the National Association and interprets decisions and policy statements to the membership. Blanche Trilling was instrumental in founding the organization at the University of Wisconsin in 1917. The ARFCW now lists more than 1200 women college students as members in some 300 colleges and universities. These women students are members of the college or university Womens Athletic Association (WAA) and are not all majors in physical education.

The association holds a national conference every two years at which members of the Representative Assembly made up of student representatives from each of the states and regional ARFCW organizations determine policies of the association. Regional and state conferences are also held. In addition, the association publishes a 16-page booklet *Sportlight* which is sent to member schools three times each year. This booklet combines student-written material with other articles on sports and recreational activities, service projects, program ideas, and news items.

INTERNATIONAL COUNCIL ON HEALTH, PHYSICAL EDUCATION, AND RECREATION

AAHPER has encouraged the use of physical education as a media for the advancement of understanding between nations since 1957 by encouraging the formating of the ICHPER. The latter is now a part of the larger body, the World Confederation of Organizations of the Teaching Profession which was formed in 1952 in Denmark. WCOTP is comprised of several of the foremost teaching federations of the world and attempts to use all areas of education in improving international understanding, in improving teaching methods, in defending the material and moral rights of its members, and in promoting closer relations between teachers throughout the world.

Some of the ways in which ICHPER has shared in this task throughout the past decade have been: (1) assisting in the exchange of personnel between countries, (2) sponsoring of international seminars in health education which are followed by regional seminars devoted to local interest, (3) encouraging countries to continuously evaluate and restate their philosophies and objectives in health, physical education, and recreation, (4) organizing seminars for classroom teachers so that they may be better qualified to teach physical education, (5) encouraging teachers of all nations to encourage their qualified and interested women to enter the physical education profession, (6) disseminating comparative education material, and (7) making it possible for students in all universities to participate in physical activity.

As the world becomes smaller because of improved transportation and communications this organization will probably take on a more important role. Those professionals who "get in on the ground floor" will receive much satisfaction from watching this organization grow.

NATIONAL COLLEGE PHYSICAL EDUCATION ASSOCIATION FOR MEN

For anyone who teaches physical education in a college or university, this is an organization which has much to offer. The NCPEAM was started in 1897 as the Society of Gymnasium Directors. After several changes of title, it adopted its present one in 1962. For years its members were primarily college physical educators in the East, but during the 1960's it became truly national in character. Its conventions are held either in December or January and their locations vary so that all regions of the country are covered within a five-year period. The Association had 631 members in 1967.[4] About 300 attend the annual meetings. This small, homogeneous group makes for a comradeship seldom equalled in professional circles. Men teaching in higher education would do well to take an active part in the NCPEAM for a number of reasons. One of the most important is that of providing an opportunity for meeting informally with outstanding men in the field – of hearing the philosophers expound on their theories, of seeing at first hand the men who play such a dominant role in the direction of the profession, and of hearing about the contemporary research that is being conducted at the leading institutions around the country.

This organization's objectives are: (1) the improvement of contributions which can be made by physical education, (2) defining the major issues in physical education in higher education, (3) gathering, analyzing, and organizing research which will attempt to resolve the major issues, (4) developing interdisciplinary relationships with kindred fields of knowledge with the hope that they may shed light on physical education, and (5) improvement of public relations through increased public understanding of the nature and purposes of physical education in our lives.

Most of its committees evolve out of the areas of the Basic Instruction, Intramurals, and Teacher Education and seldom does one attend a meeting or review the proceedings without finding something to help him solve a local problem. The new History of Sport section is giving leadership in the emerging interdisciplinary approach either through guest speakers in other fields, or through the prepared reports of its own membership. The organization is rapidly recognizing the reciprocal relationships sport has with the economic, political, social, and cultural life of man.

The National Association for Physical Education of College Women has rendered similar services to the women of the profession. Each of its five affiliated organizations in various geographical areas throughout the nation sponsor conventions, research, and professional projects. During recent years it has co-sponsored the scholarly publication QUEST along with the NCPEAM.

AMERICAN COLLEGE OF SPORTS MEDICINE

Within the period of a very short time (origin, 1954) this organization has given outstanding leadership on a national scale in scientifically determining the values of and best methods for training in all fields of sport. By the time the organization will be twenty-five years old, it will probably be judged as the foremost group in analyzing the physiologic merits and limitations of activity.

One of the reasons for its success thus far has been its ability to enlist the cooperation of three disciplines seriously concerned with the values which may accrue from participation in physical activity – medicine, physiology, and physical education.

The constitution of the ACSM states its objectives and purposes to be: (1) to promote and advance medical and other scientific studies dealing with the effect of sports and other physical activities on the health of human beings at various stages of life, (2) to cooperate with other organizations, physicians, scientists, and educators concerned with the same or related specialties, (3) to arrange for mutual meetings of physicians, educators, and allied scientists, (4) to make available post-graduate education in fields related to these sciences, (5) to initiate, promote, and correlate research in these fields, (6) to edit and publish a journal, articles, and pamphlets pertaining to various aspects of sports, other physical activities and medicine, and (7) to establish and maintain a sports medicine library.

The ACSM has several interesting projects underway for the years ahead which should shed increasing light on these fields as they relate to activity. One of these projects has involved nearly 1000 individuals from 57 countries. This project is the publication of an *Encyclopedia of Sports Medicine*. A deadline has not been established for the completion of this work which involves abstracting the research literature on all facets of sports medicine from all over the world. Some of the topics which will be included in the Encyclopedia are: Environment; Emotions and Intellect; Growth, Development and Aging; Physical Activity (General); Physical Activity (Sports, Games, and Exercise); Physical Activity (Sports, Games, and Exercise according to the listing, description, and treatment of sport injuries by anatomical location); Drugs; Prevention of Disease and Injury; Safety and Protection; Special Application of Physical Activity to the Handicapped Individual; and Rehabilitation.

Two other projects of the ACSM are: (1) the listing of speakers on various sports medicine topics and (2) the compilation of various medical data on Olympic athletes from the United States.

AMERICAN ACADEMY OF PHYSICAL EDUCATION

The American Academy of Physical Education was founded in 1930. It is the elite body of the profession and is comprised of one hundred carefully screened members. Its objectives have been to: (1) advance the understandings of the profession, (2) elect Fellows whose contributions merit membership, (3) disseminate professional information, (4) assist in the enactment of legislative measures which will benefit the profession, (5) recruit members, and (6) appropriately recognize the meritorious achievements of colleagues. It has also taken on the responsibility of sponsoring the annual R. Tait McKenzie lectureship at the national AAHPER conventions in honor of R. Tait McKenzie, its founder.

AMATEUR ATHLETIC UNION

After the middle of the nineteenth century there were a number of amateur athletic clubs in the United States that competed against one another. There was a great need for uniformity in rules and to check the evils of professionalism. As a result of this felt need, the officers of the Brooklyn and New York City Athletic Clubs formed, in 1873, the National Amateur Gymnastic and Athletic Tournament Association. They made the first efforts to establish uniform rules. This organization was superseded by the National Association of Amateur Athletics of America formed by the athletic clubs in and near New York City, in 1879. Six years later the Pacific Coast Amateur Athletic Association was formed. It operated independently of the NAAA. In 1888 the New York Athletic Club withdrew from the NAAA and organized the Amateur Athletic Union of the United States. During its first year, this association conducted national championships in boxing, wrestling, fencing, and track and field events, all held at the Detroit Athletic Club. During the summer of 1888 the NAAA and the AAU affiliated to become the first national body to represent amateur sports in the United States.

In its beginning the AAU believed it should represent all amateur sports in the United States and did claim jurisdiction over more than forty sports. By 1899, the number was reduced to sixteen and possible conflict with colleges and universities was avoided. However, conflict with colleges arose a few years later over basketball because colleges played against independent teams who were not members of the AAU. These colleges suffered the disapproval of the AAU but nevertheless resisted centralized AAU regulation.

Today the AAU governs almost all amateur sports outside the schools and colleges with the exception of football, tennis, and golf and its members number in the millions. It represents the United States in international amateur sports and holds the position of control in the United States Olympic Committee.

NATIONAL COLLEGIATE ATHLETIC ASSOCIATION

In 1873 twelve New England colleges and universities organized the Intercollegiate Association of Amateur Athletes of America (ICAAAA) to conduct track and field competition. Because there was much criticism of intercollegiate athletics, particularly of football (68 deaths and 804 serious injuries had been suffered by football players between 1901 and 1904), and because of unethical practices in recruiting and subsidizing of athletes, faculty representatives in 1906 organized the Intercollegiate Athletic Association of the United States. This association was renamed the NCAA in 1910.

The NCAA has jurisdiction over all intercollegiate sports. Many other intercollegiate athletic associations are affiliated with the NCAA.

The AAU and the NCAA have engaged in numerous conflicts over the years. Presidents Theodore Roosevelt, Woodrow Wilson, and John F. Kennedy have made efforts to arbitrate these conflicts. At the time of this writing, the two groups are in the midst of difficulties which federally appointed arbitrators have been unable to settle. One aspect of the conflict at the present time is disagreement over which group has the authority to sanction meets and to select representatives for Olympic competition. College and university coaches affiliated with NCAA have long felt they were not adequately represented in the AAU or the U.S. Olympic Committee. Until differences are settled, the American athlete will be the one to suffer in domestic competition and the nation will also suffer when it selects those who will compete in international competition.

NATIONAL ASSOCIATION OF
INTERCOLLEGIATE ATHLETICS

The NAIA is an association of small colleges which sponsors national championships in basketball, track and field events, golf, and tennis. It had its beginning in 1937 when small college basketball teams which had won their conference championship were invited to a national tournament in Kansas

City. This meeting resulted in the formation of the National Association of Intercollegiate Basketball three years later in 1940. People interested in other sports in small colleges began to request membership, were enrolled, and in 1952 the Association changed its name to the present one.

NATIONAL PARKS AND RECREATION ASSOCIATION

Although the field of recreational services is much broader than athletics, the latter is a large part of any recreational program; therefore, it is worthy of mention here. Recreation has had a laudable record since Joseph Lee founded the movement at the turn of the century. The expansion of the recreation concept is reflected in the changes in title of its publication from *Playground* in 1907 to *Playground and Recreation* in 1930, to *Recreation* in 1931, and to *National Parks and Recreation* in 1966. This association has had regional and national meetings and in many states has had its state chapters as well. It has always focused its attention on three major areas: (1) professional leadership, (2) lay leadership, and (3) the acquisition and use of space for recreation.

The importance of the National Parks and Recreation Association is vividly pointed out by Lerner as he describes the role of recreation in contemporary American life:

The greatest revolution ahead is the time revolution made possible by automation. Instead of the leisure class societies of the past, America is on the threshold of becoming a leisure society in which time is available not for the privileged few but for the many who will have a new dimension of freedom added to their lives. But America must use this time to replace the current cult of fun-tension filled and frenetic, and replace it by the idea of play as full expressiveness and harmony of body, spirit, and mind.

The people and the community must recognize how important is the role of parks, playgrounds, and recreation in this concept. There is scarcity of accessible space today and yet the workday is shorter and leisure time greater. Instead of defacing and polluting the natural environment, instead of filling space and time with unfulfilling pursuits, we must put space and time to use for all people and give them a chance to develop the values of work and play.[5]

Other professional organizations which may appeal to certain physical educators are: the National Federation of High School Athletics, specific coaches' associations within states, the National Intramural Association, the National Trainer's Association, the Fellowship of Christian Athletes, the national honorary fraternity for men, Phi Epsilon Kappa, and Delta Psi Kappa for women. There are enough professional organizations in physical education that the dedicated physical educator need not look elsewhere to perform services for mankind.

CIVIC ORGANIZATIONS

Some teachers would like to serve their community in areas other than sport or physical education. They like diversity and challenge. Civic groups often recognize and put to use the leadership abilities of physical educators. These civic groups provide an excellent avenue for extending one's circle of acquaintances in the community. Each community has its own specific organizations to meet the needs of its citizens. There are also a number of national agencies which have admirable objectives that might appeal to the physical educator. When a teacher begins his life in a new city, he should be aware of such groups, where and when they meet, what they purport to do, and how one may affiliate. It would be unwise to attempt to list all such groups in a book of this scope, but a few of the more notable ones are described throughout the remaining pages of this chapter.

American Red Cross

This is a national quasi-governmental organization with thousands of local branches and one with which most physical educators have had some contact. It is a social agency which continues to be a leader in safety education and its influence continues to be felt by literally millions of civilians during war and peace. Some of the readers have very likely been members of the Junior American Red Cross during their adolescent years. They may have participated in projects in school which helped families in such disasters as floods, fires, and hurricanes. The ARC very likely gave clothes, blankets, food, and medical care. Those who will be entering the armed services will see the Red Cross all over the world as it provides countless services to the soldier, sailor, marine, coast guardsman, and airman.

Some of the readers have had experience with this agency when they met its rigid water safety requirements prior to being awarded the certificate for Beginning, Intermediate, or Advanced Swimmer; Junior or Senior Life Saver; or Water Safety Instructor. The ARC also certifies people as Standard or Advanced First Aiders and as First Aid Instructors. It has established an enviable reputation in setting standards of safety for all kinds of waterfronts.

The ARC is constantly searching for enthusiastic volunteers not only to help enlist community support for the local chapter, but also·to guide its destiny as it endeavors to provide continued assistance to citizens in time of trouble.

Boy and Girl Scouts of America

Probably no one has ever ascertained what percentage of physical educators were once Boy or Girl Scouts but if the count were ever taken, it would probably be a sizable majority. Scouting develops many of the same qualities which are developed in physical education classes: love of action, cooperation, and independent thinking. Physical educators often have had their initial experience with boy or girl scouts during their teen-age days. The experiences may have been extended if they assumed roles of leadership as patrol leaders, camp counselors, or scoutmasters.

Most former scouts recall worthwhile and memorable incidents in their patrol meetings, at campfires, while learning swimming strokes, when going on overnight trips, and when preparing their first meal outdoors. Consequently, they are often most willing to volunteer to serve on troop committees, to help prepare scouts for merit badge requirements, to supervise them on hikes, and to assist in financial projects.

The organization has used the slogan: "Building Boys is Better than Mending Men." The physical educator can feel a part of a worthwhile endeavor when he assists in some of its many character-building projects for youth.

Young Men's and Young Women's Christian Association

Working on a lay committee of the local Y may at first appear to be a "busman's holiday" but this is not necessarily true for there are many areas besides athletics in which the physical educator may become interested. Some of these committees include: finance, membership, camp, development, personnel, public relations, and adult education.

The YM and the YWCA, like so many other service groups, operate with a small number of professional people but with many volunteers. Consequently, the YM or the YWCA deeply appreciates the professional help that physical educators can provide. Its committees, which are comprised of people from all walks of life, meet periodically to plan the specific work for which they are responsible. It is a privilege to be invited to serve with the Y in any volunteer capacity. Since businessmen normally honor such an invitation, it is a splendid opportunity for physical educators to extend their acquaintances outside of the teaching profession.

Canoeing *(Courtesy: Maine Dept. of Economic Development)*

SUMMARY

There are a number of professional and service organizations which have been established to provide assistance to physical educators and to enable physical educators to become more effective in their service to society. These include the NEA, the AAHPER, the ICHPER, the WCOTP, the NCPEAM, the NCPEAW, the ACSM, the American Academy of Physical Education, the NCAA, the AAU, the National Parks and Recreation Association, the National Federation of High School Athletics, the National Intramural Association, the National Trainers Association, the Fellowship of Christian Athletes, and honorary fraternities such as Phi Epsilon Kappa for men and Delta Psi Kappa for women.

These associations have made substantial contributions to the improved stature of physical education, health, and recreation. They have accomplished this through unified efforts of their members for improved salary structures, through provision of various fringe benefits, and by enabling their members to serve society through their work more effectively. This has been accomplished by facilitating exchange of knowledge and ideas through publications, clinics, conferences, and research and study groups.

Some of the associations such as the NEA, AAHPER, NCAA, AAU, and the National Federation of High School Athletics, which are national in scope, have such huge memberships that they have found it advisable to establish state or district (or both) associations to facilitate accomplishment of their goals. Others, such as the ACSM, the American Academy of Physical Education, the National Intramural Association, the National Trainers Association, and Phi Epsilon Kappa have members from every state in the nation but have smaller memberships because they are more specialized in their interests or carefully screen their members selecting only the most outstanding members of the profession. Others such as ICHPER and WCOTP have members from all over the world.

A number of service organizations which often call upon physical educators to assume positions of leadership or in which physical educators are likely to become involved were described. These included the American Red Cross, the Boy and Girl Scouts of America, and the YM and YWCA as well as the YMHA and YWHA.

QUESTIONS

1. How has the NEA been of service to teachers?

2. List the seven commissions of the NEA.

3. What are the services of AAHPER to physical educators?

4. How has AAHPER enabled physical education to become more effective?

5. Name the special interest divisions of the National and District Associations of AAHPER.

6. What are the services of ICHPER through which it accomplishes the objectives of WCOTP of which it is a part?

7. List the five objectives of the NCPEAM.

8. List the seven objectives and purposes of the ACSM.

9. What is the American Academy of Physical Education?

10. What are the purposes of the NCAA and the AAU?

11. Why is an acquaintance with the American Red Cross of importance to the physical educator?

12. With the Boy and Girl Scouts of America?

FOOTNOTES

1. "Know Your NEA?" *NEA Handbook*. Washington: National Education Association, 1964, p. 13.

116   PREPARATION AND WORK OF THE PHYSICAL EDUCATOR

2. Troester, Carl A., Jr., "The Work of the Association, 1964–1965," *Journal of Health, Physical Education, and Recreation, 36*:6:50, June, 1965.

3. Campbell, Walter, "Our Ultimate Goal," *The Lion, 48:*12:5, June, 1966.

4. *Proceedings: Annual Meeting of the National College Physical Education Association for Men,* American Association for Health, Physical Education, and Recreation, Washington, D.C., 1965.

5. Lerner, Max, "Excerpts from a Speech Given at the 17th Annual California and Pacific N.W. Recreation and Parks Conference, 1965," *Recreation, 58*:10:474, December, 1965.

6

Relationships of Physical Education with Other Aspects of School and Community Life

MANY PEOPLE IN physical education feel that the teaching of physical education classes or the coaching of sports constitute the entire field of sports. Such an outlook reflects a myopic view. It is suggested that the reader list the many ways in which sport cuts across not only the other courses he is taking but across other areas of life as well.

There is a large proportion of space allocated to sports in the daily newspapers. There are an increasing number of sport magazines to be found on the newsstands. Several million people across the country tune in their car radio on every Saturday afternoon in the fall to listen to the collegiate football games, or watch the game on television. In the winter they enjoy watching professional basketball on television. In the summer millions follow the fortunes of their favorite baseball team in the ball park, on radio or television or in the sports pages of the paper. Department store supplies of jewelry and ties have been designed specifically for the sportsman. The term "sport shirt" and "sport" jacket is a common one in the household, and the 'sport car" has found its way into thousands of American garages. Madison Avenue has taken advantage of the magnetism of sport by using outstanding athletes to help sell shaving lotion, cereals, beverages, and insurance policies.

Schools and universities have required their students to complete courses in physical education. All branches of the armed forces have extensive athletic programs. An increasing number of sports have been included in the interscholastic and intercollegiate programs. College administrators have recognized the publicity potential inherent in competitive athletics.

State governments have disclosed their fascination for sport when they sought to improve their recreational resources to glamorize their areas for bathers, hikers, skiers, the general vacationer, and the spectator. Cities recognized that the proximity to golf courses and playgrounds were important to industrialists who contemplated building industries in their communities.

Physical educators need to be firmly rooted in the physical education activities conducted in the gymnasium, the pool, and the athletic field, but they should extend their vision to look out on the wide world of sport in order to obtain an understanding of the ways in which sport affects the total culture – and also, how the culture affects sport. It might be best to start with the familiar – that of the relationship between physical education and athletics.

RELATIONSHIPS BETWEEN PHYSICAL EDUCATION AND ATHLETICS

A cursory look at the historical development of one aspect of the sports world – intercollegiate sports – will serve to illustrate the rapid growth of sports and also to indicate their appeal to people.

The conduct of the intercollegiate sport programs of the 1960's is the antithesis of what could have been observed at one of the earliest intercollegiate contests – the 1859 baseball game between Amherst and Williams. Today the athletic program is one of the most highly organized, most expansive, and most publicized segments of university life. In 1859 it was little more than a "pick up" game between the best of any area players who could be found by two colleges.

The initial competition was an outgrowth of student interest in activity which the college administration did not provide. Most of the college boys were living away from home, and after a day of studying, it was almost inevitable that many would engage in some type of sport. Before long the players began to wonder whether they could beat the team from the next town. As a result, the college teams played anyone they could and, since they received no support from school authorities, the conditions under which the games were played often left much to be desired. The officiating was inadequate, little regard was given to the safety of the players, and the levels of skill and social standards demonstrated were often of a low order.

School administrators were in opposition to this type of sport at first. However, when they saw their admonishments go unheeded, they decided to try to keep the play under control. This they have done since through efforts to provide safe equipment and facilities, placing limits on the number of games which may be played, on the length of the season, hiring well qualified people, and through many other measures. In some institutions, students still have a voice in decisions to be made on athletic policies. However, faculty normally represent their institutions in league discussions.

Sports, as well as institutions, began to organize. Rowing, football, and track were the first sports to organize. Today every intercollegiate sport has an organized body. In 1873 the Ivy League was started with Rutgers, Columbia, Princeton, and Yale being in the original organization. The Western Conference (Big Ten) followed in 1893, and now the majority of universities are members of an athletic conference.

The problems confronting today's conferences and those of the early 1900's are strikingly similar in many cases. Years ago the schools were concerned about eligibility. They questioned whether or not the boy who lived near the college but did not attend the school or the boy who had just transferred to the school a few weeks earlier but who had played at two other colleges the previous year could compete. Today conferences try to have a boy sign an "ironclad" agreement of "intention" which will not permit him to play for another team once he has declared his intention. When a player transfers to another college or university, he may not compete until he has been in residence for one school year. This has served to discourage students from transferring from one institution to another when they were offered greater financial aid. While it is usual for a student to participate in intercollegiate sports for three or four years, it is now quite common to "red shirt" a boy, or to withdraw him from competition for a year until he reaches greater maturity or until the better qualified players have graduated. Often, this practice delays the student's graduation for a semester or two.

A half century ago university authorities were concerned about athletes who were delinquent in their studies because of their consuming interest in sport and because they missed classes as a result of games away from home. Today, the same problem exists because greater numbers of bowl games extend the season. In addition, individual players participate in a variety of post-season all-star games. Basketball has its Christmas holiday tournaments as well as post-season tournaments. Consequently, successful teams have 25—30 game schedules and baseball teams in the warmer geographical locations normally play 25—35 games. Since intercollegiate baseball games are usually held during the day, players are required to miss many classes.

In the early days of intercollegiate athletics the coaches were hired on a seasonal basis and they did not need to present any academic qualifications. The coaches sought faculty rank and tenure on the basis that they taught students activities which the university approved and sponsored. Today there are few seasonal coaches and there are few who do not hold faculty rank. Tenure in the position is a different matter. As long as the interscholastic athletic program is regarded principally as entertainment rather than as an educational experience by many students and alumni, tenure will be difficult to attain.

As is so often the case, high schools emulate universities. This has been the case in interscholastic sports. At first the high schools permitted anyone to participate. There were no eligibility standards, nor were there any organizations of any kind. It did not take many years for school officials to recognize the need to have sports administered by competent educators who would conduct athletic programs according to educational principles.

State organizations of high school athletics were organized early in this century. By 1925 every state in the union had such organizations to administer their programs, to insure that competition was held between boys and girls of comparable ability, and to have rules adapted to their special needs. The National Federation of State High School Athletic Associations was formed in 1922. Today it keeps various statistical accounts, seeks reduced prices for insurance premiums, organizes rules committees, keeps records of the various sports, and assists with contests between teams from different states.

A recent survey done by the National Federation of State High School Athletic Associations indicates how extensive interscholastic sports are throughout the country. According to this association, the numbers which participated in interscholastic sports in 1967 were as follows:[1]

SPORTS PARTICIPATION SURVEY

Archery	64,200
Badminton	135,900
Baseball	2,668,100
Basketball	1,129,000
Billiards	9,800
Boating	9,300
Bowling	174,300
Boxing	12,400
Cross Country	164,000
Curling	7,400
Cycling	500
Fencing	27,700
Field Hockey	30,600
Football (6, 8, 9, 11, and 12-man, and touch)	1,221,200
Golf	215,900
Gymnastics	99,700
Handball	68,500
Hockey (Ice)	34,300
Horseshoes	11,200
Ice Skating	3,800

SPORTS PARTICIPATION SURVEY *(Cont.)*

Judo	8,700
Lacrosse	19,200
Shooting	15,600
Shuffleboard	8,400
Skiing	20,495
Soccer	203,600
Softball	299,800
Squash Racquets	12,600
Swimming	3,134,700
Table Tennis	34,200
Tennis	174,700
Track and Field	724,100
Volleyball	344,100
Water Polo	16,100
Weight Lifting	60,700
Wrestling	254,200

Junior high school is where many youngsters begin to compete in interscholastic athletics. By the time students reach senior high school, participation in sports has become a very important part in the lives of many. Not only does skill in athletics give boys status, but it also encourages a number of them to decide to go to college. Without varsity sport, many youngsters would be added to today's "dropout" list. The trips, the thrill of the crowd, the adulation received from the press and the players' peers, and the fun derived from playing are often more significant to the boy or girl than any other factor in influencing them to remain in school.

Physical education and athletics are part of a larger whole. Unified efforts between the two areas saves money, time, and personnel and makes for easier accomplishment of their common goals. Both use the media of games to improve students' physical fitness status and to develop desirable social and character traits. Both use the same kind of equipment and facilities. They utilize similar methods. They have similar ultimate objectives. Physical education is designed to serve large numbers of students and endeavors to bring the level of physical fitness and skills of the participants up to such a level that they will enjoy playing the game voluntarily outside of class. Varsity squads, on the other hand, are necessarily limited to a select group who have considerable talent and the interest to give considerable time to improvement of their athletic skills.

When they are well run, varsity athletics and required physical education programs complement one another. The athletic spectacles may be used to enlarge the educational arena by including comments in the printed program and by comments made by the announcer on the values of physical fitness, sportsmanship, and wise use of leisure. A display of high levels of physical fitness and athletic skill can serve to motivate beginners toward efforts to achieve a higher level of skill and physical fitness. The interscholastic athletic contests can provide exposure for sports in an attractive and stimulating setting. Interscholastic and intercollegiate athletic contests in the less popular sports can stimulate interest which will lead to greater participation in these sports.

RELATIONSHIPS BETWEEN PHYSICAL EDUCATION AND HEALTH

Any individual who has experienced the physical and mental satisfaction resulting from regular participation in vigorous physical activity does not need to see objective evidence before he believes in the therapeutic values of activity. This subjective experience is the most effective method for inducing people to adopt habits of regular participation in vigorous physical activity. However, some people might be induced to participate in vigorous physical activity by being presented objective evidence that their well-being will be enhanced by such participation.

Evidence is coming from the physical education, physiological, and psychological laboratories to show the benefits of activity. Because of the indivisibility of man, research in the physiology of exercise is a complicated process. Because we cannot sacrifice human subjects or drive them to the same extent we would animals, we will be unable to arrive at completely conclusive answers to some of the questions regarding human physiology during and after activity.

Activity and Weight

Jean Mayer has done much research on the effect of activity on weight control. His results are similar to those farmers learned years ago — that is, that activity will reduce weight and the activity does not have to be as strenuous as one might think. It merely has to be regular. He has written:

The regulation of food intake was never designed to adapt to the highly mechanized sedentary conditions of modern life any more than animals were meant to be caged. Adaptation to these conditions without development of obesity means that either the individual will have to step up his activity or that he will be mildly or actually hungry all of his life. To increase our exercising, we must be trained from youth in sports which we can pursue for a major part of the years ahead; typical of these are tennis, swimming, and mountain climbing. This necessary training requires a major reorientation of the athletic programs of our schools, and a multiplication of the generally inadequate facilities for adult exercise. The result will be worth the havoc visited upon our habits. We will be able to keep trim and hard — instead of being either obese and flabby, or thin, flabby, and starved.[2]

It is necessary to burn 3500 calories or to take in 3500 calories less to lose a pound of fat. If one applies the above concept, he will need to eat 350 fewer calories per day and burn up 150 calories more per day (350 x 7 = 2450 and 150 x 7 = 1050; 2450 + 1050 = 3500) to lose one pound in a week. A loss of one pound per week is regarded as safe and sensible by physicians. It would be possible to lose weight at a much faster rate, but this could be dangerous to health.

The number of calories used per hour in some activites are as follows: sitting at rest, 15; standing relaxed, 20; walking at four miles per hour, 350; soccer, 550; skiing, 600–700. These are based on a 150-pound subject, but naturally such figures vary according to the intensity of the activities. They also vary according to the degree of obesity of the person. A fat person participating in the same activity as a thin person will burn up more calories. The important thing is scheduling activity at a regular time – and then adhering to this schedule. Ultimately, participation in regular vigorous physical activity will become an indispensible part of complete daily living.

Insurance companies do not claim that obesity causes diseases. They assert that the obese person is more susceptible to some of the major "killers" than is the person who maintains a normal weight. Heart and circulatory diseases and nephritis are the major causes of death among obese people. This is why insurance companies normally charge a higher rate for the obese individual who is 20% above the average weight for his height.

There have been a number of studies which have shown the effect of activity on weight control. Among them are the following: Mann[3] doubled the intake of calories from 3000 to 6000 for college students. Then he markedly increased the exercise by having the subjects run outdoors and ride bicycles with brakes tightened. By doing so, he kept the weight constant. When exercise ceased, the weight rose. Similar results were shown with rats at the Massachusetts Institute of Technology. Further experimentation showed that inactivity becomes habitual with obese rats so that even with a reduced diet, but no enforced exercises, the obese rat would not lose weight because of its habits of inactivity.

Johnson[4] studied Boston school girls and learned that the girls who ate the most calories, surprisingly enough, kept their weight normal because they were also most active. The other girls studied ate fewer calories but were about half as active as their counterparts – and they were much heavier as a result.

Thompson[5] was interested in determining if actual fat was lost rather than weight, as is usually done. He made skinfold measurements of the abdomen, chest, and arms of college basketball players and hockey players before and after the season. Although the weight remained relatively constant, the weight had been redistributed, and the men had lost subcutaneous fat in all three areas. Similar results were obtained in working with football and basketball players.[6]

Activity and the Circulatory System

The mortality rate from diseases of the heart has risen sixty per cent during the past sixty years. Today about half of the deaths in the United States are from this cause. Heart disease is the ranking health problem.

There seems to be a positive relationship between the amount of activity a person engages in regularly and his susceptibility to some forms of circulatory disturbances. Several studies indicate this relationship.

Taylor's study[7] showed a relationship between coronary heart disease and the physical activity demanded by the man's occupation. His findings are summarized in the table below:

TABLE I

Death rates for the calendar year 1955 ascribed to coronary heart diseases among selected occupations of male railroad employees of all races. (Rates are expressed as number of deaths per 1000.)

Occupation	Item	40-59 years	50-59 years
Clerks	Number of Men	12,927	22,767
	Arteriosclerotic Heart Disease Rate	2.09	5.56
Switchmen	Number of Men	10,036	13,819
	Arteriosclerotic Heart Disease Rate	1.00	3.55
Maintenance of Way	Number of Men	10,808	16,390
	Arteriosclerotic Heart Disease Rate	0.93	2.87

The above-cited study seems to indicate a lesser frequency of coronary disturbances among men employed in the more active occupations. N. N. Morris studied working men in both the transport industry[8] and government postal work and found a similar association although for some unexplained reason this was not true for the angina pectoris type of ailment. The two tables below summarize his findings:

TABLE II

First clinical episodes of coronary heart disease in male drivers and conductors of London busses 1949–1950. (All figures are for a standardized annual rate per 1000 for ages 35–64.)

	Angina Pectoris	Coronary Infarction	Thrombosis	3-Day Total Mortality
Drivers	0.5	1.5	0.9	2.7
Conductors	0.8	0.8	0.4	1.9

The British bus conductors are much more active than the drivers since they normally operate on double decker busses which necessitate many steps to collect fare from the riders.

TABLE III

First clinical episodes of coronary heart disease in clerks, telegraphers, and postmen 1949–1950. (All figures are for a standardized annual rate per 1000 for ages 35–64.)

	Angina Pectoris	Surviving First 3 months	Dying first 3 months	Total
Clerks and Telegraphers	0.5	0.7	1.2	2.4
Postmen	0.7	0.6	0.6	1.9

It is obvious that the postman who walks his route daily delivering mail is receiving much more activity than the clerk who is sitting at a desk or than is the telegrapher who sits at his work.

Eckstein[9] tried to duplicate the effect of an excessive deposit of cholesterol on the interior lining of the blood vessels. An elementary explanation of atherosclerosis is that the deposition of cholesterol on the internal walls of the arteries decreases their internal diameter which results in increased blood pressure and also causes the arteries to become more brittle. Both conditions increase the likelihood of rupture of the arterial walls. Eckstein surgically restricted a small artery that supplied the heart muscle in dogs. Half the dogs were kept in their cages for six to eight weeks while the remaining half were exercised daily. A much better collateral circulation was found among the exercised dogs at the conclusion of the study. It seems likely that the same mechanism would operate in humans.

It has been shown with rabbits,[10] chickens,[11] rats,[12] and humans[13] that exercise will reduce the rate of deposition of cholesterol. Often it has appeared that the cholesterol content will go down only when fat is reduced. However, according to evidence presented earlier in this chapter, exercise assists in that respect also.

Exercise certainly is not a panacea for all ailments. It will not cure a cold, nor will it prevent malaria or smallpox. It seems logical, however, that activity will help to shorten the time it takes for one to rehabilitate himself from weakness sustained from an operation or from prolonged inactivity in a sick bed. All of the cardiovascular qualities which characterize a runner are improved with *progressively more vigorous activity of a sustained nature.* There is little question that exercise is one of the best forms of preventive medicine. Cardiovascular ailments are the leading killers today and exercise – particularly sustained running, cycling, or swimming – can decrease the likelihood of a person's suffering from a cardiovascular ailment.

It is very difficult to combat the attractiveness of the sedentary life. Dr. Paul Dudley White[14] calls the years between twenty and forty years of age the critical years. He points out that it is during these years that atherosclerosis becomes established, that during these years men lead lives of physical indolence yet expend great amounts of nervous energy; that they become twenty to thirty pounds overweight and that these conditions result in angina pectoris, myocardial infarction, strokes, and other ailments which incapacitate or kill men between forty and sixty years of age. He concludes that health status between forty and sixty years of age is influenced more by the patterns of living between twenty and forty years of age than those followed before the age of twenty.

The research indicates that people should learn sports skills well while young. These sports should be of a type which can be played throughout life.

Participation in sports, athletics, calisthenics, gymnastics, tumbling, progressive resistance exercise, running, swimming, and the other physical activities which are the bases of physical education satisfy the biologic need of the human body for activity. In so doing, they contribute, perhaps more than any other single media, to improved health and functional efficiency. While physical education has objectives other than the biologic or physiologic objectives, these are probably physical education's most important objectives.

Participation in sports can contribute to emotional health by providing a socially acceptable form of release for feelings of aggression, by satisfying the need for belonging and recognition, and by increasing the ability to withstand emotional stress through increase in the size of the adrenal and pituitary glands. These aspects will be discussed at length in chapters XII and XIV. Needless to say, a physically vigorous life contributes to good health in other ways. Physical activity promotes sound sleep and relaxation, improves elimination, and improves the functioning of all body organs.

RELATIONSHIPS BETWEEN PHYSICAL EDUCATION AND RECREATION

"Leisure for the classes" may have been the call many years ago, but today it is: "Leisure for the masses." We are technologically ready for this new concept of living which has been developing so fast that in the past decade it has rushed upon us with the thunder of an avalanche. One of America's pioneers in recreation, Joseph Lee, said: "Leisure for everybody is a new thing under the sun — the most revolutionary thing that has ever happened. It means the coming of something unheard of in all our history — the opportunity for every man to live."

President James Garfield said in 1880: "We may divide the whole struggle of the human race into two chapters: First, the fight to get leisure, and then the second fight of civilization – what shall we do with our leisure when we get it."

People are using their newly found leisure in a variety of ways. They travel more. They putter around the house with "do it yourself" kits. They read. They watch television. They also play. People no longer feel guilty when they play. Today, if you do not enjoy play, people wonder what is wrong.

Even though major league baseball and football attendance figures may be on the upward trend, these increases are small when compared with the extent of increase in participatory activities. Until the depression of the early 1930's this had been a nation content to watch the top performers of the sport world. Forced leisure owing to unemployment caused two things to happen: (1) in an effort to create employment, the federal government through the Works Progress Administration constructed 3000 athletic fields, 250 golf courses, 10,000 tennis courts, and improved state and national park resources, and (2) people now had the time to begin using these facilities.

Several million men and women were in military uniform during World War II in the 1940's and all were exposed to the athletic experiences required in all branches of the service. Service gymnasia were constructed, physical training was required, company and regimental teams were organized, and varsity teams competed on a coast-to-coast basis. It is likely that many of these servicemen and women continued to participate in sports after a return to civilian life.

The growth of aquatics has been incredible. Swimming is the leading adult participatory sport with about 35 million indulging at least once a year. The number of home pools has increased sharply as indicated by the following table:

	Swimming Pools	Residential Pools
1948		2,500
1950	12,000	3,600
1959	133,000	125,000
1963	421,000	288,800

Water skiing and scuba diving are two aquatic activities that have shown swift expansion in the past twenty-five years. Scuba diving is now attracting five million divers who are spending about fifteen million dollars for fins, goggles, tanks, and suits.

Water skiing is taking a firm hold on the public with national and international championships being held regularly. Ski shows are the principal attractions of some Florida resorts and about six million people water ski annually. The growth is summarized as follows by the American Water Ski Association, an organization conceived in 1939 by a small group of enthusiasts who recognized the need for an organization to lend purpose and direction to the future growth and development of the sport:[15]

Year	Number of water skiers	Ski Clubs	Tournaments
1939	Less than 500	6	3
1947	50,000	25	10
1961	6,000,000	500+	21 major and 100+ minor

About forty million people participate in boating. There are over eight million boats. Seattle, Washington, has 80,000 registered boats for a metropolitan population of 800,000 people. During the 1961 Fourth of July weekend, the boating fatalities exceeded that state's highway accident deaths!

Fishing is another leading aquatic sport, particularly among adults whose vigorous athletic days are only something to be remembered. Close to four million dollars are spent in this country on tackle, and several times that amount for such auxiliary equipment as tents, camp fees, transportation, food, lodging, and licenses.[16]

Skiing has also mushroomed in recent years until now the industry is experiencing almost a hundred million dollars retail sales volume which is an increase of about 75% in the past five years.

Seven million golfers spend about a hundred million dollars each year. It is an expensive game to play and the facilities required are expensive to maintain. Boyle summarizes the private country club's economy as follows:

A human becomes a bird for a moment

"There are 3,300 country clubs of all kinds in the United States with a membership of 1.7 million. Approximately 3000 of the clubs are the classic type, privately owned by the members. Nationally, they take in about $250 million a year in dues and fees. They sell $500 million worth of food and beverages. The average club has between 400–600 members, gross annual dues of $100,000 to $150,000 and has food and beverage sales of approximately $150,000 to $250,000. There is now one course for every 29,000 Americans as compared to one for every 21,000,000 in the early 1830's."[17]

We have discussed several specific sports to show how they have grown both from a participation standpoint as well as from an economic standpoint. There are several factors that have contributed to this expansion. The increase in free time was emphasized earlier as was disposable income. The promotion and encouragement of fitness from a multitude of sources has also helped considerably in this growth. Improved school and other physical education programs have made substantial contributions to the increased participation in many recreational activities by developing skills and favorable attitudes toward these activities in school children. These attitudes have persisted into adulthood.

Sporting goods economists, in explaining the growth in their business, are pointing out that changes in the population have influenced the sporting goods business. "Today 38 of 100 individuals are under twenty-one and by 1970 it is estimated that forty-three out of a hundred will be in that age range. Also, the number of 40-year olds (those who can devote more time to golf, hunting, fishing, and bowling) is increasing — thirty-five of a hundred are in that category.[18]

The proportion of those in the fifteen to twenty-four age group — the most active of all — will increase from the current 15% of the total to about 17% by 1976.[19] Earlier retirement, increased longevity, and increasing attention to personal fitness will enable older people to continue their participation in sports a few years longer.

The inclusion of sports in a recreation program has been justified for such reasons as combating delinquency, reducing crime, improving the morale of the group, and improving one's fitness. Actually, the reason for participation in sports varies with each individual and the importance of sports to each individual also varies. Our interests are so different that each individual should select his own recreational activity. Lyne[20] remarks: "We are a middle-class society with a middle-class morality of work and an aristocratic opportunity to make the most of leisure. The question, a hard one indeed, is how does one keep the middle-class backbone of the nation stiff and at the same time give to leisure and its uses the same dignity that we have long given to work?"

Physical education and recreation complement each other. Physical education has as one of its objectives that of teaching physically active recreational skills in which participation can be continued throughout a lifetime. Physical educators endeavor to instill attitudes conducive to leading a balanced life with time for work, play, relaxation and rest. Both recreation and physical education aim to improve peoples' health, both mental and physical, through enjoyable activities. Good recreational programs and facilities provide physical education a reason for being.

RELATIONSHIPS BETWEEN PHYSICAL EDUCATION AND GENERAL EDUCATION

During the early days of education in the United States every college student received an education which was entirely a liberal education inasmuch as there was little education for a specialized profession. However, it was not long before the demand for a specialized, professional education was made known. Universities sought to bring together specialized bodies of knowledge and to develop curricula that would prepare students for the professions of theology, medicine, law, and education. From a single curriculum two curricula were developed within one framework of education. These were professional education and liberal education; the latter is often called general education.

By the mid-1800's educational leaders began to take their stand on the need for general education. In 1872 President Chadbourne of Williams College said: "The college seeks to educate not the lawyer, the minister, the farmer, the artisan, the merchant, or the teacher as such — but the man."[21]

By 1900 the common curriculum for all students was practically extinct, and in its place was the university with many departments, many subjects, and distinct specialization. This complexity caused Woodrow Wilson to utter words which are still voiced by liberalists today:

"There is no common mastery, but everywhere separate baronies of knowledge where a few strong men rule and many ignorant men are held vassals, men ignorant of the freedom or more perfect, more liberal knowledge. Without a survey of the fields of knowledge, it is hard to see how a man is to discern the relations of things, upon the perception of which all just thought must rest. The separation of the general and special training is an acute symptom of the disease of specialization by which we are so sorely afflicted."[22]

The words of these men influenced educators throughout the land, and consequently, general education became more prominent in the offerings of all institutions. While the methods differ from one institution to another, the goals of general education today are not too unlike those suggested by the early proponents of general education.

McGrath interprets general education this way:

Unless men are educated to be reasonable, to be moral, and to be aware of beauty, it is a question whether the activities of educational institutions can be justified, regardless of their other achievements — general education includes the fund of knowledge and beliefs and the habits of language and thought which characterize and give stability to a particular social group. It is the unifying element of a culture. It prepares the student for a full and satisfying life as a member of a family, as a worker, as a citizen, an integrated and purposeful human being — it affords youth opportunity to know the origins and meaning of the customs and political traditions which govern the life of their time. General education seeks to instill attitudes and understandings which form the essence of good citizenship — moreover, with its interest in a sound mind in a sound body, necessary for responsible living, it supplies the factual basis of mental and physical health and encourages the proper practices of eating, sleeping, thinking, and playing. Through the sharpening of esthetic awareness it enables students to find beauty in its multiform expressions and to create it in their own lives.[23]

Notice the word *playing* in the above statement. This was something comparatively new in the concept of general education. While most universities felt, in the past, that physical education should be a common experience of its enrollees, they had hesitated to term it "General Education" per se. Physical education had to struggle for many years before it became a fully accepted part of education.

Play was not originally considered as a phase of education that could aid in developing the ability to do reflective thinking, nor was it considered something in which the mind was used. It was "physical." This attitude was demonstrated by the persistence of the old belief that the mind, the body, and the soul are separate entities and that they must be dealt with separately. The church was to be concerned with the soul, the school with the mind, and the body was to be abhorred because it was vile. There was a wide gulf between the so-called academic subjects and physical education in spite of the fact that centuries ago the Greeks expounded the theory of the whole and indivisible man. Van Dalen summarized this faculty psychology of the 18th century when he wrote: "The school, therefore, was looked upon as the primary agency to provide mental instruction. The home and the church, for the most part, were to provide moral instruction, and the body apparently could take care of itself."[24] It is a paradox to realize that today we urge children to play in order that they will know how to play when they are adults and that we use this reason to justify the existence of sports in the educational program!

Sports began to flourish in the schools following World War I. One reason for this was the disheartening draft statistics which some people thought reflected the failures of physical education. Consequently, more facilities were added, and physical education became more apparent in educational programs. A second factor was that school men were beginning to believe that schools should also concern themselves with children's social behavior.

The traits of cooperation, fair play, good citizenship, and other qualities of character were values that many educators now thought should be included as educational objectives.

Physical education is a required subject and has now been so well accepted that Irwin reports that "nine surveys conducted within the past five years on both a sectional and national scale have revealed that between 91% and 95% of higher institutions maintain required programs of physical education. The American Council on Education which collects data on the operation and status of accredited colleges and universities in the United States in the six regional accrediting agencies, states that of 952 recognized senior colleges offering general programs, 91% required physical education; 96% of all tax-supported schools required it, and 95% of land grant schools maintain the requirement."[25] In a smaller but more recent study Donnelly[26] found that 87.6% of 257 colleges required physical education and that 83.7% of those gave academic credit.

Education is liberal as it gives us increasing opportunities to make choices. The more restricted we are, the less liberal is our education. Ability to participate in a variety of sports certainly may be included in such a definition. More and more do sound thinkers recognize that general education is not to be bound by four or five of the traditional areas.

If an objective of a general education is to enhance one's leisure, physical education certainly can make contributions to this objective. Adler's views seem so pertinent that they are quoted in detail:

Liberal education is education for leisure; it is general in character; it is an intrinsic and not an extrinsic end; and as compared with vocational training, which is the education of slaves or workers, liberal education is the education of free men. According to this definition or conception of liberal education, it is not restricted in any way to training in the liberal arts. We often too narrowly identify liberal education with those arts which are genuinely the liberal arts — grammar, rhetoric, and logic, and the mathematical disciplines — because that is one of the traditional meanings of liberal education. But, as I am using the term 'liberal' here, in contradiction to 'vocational', I am not confining liberal education to intellectual education or the cultivation of the mind. On the contrary, as I am using the phrase, liberal education has three large departments, according to the division of human excellences or modes of perfection. Physical training or gymnastics in the Platonic sense, if its aim is to produce a good coordination of the body, is liberal education. So also is moral training, if its aim is to produce moral perfections, good moral habits or virtues, and so also is intellectual training, if its aim is the production of good intellectual habits or virtues. All three are liberal as distinguished from vocational. This is not, in a sense, a deviation from the conception of liberal education as being concerned only with the mind, for in all three of these the mind plays a role. All bodily skills are arts; all moral habits involve prudence; so the mind is not left out of the picture even when one is talking about moral and physical training.[27]

One of America's earliest philosophers of physical education, Thomas Wood, stressed physical education's dependence upon many disciplines if it were to find its proper place in education. He declared: "When physical education presents a program which is psychologically and physiologically sound, and therefore pedagogically acceptable, it will find itself in organic relationship with education as a whole and to the other subjects or departments represented."[28] It would appear that there is much evidence to justify physical education as a part of general education along with English, art, social science, history, literature, and music. Physical educators who are aware of their role in the process of providing a general education will strive to achieve the goals of general education through physical education, will attend school meetings, and will always keep in view the larger picture.

INFLUENCES OF SOCIAL FORCES UPON PHYSICAL EDUCATION

An editor of *Sports Illustrated* once said at a convention: "The greatest common denominator of leisure activity and of human conversation among Americans pursuing happiness is SPORT." If one questions the authenticity of this statement, it would be well for him to scan the magazines and newspapers, listen to the radio, and to watch the television programs to note how often sports confront the public.

This is an era of "image making." A company's stationary, the dress of its personnel, the avenues it uses for advertising, and its packaging all help to give a product a certain image in the public's mind. Sports have a universal fascination to many people, consequently, some companies strive to have their products, whether sticks of bubble gum or $50,000 life insurance policies, associated with sport. Even a staid institution like the Chase Manhattan Bank of New York has utilized sports in its advertising campaigns. Its "nest egg" is always shown in sporting situations. Its advertising management writes: "We carefully avoid spectator activities because we believe that the really interesting people are those who do things."[29] The sports chosen are carefully selected. All seem to appeal to the adult man and often the family is in the picture.

The change in the structure of our society has had its effect on sport. Neumeyer and Neumeyer write: "In 1800 we had about 6.1 people per square mile and this rose to 50.7 per square mile by 1950, and this has been exceeded by now."[30] The first major shift of population was from the rural areas to the cities. Now people are moving to the suburbs. Howard indicates what this population shift means when he says:

Almost all of the housing built in post World War II has been single family houses constructed on larger lots. In 1850 a standard city lot was 20 feet wide in many cities. It increased to 30 feet by 1900, and to 40 feet by 1925. For today's one-story house, 60 feet is the minimum width and 80 to 100 feet is common. Every family provided with a new house today uses about twice as much land as did a family only 30 years ago. This is as true for apartment living as for single houses – the buildings are lower and farther apart, and less of the land is covered. However, a successively smaller proportion of the metropolitan population is living in apartments."[31]

Why is so much attention given to the shift of population? Since space for living, for working, and for fun may all be the same parcel of land, there is a struggle by all parties to grasp this land. For instance, the federal government made a recent survey and learned that:

We have about 3700 miles of coastline bordering our country but only 6½ per cent or 240 miles, are in Federal and State ownership for public recreation uses. Within these 240 miles are 39 areas in 14 states: two national parks, one national seashore recreation area, and 36 state seashores. In addition, there are eight national wildlife refuges, plus a few small keys and islands, with ocean beaches that are not primarily used for public recreation. A few counties and municipalities own and operate public beaches. More than half of the 240 miles is contained in the Cape Hatteras National Seashore Recreational Area (North Carolina) and in Acadia and Everglades National Parks (Maine and Florida). Neither of the national parks contain much beach frontage suitable for seashore recreation.[32]

Robert Moses, who has planned so much of New York City's recreational space, is just as concerned with the loss of inland space to housing and industrial developments as he is with recreational space. He feels there will be inadequate space for golf courses, if the quest for space continues at its present rate. He believes that it will be very difficult for the private club to survive. He points out the decline in the number of golf courses in New York City: "The age of the private suburban golf course within 20 miles or so of any large city is drawing to a close. Although New York is an extreme example, what is true of it, in proportion, is true of every other expanding city in the United States. In 1929 there were 26 private or semi-public golf clubs within the comparatively narrow confines of New York. In 1959 there were four."[33]

In 1932 there were 64 private courses in Westchester County and 53 in Nassau County (bordering New York City). In 1959 there were 45 in the former and 26 in the latter. New highways doom many courses. When a private suburban golf course becomes surrounded by an area populated by commuters, the fate that befalls it is a rapidly rising property assessment and tax collection (jealously watched by small nonmember neighbors who insist that the club pay its share of the cost of schools and other services), greater maintenance costs, and fewer people eligible for membership. When a private 125–175 acre city or suburban gold club is assessed for 1.5 million or more and has to pay real property taxes of $60,000–$70,000 it assumes the mantle of responsibility with reticence.

Man never ceases trying to seek increased leisure, of assuring himself that having leisure time is not immoral, and of working to satisfy his material wants and his ego need for status. One of the devices Americans have invented to enjoy more leisure time is Daylight Saving Time, which provides another hour of daylight for golf, swimming, travel, and fun around the house. Where it hasn't worked, commercial lighting has been substituted. Today, it takes but a few minutes to find a lighted driving range, a pitch-and-putt golf course, an archery range, tennis courts, and shuffleboard courts.

Vacations have also been changed as well as augmented. At the turn of the century most people were entitled to a week's vacation. In 1930 two weeks became more common, and now a three-week vacation is common practice. Often vacations are taken on a split basis (summer and winter) in order to take advantage of both climates. Through intelligent promotion, Florida is becoming a very attractive summer resort and the New England and Northwest states are attracting thousands of winter tourists.

Legislators as far back as 1790 have taken an interest in the many influences of sport and physical education upon the American public. In 1790 the legislators were concerned about the unfitness of the Revolutionary War soldier, and consequently, they introduced a bill to improve his physical condition. Since that time references to the subject have been found in scores of places in the Congressional Record and numerous other publications of the federal government. In addition to the formal writings, there have been hundreds of speeches and a multitude of references made to participation in sports by congressmen.

States are also interested in sport. Each state has an Economic Development Commission whose purpose is to acquaint industry and individuals with those state resources which would interest them in spending both time and money. Millions of dollars are spent annually publishing and mailing promotional packets, advertising on billboards and in magazines, producing movies, and holding planning conferences. Camping folders, hunting and fishing regulations, road maps, vacation guide brochures, and industrial site brochures are always available.

Connecticut, for example, recognizes the interest people have in its recreational facilities and points out that because of the compactness of the state, one is always close to its 245 miles of beaches. It has advocated regional planning agencies to assist cities in acquiring, developing, and operating land for play purposes. A study of the state's present and future economic growth showed that if the state were to prosper — meaning to have its constituents live happily at a high standard of living — it must have good roads, superior education (resulting in a skilled work force), reasonable taxation, adequate health and welfare programs, forward-looking urban renewal plans, and *recreational opportunities that are so broad that they can offer any person a constructive way of using his increasing leisure.* (Italics the authors!) It can be seen that state governments do concern themselves with sports and recreation and regard them as a necessary component of its total welfare.

Recreation on a public level was initiated when the Boston Sand Garden was constructed in 1885. By 1897 New York acquired a tract of land for $1.8 million which it made into a neighborhood playground. By 1902, 796 other cities acknowledged their responsibility for recreation when they provided playgrounds. The concept of parks in the early days was that of a place of beauty and quiet — not of boisterous sport. Now it is common for cities to have recreation buildings, baseball diamonds, bathing beaches, boating centers, golf courses, ice skating rinks, and tennis courts for their citizens.

The city, like the state, must look after its economic interests in the promotion of sport. Municipal recreation has become a necessary and worthwhile investment. However, there is little likelihood that municipal recreation programs can become self-supporting. Some imaginative communities have promoted certain sporting events that not only bring money into the town but provide them with national publicity as well. The majority of the 24 big league baseball teams, for example, have been lured to Florida cities, where they serve as tourist attractions for the state. Las Vegas, through vigorous promotion, has used athletic events frequently to help attract over 11 million tourists yearly. Not only does it have more swimming pools at its thirteen major resort hotels than does any other comparable resort area, but it also has six eighteen-hole championship golf courses, two nine-hole pitch-and-putt layouts, and seven driving ranges.

Sport has also been a wedge in assisting in the acquiring of new civil rights for Negroes in recent years. Swimming pools, recreational areas, and parks have been opened to Negroes. Negroes have been nominated to All Star teams which have played games in the South. They are also being accepted for athletic scholarships in the South.

Social forces such as racial unrest, disposable income, population density and movement, highways, roads and transportation, amount of leisure time, and competition in business influence patterns of recreational and sports behavior. In turn, recreational interests of people influence many aspects of society.

SUMMARY

Physical education does not operate in a vacuum. It influences and in turn it is influenced by man's values, mores and customs; his economy; geography; climate; and religious and political beliefs. Within the school setting there are interrelationships between physical education and varsity athletics, health, and general education. The physical educator who is aware of these interrelationships and aware of the scope of the influences of physical education, will probably be more effective than one who is not.

Physical education is but a small part of the total sports scene but it is one of the areas where the seed of interest in sport is planted and nourished.

The innate appeal of sports is manifested in many ways – the large numbers of participants and spectators, the efforts of business concerns of all kinds to identify with sports, the concern of federal, state, and city governments with sports and recreational facilities, the rapid growth of sports programs in schools and colleges, the increase in private and public sports facilities, and the rapid growth of relatively new sports such as scuba diving, water skiing, and boating.

While there are problems in the interrelationships between physical education and interscholastic athletics, they are not insurmountable. Both physical education and interscholastic and intercollegiate athletics would benefit as a result of a dedication to achievement of educational objectives, conduct of programs according to sound educational principles, and gratuitous cooperative efforts. Both have much in common – in the areas of methods, objectives, facilities, and interests.

Physical education contributes to improved health through correction or prevention of obesity, improvement of cardiac and respiratory efficiency, improvement of the vascular system and of the blood itself, and through satisfaction of psychologic needs such as recognition, self-realization, belonging, and affection.

The teaching of physical education in the schools has very likely contributed to the growth of recreational facilities, quality of equipment, and extent of participation. Physical educators should take their cues for activities to be taught in their classes from the recreational interests of people as manifested by the extent of participation in the various recreational activities.

The major objectives of a general education are to teach the student to live life more fully – to learn to enjoy beauty, to have a diversity of interests, and to become an effective member of social groups. Physical education, along with such subjects as music, art, English, social science, and history, is a part of general education since it teaches students to enjoy themselves in wholesome manners and to function as members of social groups.

Social forces influence peoples' recreational and sports practices. Population increases cause people to covet land and make more necessary the provision of recreational facilities by federal, state, and city governments. Public beaches, national parks, and state parks are particularly needed.

QUESTIONS

1. Discuss some of the perennial problems facing educators in the area of intercollegiate athletics.

2. Why has the solution of these problems been so difficult?

3. Discuss the merits and demerits of conducting intercollegiate athletics as a business. From general funds provided by taxpayers. Of doing away with intercollegiate athletics.

4. Discuss the benefits and the harm which may come to a high school athlete as a result of offers of great financial aid in return for agreeing to play for a certain university.

5. Present evidence of the relationship between regular participation in vigorous physical activity and good health.

6. Present evidence of the beneficial effects of regular physical activity upon circulatory fitness.

7. What is atherosclerosis and why is it hazardous?

8. Present evidence of the growth of recreation in the United States.

9. How has physical education contributed to the growth of recreation?

10. What are the purposes and objectives of general education?

11. Why is physical education a part of general education?

12. Why should a physical education major receive a good general education?

13. Present evidence of the high regard for sports possessed by the advertising industry.

14. Why should large cities reserve space for sports and other recreational activities?

FOOTNOTES

1. Athletic Institute, *Sportscope,* 8:6, July 5, 1967.

2. Mayer, Jean, "Exercise Does Keep Weight Down," *The Atlantic Monthly, 196*:1, July, 1955, p. 55. Copyright © 1955, by The Atlantic Monthly Company, Boston, Mass. 02116. Reprinted with permission.

3. Mann, B.V., K. Teel, O. Hayes, A. McNally, and D. Bruno, "Exercise in the Deposition of Dietary Calories: Regulation of Serum Cipoprotein and Cholesterol in Human Subjects," *New England Journal of Medicine, 253*:1349, 1955.

4. Johnson, M., B.S. Burke, J. Mayer, "Relative Importance of Inactivity and Overeating in Energy Balance of Obese High School Girls," *American Journal of Clinical Nutrition, 4*:37, 1956.

5. Thompson, C.W., "Changes in Body Fat Estimated from Skinfold Measurement of College Basketball and Hockey Players During a Season," *Research Quarterly, 23*:100-108, March, 1954.

6. Thompson, C.W., "Changes in Body Fat Estimated from Skinfold Measurements of Varsity College Football Players During a Season," *Research Quarterly, 30*:1:93, March, 1959.

7. Taylor, Henry L., "Coronary Heart Disease in Physically Active and Sedentary Populations," *Journal of Sports Medicine and Physical Fitness, 2*:2:78-79, June, 1962.

8. Morris, N. N., J. A. Heady, P.A.B. Raffle, C. B. Roberts, and J. Parks, "Coronary Heart Diseases and Physical Activity of Work," *Lancet, 2*:1053, 1111, 1953.

9. Eckstein, Richard W., "Effect of Exercise and Coronary Artery Narrowing on Coronary Collateral Circulation," *Circulation Research, 5*:230-235, 1957.

10. Brown, C.E., T.C. Huang, E.L. Bortz, and C.M. McCay, "Observations on Blood Vessels and Exercise," *Journal of Geriatrics, 11*:292-297, 1956.

11. Wrong, H. Y., R. L. Simons, E. W. Hawthorne, "Effects of Controlled Exercise on Experimental Atherosclerosis in Androgen-treated Chicks," *Fed. Proc., 15*:203, 1956.

12. Montoye, Henry J., "Summary of Research on the Relationship of Exercise to Heart Disease," *Journal of Sports Medicine and Physical Fitness,* March, 1962, p. 37.

13. Mann, C. V., K. Teel, D. Hayes, A. McNally, and D. Bruno, "Exercise in the Disposition of Dietary Calories," *New England Journal of Medicine, 253*:349-355, 1955.

14. White, Paul Dudley, "From the Wisdom of Dr. Paul Dudley White," *Wisdom, 37,* 1961.

15. *The Athletic Institute Sportscope, 7*:12:2, September, 1962.

16. Morris, Robert, *Jarman Journal of All Sports.* Berkley, Michigan: 1963, p. 23.

17. Boyle, Robert H., "The Ways of Life at the Country Club," *Sports Illustrated,* March 5, 1962, p. 74.

18. "Sporting Goods Sales Boom," *Printer's Ink, 262*:4, Jan. 3, 1962.

19. *Outdoor Recreation for American Outdoor Recreation Resources Commission.* Washington: Department of Interior, 1962, p. 30.

20. Lyne, Russell, "The Pressures of Leisure," *What's New* (Early Winter, 1958), No. 208, p. 17. Copyrighted by Abbott Laboratories.

21. Chadbourne, Paul A., "Colleges and College Education," *Putnam's Magazine,* p.s. 4, 1869, pp. 335-336.

22. Wilson, Woodrow, "Should an Antecedent Liberal Education Be Required of Students in Law, Medicine, and Theology?" *College and State: Educational, Literary, and Political Papers.* New York: Harper and Brothers, 1923, p. 224.

23. McGrath, Earl J., *Toward General Education.* New York: Macmillan Co., 1948, pp. 8-9.

24. Van Dalen, Deobold B., Elmer D. Mitchell, Bruce L. Bennett, *A World History of Physical Education.* Englewood Cliffs, N.J.: Prentice-Hall, Inc., © 1953, p. 425. Reprinted by permission.

25. Irwin, Mary, editor, *American Universities and Colleges,* 8th edition. Washington: American Council on Education, 1960.

26. Donnelly, Rich, *Summary of Recent Trends in Organizational Structure of College Physical Education Programs for Men.* Unpublished study, University of Minnesota, 1963.

27. Adler, Mortimer J., "Labor, Leisure, and Liberal Education," *Toward the Liberally Educated Executive.* White Plains, N.Y.: Foundation for Adult Education, pp. 50-59.

28. Wood, Thomas D., *Health and Education*, Part I, Ninth Yearbook of the National Society for the Study of Education. Chicago: University of Chicago Press, 1910, p. 82.

29. Coords, Deane, personal correspondence, March 15, 1963.

30. Neumeyer, Martin H., and Esther S. Neumeyer, *Leisure and Recreation.* New York: Ronald Press, 1958, p. 155.

31. "Suburban Population Increasing Rapidly," *Statistical Bulletin,* Metropolitan Life Insurance Co., July, 1961, *42*:1-3.

32. *A Report on Our Vanishing Shoreline.* Washington: Department of Interior, 1965, p. 27.

33. Moses, Robert T., "Population's Pressure on Golf," *Sports Illustrated,* April 27, 1959, p. 7.

Part II

THE ROLE OF PHYSICAL EDUCATION IN SOCIETY

7

Physical Education in Ancient Societies

PHYSICAL EDUCATION, LIKE all aspects of our life, is influenced by climate, topography, economy, political structures, prevailing philosophic beliefs, and many other forces. An understanding of how these forces do and have influenced physical education is necessary in order to enable physical educators to formulate aims and objectives, select activities to be taught, determine methods to be utilized, and to determine and to select criteria for evaluation of existing programs. An understanding of present day forces is obviously essential. It is more difficult to understand the forces and influences which surround us today than it is those of the past because we have been indoctrinated in and have emotionalized attitudes toward today's forces. For these reasons, a study of the history of physical education can be very helpful in developing better physical educators.

A study of the past will help us to understand the present better and to help prepare for the future. In our study of the past we should endeavor to select those values, aims, objectives, principles and methods which have proven fruitful and are appropriate to our present situation. We should discard those which have proven ineffective or dangerous.

JAVA, NEANDERTHAL, AND CRO-MAGNON MAN

When man first appeared upon this earth, he was not very impressive. He was a beast among beasts. He was not the largest, fastest, strongest, most ferocious, or the most agile. He could not fly or swim. He did not have fur to protect himself from the cold or canine teeth or claws with which to fight and to kill. In comparison with *Tyrannosaurus rex,* the mastodon, or the saber-tooth tiger, he was indeed a puny creature. When one looks at his physical equipment, it is difficult to understand how he was able to survive.

However, because of his lack of physical endowments, he was forced to develop those qualities which he possessed in greater abundance than any of the other animals — qualities which enabled him to control or to utilize most of the forces and materials around him. These qualities were his ability to reason, his faculty for organization, and his powers of imagination. It is probably because life was arduous and difficult for him that he developed as he did. If his life had been easy and comfortable he would not have been challenged to develop his native powers.

During the Eolithic age, man wandered about naked, searching for raw food, sleeping on the ground without shelter and using sticks and stones to protect himself. Somewhat later, in the Paleolithic age, man still wandered about seeking food but had learned to utilize caves and other natural shelters, kept himself warm with dried animal skins, used fire to cook his food, made tools and weapons of flint, and had begun to develop crude forms of art. In the Neolithic age man made bows and arrows to make possible the killing of game and enemies at greater distances, pottery to store food, textiles to clothe himself more effectively, and domesticated plants and animals to feed himself better and to make unnecessary the constant wandering in search of food.

The many emotions experienced by man such as fear of the ferocious beasts and of death, awe of the forces of nature such as floods, hurricanes and tornadoes, joy in the abundance of food, and perplexity in the many things he could not understand, caused his mind to be filled with wonder and questioning. Sometimes he was fortunate and was well fed and his home was secure, but at other times he was unfortunate and he knew hunger and hardship. As a result, he pondered the reason for his variable fortunes and concluded that the good and evil which befell him were evidences of supernatural forces which he could not conquer or subjugate but which he could appease and supplicate.

Because he had powers of imagination and because he visualized all things in terms of his own experiences, he endowed these forces with personalities similar to his own or with the characteristics of those creatures with which he was familiar. These supernatural beings, he believed, controlled his destiny. Primitive man believed that to develop his own physical powers was not enough to insure his security. He believed he must also appease the gods. Consequently, he developed a body of religious customs and usages to insure his collective security. Every child was trained to conform to the prescribed methods of obtaining the favor of these gods which had such great control over his life. No one was permitted to deviate from the rigid body of rituals, traditions, laws, and ceremonies. Conformity to the group patterns had precedence over individual rights. Things always had to be done in the same way according to prescribed group patterns. This, of course, stifled experimentation and learning and accounts for the extremely slow progress made by man for so many centuries.

Obviously, the rigorous primitive life demanded that man possess a strong, agile, powerful body. In his hard outdoor life it was necessary that he carry heavy loads, fight, stalk game, and run from his enemies. One who lacked physical stamina and physical skills was a danger not only to himself but to his tribe as well. Consequently, physical efficiency was encouraged to increase the probability of individual as well as group survival.

Primitive man, like modern man, needed recreational activities to find relief from the tedium of routine activities and work necessary for survival. Activities such as hunting and fishing, which are regarded as recreational by modern man, were part of the daily toil necessary for survival. Mimetic games provided children preparation for adult responsibilities, just as they do for today's children. Primitive children pretended to hunt, fish, build houses, and make weapons. Toys were made for children which were similar to some of the toys with which children play today. Archeologists have discovered many such toys.

Boys and young men competed in many games of strength and skill such as wrestling, boxing, fighting, jumping, running, swimming, climbing, and bat and ball games. Dancing played a most important role in primitive cultures because through their dances the people communicated with their gods. The body movements utilized in the dances represented not only the movements in nature such as the leap of the tiger, trees being bent by the wind, the slithering of the serpent, or the motion of the waves, but also basic emotions such as anger, fear, love, and victory. There were special dances for a variety of situations. There were war dances to solicit the aid of the gods in attaining victory and to incite an emotionalized frenzy, dances after the conflict to celebrate victory and to thank the gods, dances to initiate the adolescent into adulthood, dances performed by the medicine man to heal the sick by chasing out the evil spirits, and dances for many other situations.

The parents were primarily responsible for the child's physical education. They, like today's parents, taught their baby to reach for brightly colored objects, to roll over, to sit up, to crawl, to walk, and to run. But unlike most of today's parents, they also taught him to stalk game, to fish, to shoot arrows, to throw spears, and to escape from animals by climbing trees or swimming across a river. Motivation of the learner was never a problem because the relevance of the skill or knowledge to survival was immediately obvious. The skill or knowledge was immediately applied or used. All education was practical. It was obvious to the learner that if he did not learn his lesson well, he might not survive. The selective process was a highly rigorous and brutal one by our standards today! Those who had not inherited the physical and mental qualities necessary to mastery of the curriculum or who were too lazy to work for mastery did not survive. If they had not learned to throw the spear with accuracy, they did not receive a second or third chance. The wild beast devoured them! Today's students are seldom so highly motivated.

Later, when the educational process became more organized and was placed under the village medicine man or priest, the reasons or the "why" of the prescribed procedures became less obvious and motivation for learning became a problem.

Man lived at this level roughly 1,995,000 years of his 2,000,000 years on this planet. Progress was slow and often painful. One of the principal reasons for this was early man's insistence upon conformity, his persistence in continuing to do things in the established ways, and his suppression of freedom of thought or individuality whenever it conflicted in any way with the fundamental beliefs of his tribe or group. With encouragement of individual initiative, freedom of expression, research, and increased respect for the individual, man's progress in controlling his environment accelerated at an ever increasing rate until *today more scientific advance is made in one day than was made in thousands of years during man's early history!*

EGYPT – BIRTHPLACE OF CIVILIZATION

It is extremely difficult, if not impossible, for man to make scientific and social progress when all his energies and time are taken up with survival – with combating nature, with gathering food, and with securing shelter. He needs leisure during which to think, to study, to write, to exchange ideas, to experiment, and to invent if he is to progress. Today, machinery, automation, computerization, and cybernetics provide this leisure over and above the time needed for the activities of survival. In societies of the past, slaves provided leisure for the fortunate few. When survival is difficult, strong young bodies cannot be spared to study and to read. They are needed to accomplish the necessary work.

The eastern shores of the Mediterranean Sea, the lower valleys of the Nile and the area between the Tigris and the Euphrates Rivers provided man with fertile soil where he could easily grow the food necessary for survival. The climate was mild. Increasing numbers of people came to live in the fertile valleys. This increased the need for cooperative living and facilitated the exchange of ideas. Man gained leisure. He grew in numbers, in knowledge, in his social institutions, and in material wealth. The Phoenicians, Philistines,

Hebrews, and Canaanites of Syria and the people of Egypt and Mesopotamia gave birth to civilization.

The oldest records of Egyptian civilization go back to 5000 B.C. Egypt reached its zenith with the conquest of Ethiopia in 1500 B.C. During this time the people made many lasting contributions to the forward march of man. These included furniture, eating utensils, principles of farming and irrigation, the twelve-month calendar, an alphabet which was principally pictorial but partly phonetic, and advances in astronomy, architecture, hydraulics, navigation, engineering and medicine. They devised papyrus from which the word *paper* came. After the conquest of Ethiopia, the Egyptian Empire began to decline until it was conquered by Assyria in about 700 B.C.

With the invention of an alphabet, the development of writing and record keeping, and the increasing importance of these as the society became more complex, the ability to write became very important. Only through serving as a scribe could a boy raise himself above the class of his parents. The principal aim of education, consequently, was to learn to read and write — not for cultural appreciation and enjoyment of life but for the utilitarian objective of earning a living. For this purpose, schools for scribes were established in which boys could enroll upon payment of a tuition fee.

Formal physical education programs were not included in these schools. However, Egyptian people of this period did enjoy participating in sports. Swimming was one of the most popular and was enjoyed by both the noble and the poor and by both men and women. A hieroglyphic symbol for swimming shows that an alternating overhand stroke was being used even at this early date. Instruction in swimming was given the members of noble families in their private pools by slaves of high status. Wrestling was participated in by the nobility, the soldiers, the merchants, and the unskilled laborors. Military men wrestled in order to condition themselves. Professional wrestlers entertained at festive occasions. The lower classes hunted, trapped, and fished with bows and arrows, spears, harpoons, and crude fishing tackle. Dancing continued in popularity. There were both religious and folk dances which were accompanied by flutes, lyres, castanets, and tympani. Some of the dances included acrobatic stunts. Small children played with marbles, tops, dolls, jacks, hoops, and balls, while older children did tumbling and gymnastic stunts.

CHINA

The Orientals were among the first peoples to rise to higher levels of civilization. The history of China predates Christianity by approximately

2500 years. Chinese education was designed to perpetuate the state by training each individual to perform his specialized duties. To insure the preservation of ancient values, the government set up examinations to test mastery of ancient rites, rituals, teachings. Those scoring highest received the most important governmental jobs. The entire Chinese educational program was designed to maintain the status quo. It was not the military, laboring, or religious man who was the national idol but the aged scholar. An aged scholar then, as now, did not do physical work or exercise. Consequently, physical work and exercise were not valued.

Physical fitness and sports skills were valued only for their military usefulness. National leaders were expected to be proficient in playing a musical instrument, shooting a bow, horseback riding, writing, and arithmetic. Military men were not expected to possess literary skills but were given special examinations in the lifting of weights, shooting the bow, and handling the sword. Military men boxed, played football, practised jiu-jitsu, and "butted." In "butting" the contestants placed ox skins with horns over their heads, got on the backs of their partners and proceeded to butt other opposing two-man teams.

INDIA

It is suspected that a branch of the European Aryan race conquered the people of India about 2000 B.C. The hot, humid climate, the high mortality rate from contagious and other diseases, and the abject poverty led the people to develop religious beliefs which would better enable them to tolerate the harsh realities of their lives. They renounced the joys and satisfactions of life, personal ambition, and activity in order to be absorbed by the "Eternal Spirit" or Brahma. Such a philosophy serves as a deterrent to efforts to improve one's situation, to a life of vigor and activity, to a search for excellence, and to assumption of individual responsibility. The rigid caste system with five major castes (Brahmans, Kshatriyas, Vaisyas, Sudraws, and Outcasts or "Untouchables"), and hundreds of subgroups also served to maintain a stagnant society. The aim of the educational program was to achieve fusion with Brahma by practicing the caste rules and rituals. Emphasis was upon life after death rather than upon achievement, helping others, or serving the nation. They believed they could achieve fusion with Brahma by subjecting their bodies to pain and discomfort through Yoga, enduring extremes of temperature, maintenance of silence, and by other means.

Physical education was of no consequence to the Hindus of India. However, they did make some contributions in the areas of health. A daily bath was required by members of the three highest castes. They objected to the use of intoxicating liquors and they prescribed fasting for the cure of disease.

PERSIA

Another branch of the Aryan race conquered the people of Persia and settled there. Unlike that of India, the climate of Persia was invigorating. It was dry, had great climatic variations and had high tablelands, rich valleys, and barren plateaus. These conditions gave rise to a strong, vigorous, and warlike people who built the great Persian Empire which lasted from 558 B.C. until 331 B.C. when it was defeated by Alexander the Great of Greece. The Persian religion was militant and ethical. Persians believed that there was a constant conflict between good and evil and that the individual must fight for the triumph of good. Contrary to the religion of the Hindus, theirs was a religion of hope, activity, and individual responsibility. The primary educational aim of the Persians was to develop in their young men military skills, high moral principles, and patriotism so that they could strengthen and extend their empire. Physical education was *the* modality used to accomplish these aims. Physical education was the total educational program; however, it was conceived in narrow militaristic terms. The mother raised the child until he was seven years old at which time his military training began at the court of the Great King or one of his governors. This training continued until the boy was fifteen years old at which time he entered the regular army where he served until his retirement at age fifty.

White sport *(Courtesy: Vermont Development Commission)*

During their military training, boys learned to shoot the bow, sling stones, throw javelins, bear extremes in temperatures, endure long marches, live on little food, swim across rivers while keeping their equipment dry, and to ride so well that they could mount and dismount a horse and hit targets with javelins or arrows while galloping at full speed.

SUMMARY

We have seen that while the stresses of a hard life will cause man to become tougher and to achieve a higher level of physical fitness, leisure is essential to the development of recreational, play, and sports facilities and skills. When life is too arduous because of unfavorable climate, topography, or other conditions all the time of people must be used for survival purposes leaving no time to develop in the areas of sports, music, arts, literature, science, and invention. For this a people can be forgiven.

People cannot be forgiven, however, for allowing themselves to become so fearful of innovation and change that they insist upon conformity, ritual, and maintenance of the status quo. This attitude results in stagnation, lack of progress and ultimate defeat. A contrast between the philosophic beliefs of the Persians and the people of India illustrates the reasons for great differences in the degree of the progress they had made.

QUESTIONS

1. Why was Java, Neanderthal and Cro-Magnon man able to make so little cultural progress?

2. Provide illustrations from modern life of adaptations to stress which make a person tougher. Clues: athletics, disease, climatic adaptations.

3. Why is it more difficult for students of today to see the relevance of what they are required to learn than it was for "students" of primitive times?

4. How did the relationship between parents and their children of primitive times differ from these relationships today?

5. Why were the Egyptians able to make great cultural progress?

6. What were the characteristics of Oriental education which served as a deterrent to progress?

7. What were the climatic and philosophic differences between India and Persia which were responsible for differences in cultural progress?

See bibliography listings on page 199.

8

Physical Education in Early Greece and Rome

THE GREEKS WERE among the first peoples of the western world to attain a high level of civilization. Their beginnings, however, were humble. During the Homeric period, around 1000 B.C., the period about which the blind poet Homer wrote in the *Iliad* and the *Odyssey,* their society was almost primitive. They lived a rustic, pastoral life, cultivated nearby fields, and grazed their flocks on the nearby mountain sides. Their religious beliefs influenced them strongly but in a somewhat different manner from the way other people of other nations and times have been influenced by their religious beliefs. Their twelve major gods resembled humans in that they possessed the good and bad qualities, the moods and whims, and the likes and dislikes of humans. However, they possessed far greater ability and power than did humans. The Greeks did not fear their gods as much as they were entertained by their antics, escapades and accomplishments. Greek religion did not have a code of right, just, and virtuous behavior and consequently had little influence upon the moral behavior of the people. The early Greeks did, however, strive to emulate the superior intellect and physical accomplishments of their gods. This attitude caused them to constantly seek perfection and to enjoy rivalry.

Greece, which is a tiny peninsula, juts out into the Mediterranean Sea toward Asia. This aspect of its geography provided its people contact with the Asian civilizations. Partly because of this, they became a composite people with the attributes and characteristics of many races and utilized elements of many ancient cultures. The sea around them provided them with protection from their enemies while at the same time permitting them to meet and to communicate with people of other countries and to learn from them. The soil was fertile and the climate was mild. This enabled them to have leisure after their needs for survival were met. They used this leisure for self-improvement and for the development of creative abilities. The short mild winters were energizing and the long dry summers made it possible for them to live a vigorous outdoor life. The mountains which divided Greece were in large part responsible for its development into a number of small political units instead of as a united nation.

One of the most wealthy landowners in a valley became the tribal leader and in later years this person became the ruler of the city-state. Many such city-states existed at first, but in time the city-states consolidated into twenty leagues, each being under the largest city-state in its league. In time, many city-states changed from monarchies to aristocracies and, in some, the form of government approached democracy. Sparta, however, developed a totalitarian form of government. Even in Athens (which had the most democratic form of government) only the twenty per cent of the people who were citizens could become educated, own land, and participate in government. Of the remaining people, seventy-four per cent were slaves while six per cent were foreigners. The slaves, who were captives from conquered lands, performed almost all the necessary labor. It should be remembered that we are describing the life and accomplishments of the twenty per cent of the Greeks who were citizens. They were the only segment of the population who possessed the education and leisure necessary to pursue excellence, to undertake creative enterprise, and to philosophize.

HOMERIC GREEKS

In Early Greece – roughly prior to 800 B.C. – Grecian life was simple, rustic, and vigorous. Everyone, even the most wealthy, engaged in physical labor. Odysseus, the King of Ithaca, for example, was a skilled ploughman, shipwright, and carpenter. It was a time when all Greek citizens enjoyed competition and participation in vigorous physical contests. It was also a time when Greece was progressing toward its ultimate achievement of becoming one of the great civilizations. History shows that when the people of a nation are vigorous, ambitious, and hard working, that nation is on the ascendency and when they overindulge themselves in "soft" living, that nation is on the way down.

Homer, in the *Iliad*, tells us of some of the games of this period. There were chariot races, boxing matches, wrestling matches, foot races, and throwing matches. Prizes such as oxen and a "maiden skilled in manifold work" were awarded the winners. Sportsmanlike conduct and attitudes were manifest. Homer tells of the boxing match between Epeios and Euryalos:

"When Euryalos' limbs failed straightway under him and he lay upon the ground, great-hearted Epeios took him in his hands and set him upright."

Since the people of Homer's time were almost constantly at war, the principal aim of their physical education was to develop strength, endurance, agility and courage — qualities needed by fighting men. They sought well-rounded physical development rather than mere strength and bulk. They were not as tall as the people of central Europe, nor did they possess the muscular development of the Romans; however, in symmetry and beauty of body they had no peers.

SPARTAN GREEKS

About 800 B.C., the city-state of Sparta became desirous of dominating other people and of extending its boundaries. They were so successful that the population of Sparta came to be composed of only 9000 Spartans and 250,000 slaves — an average of almost twenty-eight slaves per person! As a result, all Spartan citizens had only one profession — that of serving their country as a soldier. The state provided each citizen with land and with slaves to do the necessary work. Boys were trained to become obedient and courageous soldiers who could stoically endure the pain and discomfort of battle. Girls were exercised in order that they would bear healthy and strong children — children who belonged from birth to the state. Girls and women were conditioned to expect a feeling of joy and self-esteem when a husband or son gave his life in battle. A council of elders examined each newborn male baby to determine whether or not he was physically and organically perfect enough to be permitted to live in order to spend his life in service to the state. Those deemed unworthy were taken to Mount Taygetus and left to die.

The mother reared the child according to instructions received from the state until he was seven years old. From the age of seven until fifteen, he received a strenuous military training during which time he lived in crude barracks. Boys were grouped into companies of sixty-four. One of the boys was elected leader. Four companies combined into a troop which was led by a boy of about twenty years of age. This youthful leader gave orders and inflicted punishment to the 256 boys in his troop, in which task he was assisted by officials called "whip bearers." At the age of eighteen the boys went on military maneuvers, scouted outlying districts of the state, trained younger boys, and underwent numerous tests of their military skill. At the age of twenty, they took an oath of allegiance to the state and from then until they were fifty years of age they engaged in intensive military maneuvers and warfare. Even after the age of fifty, a man might be called to active duty if the state needed his services. All men were required to exercise twice each day until they were thirty years old. At the age of thirty every man was compelled to take a wife, gained full citizenship, and took a seat in the council. However, he lived and ate in the barracks rather than with his wife and family.

The Spartans dominated the Olympic Games for 144 years (from 720 B.C. until 576 B.C.) Their rigid and severe physical conditioning program brought results in this area as well as on the battlefield! However, after the fiftieth Olympiad, the Spartans were no longer successful in dominating the Olympic Games. This was due, historians believe, to their increasingly conservative, narrow, and static society which discouraged individual initiative and ambition.

The Spartans produced a stable government which remained unchanged for centuries. However, because of their conservativeness, they contributed very little to art, literature, science, or philosophy. Their militarism enabled them to conquer others but prevented them from making any lasting contributions to mankind.

ATHENIAN GREEKS

To the north of Sparta, in the city-state of Athens, a culture developed which has had a profound influence upon the thought and practices of mankind through the ages in almost all areas of life — art, literature, philosophy, sports, medicine, and architecture. The Athenians developed a liberal, progressive, and democratic society which encouraged intellectual curiosity and participation in cultural activities. From the eighth to the fifth century B.C., Athens changed from a country made up of herdsmen who were ruled by a monarch to an oligarchy ruled by the few who owned the most land, and finally, to a more democratic form of government in which many governed.

The aim of education for early Athenian youth was to develop a well-proportioned and harmonious personality capable of serving the state during both war and peace. Like the people of Sparta, Athenians wanted to train their youth to perform their military duties effectively but, unlike the rulers of Sparta, they also wanted their youth to develop the qualities needed during peacetime. They wanted to develop men who were both capable warriors and men of wisdom. They sought to develop the well-integrated and well-balanced personality.

The Athenians were the first to utilize physical education consciously as a media for development of the total individual. They endeavored to educate *through* the physical. They did not seek to develop only physical qualities through physical education and sports. They valued the form, grace, and skill with which athletic activities were executed even more than they did the establishment of records or of great strength, speed, or endurance. Beyond the esthetic qualities in the execution of sports skills, they sought to develop through sports those moral qualities which they valued such as self-discipline, courage, humility, determination, and sportsmanship. More emphasis was given to the formation of these qualities than was given to the development of strength and athletic prowess.

The child was educated at home until he was seven years old. At this time he began to attend two different schools. The *palaestra* or wrestling school was one of these. Some of these were simply a room attached to a private dwelling. Others, which were more elaborate, were separate buildings with an open court in the center for wrestling, boxing, jumping, and gymnastic exercises; rooms for dressing, oiling, bathing, and sanding the body; and an exercise room with punching bags and balls. The palaestra was owned by a paidotribe, or physical education teacher, who hired assistants and professional flute players. He charged a fee for his services. An old slave, known as a paidagogus, or pedagogue, served the boys as chaperon, valet, counselor, tutor, and guardian. The other school attended by boys from the age of seven until eighteen was called the *didascaleum* Here boys were taught literature, music, and arithmetic.

Adult men of all ages made extensive use of the *gymnasia,* which were usually located in a grove of trees near a stream just outside the city. The gymnasium included a central court which was surrounded by a covered track. In other respects they were quite similar to the palaestra. The most famous of the gymnasia of Athens were the Academy, the Lyceum, and the Cynosarges. Men came to the gymnasia not only to exercise but also to philosophize, to exchange ideas and to discuss politics. These gymnasia were financed by the state and administered by public officials. They had no formal curriculum or courses but served adult citizens in a manner similar to modern country clubs or athletic clubs except that there was no fee charged.

All Greek city-states had numerous local athletic celebrations but the biggest athletic celebrations were the Panhellenic games. These were national in scope. The Panhellenic games included the Olympian, Isthmian, Pythian, and Nemean festivals. Of these, the most famous were those conducted every four years, beginning in 776 B.C., at Olympia and called the Olympic Games. During the five days of the games all warfare ceased. People from all over the nation and from all walks of life came to Olympia to pitch their tents and to watch or to participate in the festivities. While the contests were conducted in a democratic manner and noblemen and peasants competed against one another, no woman except the priestess of Demeter was permitted to watch. The prizes awarded at all four Panhellenic games were of insignificant value but the awards were made with much ceremony and were greatly coveted. The award at Olympia was a palm branch, at Pythea a wreath of bay leaves, at

Isthmia a wreath of dry parsley leaves, and at Nemea a wreath of fresh parsley.

The Olympic games included foot races, the pentathlon, pancratium, wrestling, boxing, and chariot racing. There were foot races of various distances and runners ran in heats, the winners of each heat running in the finale. Racing in armor was also included as were night torch races. The pentathlon included running, jumping, throwing the discus, throwing the javelin, and wrestling. This event was most appreciated by the Greeks because it helped, more than any other event, to achieve the Greek ideal of harmony and balance in physical development. The Athenians held hand weights called *halteres* while jumping. These weighed about ten pounds each. The broad jumper took a few short, springy steps and just before his takeoff, checked his run and synchronized the upward and downward swing of the arms with the halteres with his takeoff. Their discus was about a foot in diameter, weighed about five pounds and was made of polished stone or metal. Greek discus throwers did not rotate the body as do modern throwers but threw from a fixed position. Wrestling, which was most popular, was of two styles — standing and ground wrestling. In stand-up wrestling, the competitor tried to throw his opponent to the ground three times. In ground wrestling, he threw his opponent to the ground and continued wrestling until one competitor admitted defeat. Boxing resembled modern boxing except that all blows were directed at the head and none at the body. Also, a man could be hit when he was down. Thongs of dry, hardened leather about ten feet long were wound around the hands. There were no rounds — the match continued until one of the contestants was rendered unconscious or admitted defeat because of wounds or fatigue. Most of the Greeks knew how to swim. The overhand stroke was most commonly used but they also knew how to do the backstroke, breast stroke, sidestroke, float, and how to tread water.

After they defeated the Persians, the Greeks entered upon a period of changing values, a changing way of life, and upon a period of slow and insidious decay of moral fiber which ultimately led to defeat by the Romans. After the Persian Wars, there was a period of expansion and the Athenians no longer lived in a simple, conservative, agricultural community but in a commercial and cosmopolitan capital. Citizens became immensely wealthy, owned many slaves, and had much leisure. People became less interested in performing civic service and more interested in accumulating personal wealth and possessions. The educational program became increasingly intellectualized while the civic and physical goals were deemphasized. Wealth and power instead of service to the state brought prestige. Many of the Sophist teachers of this period taught that a morality based on religion and tradition was wrong and that every man should determine for himself what was moral and what was not. The great thinkers such as Socrates, Plato, and

Aristotle recognized the folly of these new points of view but were unable to stem the rising tide of individualism which completely demoralized the once great empire.

Most young men were no longer interested in their own physical development and, as a result, highly paid professional athletes took over the contests in the Panhellenic games and in the lesser festivals. Professional athletes sold their services to that city-state which offered them the most money. Participants in the games were no longer citizens who were useful to society in other ways, who practiced morality and sportsmanship during their athletic participation, and who utilized participation in sports to make themselves more effective in achieving ends more useful than victory in athletics. The professional athletes became self-centered, narrow, brutal, and selfish. They trained so diligently all year that they had no time left to develop abilities other than those required in their specialized sports skill.

The gymnasia became increasingly luxurious – a place to watch the professional athletes train or to luxuriate in the hot baths. It was no longer a place to seek physical perfection through the stress and strain of vigorous physical activity. It became necessary to employ professional soldiers because there were so few volunteers for military service. The athletic festivals became commercial enterprises where merchants, peddlers, and quacks could make money. Politicians used the festivals to announce treaties and truces and to solicit the votes of their subjects. Many used the festivals to display their wealth.

The dance, which had possessed artistic standards of balance, harmony, and order, increasingly catered to the spectators and became more profane and vulgar and less artistic.

THE ROMANS

Rome began its march toward control of one of the greatest empires of all time in 309 B.C. when it threw out its foreign Etruscan ruler and declared itself a republic. The small country town of Latium on the banks of the Tiber River near the seven hills of Rome in Italy ultimately became a luxurious, cosmopolitan, and corrupt metropolis which ruled the major portion of the civilized world – an area as large as the United States with a population of seventy to ninety million people. Its subjects included the half-savage Britons, who had just given up wearing animal skins and dyeing their skins blue, and the urbane and suave Greeks.

During its beginning, Italy contained many tribal communities. Every summer the Roman farmers had to leave their plows and snatch up their swords and oxhide shields to defend their families and property from the

Etruscans, or rough tribesmen, who came out of the surrounding hills to rape and pillage. Ultimately, Latium extended its rule over the neighboring tribes and united the entire Italian peninsula. The simple, uncomplicated, hard-working farmers of early Rome were conditioned to physically exhausting work and consequently became tough fighters when the occasion demanded it. At first, they were not very efficient in governmental matters. Political rights were determined principally by a man's wealth. The republic, which they formed after casting out the Etruscans, was in reality an aristocratic oligarchy. Their government was so inequitable and inefficient that in times of emergency they had to appoint a dictator. Such an emergency occurred in 390 B.C. when marauding Gauls surprised and sacked Rome. The Gauls had to be bought off with a large ransom. This experience caused the Romans to reach the decision that they would make Rome so invincible that no enemy could ever conquer it again. To make themselves invincible, they began to conquer their neighbors until, in a little more than a hundred years, they had conquered all of Italy.

During the third century B.C. the only power great enough to challenge Rome was that of Carthage on the shores of North Africa. Sicily, a Carthaginian stronghold, was barely off the Italian Coast. The Romans and the Carthaginians regarded one another as threats and began a conflict which was to last sixty-three years and which the Romans finally won. In 241 B.C. the Romans won the battle for Sicily and in 202 B.C. the Roman general Scipio Africanus defeated the Carthaginian general Hannibal in Africa. This marked the end of the Carthaginian empire and the beginnings of Rome's passage from a nation to an empire.

Rome, as the center of an empire, had an overabundance of money, material wealth, and luxuries of all sorts. People of all occupations and from all parts of the Mediterranean world came to live there. The new wealth and power brought out the baser instincts of the Roman people. In 146 B.C., they demolished Carthage and sacked, plundered, and burned Corinth and sold its citizens into slavery. While on the one hand the senators and generals became tremendously wealthy and possessed hundreds of slaves, on the other hand, the peasant soldiers came home from long campaigns to their neglected farms to find that the wealthy had taken them over. When in 133 B.C. Tiberius Gracchus urged the people to clamor for land reforms, he and three hundred of his followers were massacred by the Senators and thrown into the river. However, with the passage of time, the masses gained greater consideration of their plight and the government became increasingly efficient until it reached its zenith with the rise to power of Caesar's sickly, scheming, and cold-blooded great-nephew Octavian who, in 27 B.C., was given the title Augustus.

Augustus developed the worship of Rome — and of Augustus — which he accomplished in part by commissioning of the great writers Virgil and Horace to extol the virtues of Rome in stirring poetry. But he also built a stable government, improved the lives of the people, and improved the efficiency of the government. Always, he offered the prize of Roman citizenship as an inducement to conformity to the Roman will. Taxes were surprisingly low; peace was maintained; law and order was observed; trade over land and sea was booming; and agriculture was flourishing. However, inherent weaknesses were beginning to become manifest.

The Romans were a serious and industrious people with natural administrative ability but they lacked in artistic and philosophic ability. They left no scientific discoveries, no new philosophic concepts, and no new art forms. However, because of their practical abilities, they were able to apply the theoretical knowledge of others in building bridges, roads, aqueducts, and buildings. They organized laws for institutions, education, and government, many of which are followed to this day. Because of their utilitarian and practical point of view toward all things, they could appreciate sports and physical education only for their usefulness in achieving a specific purpose. This purpose was training for military service. To the Romans, the Greeks' interest in beauty, form, grace, and joy through sports was a waste of time.

Boys accepted the responsibilities of citizenship in a formal ceremony between the age of fourteen and seventeen and shortly after were conscripted into military service, if they were needed for active service — which was most of the time since Rome was almost constantly at war. During the early history of Rome, men enjoyed competing in the athletic events which were a part of the festivals and religious rites. Later, they preferred to observe the performance of slaves and professional athletes. They continued, however, to participate in horse and chariot races. Older boys did not participate in competitive games. But they did maintain a high level of physical fitness as a result of their hard farm labor and the training in military skills provided by their fathers at the Campus Martius and other military camps. At the Campus Martius they were taught to box, wrestle, ride, shoot an arrow, swim, fight, to endure heat and cold, to run, jump, throw a javelin, and to fence. Twenty-mile forced marches with thirty to eighty-five pounds of armor, weapons, food and cooking utensils were made about three times a month.

Ultimately, Rome conquered almost all of its known world and its empire stretched from the Rhine and Danube rivers on the north, to the Sahara Desert on the south, and Persia on the east and included Britain, Spain, Greece, France, and the northern portions of Africa, Arabia, and Egypt. When the farmers of early Rome had to worry about the surprise raids by the northern barbarians and every male was subject to military service, all men saw a reason for maintaining a high level of physical efficiency. However, when they were no longer subject to military draft and did not have to fear invasion, they saw no reason for continuing the arduous work of keeping themselves physically fit as had the Greeks who enjoyed athletic competition and who appreciated the form, grace, and beauty of the human body in motion. The valuing of sports only for military purposes, the large numbers of slaves, and the new wealth caused the Romans to indulge themselves in a soft, comfortable life, and to overindulge in food, wine, and riotous living. An attitude of self-seeking individualism became widespread. Corruption, bribery, and ruthless exploitation became rampant. Emperors became despots. Civil freedom and self-government disappeared. The democratic rights of the lower classes were disregarded. Some became tenant serfs, while those in the city lived on public welfare and attended the brutal and sadistic gladiatorial contests. Divorce rates increased. Birth rates decreased. Morality deteriorated.

Ambitious politicians competed with one another in endeavoring to present the most ostentatious games to please the savage mobs and to obtain their votes. To defray expenses, they used government funds in addition to their own money (which they hoped to recoup by securing profitable political appointments in the provinces). Some of the leaders saw the evils in this but were unwilling to hazard their political future by taking an unpopular position. Festivals (ludi) became so numerous that by A.D. 354 there were 175 such celebrations each year or about one every other day. About 50 B.C., they began to build wooden bleachers but later they built lavish facilities of stone and marble such as the Circus Maximus which was 2000 feet long and 600 feet wide and could accommodate 150,000 spectators. The famed Colosseum covered six acres and had walls 160 feet high. Van Dalen, Mitchell, and Bennett write: "The subterranean area contained chambers for gladiators, dens for animals, and labyrinths of pipes to flood and drain the arena for water battles. In the Flavian amphitheatre (Colosseum) the marble seats were covered with cushions, awnings protected the citizens from sun and rain, the air was refreshed by perfumed fountains, and sixty-four exits minimized congestion as the crowd left at the conclusion of the combats."[2]

Almost all the gladiators were slaves, criminals, or captives although a few were citizens who voluntarily became gladiators in order to obtain sustenance. Most of the gladiators were owned by wealthy men.

In their efforts to curry the favor of the unemployed, restless, indolent, and brutal mobs whose votes they coveted, the politicians extended themselves in presenting ever more lavish and splendid spectacles until they became quite ridiculous. Men, beasts, and even women were matched in all conceivable combinations. Miniature wars were held in which hundreds were killed. Arenas were flooded to permit the presentation of naval battles. Huge sums were bet on the outcomes of these contests. In dual contests the men fought in armor and used various types of weapons. The fighting continued until one of the contestants was killed unless the mob gave the "thumbs up" sign to spare his life. More often, however, they gave the "thumbs down" sign. The Romans were unable to enjoy the jumping, throwing, and running events which the Greeks had enjoyed. Under the Romans, boxing became a murderous sport when they inserted two or three spikes of lead or iron into the *caestus* or glove.

The Roman *thermae* and the Greek gymnasia were similar in that both had facilities for bathing and exercising but in the thermae the facilities for exercise were meager while those for bathing were sumptuous. In the days of the Empire the baths were huge structures made of granite and marble with floors of mosaic and tile. Ceilings had intricate designs and were supported by great arches. There were hot, tepid, and cold baths in which the water was often perfumed. There were steam baths, drying rooms, and chambers where the patrons were massaged with scented oils. The Romans had reached the zenith in their search for an indolent, self-indulgent, and comfortable life. It is not surprising that their society began to rot and to decay from within.

The large number of indolent unemployed who subsisted on the dole, the inequitable distribution of wealth (at one time six men owned one sixth of the province of Africa), their consumption of more than they produced, their overspending on luxuries and upon ostentatious buildings, and the increasing cost of supporting distant armies whose loyalties were questionable, all contributed to the decline of this once great empire. An iron totalitarianism gave the Empire another hundred years of life but in A.D. 410 Rome was sacked by the Goths — the first time it had been conquered in 800 years.

SUMMARY

From the Greeks we have learned that the professionalizing of athletes greatly decreases the effectiveness and usefulness of athletics, in that fewer people participate in sports since they can receive satisfaction of their needs through vicarious participation and avoid the struggle and strain of vigorous participation. Furthermore, those who become professional athletes are harmed rather than bettered as a result of their experiences because their interests, knowledges, and skills become narrowed. We have also seen that while favorable climatic and geographic conditions and fertility of the soil (which made survival easier) are prerequisite to the development of a culture, excessive amounts of ease, comfort and security are detrimental to a society unless new challenges and stresses are introduced.

From the Romans, we have learned the error in conceiving the purposes of sports and athletics in narrow militaristic terms. When military needs are no longer present, participation in sports and athletics are discontinued by the majority of the people, and instead they participate vicariously by paying and watching professional athletes. Professional athletic spectacles are likely to degenerate into events designed to appeal to the baser instincts of people. We have seen, too, how power- and money-hungry politicians can use sports festivals to further their own personal ends.

From both cultures we have learned of the dangers inherent in a life of excessive ease and luxury. Athletics can provide the necessary stresses to offset the deleterious effects of an excessively soft and comfortable life, whether made so by human or by mechanical slaves.

QUESTIONS

1. Describe the conditions under which they lived and the beliefs of the Early Greeks from the Homeric period (about 1000 B.C.) until they conquered the Persians which contributed to and made possible the development of a great civilization.

2. Since the Greeks did not have the labor-saving machinery which people of today have, how was it possible that they had so much leisure?

3. Discuss the differences between Sparta and Athens.

4. Describe the palaestra. The gymnasia.

5. Discuss the Panhellenic games.

6. Describe some of the events included in the early Olympic Games.

7. Why did the Greek civilization begin to decline after the Greeks had conquered the Persians?

8. What were the qualities of the Romans which contributed to their ability to build great cities?

9. How did the Romans' point of view toward sports and athletics differ from that of the early Athenian Greeks? Why did this point of view cause the Romans to discontinue participating in sports after they had won all their military campaigns?

10. Why did the Roman festivals (ludi) become so numerous, ridiculously lavish, and so designed as to appeal to the baser instincts of man?

11. What were the similarities and the differences between the Roman thermae and the Greek gymnasia?

12. What implications for the conduct of modern athletic programs can one draw from a study of early Greek and Roman athletic programs?

See bibliography listings on page 199.

9

Physical Education in Europe from the Dark Ages to Modern Times

AS ROME LOST control of her provinces and as the barbarians swept down from the north, in ever-greater numbers and with increasing frequency to rape, slaughter and pillage, the people became filled with fear and terror. The weak gave up their freedom to labor in servitude in the castles of the strong in return for their protection. The fall of Rome was followed by five centuries of chaos and darkness and men regressed almost to a tribal form of life. Trade, commerce, and education became almost nonexistent.

The only stability and hope for improvement in the situation was provided by Christianity. Christianity provided doctrines and ideals which could be accepted by almost all men and which, once accepted, could lead men out of the abyss in which they found themselves. Christianity's then new idea that all men are equal in the eyes of God gave the lower classes a new sense of dignity and worth. The emotionalized approach to the promulgation of the ideas of love and sympathy for others, of fear of eternal retribution, and of love for a benevolent God appealed to both the Romans and the Northmen. As a consequence, the Church not only survived the barbarian invasions but was also able to serve as a unifying force, perpetuate a measure of learning, and preserve some of the knowledge of the Greeks and Romans. While Jesus had healthy out-of-door interests, was obviously vigorous and fit, and never condemned the joys and relaxations of this world in themselves, some early churchmen did condemn all things of the body and along with them all sports and physical contests. In their defense, it must be said that they were justified in doing so from their point of view. They had seen or heard of the sports of the later Athenians and the gladiatorial contests of the Romans and believed them to be brutalizing. They feared the effects of the mixed nude bathing of the Roman thermae upon morality. They abhorred the remnants of worship of pagan gods at the athletic festivals. To discourage interest in sports, the Church denied communion to those who attended the gladiatorial contests and baptism was denied gladiators until they had given up their profession.

The churchmen persisted in their campaign against the athletic festivals and the gladiatorial contests until, in A.D. 394, Emperor Theodosius abolished the Olympic Games and in A.D. 404 the last gladiatorial contest was held.

MONASTICISM, FEUDALISM, MANORIALISM, AND CHIVALRY

It can be seen that religious beliefs powerfully influence sports and physical education and that when sports are conducted in unwholesome manners people will discontinue their practice. *Monasticism*, which had been practiced earlier by the Hindus, Persians, and Egyptians, became one of the institutions through which men could seek salvation for their souls by means of bodily mortification, silence, and world renunciation. The monks censured all activities pursued solely for pleasure. While the program in the monasteries made no place for sports or recreational activities, the monks themselves were quite robust because they had to do seven hours of hard labor each day. In addition, they were required to read or to transcribe from the writings of the Greeks and Romans for two hours each day. These practices served to preserve some of the learnings of the Greeks and Romans, to give labor a new dignity, and provided a "softening" influence upon the tough Teutons.

The monks got a minimum of food and sleep. Sanitation was nonexistent. Swimming and baths were frowned upon. The "odor of sanctity" was not just a phrase. It is not surprising that there were so many plagues and that contagious diseases spread so rapidly. Nothing was done to discover the causes of these misfortunes or to improve the situation because they were regarded as acts of God in punishment for sin. The Church helped to solve some of the peoples' problems. Other institutions were developed to solve other problems.

Feudalism helped to solve some of the social, economic, and political problems. It developed in this way: The king, who was regarded as the vassal of God, owned all the land. However, he was unable to rule the vast areas during such unstable times; therefore, he delegated some of his power and land to a nobleman who in turn further subdivided the land and the power. Each noble reciprocated by pledging loyalty to and promising to fight for the king.

Manorialism was a system in which those unable to fight effectively traded their servitude for the protection which the noblemen could provide by means of their fighting skills and the stone walls of their castles. The peasants, who did all the work, had no time for recreation or for education and consequently they remained ignorant, superstitious, and humble. The nobles themselves did not have the kind of life some of our romantic writers have pictured. The castle was dark, cold, damp, and drafty. The diet was monotonous. Nobles slept in their clothes, went unbathed, and ate with their fingers.

Chivalry was the institution which was formulated to preserve the social and moral customs of war, religion, and gallantry toward ladies. The ideals of chivalry came from the military, from the Church, and from contact with the Saracens of the East during the holy wars. Chivalry reached its zenith between A.D. 1250 and 1350. The knight pledged in a solemn and sacred ceremony to fight for his lord and to give him his loyalty; to defend the Church; protect the poor and oppressed; redress wrong; avoid sin; uphold Christian ideals, perform religious ceremonies; and protect women, widows, and orphans.

Education in chivalry, which was provided only for the sons of noblemen, was achieved principally through physical education. From the age of seven until fourteen the boy was called a page or henchman. During this period he learned to shoot a bow, to throw heavy weights, and to use a sword and cudgel. He also received religious training and was drilled in etiquette. From the age of fourteen to twenty-one he was called a squire. During this period he served his noble and underwent a very strenuous physical training program which included distance running, swimming with armor, throwing spears, mounting or exchanging horses at a full gallop, swordplay, use of the mace, battle-axe, and shield; wrestling; jumping; climbing; use of the bow and crossbow; vaulting; and use of the lance. He took care of his noble's armor, waited upon him and assisted him in battle or in the lists. At the age of twenty-one he was inducted as a knight in a solemn and impressive religious ceremony. The night previous to the ceremony he spent in prayer and after the ceremony there were gala festivities, banquets, and a tournament. Young men endeavored to earn knighthood before their twenty-first birthday by distinguishing themselves in a deed of valor during battle.

The pages, squires, and knights played a number of games which were designed to improve their combat skills. In quintain the squires utilized a device which encouraged them to improve their marksmanship with a lance. A dummy target, made up to look like a Saracen and with a sword or lance in one hand and a shield in the other, was so mounted on a post that if it were not struck in the center it would revolve. The squire charged at the quintain on foot or horseback and attempted to strike it in the center with his lance. If he struck it off-center, it spun and he received a resounding, humiliating and sometimes painful whack on his back from the sword or shield in the dummy's hand. In human quintain, one young man sat on a three-legged stool and endeavored to parry with a sword the thrusts of a lance by his opponent who endeavored to knock him off the stool. Another game, which the nobility played, was called behourd. In this game one team attempted to defend a small fortress from attack by another group.

The tournaments were the most popular of the sporting events. They were held from the eleventh until the sixteenth century. The grand tourney or *melee* was the most popular event. The melee began with thirty or forty knights charging one another on horseback from opposite sides of the arena. After the initial thunderous crash of lance against armor, those who were not thrown violently to the ground or run through by a lance, continued to charge and fight with fury. While the regulations required use of blunt weapons, sharp ones were often used. Clubs and the battle-axe were also used occasionally. Injuries occurred in every melee and fatalities were fairly frequent. The joust, which was also a part of the tournament, was a combat between two armed horsemen who fought with blunted weapons. After a blare of the trumpet, the horsemen charged at one another and endeavored to knock the other off his horse by means of a well-directed blow with the lance. If neither man became unseated, they wheeled and charged again. Sometimes the fight was continued on foot.

THE GROWTH OF GUILDS

The invention and use of gunpowder, the emergence of greater nationalistic feelings, more effective monarchies, substitution of royal law for feudal law, greater trade and commerce, the growth of towns, and the rise of the burgher or merchant class, all served to make obsolete the noble class, the knights, and the institutions of feudalism, manorialism, and chivalry. However, this progress gave rise to new problems, hence new organizations were formed to solve or alleviate these problems. *Religious* and *social guilds* were organized to provide social recreation, to perform charitable functions, and to perform community services. *Merchant guilds* were organized by businessmen engaged in wholesale trade to protect and promote their interests. *Craft guilds* were organized by men engaged in certain trades in an attempt to rectify the injustices to which they had been subjected — such as carrying a disproportionate amount of the tax load. The craft guilds also regulated hours of work and wages, established standards for workmanship and materials, determined the amount of preparation needed to practice a craft (apprenticeship), and promoted religious and social functions. The craft guilds succeeded in giving a dignity to work which it had never enjoyed when it was done by slaves or serfs.

Physical education during the later Middle Ages did not play as important a role as it did during the feudal period. The townspeople during the later Middle Ages performed functions other than military whereas the function of the knights had been almost exclusively military. However, physical education was used by town leaders to increase the feeling of unity and to provide the workers with activities through which they could release their frustrations, irritations, and angers in forms other than peasant revolts. The peasant's monotonous life of drudgery did not permit him to develop the ability to be discriminating in the use of the little leisure he had. To him, sports and games were merely fun and he combined them with drinking and violence. In spite of opposition from the Church, from the kings, and from the merchant guilds, men continued to participate in sports. Edward II in England in 1314 threatened to jail men playing soccer. Edward III declared all sports illegal with the exception of archery. Archery was exempted only because it had military usefulness.

From the eleventh through the fourteenth centuries, men and boys and girls and women participated in many different games and sports. In England there was cockfighting, ball playing, war games, boat quintain, dancing, shooting, wrestling, sled riding, ice skating (bones were tied to the shoes), hawking, hunting, and burlesques of the tourneys in which the contestants mounted an assortment of animals such as donkeys, cows, and goats and swung at one another with flails. In Italy men engaged in various forms of combatives such as the mass battle with shields and clubs which was continued until one team retreated. In the "battle of the bridge," thirty to sixty men fought against a like number of opponents for possession of a bridge. They used a narrow shield as a weapon. With this shield they could parry and thrust and, when the press of bodies on the narrow bridge was relieved as one side pushed the other across, they could grasp the shield by its narrow end and use it as a club. Not many contestants were killed because they were well protected by armor of iron and leather. Other games which were played throughout Europe included quoits, bowling, tennis, handball, billiards, croquet, rugby, soccer, horseracing, and dancing. Many of the games which have continued to be played to this day were then in their primitive form. For example, in tennis, a rather large leather ball stuffed with wool was struck with the hand over a dirt embankment.

SCHOLASTICISM

There was a gradual intellectual awakening in the Christian world from the eleventh through the fifteenth centuries; however, this awakening was accelerated near the end of this period. This occurred for several reasons. People who had traveled on the Crusades to Spain had come in contact with Saracenic ideas and had returned with a different point of view and new ideas. Previously, no one had questioned the teachings and dogma of the Church. Also, the Church resented efforts to rationalize its doctrines and truths, believing they should be accepted without question and needed no justification. Now, theologians themselves felt they had to bring all people to believe by appealing to reason. They sought to answer all doubts and questions through a philosophic process which came to be known as *scholasticism.* They established procedures for the art of disputation and reasoning about matters of opinion which is today called the *dialectic* method. Cathedral schools, at which theologians lectured and engaged in the dialectic process, attracted large numbers of students who were anxious to learn. These *cathedral schools* developed into the great universities. Other universities developed in cities which had served as repositories for some of the ancient writings of the Greeks and Romans. For example, Bologna became a famous law school because the Roman legal codes had been retained there.

The universities were loosely organized institutions with no complex of buildings and grounds as they have today. There were no facilities for physical education activities and there was no physical education program. Students gave expression to their animal vitality through street fights, drinking, gambling, fights between "town and gown," and fights between the various fraternities which were made up of national groups. University officials made no effort to provide recreational facilities or programs for the students but they did make effort to curb or stop student recreational activities.

HUMANISM, MORALISM, AND REALISM

Van Dalen, Mitchell, and Bennett point out that education in Europe was powerfully influenced between the fourteenth and seventeenth centuries by three great movements. These were: *humanism* which originated in Italy; *moralism* which originated in different forms in Germany, Switzerland, the Scandinavian countries, and Spain; and *realism* which had its beginnings in Spain, France, and England.

Humanism sought the educational goals of the early Athenians; that is, the harmonious development of the entire person — his intellectual abilities, his physical abilities, his social skills, his artistic abilities and appreciations, his political interests, his military abilities, and his literary skills. It endeavored to bring together the values of Christian morality and Greek individualism. Unfortunately, it was unable to achieve its goals because most people were unable to understand the duality of its preachments for both individual freedom and social responsibility and could only see its advocacy of freedom, self-expression, and license.

Individual Humanism

Some of the early proponents of *individual humanism* were Petrarch, Vergerius, Feltre, Verone, Alberti, Vegius, and Piccolomini (who later became Pope Pius II), and the physicians Cordano and Mercurialis. Almost every humanist philosopher believed physical education played an important role in the educational process. The Individual Humanists held that if intellectual efforts are to be effective it is necessary that the body be healthy and that the spirit be joyous. They recommended inclusion of physical education in the curriculum because it develops self-discipline. Vergerius recommended activities for pleasant relaxation as well as military exercises. However, he rejected on the one hand, coarse and brutal activities and, on the other, effeminate activities. Pope Pius II (Piccolomini) wrote to the King of Bohemia to advocate that boys be taught games and exercises in order to improve their posture and carriage. During this time many papers were being written about the causes, symptoms, and treatment of the Black Plague. These were among the first efforts at instruction in public health. While most of the articles were reasonably scientific, some attributed the cause of the illness to poisonous vapors and to the positions of the planets.

Humanist educators were among the first to be concerned with teaching methods as well as content. They advocated methods which many teachers of today believe are new and modern. They discussed consideration for individual differences, progressive education, respect for each individual personality, limitation of class size, encouragement of cooperation among students, and utilization of competitive situations as motivating forces.

Social Humanism

Because the people of France, Germany, and the Slavic countries were more religious than those of Italy, they were less interested in personal development, self-realization, and individual achievement and more interested in advancing mankind as a whole through improving his social and moral behavior. Consequently, in these countries humanism had a slightly different emphasis and was called *Social Humanism.* Because in these northern countries scholasticism was thoroughly entrenched, it took considerable courage to espouse new and different ideas. The men who possessed this courage included Erasmus, Agricola, Melanchthon, Thomas Kempis, Reuchlin, Wimpfeling, Sturm, Ascham, Elyot, Budeous, Corderius and More.

Few of the social humanists were able to understand the deeper meanings of physical education and as a result few of their schools had physical education programs. Their emphasis was upon the classical subjects. While in its beginnings the movement possessed a critical, investigative, and intellectual spirit, after 1600 the classics were no longer read to capture their flavor and meaning but to commit to memory; consequently, learning became a formal study of language, style, and form. Students participated in sports and games as extracurricular activities, many of which were sponsored by nonschool recreational agencies. Activities included bowling, tennis, fencing, archery, cockfighting, bull and bear baiting with dogs, golf, card playing, dancing, the ballet, exercising with dumbbells, hawking, hunting, wrestling, running, swimming, horseback riding, chess, and dice. Archery which had been very popular, partly because of its military usefulness, became less popular after 1588 when the English, using firearms, defeated the Spanish who used bows and arrows. Golf was invented in Holland and was adopted by the Scots and the English as their national sport.

Books written for the layman on health and sports and games began to appear at this time. The first book on sports and games was written by a woman, Dame Juliana Bernos. It was on hawking, hunting, and heraldry.

Moralism

Humanist scholars, as a result of studying the classics, scriptures, and writings of the theologians, were led to criticize the spiritual leaders. The kings of the sixteenth century felt that the church held many civil powers which rightfully belonged to the state. The merchants and businessmen, who were granted many privileges, rights, and protection by the king, found it to their advantage to support the king in any disagreement. The first two situations led to the church reformation and the third gave it impetus. The church revolt and reformation which followed resulted in doctrinaire and procedural changes in church affairs which brought its functions into greater conformity with the needs and beliefs of the people at that time. Because the emphasis was placed upon social conscience and morality and also because efforts were made to rationalize current practices on the basis of morality, the movement has been called *moralism.* It took two principal forms, *Protestant moralism* and *Catholic moralism.*

In their beginnings the Protestant moralists taught that each individual should discover for himself the eternal truths contained in the Bible rather than accept blindly the interpretation of the churchmen. However, after the new religious sects became better organized, they became more dogmatic and less liberal. Because of the disagreements which arose, Protestantism took different forms. In Germany it was *Lutheranism;* in Switzerland, *Calvinism;* France had the *Huguenots;* Scotland, the *Presbyterians;* Netherlands, the *Dutch Reformed;* England, the *Anglicans;* and others, the *Reformed Faith.*

In all of these countries, religious leaders found it necessary to make efforts in the area of education. Protestant education concerned itself not only with personal salvation but also with training in home, occupational, and state duties. Early Protestants believed each man should determine for himself what was moral. Later, Protestants felt they had to supervise other men closely in order to insure that they would conform to their own rigid code of behavior. They wished to develop good citizens who could work in harmony with the growing capitalistic system. They taught that hard work and thrift were an expression of service to God and consequently constituted moral behavior. Idleness, frivolity, and worldly pleasures were to be avoided.

Though Martin Luther pronounced in favor of physical activities, many of his followers vigorously condemned them through their sermons and through passage of the "blue laws." Martin Luther advocated the seeking of good health in order that men could labor more energetically and serve the church more effectively. Calvin was so concerned with moral discipline that he completely restrained physical education with prohibitions which prevented its goals from being achieved. Another factor which restrained physical education under Protestantism was the desire of its leaders to eliminate any activity that was of Catholic origin or which was similar to activities of the Catholics. As a result, Protestant leaders did away with many of the medieval religious holidays and prohibited Sunday amusements which had presented opportunities for men to pursue the social-recreational objectives of sports and games.

Among the early American colonists, the harsh demands of survival left little time or energy for play and so it was necessary that play be condemned. Unfortunately, the Puritans persisted in this point of view long after it had become unnecessary. In the southern United States several factors combined to encourage a greater degree of participation in sports and recreational activities. First, the Southerners were principally Anglican and consequently were subjected to fewer restraints. Second, the warm climate and fertile soil made survival somewhat easier leaving more time for leisure after the survival needs had been met. And finally, slave labor permitted them more time for leisure.

Having succeeded in removing the Roman Catholic Church as the official agency of education, the Protestant reformers found it necessary to establish their own schools. Since the governments had supported them in their revolt, they turned to them for aid in this new task. This was the beginning of state control and support of education. A dual system of education developed. Most boys and girls attended the Dame or parish schools and then went into apprenticeship to learn a trade. This gave them a very limited education. Children who demonstrated unusual intellectual ability or whose parents were wealthy, attended the Latin grammar schools from which many went on to study at the universities.

Protestantism discouraged participation in sports and recreational activities. In a few schools, students were given two or three hours to do as they pleased one afternoon each week. The Puritans made it illegal to even celebrate Christmas. The early American Puritans punished those who played on Sunday rather severely by inflicting large fines or public whippings. Even sled-riding on a Sunday by small children would result in eternal damnation, it was believed. However, as time passed and increasing prosperity came to the colonists, a greater number became more bold about their pursuit of life's pleasures. Fewer found their pleasures in attending funerals, public whippings, and long sermons while an increasing number attended cockfights, animal baitings and shooting matches; competed in billiards, dice, card games, quoits and bowling; and participated in dancing, fishing, hunting, boating, fox hunts, coasting, ice skating, and sleigh-ride parties.

The Counter-Reformation

In the countries of southern Europe such as Italy, Spain, and France, Catholicism remained the dominant force. One of the reasons for this was the movement which came to be known as the *Counter-Reformation.* The Counter-Reformation consisted of vigorous and militant efforts to revitalize the church by improving the quality of the clergy and the practices of the church. Great improvements resulted from the Council of Trent of 1545–1563. The efforts of the Jesuits, which were established by a Spanish knight, Ignatius de Loyola, illustrate the Catholic Church's recognition of the value of education in winning back dissenters. The Jesuits rejected the medieval idea of religious withdrawal from this world and sought instead a life of practical activity dedicated to the training of Christian leaders. The Jesuits assigned an important role to physical education when they taught that the body was divinely created to serve as the receptacle of the soul and the tool of the spirit. They also recognized that qualities of character could be developed through sports.

The Catholics established many new teaching orders at this time. In addition to the Jesuits, there were the Oratorians and Port Royalists teaching at the secondary level and the Brethren of the Christian Schools, the Piscrists, the Order of the Ursulines, and the Sisters of Notre Dame teaching at the elementary level. The first teacher-training program was established by the Brethren of the Christian Schools. Later, the Jesuits, Oratorians, and Port Royalists developed such programs. In the elementary schools conducted by the Brethren of the Christian Schools, teachers were required to examine each child's state of cleanliness twice each day. The Jesuit schools motivated boys toward greater intellectual efforts through use of such devices as honor societies, competition between paired individuals and matched groups, and through the awarding of a leadership position to those doing superior work. At some of the girls' schools, girls who won games were given money prizes which they donated to charity.

Realism

As the humanistic studies narrowed to an emphasis upon the works of Cicero and the different Protestant sects increasingly suppressed individual judgment and required a greater degree of unquestioning obedience, more men demanded a broader curriculum and one which was more directly related to the realities of life. A growing awareness that a few classics did not hold the total and final sum of all human knowledge gave rise to the movement known as *realism*. Realism manifested itself in three stages known as *verbal realism*, *social realism*, and *sense realism*.

Juan Luis Vives (1492–1540), François Rabelais (1483–1553), and John Milton (1608–1674) were the leaders in *verbal realism*. Like the humanists, they believed the classics were the bases of all learning, but unlike the humanists, they tried to make learning as practical as possible. They believed that the meaning of the classics was of greater importance than their style or form. Vives believed that physical exercises were useful to build energy which could be drawn upon to support greater mental efforts. He censored activity which depleted the body's stores of energy. He also censored activity whose purpose was increased military efficiency because war was not consistent with the Christian principle of brotherly love. Both Rabelais and Milton advocated daily periods for physical education. Milton recommended a militaristic type of training while Rabelais advised that a program so vigorous be presented that it is doubtful that anyone could have adhered to it. While none of the ideas of these men were incorporated into the schools of their day, their writings influenced educational thinking for many years afterward.

Michel de Montaigne (1535–1592) was the leading exponent of *social realism*. While he advocated a bookish instruction consisting of the classics, he demanded that it be made as utilitarian as possible. He recommended a liberal education in which the whole man was taught. His manners, his social behavior, and his posture as well as his skill in grammar and logic were to be improved. Montaigne was especially critical of those who emphasized the acquisition of knowledge to the detriment of the development of virtue and judgment. He endeavored to develop the fully integrated personality and in this process physical education played an important role for, he believed, it is through the physical that man's moral and intellectual powers come to fruition. Montaigne believed that an education supplied by a tutor was superior to either that which could be provided by parents (who are too soft) or by schools (which make the boy vain). He was among the first to condemn memorizing as an educational procedure and to recommend the classroom discussion technique.

With the acceleration of scientific discoveries such as the circulation of the blood, dissection of the human body, the invention of the barometer, and new procedures in mathematics, geometry, and astronomy, men began to develop greater appreciation of the value of observing nature and of utilizing independent judgment. The leaders in this movement came to be called *sense realists.* They included Francis Bacon (1561–1626) of England and Richard Mulcaster (1531–1611), and John Amos Comenius (1593–1670) of Czechoslovakia. The sense realists contended that learning takes place most effectively through the senses – seeing, touching, hearing, feeling, and tasting – and that this learning must be utilized in the service of mankind. Sense realists, as a result of their emphasis upon the senses as the media for learning, attributed to physical education an important role in the educational process.

Bacon, who wrote before the germ theory of disease was known, believed that disease could be prevented by proper exercise. Mulcaster advised that people not wait until beset by illness or old age before becoming concerned with their health but that they should concern themselves with it from infancy. Comenius was among the first to see the role of play in the lives of children in insuring sound mental-emotional health. Mulcaster advised that colleges and universities establish specialized curricula for the training of teachers as had been done for the training of physicians and lawyers. This suggestion was not to be implemented until some 300 years later. Bacon publicized the *inductive method* of thinking in which many observations are made and facts are collected before general principles are arrived at. Previous to this, the common method of thinking was *deductive logic,* in which the person tries to prove what is already known or thought to be known. This new emphasis upon the inductive method of science was to have a profound influence upon teaching methods. Comenius presented many ideas concerning teaching methods which today are often presented as new ideas. He advocated proceeding from the simple to the complex, from the known to the unknown, frequent repetition, basing selection of materials upon the child's experiences, use of clear, simple, and humorous explanations, and wide use of visual aids.

DISCIPLINARIAN EDUCATION

By the end of the seventeenth century the world was aflame with intellectual curiosity and scientific interest. John Locke (1632–1704) was one of the leading men in giving this curisoity and interest direction and guidance. His ideas on religious tolerance and on the political rights of man influence our thinking and practices to this day. Previous to his time, it had been generally believed that the child was born with information and beliefs which would have to be developed and drawn out. Locke described the child's mind as a blank blackboard upon which his parents, teachers, and life experiences slowly write the story of life. This meant that learning had to be mediated through the senses and that it is a process of combining sensations and reasoning to formulate generalizations, principles, and concepts. No longer could men think of a child as a miniature adult. This idea had important implications for teaching methods, content, and philosophy. He did not view learning as the accumulation of a quantity of knowledge but rather as an increase in the powers and activity of the mind. He has been regarded as one of the leaders in *disciplinarian education* which attempted to develop qualities of character and refinement in aristocratic young men.

Locke believed that physical education is the base of the educational program and that all other parts rest upon it. He believed that physical education should develop in children a strong and healthy body, good health habits, and the physical skills used by a gentleman of society. He was aware, as well, of both the recreational values and the social values of physical education.

He recommended inclusion of a variety of learnings in physical education such as swimming, wrestling, fencing, riding, dancing, and manual skills including gardening, carpentry, and iron work. While Locke believed the child should submit to authority, he did not favor physical punishment or nagging. Discipline should be exercised skillfully. He advised public praise and private censure as one method to secure conformity. Another method which he advocated was the invention and use of games to make learning more pleasurable.

NATURALISM

The work of pioneer scientists of the eighteenth century, which demonstrated explanation of certain universal truths through observation of nature, caused other men to wonder whether such universal truths concerning man's social structures could not be discovered through observation and study. Jean-Jacques Rousseau (1712–1778) was one of those who thoroughly examined governmental and educational institutions. His conclusions were not very complimentary to French society. He complained of excessive taxation, arbitrary arrest, and excessive regulation of business. He contended that men lived and died in slavery but that the laws of nature endowed men with certain inalienable rights and that these rights had precedence over inherited rights. Rousseau was as harsh in his criticism of French educational practices as he was of French society in general. Like Comenius and Locke before him, he believed children should learn about their environment through use of their senses but, unlike them, he believed that they should be free from any authority in order to allow a natural development of their personalities. Comenius had believed that the child should be subject to the authority of the Bible while Locke had believed that he should be subject to the demands of society. Rousseau would set the child completely free to develop according to his own natural inclinations and thereby avoid his enslavement by society and his contamination by man. Children were to develop according to the laws of nature rather than those of man. This was the major thesis of *educational naturalism* which Rousseau had fathered. Rousseau's theories concerning individual and personal rights greatly influenced the democratic structure of early American government and education.

The naturalists believed that children were not sufficiently mature to achieve the moral and intellectual goals established for them by educators but that youth was the time to build a strong and skillful physical organism. They believed that it is not as important for education to develop knowledge, social accomplishments, or elegant manners as it is to develop a contented and cheerful disposition, a virtuous character, and a healthy body. Physical education constituted the major portion of their program until the child was twelve years old and it continued to play an important role until the child was fifteen years old. After the age of fifteen the child was given a rigorously intellectual program.

It is obvious that with such a point of view, physical education played a very important role in naturalistic education. At Basedow's Philanthropinum, the first school organized according to a naturalistic philosophy, three hours daily were devoted to physical education and another two hours to manual labor. Basedow's school had high jumping pits, balance beams, seesaws, hoops, tennis courts, and badminton courts. Later skating, gardening, woodworking, and marching were introduced along with posture exercises. These posture exercises were the forerunners of today's floor exercises done in gymnastics. Basedow ran one of the first summer camps. Naturalists did not believe that children should compete against one another but rather that they should compete against their own former performance. The school and its program was child centered in that it was made to fit the child. Physical education was to prepare children for democratic citizenship by accustoming them to equality, fraternity, rivalry, and to the seeking of public commendation.

NATIONALISM

A number of developments and inventions coalesced during the nineteenth century which fostered the development of nationalistic spirit. The Crusades and the Christian-Moslem wars contributed to the development of a spirit of national unity. The growth of factories resulting from the Industrial Revolution created demands for raw materials which often had to be secured from other countries. The new factories also created a desire for new markets for manufactured goods in other countries. The economic welfare of the people became identified with that of the nation. The newly invented printing press made possible the mass dissemination of ideas and information of concern to the entire nation and broke down provincialism. The American and French revolutions provided examples and inspiration to liberals throughout the world and served to point out the relationships between individual and national welfare.

This nationalistic spirit infused a number of educators who saw in physical education a means for nurturing this spirit in others. Education under nationalism promotes civic ideals, social and political homogeneity, and patriotism. Physical education is used to develop physical fitness in order that citizens will be enabled to become maximally productive and better able to defend their country.

Germany did not exist as a true nation in the early 1800's. However, the defeat of the professional Prussian soldiers by Napoleon's citizen armies, and the ensuing threat of the dissolution of all of Germany, caused the German kings and nobility to become more willing to utilize the spirit of nationalism and democratic aspirations of the common people. Although the kings and nobles were fearful of the democratic aspirations of the people, they did want to harness their nationalistic feelings to help conquer the French. After some hesitation, they did mobilize the common people. With the aid of the common people, the Prussians defeated the French in 1813. Although the German people had won the battle for national freedom, they did not win the battle for individual freedom because after the war severe methods were used to silence all liberals and the constitutional liberties for which they had argued were denied the people.

Frederick Ludwig Jahn (1778–1852), who was the physical education leader of this era, lived during this period of developing nationalism and aspiration for individual liberty. Jahn's great national pride and love of liberty were the principal detriments of the kind of physical education program which he developed. He believed that physical education should develop love for the country as well as the physical powers essential to national defense and combat. However, his militaristic aspirations did not prevent him from using physical activities as a means for developing individualism and freedom. He abhorred systems of exercise and rigid formality. He believed that the physical educator should lead through example and should obtain coopera- tion rather than obedience. Consistent with his belief in individualism, he was always conscious of the individual differences in pupils and urged classifica- tion according to age, size, and ability.

Jahn was not a physical educator until he was about thirty-two years old. He was a teacher who accompanied the students on hikes into the country on Wednesday and Saturday afternoons when they were given the afternoon off. On these hikes he encouraged such big muscle activities as running, jumping, wrestling, climbing, swimming, and stunts. He led them in patriotic songs, told of German history, and urged them to work for liberty and for their country. He improvised horizontal bars (a horizontal oak limb), javelins (straight sticks), and jumping standards. In 1811, he opened his first Turnplatz outside Berlin. Patterned after the Greek palaestra, it consisted of a fenced-in rectangular area enclosing home-made inclined and horizontal ladders, jumping standards, horizontal bars, climbing poles, balance beams, climbing ropes, pole vaulting equipment, broad jumping pits, a running track, a wrestling ring, and a hut for dressing. The following year a greater diversity of and better equipment was added. The next year (1813) the War of Liberation with the French broke out and Jahn and most of his Turner members joined in the battle. The great surge in patriotism which followed the victorious efforts caused a rapid growth in the Turner clubs and Jahn became a public hero. However, Jahn's effectiveness was relatively short lived since in 1818 the Turner organization was outlawed by most of the German states because the authorities feared the liberal teachings of the organization. Jahn was arrested the following year for allegedly inciting revolutionary practices.

A few Turners met secretly while the organization was outlawed but the organization did not enjoy a true revival until 1860 when its members decided to avoid all political activity. After this, the organization grew to number many thousands of clubs all over the world and many more thousands of members.

Adolph Spiess (1810–1855) was responsible for bringing gymnastics and physical education into the schools of Germany. Spiess was concerned with gymnastics as an important part of the educational curriculum while Jahn viewed it primarily in nationalistic terms and as an out-of-school activity for both adults and students. Jahn emphasized freedom and liberty while Spiess believed that physical fitness could be most effectively improved through quick and accurate response to commands. He believed in order and precision. He preferred activities and methods which would enable one instructor to lead large groups exercising simultaneously and in unison. Consequently, he stressed calisthenics and marching. Since he was gifted musically, Spiess arranged many of the exercises and marching drills so that they could be done to music. In most of his drills, the students stood in circles or rows and performed the exercises to count. The indoor gymnasium which Spiess opened could be divided into two rooms by a movable partition. The Spiess system was adopted by most of the German schools although later it was modified to include some aspects of Swedish gymnastics.

Under the Nazi regime, physical education became the most important aspect of the entire educational curriculum, and adult sports and recreational and physical fitness activities enjoyed a promotion and prominence they had never before enjoyed. However, the activities and organizations were completely subverted in order to achieve the goals of the National Socialists. The development of physical fitness was assigned priority over all other educational objectives. The Spartan program, rigid discipline, and strenuous activity were conducted in such a manner as to develop fanatical loyalty and unquestioning obedience. The goal was not development of personality but development of the nation. Physical fitness was to be developed as an obligation to the Nazi party.

The Nazi party immediately seized control of all sport and youth organizations and of school physical education programs. A complete reorganization was made in order to bring all organizations under centralized control.

Children who could not withstand physical hardship could be expelled from school. After the school day, children were active in youth clubs where they received instruction in Nazi ideology, practiced military drills, and performed work for the party. After leaving school, children were required to spend about one year in farm work (usually in another part of the country to break down provincialism) where they received physical training and indoctrination in addition to having to do the heavy farm work. A period of six months of Labor Service was also required. After this they were required to perform two years of military service.

Almost all teachers wore the Storm Trooper's uniform. Control of the teachers' organizations was seized by the party. Hikes were disciplined marches. Woodcraft was used to teach army maneuvers. Children were taken on marches of eight to nineteen miles at least once each month. These marches were utilized to teach the children a variety of military skills such as tracking, spying, and throwing of hand grenades.

Sweden, in the seventeenth century, was one of the most powerful countries in Northern Europe but by the beginning of the nineteenth century had lost a large amount of its territory to Russia. As a result of the loss of status of their once great empire, the Swedish people developed an intensely patriotic spirit.

Per Henrik Ling (1776–1839), who became the founder of Swedish gymnastics, attended school in Sweden and Denmark. As a student he took fencing lessons and during the course of the lessons noted improvement in an afflicted arm. As a result, he became interested in the effects of exercise upon the body – particularly in the amelioration of physical anamolies. He also became imbued with patriotism as a result of the teachings of the philosophers and poets. Ling returned to Sweden from Denmark to take a position as fencing master and lecturer in Norse mythology, poetry, and history in the year that Sweden was forced to surrender Finland to Russia. His patriotic zeal led him to write a number of patriotic poems, epics, and plays, and he became recognized as a literary leader. He used literature to incite patriotic feelings and to motivate toward action but he saw in physical education a means for strengthening the people so that they could recapture their former glory.

He believed that physical education should develop endurance, agility, and power but that it also should always be conducted according to the known facts of the human organism. He believed that the military, medical, pedagogical, and esthetic goals of physical education are a unity and that all should be pursued simultaneously. Ling began with the Guts Muths-Nachtegall program which he had learned in Denmark but gradually he rejected the exercises which did not conform to his scientific theories and finally evolved a program which consisted of fencing, vaulting, free exercises, and light apparatus work. He made use of stall bars, booms, saddles, window ladders, vaulting boxes, climbing poles, and horizontal, vertical, and oblique ropes. After he became director of the Royal Central Institute of Gymnastics in Stockholm, he began to experiment with medical gymnastics for physical disabilities.

Ling's system has continued to serve as the basis for Swedish physical education programs but in recent years modifications are being made due to a greater diversity of sports interests among people, and also as a result of recent research. These changes include greater attention to sports, activities for women and older people, and dynamic rather than static activities.

Denmark, like Germany and Sweden, was influenced by the Industrial Revolution, the French Revolution, and the Napoleonic Wars. The leader in physical education in Denmark during these turbulent times was Franz Nachtegall (1777–1847), who held the title "Director of Gymnastics." Although he believed in a broadly based program, the Napoleonic Wars forced him to conduct physical education in such a manner as to achieve military

Stamina, courage, skill, and knowledge
(Courtesy: New England Council, Inc.)

goals. He advocated activities on hanging ladders, climbing poles, rope ladders, and wooden horses, jumping, running, vaulting, balancing, swimming, and military drills were also included. His writings are the first to mention the use of mats as a safety procedure. Exercises were done to command in a precise and military manner, and individual expression was prohibited.

The Danish-German gymnastics of Nachtegall were superseded, for the most part, by Ling's Swedish gymnastics after Nachtegall's death. Today, gymnastic exercises (which emphasize a continuity of movement and intensive stretching while marching or while standing in position and use of wall bars and the vaulting box), comprise a major portion of the Danish school physical education program. However, during the spring, games, dances, and sports receive the major attention. Sports played by the Danish people today include soccer, tennis, squash, badminton, cricket, boxing, wrestling, handball, track and field events, archery, rowing, and swimming. Hiking, cycling, and folk dancing are also very popular.

France was essentially a feudal state before the French Revolution. There were great contrasts between the few self-indulgent aristocrats and the many oppressed and poor common people. After the overthrow of the aristocracy, there was an increase in the nationalistic feelings of the French people which were further increased by the successes of the Napoleonic Wars. French leaders planned to sustain these nationalistic sentiments by establishing a strongly centralized form of government. A centralized system of education (which has endured to this day) was also established. French nationalism is, even today, nurtured in such courses as history, geography, civics, music, literature, and physical education.

A Spaniard, Colonel Francisco Amoras (1770–1848), established the foundation for the French military and school physical education program. A Swiss, Pkokion Clias (1782–1854), established a program in the elementary schools patterned after that of Guts Muths and Jahn. Both men directed their programs primarily toward the achievement of military objectives.

Amoras' program utilized progression with stretching exercises accompanied by singing or a metronome and then followed by more vigorous activities such as apparatus stunts, balancing, marching, leaping, climbing, vaulting, and jumping. Amoras was one of the first to use rings, the trapeze, inclined boards and ladders, rope ladders, the giant stride, and a machine to measure strength.

It was a Frenchman who made one of the greatest contributions to athletics when he revived the Olympic Games. Baron Pierre de Coubertin (1863–1937) became concerned about the Frenchmens' lack of participation in gymnastics and sports as compared to that of members of other countries. As a means of encouraging greater participation, he organized the Union of Athletic Sports Societies to give some 200 French athletic clubs unity. Then

Czechoslovak Sportskrade

he organized matches between France and England. In 1892 he initiated efforts to revive the Olympic Games. These came to fruition in 1896 when the first modern Olympic Games were held in Athens, Greece.

Today physical education is required for French children in all schools. Body-building activities including games and dances are emphasized for children seven and eight years old, while corrective exercises for those nine to twelve years old are stressed. Athletic skills are introduced when children are eleven or twelve years old. Track and field and swimming are regarded as basic to all other sports. Interscholastic sports are not sanctioned by the schools. The office of the Minister of National Education supervises both private and public education including selection of textbooks, courses of study, examinations, and teacher education and certification.

The masses of French workers have not had leisure until recent times. Perhaps this is one reason why so few Frenchmen today participate in recreational activities such as sports, games, and exercises and why so many prefer to spend their leisure in the home, cafe, or the theater.

The development of physical education programs in England, Russia, and the countries of Continental Europe followed a similar nationalistic direction during the years following the French Revolution, Napoleonic Wars, Industrial Revolution, and the invention of the printing press. Unfortunately, we cannot present these developments here. The interested reader will find that the sources cited in the bibliography at the end of Chapter X are excellent.

SUMMARY

Educational philosophies, theories, and practices have influenced the quality, quantity, and content of school physical education programs throughout the centuries as they have other subject areas. Undoubtedly, they will continue to do so. Physical educators need to be aware of these constantly changing emphases and points of view and of their implications for physical education in order that they be enabled to evaluate them and reject the harmful ones and accept the good ones.

We have seen that many early churchmen reacted to the brutalized Roman gladiatorial contests, the morally questionable goings-on at the thermae, and the self-indulgence of the later Greeks and Romans by condemning sports and athletic contests. Some went so far as to preach and to practice the opposite of self-indulgence by exposing themselves to the elements and denying themselves food. Boxing today is undergoing similar criticism because many feel it is a brutalizing activity to both participants and spectators. Physical educators and athletic coaches must consider possible public reactions to activities which they promulgate.

We have again seen that physical education continued to be utilized to serve military objectives. However, physical educators must realize that this is inadequate justification for physical education because as soon as the military emergency is over, physical education will be de-emphasized.

We have seen how thought, intellectualizing, and writings have stimulated further thought, intellectualizing, and writing thereby accelerating man's progress. Progress has often been initiated by discontent or injustices which led to criticism and analysis which led to justification, rationalization, further analysis and ultimately to corrective measures.

It has been illustrated that some philosophic positions are more favorable to the growth of physical education than are others. Contrast, for example, attitudes of the social humanists toward physical education with those of naturalists.

It has been seen that institutions which have originated and developed as a result of reaction to the dogmatism and inflexibility of other institutions (Protestant and Catholic churches, for example) and which are quite liberal at the beginning tend to become increasingly dogmatic and inflexible themselves. This tendency must be checked in all forms of organizations — including the physical education organizations. Often, attitudes and procedures which had been appropriate to the circumstances are no longer appropriate because of changed circumstances, yet the outmoded attitudes and procedures persist. This was the case of the Puritans in Colonial America. This phenomenon too should be guarded against.

Now let's see what has happened in physical education in the United States.

QUESTIONS

1. What were the conditions prevailing after the fall of Rome and what were the characteristics of Christianity which enabled it to serve as a unifying force and to provide a measure of learning?

2. Why did some of the early churchmen object to sports and athletic contests?

3. Discuss chivalry — its purposes, ideals, educational program and sports and military training activities.

4. Compare and contrast the social, merchant, and craft guilds of medieval times with civic and fraternal clubs (Kiwanis, Civitans, Rotary, Elks, Moose, etc.), Chamber of Commerce and trade unions of today.

5. Discuss some of the sports and recreational activities popular from the eleventh through the fourteenth century.

6. Discuss the reasons for the intellectual awakening which took place in the Christian world from the eleventh through the fifteenth centuries.

7. On what bases did the individual humanists justify the inclusion of physical education in the school program?

8. What were the reasons for the earlier acceptance of sports and other recreational activities in the southern states of the United States than in the northern states?

9. What were the differences in the philosophic beliefs of the individual humanists and the social humanists which enabled the individual humanists to promote physical education with greater enthusiasm?

10. What were the reasons for the establishment and growth of moralism?

11. Why do institutions (including religious institutions) tend to become more dogmatic and inflexible about their preachments, teachings, and methods after they become established?

12. Why did the Puritans in Colonial America condemn nonproductive use of time?

13. What was the idea promulgated by the Jesuits that assigned to physical education an important role?

14. Who were some of the leaders and what were the similarities and differences in beliefs among the verbal, social, and sense realists?

15. How did the accelerated pace of scientific discovery contribute to the development of sense realism?

16. Who was John Locke and what were some of his beliefs regarding education in general and physical education in particular?

17. Who was Jean-Jacques Rousseau and what were some of his beliefs concerning education and physical education?

18. Discuss Basedow's Philanthropinum.

19. Discuss the similarities and differences in the physical education programs of Jahn, Spiess, and Ling.

20. What were the developments and inventions which occurred in the nineteenth century which influenced the patterns of living and, consequently, of physical education? How did they influence physical education?

21. How did the Nazis utilize physical education to achieve nationalistic purposes?

See bibliography listings on page 199.

10

Physical Education in the United States

THE SETTLERS COMING to Colonial America in the seventeenth century were principally farmers, craftsmen, and seafaring men. They faced a most difficult task in conquering the wilderness and consequently became a rugged, hardy, self-disciplined people able to survive many hardships. Their survival depended principally upon capacity for physical activity and stamina. The rigors of their life demanded that pleasures arise from productive efforts. They got their recreation through the sociability provided in barn raisings, husking bees, log rolling, planting and harvesting exploits, hunting and fishing, and through the feeling of accomplishment of successfully fighting a hostile environment.

EARLY SETTLERS

The English settlers brought with them the values and customs of England. These included the social and political customs such as willingness to assume civic responsibilities through service in local governmental positions, use of the common law and jury system, a conviction of the precedence of individual rights over those of the king or the government, and a preference for the sports and games of England to the gymnastics of Central Europe.

In the beginning, what little educating was done, was done by the parents. Often one of the mothers volunteered to teach a group of children. In these *Dame* or *Kitchen Schools*, as they came to be called, children were taught reading and religion and occasionally some writing and arithmetic. Toward the end of the seventeenth century an increasing number of schools were initiated which patterned themselves after those of England. These were called *Latin grammar schools* because the emphasis was upon the teaching of

188

Latin grammar. One of the earliest and best known of these schools was the Boston Latin School founded in 1635. Two colleges were founded quite early – Harvard in 1636 and William and Mary in 1693. Princeton, Kings College (now Columbia University), Brown, Rutgers, and Dartmouth were founded about 1750. Physical education played little or no role in the curricula of any of these schools. Benjamin Franklin established the Philadelphia Public Academy in 1749, which became the University of Pennsylvania in 1791.[1] Franklin and Noah Webster were among the first writers on the subject of education in the United States who advocated the inclusion of physical activities in the educational program.

Fundamental changes were occurring in American education during the nineteenth century. One of the most important was the principle of free public education which had been advocated by Horace Mann of Massachusetts and Henry Barnard of Connecticut. Another factor bringing about these changes was the amazing increase in the number of school children – from a half million in 1865 to almost fifteen million by 1900 – a huge increase in the short span of forty-five years. A third factor was the signing of the Morrill Land Grant Act in 1862 by President Abraham Lincoln. This act provided public land to each state for the establishment of a state university. It required that all state institutions receiving this land endowment institute a program of military science and drill for all male students. Unfortunately, most of the institutions which received these land grants discontinued gymnastics and physical education when military science and drill were added to the required curriculum. Some university administrators believed that the outcomes of both programs were similar. This belief has persisted, in some quarters, to this day. It is the responsibility of physical educators to indicate that the two courses are entirely different.

INTRODUCTION OF FOREIGN PHYSICAL EDUCATION PROGRAMS

In 1825, the Round Hill School in Northampton, Massachusetts, appointed Dr. Charles Beck, a former student of Jahn in German gymnastics, to direct its physical education program. Dr. Charles Follen, another advocate of Jahn gymnastics, was appointed at the same time to establish a gymnastic program at Harvard University. German gymnastics flourished for a few years in the New England area and in New York, particularly in the areas with large numbers of German immigrants. By 1860, there were over 150 German Turnvereins in this country. At the Chicago World's Fair of 1893, 4000 Turners participated. However, German gymnastics did not persist in the schools principally because the highly formal teaching methods making use of command-response techniques were not adapted to the culture, values, and way of life of the people in the United States. People in the United States value individual freedom and self-expression. They live and work in a competitive economy where one's success depends primarily upon his own individual efforts. These values and practices are not favorable to the Jahn German gymnastics which were designed to achieve German nationalistic objectives. In defense of the gymnastics of today, it must be pointed out that the highly formal teaching methods of former years have been discarded long ago. Gymnastics today encourages individual freedom and self-expression. Modern gymnastics initiated by Hartley Price of Florida State University, Gene Wettstone of Pennsylvania State University, Leslie Judd of Springfield College, Lyle Welser of Georgia Tech University, Paul Romeo of Syracuse University, Ralph Piper of the University of Minnesota, and others have made gymnastics one of the best sports for permitting individual freedom and giving opportunities for self-expression.

EARLY EFFORTS OF AMERICAN PHYSICAL EDUCATORS

Catherine E. Beecher, who was Director of the Hartford Seminary for Girls, introduced a method of physical education which utilized posture exercises, wand drills, archery, swimming, and horseback riding. She believed that the gymnastic programs were too vigorous and demanded strength which girls do not possess. The program which she advocated was not widely accepted because girls and women were expected to play a weak and helpless role. Yet women were called upon to do heavy housework. Dio Lewis (1823–1886) attempted to combine the calisthenics program of Catherine Beecher with the Swedish gymnastics of Per Henrik Ling to produce a program tailored to the needs and interests of young people. In addition, his program of "new gymnastics" included bean bag throwing, ball games, social games, and dance routines, many of which were done to musical accompaniment. This magnetic personality and brilliant speaker also founded the Boston Normal Institute for Physical Education and published the first American physical education periodical called *Gymnastic Monthly and Journal of Physical Culture*. Like the programs of Beck, Follen, Beecher, and Lewis, his program was never fully accepted. This was due in part to the interference of the Civil War.

Dr. Edward Hitchcock became the first college director of physical education and hygiene with full faculty status when he assumed his duties at Amherst College in 1861. His program became the foundation of twentieth century physical education. It included marching, calisthenics, sports and games, vaulting, rope climbing, weight lifting, Indian club swinging, and stunts on horizontal bars, rings, and ladders. He became a pioneer in anthropometrics when he established a battery of anthropometric tests for Amherst students. For twenty years, until the appearance of Sargent's system, Hitchcock's program was the outstanding program in the United States.

Dr. Dudley A. Sargent developed, in the late eighteen hundreds at Harvard University, a program incorporating features of German and Swedish gymnastics, calisthenics, and strength building exercises and utilizing some forty different kinds of machines which he invented. Many of the strength testing devices used today bear Sargent's name. In 1881 he established the Sanatory Gymnasium in Cambridge, Massachusetts which became the Sargent School of Physical Education and is now the Sargent College of Boston University. During the years 1883 to about 1910 Swedish gymnastics were vigorously promoted in the Boston area by Amy Morris Homans, Baron Nils Posse, and Dr. Edward M. Hartwell, all physical educators, and Mary Hemenway, a wealthy widow who was interested in physical education. Nils Posse was a graduate of the Royal Central Institute of Gymnastics in Stockholm. He organized the Posse Normal School in Boston in 1890 and in addition assisted, along with Amy Homans, in the teacher preparation program at the newly organized Boston Normal School of Gymnastics. In 1909 this school affiliated with Wellesley College when it became the Department of Hygiene and Physical Education.

William G. Anderson, a young physician who was greatly interested in physical education and a highly skilled gymnast, was responsible for the founding of the American Association for Health, Physical Education, and Recreation. When he came to Adelphi Academy in 1885 as instructor in physical education, he felt that there was a need to bring the leaders of the diverse physical education programs together to share ideas and to establish common bases. The meeting was called for November 27, 1885 and there were sixty people in attendance. Dr. Edward Hitchcock was elected president of this new organization which the original members decided to call the Association for the Advancement of Physical Education.

One of the most important physical education conferences ever held in the United States was the Boston Conference held November 28–29, 1889, at the Massachusetts Institute of Technology. It was promoted and financed by the philanthropist Mary Hemenway who was aided by Amy Morris Homans and Dr. William T. Harris, the United States Commissioner of Education. The tone of the meeting was established at its outset when it was determined to evaluate the entire area of physical education rather than the merits of specific systems. The most important conclusion reached by the conferees was that physical education should concern itself with the total physiologic development of men – their cardiovascular and metabolic functioning – as well as their muscular development.

PERIOD OF RAPID GROWTH

Interest in physical education was beginning to mount as indicated by the passage of laws requiring schools to provide physical education programs. California passed such a law in 1866, Ohio in 1892, Wisconsin in 1897, North Dakota in 1899, and Pennsylvania in 1901. It is interesting that the Eastern states, where most of the pioneering activity had been done, were not among the first to pass such laws. It was also during this period that the interpretation of physical education began to become more uniform as indicated by the more frequent use of the term *physical education*. Previously, it had been called drill, gymnastics, hygiene, physical culture, and physical training.

The seed was planted to affiliate physical education with the National Education Association in 1893 when the NEA was asked by the directors of the Chicago World's Fair to sponsor an International Congress on Education. The NEA then organized a temporary department of physical education and hygiene as a division of the Congress. Two years later it organized a Department of Physical Education which in 1924 became the Department of School Health and Physical Education. It was not until 1937, however, that the American Association for Health, Physical Education and Recreation became a part of the National Education Association.

As a result of the spread of the Industrial Revolution, which increased the leisure at people's disposal, and the increase in tensions and frustrations associated with urban living and industrial labor, an increasing number of people turned to sports and games as a means of catharsis. Evidence of the turning of people to sports and games is provided in the formation of associations, leagues, and athletic clubs, the invention of new sports, and the initiation of new national tournaments. The National Association of Baseball Players held its first conference in 1867. The first intercollegiate football game was held between Rutgers and Princeton in 1869. The National Bowling League was organized in 1875. The New York Athletic Club was initiated in 1868. New York and San Francisco built the first YMCA gymnasiums in 1869. Eighteen years later there were 348 YMCA's with gymnasia in the United States. The first country clubs were opened in Boston and New York in 1886. Dr. James A. Naismith invented basketball at what is now Springfield College in 1891. The American Lawn Tennis Association was formed in 1882. *The New York Journal* introduced the first sports page in 1895. This was indeed a period of remarkable growth in sports participation in only a twenty-eight year period!

Participation in intercollegiate sports in the colleges and universities (without faculty supervision and directed entirely by students) was increasing at a very fast pace. However, sports were presenting many problems to school administrators, faculty, and students since there was little or no training, conditioning, protective equipment, schedule control, or playing and eligibility rules. School administrators ultimately found it advisable to provide a measure of control and direction. During this period men like Walter Camp, Fielding H. Yost, George Huff, and Amos Alonzo Stagg provided the guidance and direction which brought to school athletics a measure of academic respectability and acceptance. Other efforts were made to control intercollegiate and amateur athletics. The Intercollegiate Association of Amateur Athletes (now the NCAA) was initiated in 1885. In 1876 the Intercollegiate Football Association and in 1883 the Intercollegiate Athletic Conference were organized. The National Association of Amateur Athletes, which became the Amateur Athletic Union eleven years later, was formed in 1879.

The growth of industry in the larger cities brought increasing numbers of people to live there. Leaders became concerned about the deleterious effects of living in the crowded and unsanitary tenement buildings of the slums and made efforts to assist children living there. Dr. Maria Zakerzewska, who had seen the sand piles placed in Berlin parks for children, suggested a similar plan for Boston. A philanthropic group accepted her plan and playgrounds were born. The plan was quickly adopted by other large industrial cities. New York legislated an organized play area for children in 1888 and in Chicago the Hull House constructed a playground and organized a program which developed into the Chicago playground system.

A salesman, George Williams, organized the first YMCA in England in 1841 to minister to the moral and spiritual needs of English youth. In 1851 a YMCA was started in Boston and from there spread like wildfire across the United States. In 1856 YMCA leaders at their national convention decided to include gymnasia in their facilities. The YWCA, like the YMCA, was initiated in England to provide for the religious needs of girls. The first YWCA in the United States was started by Mrs. Henry Durant of Boston.

NEW FORCES AND NEW EMPHASES

A number of forces combined during the period from 1900 to 1918 to powerfully influence the development of physical education. Henry Ford's ubiquitous "Model T," the introduction of trolley cars, Edison's incandescent lamp, Bell's telephone, the motion picture industry, and the growth of railroads greatly changed the living habits of people. People became more mobile and developed a taste for leisure heretofore thought available only to the wealthy. Businesses combined and became greatly enlarged since, with improved communication and transportation, their markets became national in scope. More people moved to the cities. People became concerned about the unhealthful, unsanitary, and dangerous conditions in factories, brutal use of child labor, a federal government responsive only to the privileged few, finance and industry, corruption and bossism in the city government, and in other social and political reform.

This concern resulted in a movement which became known as the *Progressive Movement.* It was led on the political front by Theodore Roosevelt and Woodrow Wilson, in psychology by William James, G. Stanley Hall, and Edward L. Thorndike, and on the educational front by John Dewey and William H. Kilpatrick. The politicians urged greater use of democratic procedures. The psychologists asked the schools to produce individuals bold enough to shape society and to construct curricula on the basis of the child's growth, nature, and development. They pointed out that no subject had innate disciplinary value which could transfer to other areas. They also urged a broader and more useful curriculum. The educators urged that the school be child-centered, participate in community activities, and bring the community into the school. The school, they believed, should participate in social change. Dewey's "progressive education" resulted in great changes in method, content, and emphases in all subject matter areas throughout that period and to this day. There can be no doubt that the dynamism of the Progressive Movement hastened many of the changes but they would have had to occur sooner or later because the number of children in high schools had grown from 350,000 in 1895 to 1,300,000 by 1915.

In the early part of the twentieth century, Dr. Thomas D. Wood, Clark W. Hetherington, and Dr. Luther H. Gulick urged discontinuance of the older types of physical education programs which focused upon physiologic outcomes. These men urged that physical education be utilized to achieve the objectives of a general education. Their programs came to be known by various names such as: "new physical education," "natural program," and "natural gymnastics." The programs included sports, games, outdoor activities, and selected gymnastic progressions. Wood, Hetherington, and Gulick insisted that the program be rooted in American society, educate children for democratic citizenship, and be based upon the age, needs, and interests of the children being served. They fully realized that the task of physical educators was made infinitely more complex if it was to be responsible for transforming the mental, emotional, and social qualities of the individual, as well as his physical fitness status.

The changed emphasis and enlarged concepts of the role of physical education resulted in the construction of a different type of facility. Gymnasia were built with large open spaces for the playing of games — principally basketball — and the facilities for spectators were greatly increased. An increasing number of men hired as college directors of physical education, held a degree of doctor of philosophy or doctor of education, and a smaller number the degree of doctor of medicine. Teacher training institutions in physical education required fewer courses in physiology and anatomy and a greater number in psychology and sociology. Many private, noncollegiate, teacher-training schools in physical education affiliated with colleges and universities. These mergers improved the academic respectability of physical education. The Anderson School of Physical Education, which in 1901 became the New Haven Normal School of Gymnastics and later Arnold College, affiliated with the University of Bridgeport where today it is known as the Arnold College Division of the University of Bridgeport. The Boston Normal School of Gymnastics became the Department of Hygiene and Physical Education at Wellesley College in 1909. The Bouvé School of Physical Education affiliated with Simmons College, the Savage School of Physical Education with New York University, the Sargent School of Physical Education with Boston University, and the North American Gymnastic Union with the University of Indiana.

Whereas early research activity had been in the area of anthropometrics and strength, during this period it was principally in the areas of cardiovascular fitness and physical-achievement tests. This redirected research emphasis came about because of the new program content. Sports and games do not contribute as much to strength as they do to cardiovascular fitness and to skill in sports and games.

School health education became established largely as a result of the efforts of Dr. Thomas D. Wood. School health examinations became more thorough and an increasing number of physicians and nurses came to be employed in the schools in spite of vigorous opposition from some quarters.

Sports continued to grow in number. Playground ball, which was invented in 1907 and renamed softball in 1930, was growing in popularity. Outing clubs were started in 1910 with the development of such a club at Dartmouth College. Golf was not yet a game for everyone but it continued to grow. Municipalities began to build swimming pools and a few schools added swimming pools to their facilities. Dr. Luther H. Gulick, Dr. Dudley A. Sargent, and Dr. Henry Curtis led in the founding of the Playground Association of America in 1906. School buildings began to be used as recreation centers after school hours when in 1911 the National Education Association passed a resolution which urged that this be done. The many-faceted Dr. Gulick also contributed greatly to the growth of the camping movement. The growth of the camping movement became manifest when the Camp Directors' Association was organized in 1910. An indication of the achievement of academic respectability by the relatively new profession of physical education was the granting of permission by the Massachusetts Legislature to Springfield College to award bachelor's and master's degrees in physical education in 1905.

With the entry by the United States into the First World War, there was danger that the emphasis in physical education might become narrowed to exclusively physiologic outcomes. Fortunately, this did not occur. At the beginning of the period of conflict, two programs were developed. One was a fitness program including combatives, marching, drill, and calisthenics and the other was a sports and games program. The two programs coalesced as time passed and became the program of the allied forces. Comments in speeches by Newton D. Baker, then Secretary of War, and the writings of James H. McCurdy of Springfield College helped to stem the movement for substitution of military training in the schools for physical education.

There were many forces operating between the first and second world wars which influenced health, physical education, and recreation. There were the ideas and writings of Marx, Freud, and Einstein, the prosperity of 1920–1929, and the Great Depression of 1929–1937. President Franklin D. Roosevelt inaugurated a great variety of programs such as the Social Security Act of 1935, the Civilian Conservation Corps, the Works Progress Administration, the National Youth Administration, and the Wagner Act of 1935 to stem the depression. Many sports and recreational facilities were built by these groups. Another influence upon physical education was that the international balance was being upset by acts of aggression by Tojo's Japan, Hitler's Germany, and Mussolini's Italy. This led to World War II and a renewed emphasis upon physical fitness.

Health, physical education, and recreation continued to grow. Between 1919 and 1930, thirty-nine states enacted physical education legislation. This legislation made it mandatory that schools require all students to take physical education for a specified number of hours each week. It also specified the type of program. An increasing number of state departments of education employed a state director of physical education. The professional preparation of teachers of physical education became strengthened as a result of a report by the California State Department of Education in which it was pointed out that twenty-eight college catalogs listed a total of 671 different course titles for teacher preparation in physical education. The Department of School Health and Physical Education of the National Education Association made an effort to solve this problem when it authorized Dr. Jay B. Nash, the president of the department, to organize a National Committee to develop standards by which teacher training programs in physical education could be evaluated. Dr. Nash appointed Dr. Niels P. Neilson to serve as chairman of the national committee. Representatives of a large number of interested organizations and groups were appointed to membership. This committee made important and far-reaching recommendations. Remarkable progress has been made since World War II by the profession.

The Athletic Institute, founded by manufacturers of sporting goods in 1934, sponsored the National Conference on Undergraduate Professional Preparation in Health Education, Physical Education and Recreation Education which was held at Jackson's Mill in West Virginia in 1948. At this conference recommendations were made concerning principles, standards, and programs in teacher education in physical education. A similar conference concerning graduate study was also sponsored by the Athletic Institute at Pere Marquette State Park in Illinois in 1950. These conferences illustrate that business interests can make contributions to physical education as they do in other areas.

In 1960 at its national convention in Miami, Florida, the American Association for Health, Physical Education, and Recreation decided to accept the National Council for Accreditation of Teacher Education (NCATE) as the official accrediting agency for teacher education in health, physical, and recreation education. The quality and quantity of research is growing as a result of publication of research studies in the *Research Quarterly of the American Association for Health, Physical Education, and Recreation,* construction of research laboratories in physical education at colleges and universities, and cooperation with other disciplines.

Competitive sports programs are growing in the elementary and junior high schools. Sports programs for children are also being sponsored by organizations outside the schools such as Little League, Church Leagues, Pop Warner Leagues, Dads' Clubs, and others. Opportunities for competition for girls and women in high schools and colleges are increasing. However, programs for women have avoided many of the problems which have beset intercollegiate and interscholastic sports for men. This has been true principally because of the efforts of the Division of Girls' and Women's Sports (DGWS) of the American Association for Health, Physical Education, and Recreation. Intramural sports, in the colleges and universities since 1919 and in the high schools since 1925, have grown rapidly and have received the recognition of school administrators. The National Recreation Association, which changed its name in 1930 from The Playground and Recreation Association, has vigorously promoted the growth of the recreation movement. The American Camping Association has also promoted the growth of camping.

In recent years, there has been a return to greater emphasis upon the physiologic outcomes of physical education. In 1953 Dr. Hans Kraus and Ruth Hirschland reported the results of their study in which they compared the performance of American children with that of European children in tests of minimal muscular fitness. Among American children 57.9 per cent failed one or more of the six tests while only 8.7 per cent of European children did so. Other studies comparing children of other nations with American children produced similar results. This test measured only the flexibility of several selected joints and the minimal strength of a few selected muscle groups on a mere pass or fail basis. It did not measure endurance, power, agility, speed, or balance which are the other recognized aspects of physical fitness. However, since the Kraus-Weber research received wide publicity which attracted the attention of President Eisenhower, it did serve a most important purpose. President Eisenhower consequently called a National Conference on Physical Fitness of American Youth which was held at the U.S. Naval Academy in 1956. President Eisenhower then appointed a National Council on Youth Fitness with Dr. Shane MacCarthy as executive director. Other conferences on youth fitness were called by the AAHPER, the NCAA, and a number of state governors. The AAHPER, on January 21, 1959, announced its sponsorship of a nationwide fitness program called Operation Fitness – U.S.A. The American Medical Association endorsed physical education at its House of Delegates Meeting in June, 1960 in Miami, Florida. The late President Kennedy, on numerous occasions and with great vigor, endorsed physical fitness and physical education. He endorsed physical education through the calling of national conferences, by appointing Charles "Bud" Wilkinson, Athletic Director and Coach of Football at Oklahoma University, as his personal consultant on youth fitness. President Lyndon B. Johnson continued this endorsement of physical education.

Physical education today is experiencing a growth and prosperity comparable to that of Early Greece.

SUMMARY

There were deterrents to the growth of physical education in Colonial America. These were the Puritan influence and the necessity for long hours of hard work leaving little time or energy for recreational activities. There were also a number of false starts such as the efforts to introduce German gymnastics, Swedish exercises, and calisthenic programs. When the athletic programs became indigenous to the United States, satisfied the needs and desires of the people, and were in conformity with the values and beliefs of the people, physical education prospered and grew very rapidly.

A number of dedicated and energetic men and women have made lasting contributions to physical education. These have included Charles Beck, Charles Follen, Catherine Beecher, Dio Lewis, Edward Hitchcock, Dudley Sargent, Amy Homans, Baron Nils Posse, Edward Hartwell, Mary Hemenway, William Anderson, James Naismith, Walter Camp, Amos Alanzo Stagg, Fielding Yost, George Huff, Maria Zakerzowska, Thomas Wood, Clark

Hetherington, Luther Gulick, Henry Curtis, James MacCurdy, Jay Nash, and Niels Nielson. Others include Delbert Oberteuffer, Charles McCloy, Tom Cureton, Art Daniels, Chester Jackson and Seward Staley. These men and women can provide a model and an inspiration to young physical educators.

QUESTIONS

1. What were the reasons for the failure of German gymnastics to achieve acceptance in the United States?

2. What were the reasons for the rapid growth of physical education from 1850 to 1900?

3. What were the forces which combined during the period from 1900 to 1918 to powerfully influence the development of physical education?

4. Who were the leaders in the Progressive Movement in the areas of politics, psychology, and education? What changes did they recommend?

5. What changes occurred in physical education in part as a result of the efforts of Wood, Hetherington, and Gulick?

6. Review some of the evidences of the continuing growth of physical education between the first and second World Wars.

7. Review evidences of growth of physical education between World War II and the present time.

BIBLIOGRAPHY (Chapters 7—10)

1. Deschner, Ramy B., *The Evolution of Sports and the Cultural Implications of Physical Education*. St. Louis, Mo.:Fred Medart Manufacturing Co., 1946.

2. Van Dalen, Deobold B., Elmer D. Mitchell, and Bruce L. Bennett, *A World History of Physical Education*. Englewood Cliffs, N.J.: Prentice-Hall, Inc., 1953.

3. Weston, Arthur, *The Making of American Physical Education*. New York: Appleton-Century-Crofts, 1962.

4. Hackensmith, C. W., *History of Physical Education*. New York: Harper and Row, Publishers, 1966.

5. Leonard, Fred Eugene, and George B. Affleck, *A Guide to the History of Physical Education*. Philadelphia: Lea and Febiger, 1949.

Part III

PHILOSOPHY AND PHYSICAL EDUCATION

11

Philosophies Influencing Education

WHAT PHILOSOPHY IS

Webster defines philosophy as the "love of wisdom" and as "the science which investigates the facts and principles of reality and human nature and conduct." While it is true that philosophers spend a lifetime in the study of many disciplines and must possess a high order of intelligence in order to be able to relate the knowledge gained from this study, almost everyone has engaged in the *philosophic process.* Anyone who has gazed into a campfire, contemplated the stars in the night skies, looked out over the ocean or a lake and pondered the nature of the universe, man's place in the universe, or the nature of God has engaged in this process. Anyone who, during a "bull session" has discussed such topics as what is moral and what is immoral, whether we can direct our destiny or whether it is determined for us by fate, the relationships between man and the state or individuals and government, or the role of education, has engaged in the *philosophic process.*

Man is a thinking animal and if he thinks, it is inevitable that he will wonder about these questions and that he will arrive at tentative answers most satisfactory to himself. The answers most satisfactory to him will be those most consistent with his early training, his experiences, his state of knowledge, and the situation in which he finds himself. This will become his own philosophy. It will guide him in his decisions, his reactions, and his behaviors. While it may not be as complete, as all-inclusive, as logical, as consistent, or as accurate as the philosophies of the great philosophers of the ages such as Socrates, Plato, Aristotle, Comenius, Locke, James, or Dewey, it is his own. It can give direction, meaning, and consistency to the pattern of his life. This is called an *eclectic philosophy* because it incorporates something from every philosophic school.

203

One's philosophy should be a growing, dynamic thing which becomes more complete, more inclusive, more logical, more consistent, more accurate, and more unified as his knowledge increases, as he grows in maturity, and as situations change. A study of the reasoning and conclusions of the great philosophers and of the major philosophic schools of thought will enhance this process. This study may lead to identification with one of these schools of thought. In this chapter we will study the three major philosophic schools to an extent consistent with the time available in a course such as this and to an extent consistent with the space available in a textbook of this kind. The student will study philosophy in greater depth in courses such as "History and Principles of Physical Education" and again, very likely, in a philosophy course in graduate school. We can only hope here to stimulate the reader's desire to learn more of philosophy, to help him to begin to understand that philosophic beliefs do influence the conduct of physical education, and to bring him to a realization that physical educators need to know and to understand these influences. This knowledge and these understandings should continue to grow thoughout the physical educator's lifetime. A thorough understanding of philosophy, which would require a study of the earliest philosophic beliefs and continued study of how these beliefs were modified throughout the centuries to evolve to their present form, could not be developed through the reading of only one chapter. For this reason, we will present the earliest philosophic beliefs (which are also likely the simplest and easiest to understand). Then we will indicate what the modern descendants of these earliest philosophic schools believe that philosophic school's beliefs imply for the conduct of physical education. It is hoped the reader will gain respect for the philosophic process.

The Word *philosophy* is derived from Latin and Greek. It means the desire to search for facts and values in life and the universe and to evaluate and to interpret these in an unbiased and unprejudiced manner. Philosophy is like science in that it organizes knowledge about man and the universe in order to better evaluate and comprehend it.

The philosophy of the early Greeks and of the Renaissance period encompassed all of the physical and social sciences but as man's knowledge increased, special disciplines were developed such as astronomy, chemistry, physics, medicine, and dentistry in the physical sciences and economics, psychology, sociology, and law, in the social sciences. These disciplines grew out of philosophy.

Philosophy can be divided into several basic areas of study. *Ethics* is the study of morality or of right and wrong. *Metaphysics* is the study of the ultimate nature of man and the universe. It attempts to determine the exact nature of reality. Modern philosophers, however, do not concern themselves greatly with the nature of reality. *Politics* is the study of government.

Esthetics is the study of the nature of beauty. *Logic* is the study of the methods for investigating truth through such methods of reasoning as induction and deduction. *Epistemology* is the study of the origin, limits, and nature of knowledge.

While science describes, discovers, and analyzes facts, it is philosophy which criticizes, evaluates, and synthesizes these facts. Science teaches how to put men on the moon but philosophy determines the worth of these efforts. Science determines how to increase man's strength and power most effectively, but philosophy evaluates the relative worth of these efforts. Both science and philosophy involve critical thinking and reflection, construct theories and principles, and prove and disprove theories to form new hypotheses; however, philosophy is additionally concerned with values. Philosophy endeavors to integrate and to relate the entire spectrum of human knowledge to determine what kind of life we should lead. Philosophy endeavors to see man and the universe in a coherent, systematic, and meaningful way. In doing so it gives direction to our actions.

Unfortunately, some people hold a negative or destructive philosophy based on selfishness, greed, and pleasure. These simple philosophies are illustrated by the coach who uses such cliches as: "It's not how you play the game but whether you win or lose which is important," "You've gotta win at all costs," or "Dog eat dog!" Other examples of destructive philosophies are illustrated by the expressions: "God helps those who help themselves!" "Might makes right," "Big 'I' first," "Live it up today for tomorrow we may die." Obviously, our society would be a greatly disorganized one if all people held these points of view. If there were no one with honesty, integrity, concern for others, feelings of sympathy and kindness, thrift, or a desire to build for future usefulness, it would indeed be a chaotic world.

Athletic contests would become brutal gladiatorial contests. It would be necessary to have one extremely alert official for each player in the game. It would be necessary to maintain constant surveillance over all players, coaches, officials, school administrators, alumni, and fans to insure that there was no bribing, "throwing" of games, or other violations of rules. Telephones would be tapped, rooms would be "bugged," men would be "shadowed" and no one would be believed. Productivity would be greatly decreased because the major portion of a person's time would necessarily be spent in protecting his possessions and most of the remaining time would be spent in attempting to take away the possessions of others. Money would be useless because a monetary system depends upon mutual trust. Loans could be made only by those who could evoke fear because the loans probably would not be repaid otherwise. Traffic laws would become unenforceable. Carried to their ultimate conclusion, these philosophies would make the world a fearful place in which to live.

Fortunately, these points of view have found little acceptance. The great philosophers whose thoughts have influenced mankind throughout history have taught the necessity of honesty, integrity, cooperativeness, sportsmanship, fair play, consideration for others, kindness, and thrift. This was true of Heraclitus (535–475 B.C.) and of Aristotle (384–322 B.C.) and it was true of the modern philosophers such as Bertrand Russell, George Santayana, William James, and John Dewey. This was also true of such well-known philosophers as Plato (427–347 B.C.), Epicurus (341–270 B.C.), Cicero (106–43 B.C.), Socrates (469–399 B.C.), Comenius (1592–1670), Descartes (1596–1650), Locke (1632–1704), Pestalozzi (1746–1827), and Nietzsche (1844–1900).

While these men had different ideas about the nature of the universe, man's place in the universe, the nature of God, the soul and immortality, man's relationship to the state, the role of education, and the relationship between mind and matter, they had surprisingly similar ideas about what is good and what is evil. While the methods which they advocated to achieve the "good life" differed, their ideas on what constituted the "good life" were very much alike. Undoubtedly, their philosophy, like yours and mine, was influenced by qualities which they had inherited and by their environment. Their social and economic status; the amount, quality, and kind of education which they had received; the prevailing political and religious views; and the customs, traditions, and mores of their society also influenced their philosophy. We will look briefly at the views of several of these men and of the philosophic schools of which they were members. This should help the reader to formulate his own philosophy.

MAJOR CONCERNS OF PHILOSOPHY

The three leading schools of philosophic thought are *idealism, pragmatism,* and *realism. Existentialism* which is the most recently organized point of view is not a systematic philosophy in the traditional sense; rather it permeates many philosophies. *Gestalt psychology* provides a unity and continuity for the individual and his relationships with society but it cannot yet, it is felt, be called a philosophy. There are a number of other philosophies such as Naturalism, Christian Idealism, Neo-Aristotelianism, and others. These will probably be studied by students of physical education in philosophy courses.

We will look at each of the three leading philosophic schools through the eyes of their first and leading proponents. Some of the beliefs of the early leaders have been modified by their followers. We will point out their beliefs under such headings as:

1. The nature of the universe

2. Man's place in the universe

3. Determination of good and evil

4. The nature of God

5. The soul and immortality

6. Man's relationship to the state

7. The role of education

8. The relationships between mind and matter

9. Implications for the conduct of health, physical education, and recreation programs.

The Nature of the Universe

The earliest philosophers were greatly concerned with the problem of the *nature of the universe*. They wanted to solve the mystery of how the world was made — to determine the "stuff" from which the many objects in the world were made. Philosophers of today do not concern themselves greatly with this problem. However, methods used for the solution of this problem do illustrate the philosophic process.

Thales, who lived in Ancient Greece about 600 B.C., concluded that water was the original "stuff." He reasoned that since water turned to a solid (ice) when frozen and into air (steam) when heated, everything originally came from water, and in the end returned to water. Anaximines, also of Ancient Greece, believed that the original "stuff" was air. He reasoned that since men and animals breathe air and this air turns into flesh, bone, and blood and that since air becomes wind, clouds, water, earth, and stone, air must be the original "stuff."

Man's Place in the Universe

All philosophers have been concerned with man's role in the universe. Some have crowned him with glory and honor just a little below that which they gave to God. Others attributed to man no greater eminence than they attributed to animals. Thales believed that, since man (as everything else in the universe) is made of water, he evolved by a natural process and consequently returned to the original "stuff" of the universe — water. The Sophists, a philosophic group of Ancient Greece, placed man at the center of the universe. They believed that man could determine his own fate and could satisfy his needs and desires by molding that part of the universe which was useful to him.

Determination of Good and Evil

The determination of what is good and what is evil has challenged philosophers since the times of the Ancient Greeks. Some have believed that there is an absolute and unquestionable means for measuring good and evil which is applicable to all situations and for all time. The Ten Commandments of the ancient Hebrews exemplify this belief. Some philosophers have believed that an act which is good under one set of circumstances may be evil under another set of circumstances and vice versa. Other philosophers have been troubled over the inconsistency between the idea of an absolutely good God and the existence in the world of death, suffering, conflict, and immorality which goes unpunished. Heraclitus believed that the combination of opposites, such as good and evil, resulted in a whole in which there is harmony. He believed that while mortals can only see the opposites, good and evil, God can see the harmony so that everything is good in that it produces harmony.

As the interest of philosophers in the nature of the universe decreased and their interest in the nature of man increased, they became more interested in defining the good life. Democritus believed that the goal of life is happiness. He believed that happiness does not depend upon worldly things but rather upon a state of tranquility or harmony of the soul made possible through reflection and reason. The good man to Democritus was not the man who did good but the man who wanted to do good at all times. Protagoras, a Sophist, believed that each man has the right to determine for himself what is good and what is evil. Other Sophists such as Esthydemus, Thrasymachus, and Callicles taught that morality was merely convention, that there were no moral laws, no principles of right or wrong, and that each man should live as he wished and get what he wanted by any means possible. These beliefs would, obviously, lead to thorough selfishness, moral anarchy, and chaos. It may be no coincidence that their teaching was done just before and during the decline of the Greek civilization.

The Nature of God

The earliest people believed in numerous gods. The Ancient Greeks believed there was a community of gods made up of gods of varying degrees of power and with specialized functions. At the head was Zeus. His wife was Hera. Their offspring were Apollo, Hermes, and Aphrodite. These gods were vested with human frailties as well as virtues. Xenophanes, who lived about 600 B.C., believed that there is only one God and that he is unlike human beings in every way. Xenophanes believed God is in one place, never moves, has no beginning or ending, and is an eternal unity.

The Soul and Immortality

The passing away of loved ones has been a powerful emotional experience for man since he has been on this earth. The knowledge that he too must someday die has caused him to wonder about man's immortality. Always man has wished to believe that death cannot be the end, that death is not the victory of one's enemies, and that humanity persists in some form after death. Early man probably dreamed that he roamed far and wide to new and distant lands on hunting and fishing expeditions. When he awoke from his sleep, his friends assured him that he had not moved from his cave or tent. Since this happened often to each man and to all men, men came to believe that there was some part of man which could free itself of his body and live its own life. This was probably the beginning of a belief in the human soul. Early man also believed that trees, rivers, animals, and everything in nature possessed a soul and that the soul was unaffected by things which affected the body. Anaximines believed that the soul was thin or rarefied air, that it held the individual together, and that when it left the body, the body was destroyed. Empedocles thought that the soul left the body when it died and took up residence in another body. This is called the *doctrine of the transmigration of souls.*

Man's Relationship to the State

Primitive man lived with others in his cave or shelter of branches and leaves because he learned early that two or more men are better able to protect themselves and are more secure than one man alone. However, when two or more people lived together, it was inevitable that there would be conflict of purpose and desire and, consequently, rules were established. Those rules which protected the group against its enemies from within and without were preserved and those which did not were discarded. Most of the rules were learned by people while they were children by observing and imitating elders. Others were learned during solemn ceremonies such as the puberty rites. Later, during man's development, rules were written down and a code of laws resulted. This was the beginning of society and of the state. Centuries later philosophers began to question the beginnings of society, its nature, and its meaning. They wondered whether social organization resulted naturally from man's living together or whether it was of divine origin; whether the power of the state rested in the people or in the rulers who received it from God; and they wondered what was the best form of social organization. These questions have not only stimulated philosophic speculation but have also driven men to revolutions and to war. The French and Russian revolutions and the Korean and Vietnam conflicts in modern times are examples of this disagreement over the best form of social organization. Democritus held that since the ultimate welfare of everyone depended upon the state, the welfare of the state should be everyone's primary concern and the state should be primary. Callicles, on the other hand, urged those with sufficient strength to refuse to obey those laws which were against nature and to assert their independence. The ultimate realization of Democritus's point of view (that the state should be primary) found expression in Hitler's Nazi Germany and in Communism while that of Callicles finds expression in lawlessness, civil disobedience, riots, and mob rule.

The Role of Education

Education has always played an important role in man's social structure. Among primitive man the child learned as he associated with his parents and other members of the family, tribe, or clan. However, as the traditions and customs of the tribe or clan increased in number, it became necessary that the older men instruct the younger in some of the traditions and customs of the tribe during ceremonial occasions. When group life became still more complex, certain members devoted a major portion of their time to teaching the young. Because traditions and customs were closely related to religious beliefs, the education provided was largely a religious education. In time, the philosophers began to think about what should be taught to the young, how it should be taught, education's relationship to group life, and the aims and purposes of education.

Relationships Between Mind and Matter

Earliest man noted that some objects in his environment could be kicked, broken, smashed, moved about, shaped and molded, and that these objects seemed indifferent to this treatment. He also noted that man did seem to care what happened to him and that he could make plans which would enable him to survive at a higher level. He could plan and then build a house, a garden, or a road according to those plans. The earliest philosophers concluded that the difference between inanimate objects and man is that man possesses a mind which enables him to plan and to think. Further, they concluded that that part of man which is mind controls the rest of the body-matter. They concluded that the universe was composed of one or more original and basic substances and that some force moved these substances to produce the different forms in the universe.

Anaximander believed that the basic substance of the universe was "the infinite," an eternal and imperishable substance. He believed this substance had eternal motion and that this explained how the universe came into being. Heraclitus believed that the basic substance and the forms which it takes are the same. The substance and form were both fire. Fire produced ceaseless activity and change and these, he believed, were the outstanding characteristics of the universe. Parmenides believed that being and thought are the same for, he reasoned, that which cannot be thought cannot be and what cannot be cannot be thought. In saying this, he concluded that thought or mind is the creator of matter. To Parmenides mind and matter are one and the same. This primacy of the mind served as the basic tenet of the idealistic philosophy.

Implications for Health, Physical Education, and Recreation

A physical educator's philosophy will obviously determine the content, the objectives, the principles, and the methods which he will utilize in his physical education and athletic program. His philosophy defines what he believes to be the nature of the universe, man's role, God, man's relationship to the state, the role of education, and what is good and evil.

We will discuss the implications of the three principal philosophic positions for physical education in greater detail as we look at them. It is important to realize that one's philosophic position does influence the kind of program he will wish to develop. On one hand, the *realist* with his belief in the reality of the world and that man must discover this reality is likely to develop a rigorous, systematically organized program with emphasis upon discipline and mastery. Since he believes that natural laws are unchanging, he believes that students must learn these laws and live by them in order to function most effectively. Consequently, he believes in teacher planning and in discipline. The *pragmatist*, on the other hand, believes that reality is ever-changing, that the only reality is that which we experience every day. He believes that knowledge is discovered through experience and he doubts that truth is the same for all time — that what is true today under one set of circumstances will be true tomorrow under another set of circumstances. Consequently, the pragmatist does not believe in a systematically organized curriculum or in teacher planning to the extent that the realist does. He believes it is important that students be given experiences in applying the scientific method in solving problems, hence he places emphasis upon problem solving.

Philosophy is man's effort to see the universe in a coherent, systematic, and meaningful way. It gives our actions direction. If our objectives, principles, and methods are to be consistent we must possess a reasonably well thought-out philosophic position. Otherwise, we are likely to be like the horseman who tried to run off in all directions at once.

One's philosophy will influence the determination of the aims or general objectives of education and these will serve as guides in the determination of the specific or immediate objectives of education. The general objectives of physical education (improved physical fitness, social behavior, and emotional health, for example) should conform to the general objectives of education. The specific objectives of physical education (ability to do twenty pull-ups, to do a kip, or to kick a football thirty yards, for example) should lead to the achievement of the general objectives of physical education. Principles, which serve as guides for the conduct of the program, should be formulated which will insure achievement of the specific objectives. Examples of principles are: "Classes should be conducted in a democractic manner" and "Respect should be shown for individual differences." The learning experiences, activities, or the content of the program should be so selected as to contribute toward achievement of both the specific and the general or more remote objectives. Finally, the teaching methods utilized should be in conformity with the principles and lead to achievement of the specific and general objectives.

This entire process might be compared to a vacation trip. One's philosophy is analogous to the part of the country he enjoys most. Idealism will appeal to some, realism to others, pragmatism to others, and existentialism to still others. Similarly, some will prefer the Smokey Mountains, others Florida, and still others Cape Cod. Theoretically, idealists will select certain general objectives (goals), realists others, and pragmatists still others. (Actually, their general objectives are quite similar as we shall see.)

Teachers must begin where they find the students in skill, understanding, and knowledge. Let us say this starting point is Chicago, Illinois, and the ultimate destination selected is Provincetown on Cape Cod. Provincetown becomes the general objective just as a level of skill in swimming adequate to swim 440 yards in fifteen minutes is a general objective. The intermediate or specific objectives could be Cleveland, Ohio (ability to do rhythmic breathing) on the first night; Buffalo, New York (ability to do the prone float) on the second night; Hartford, Connecticut (ability to swim one length of the pool); Cape Cod Canal (ability to swim four lengths of the pool); and Provincetown (ability to swim 440 yards in fifteen minutes). The principles, or guides, might be compared to the routes selected since they define the limits and indicate the direction taken. The teaching methods which we select could be compared to the method of conveyance selected – bicycle, horse and wagon, or automobile.

Plans are as essential to the conduct of an effective educational program as they are to the taking of a trip or the building of a house or a product. Bus drivers have routes to follow, carpenters follow architects' plans, and manufacturers follow designs. Educators, too, need to follow plans. These plans must begin with a reasonably coherent, consistent, and logical philosophic position.

IDEALISM

The Nature of the Universe

Although idealism antedates Plato by some 3000 years, having been started in China or India, Plato was among the first to organize and systematize its teachings in writing. While the fundamental beliefs of the idealists of Plato's time are, in the main, accepted by today's idealists, their concepts today are considerably more complete and sophisticated, as one would expect, because of the greater knowledge possessed by man about his universe, man, and society.

We can here only introduce the reader to philosophy but we hope that we will stimulate his desire to pursue the study of this fascinating subject further. Consequently, we can present the beliefs of only a few outstanding philosophers. The reader should realize that there are several branches of each of the three major philosophies which we will discuss. There are, for example, differences among the Idealists of different nations and there are the Subjective, Platonic, Personalistic, Realistic, Objective, and Pluralistic branches of Idealism.

Plato believed that the world which we see and experience through our senses is not a real world, but only a copy world. The real world for him was the world of "ideas." In the world of "ideas" is to be found the ideal tree from which all trees are copied. The ideal tree is not only perfect but never changes nor does it die. The ideal tree has existed from the beginning of time. This, Plato believed to be true of all objects in the world.

Plato's second principle regarding the nature of the universe was that "matter" is all that "ideas" are not. Matter is the raw material upon which "ideas" are impressed. Everything in nature came about as a result of the molding and forming of matter by ideas much as the sculptor's ideas are impressed upon stone. He believed that all the imperfections and all the differences between objects of the same kind which our eyes and ears perceive are due to "ideas" not being perfectly impressed upon matter. "Ideas" are perfect and unchanging but imperfections arise because it is impossible to impress the idea perfectly upon matter since matter is imperfect.

Man's Place in the Universe

In this area we again report the beliefs of Plato. He believed that man is a creation of the universe like animals but that man is the only creation which possesses universal principles, notions, concepts, and ideas which are basic to true understanding of the universe. This understanding is possible because part of the divine reason has entered his body. This portion of the divine reason he called the "soul." The "soul" is restrained and hindered by the body which is matter. Plato believed that only in the philosopher has the "soul" mastered the body.

Determination of Good and Evil

Plato's beliefs concerning good and evil were consistent with his beliefs concerning the nature of the universe in that he believed that our senses inform us of an imperfect world of matter upon which ideas had been unsuccessfully impressed. This world is evil. Ideas are good. Man can know the ideal world only through knowledge and reason. The goal of life should be to release the soul or mind from the body so that it can contemplate the true world of ideas. Man's mind must rule his every action. Plato viewed man as consisting of three parts: the appetites which concern physiologic functions and desires; the will which is concerned with action and courage; and reason. Reason should rule over the appetites and the will, and when it does man will possess wisdom, courage, and self-control and will be happy. A good life and not sensual pleasures, he believed, leads to happiness.

The Nature of God

Plato's writings about the nature of God seem confused. This may be because his mentor, Socrates, was condemned to death for teaching that there was only one God and because Plato planned to lead the masses from a belief in many gods more gradually. On the other hand, it may have been because Plato himself was unable to break away from the then current belief in many gods. He believed that a "Demiurge" created the universe by impressing ideas upon matter. Ideas, matter, and the "Demiurge" were always there but the "Demiurge" gave form to matter by impressing his ideas upon it. The "Demiurge" also created all the gods in whom the masses believed.

The Soul and Immortality

Plato believed that the "Demiurge" gave the world a soul and that this world soul was the cause of all motion, beauty, order, harmony, law, life, and knowledge. The "Demiurge" also gave souls to all planets and to all individuals. Each individual soul is eternal, having resided on a star before entering the body. It constantly struggles to free itself from the body. If it succeeds, it returns to its star but if it fails to free itself, it will move from one body when it dies to another, sinking lower and lower. The body is like a prison for the soul causing it to forget some of its perfect ideas. Under certain conditions (such as during association with an outstanding teacher) the soul recalls some of the pure ideas with which it was possessed while it resided on the star.

Man's Relationship to the State

Plato's theories regarding the relationship between man and the state were both autocratic and socialistic. They very likely were autocratic principally because Plato was wealthy and the son of aristocratic parents. He believed that philosophers should rule the country and that their authority should not be questioned. Citizens of the state should be placed in classes suited to their talents. Those with skill in warfare should be placed in the warrior class. Those with skill in selling should be placed in the trade and merchant class. At the bottom of the hierarchy would be the slaves. The rulers should determine each individual's class. Plato believed that all citizens should have a voice in the government. Slaves should do all the work. (At that time, Greece had many slaves.) All property was to be owned by the state and be distributed by the state according to merit and need. He believed that the individual could achieve his most perfect development only by completely subordinating himself to the state. A man could become "good" by being a good citizen.

The Role of Education

Plato developed one of the first theories of education. This theory he explained in his great work the *Republic*. He believed that education should be supported and controlled by the state and that its major objective should be to select and train men to serve the state. A person's educability would determine in what class he would serve. He was aware of the variability in human abilities and advised that students be placed in classes according to their abilities. According to his plan, a boy, for his first eighteen years, would be trained in gymnastics, sports, music, singing, literature, reading, and writing. At the age of eighteen, those boys who demonstrated little aptitude for further schooling were to be dropped from school. These would make up the trade and merchant class. Those remaining were to be given two years of military training. Those who demonstrated little aptitude for further schooling beyond the two years of military training were to be dropped from school and placed in the army. They would make up the military class. Those remaining were to be given an extensive education in philosophy, mathematics, music, and science. They would make up the ruling class.

Relationships Between Mind and Matter

The mind, or the soul, for he believed they were the same, was for Plato the seat of all knowledge. At the time the mind left the star, it was possessed of perfect knowledge but when it became imbedded in the body, it became foggy and forgot all it knew. Questioning would cause it to remember what it had known. Plato believed that mind molds matter; that matter has no form or reality; and that mind is the only true reality and of greatest worth. Mind impresses matter with ideas. Matter takes the shape of ideas in our mind. Plato believed that the tree which we see is not a real tree. Our mind has impressed the idea of a tree upon the matter of which the tree is made. The real tree is in our mind and was in our mind before we were born.

Implications for Health, Physical Education, and Recreation

The basic philosophic beliefs which we have presented are the earliest of the idealistic philosophic school, those of Plato. While they may seem fantastic today, it must be remembered that at the time Plato lived, knowledge in physiology, physics, astronomy, and all other areas was very limited. Nevertheless, Plato developed a consistent and, in view of the limited knowledge of his time, a logical philosophy. Modern philosophers are still struggling for complete answers to the eight problems which we have discussed.

It will be recalled that according to the idealistic point of view, finite mind springs from infinite mind. According to this point of view all minds would be fundamentally the same. The idealistic point of view tends to discount the influence of society upon the individual.

Idealism emphasizes man's rationality and the cultivation of reason. Idealists tend to do little counseling beyond the academic areas of the school. They believe that if students learn the "true" principles they will be guided throughout their lives by these principles.

The curriculum and course content in idealistic schools is likely to be teacher determined. Emphasis would be placed upon developing ethical behavior and sportsmanship through physical education and athletic programs. In classrooms the dialectic or "Socratic" method is likely to be used. In this method, a statement made by another person is analyzed so as to reveal its inconsistencies. Then, after the other person recognizes the errors in his views, he is asked a series of questions by means of which the questioner brings out what he believes to be the truth.

The idealistic school would not be likely to make efforts to reconstruct the social order. The school would likely reflect the kind of society in which it is maintained. It would be reactionary, conservative, liberal, or radical according to its economic, political, and social context.

The idealist-administrator has a sincere and genuine concern for the self-development of both teachers and students and is likely to treat those under him humanly, warmly, and with understanding since he sees himself as the father of the school family.

Since Idealism is idea and ideal centered, idealist teachers place great importance upon development of the mind and the intellect and upon the eternal truths such as Truth, Beauty, and the Good. The eternal truths are best discovered through reading, particularly of great books, and through the exemplary behavior and skilled, vigorous, and dedicated teaching of well-established knowledge by the teacher. The idealist teacher tends to prefer the well-established method and content to new innovations. Although the teacher is the center of the learning process and selects and interprets the teaching materials, guides the discussion, selects the experiments, outlines the steps and does the lecturing, he does invite the students to share these experiences with him. Major objectives of the idealist-teacher are to increase the students' store of knowledge, to help him to understand himself, and to develop in him such qualities as self-initiative, self-responsibility, self-decision, and self-restraint.

The idealist teacher prefers the lecture method to discussion by students or to field experiences for he believes that when students are not guided they may learn things which are not good for them or that at best that what they do learn could be learned much more expeditiously via lectures and assigned readings.

The idealist teacher of physical activities believes the teacher needs to develop skill in making verbal explanations of movement skills. He asks questions of students to find out how much they know, to test their intellect and to express curiosity or doubt. It will be recalled that Plato had Socrates teach principally through asking questions. The physical educator can ask after a demonstration of the neck spring: "What was the angle of the back with respect to the floor when the hips extended?" "Were the knees flexed or extended during the early part of the hip extension?" After the students try the neck spring, he can ask them: "What did you do incorrectly that caused you to fail?" "How did it feel during that successful effort?"

The idealist teacher feels no hesitancy in using subjective evaluations because he wishes to grade such elements as social behavior and citizenship and these cannot be evaluated objectively. He will compare his students' performances to norms and objective tests but he regards these measurements as only a small part of the total evaluation.

PRAGMATISM

The Nature of the Universe

John Locke (1632–1704) concluded that all our knowledge of the universe comes through the senses but whether or not there is a real world cannot be certain. George Berkeley (1685–1753) carried Locke's beliefs to the next step – one which would help stem the tide of increasing atheism and disbelief in God. Berkeley was a deeply religious man. He asked how it could be known that a world of matter actually exists. He answered that there is no universe of material bodies but only ideas. He taught that the cause of all sensations and consequently of all ideas is God. He believed that nothing in the universe exists unless it is perceived. The table in the room exists only as long as it is perceived by someone. The table is an idea, not a material object. If there is no one in the room the table may still exist in the mind of God. For Berkeley nothing existed except as ideas in the mind.

David Hume, who lived in Scotland from 1711–1776, agreed with Berkeley that all we have are ideas but he denied the existence of God since we cannot prove that He exists.

Man's Place in the Universe

Berkeley believed there is no material universe outside the mind of man or the mind of God. He believed that our sensations came to us from the mind of God, not from material objects.

David Hume contended that we can no more prove the existence of God than we can prove the existence of a material world. He believed that all of the universe that we can prove is the conscious stream of our ideas. He made man alone the center and the whole of the universe.

Determination of Good and Evil

John Dewey (1859–1952), an internationally known philosopher from Vermont and leader of the pragmatic school, believed that whatever improves the life of the individual improves the lives of all members of the group. He believed that the individual and the group are an entity since individuality is a product of social living and no one has true individuality except as a member of a group. Social groups are established to serve the individual. The individual must not be regarded as a means to serve the group. He believed that good and bad are relative terms depending upon the circumstances of the situation. What is good in one situation may be bad in another. In modern society, preservation of the aged and infirm is good but in a social group which is struggling for the survival of everyone because there is little food and all must work and fight hard for long hours to eke out a living, preservation of the weak and aged may be evil.

The Nature of God

William James (1842–1910), a pragmatist who taught at Harvard University and the universities of Edinburgh and Oxford, believed that while we cannot prove that God exists or can prove anything about Him, we do have a will to believe in God, and we must satisfy this will. James believed that God is a part of the universe and aids man to realize his goals. He regarded God as being like man but more powerful.

When John Dewey uses the term *God* he feels compelled to define it in such a way that it has no real meaning. He contends that while men have had certain experiences which they have believed gave evidence of the influence of God, this interpretation cannot be proved and consequently should not be made.

The Soul and Immortality

It is necessary to point out that where we cite the beliefs of Dewey and James, the differences manifested between their beliefs and those of Plato and other Early Greek philosophers represent not only the differences between idealism and pragmatism but also the differences between an earlier naive thinking and the more sophisticated thinking of people twenty or more centuries later who had the advantage of considerably more scientific evidence. Almost no modern philosophers believe in the traditional dualism of body and mind or soul with separate lives. Obviously, if there is no soul separate from the body, there can be no life for the soul in Shoel, Hades, or Heaven after the death of the body. Modern philosophers can find enough to concern themselves about in study of the life of man between birth and death. Consequently, they do not discuss the soul and immortality.

James felt that man's belief in the existence of a soul which had immortality after death had usefulness in helping man to lead a more moral life. Dewey believed that such a belief was harmful in that it causes men to cease trying to understand experiences which have religious qualities.

Man and the State

John Dewey thought of a democratic society as a group of individuals sharing their experiences and growing through this sharing. He conceived of the ideal society as one in which there is a reciprocal relationship between the individual and the group. The individual contributes to and receives from the group. Perhaps the only absolute preached by Dewey was that the human personality must be respected. Social groups exist to enrich the life of the individual. A man can grow and develop fully only as a member of a social group.

Dewey believed in the American tradition that all men are by nature free and equal. He would affirm that there are certain rights with which all men are endowed such as "life, liberty, and the pursuit of happiness." However, he did not believe in the policy of laissez-faire which limits the authority of the state while it enlarges the freedom of the individual and which, carried to the extreme, would result in chaos and anarchy. Dewey tried to find individual freedom within the social group so that both the group and the individual would prosper.

Man and Education

Dewey believed that education should be concerned with the individual as a functioning and contributing member of society and not with the individual isolated from society. He believed that neither the individual nor the group should be given exclusive emphasis. The child can only develop as a member of society. The individual must prepare himself to serve society by developing his own unique talents. While some of Dewey's followers developed the "child centered" or so-called progressive schools in which the child's interests alone determined course content, Dewey himself worked toward a harmonizing of needs of the individual and society.

Mind and Matter

William James and John Dewey believed that mind is a kind of behavior and not a thing. Some of our acts occur without the intervention of mind while others have the characteristics of mind. Dewey believed that man does not think unless he has a problem to solve. Daydreaming or idle thoughts are not thinking. One of Dewey's major contributions was defining the steps in reaching a solution to a problem. The first step is defining the problem. The second is collecting data relative to the problem. The third is formulation of a possible solution or hypothesis. The fourth is a testing of the hypothesis on a mental level. The fifth involves putting the hypothesis into action and noting the results. The final or sixth step is the formulation of a general principle from the knowledge gained which is applicable to other similar situations. This reflective thinking, according to Dewey, will lead to the solution of any problem if carefully done.

Implications for Health, Physical Education, and Recreation

The pragmatist believes that the primary aim of the educational process is to teach the child to live the life of the group and to acquire the disposition, the skill, and knowledge to contribute to its welfare. However, since change is occurring at an ever-accelerating rate, education must prepare children to live in conditions as yet unknown to us. It is for this reason that pragmatists place so much attention upon problem solving. Problem solving is also applied to the determination of moral conduct since pragmatists do not believe in absolutes or constant, never-changing principles for determining what is moral and what is immoral. The obligation for moral conduct rests in the social experience; that is, that action is most moral which produces the most good for the greatest number. The pragmatists would not be likely to pass immediate judgment as to the morality of an act but would feel compelled to discuss and to evaluate all aspects and outcomes of the behavior.

They believe that the individual should be the central focus of education and that the claims of society or the state are subordinate to him. They would endeavor to educate the individual in good citizenship. Totalitarianism and socialism would find it difficult to function where all schools were organized according to the pragmatic beliefs. Pragmatism is unique to democratic countries and functions best in such countries.

Pragmatists believe that the school should make an active effort to improve the culture of which it is a part. They believe it is not only the right but also the responsibility of educational institutions to evaluate, comment upon, and criticize government in the hope of effecting improvement and change. They attempt to teach the child to participate in the existing group culture by giving him an understanding of and practice in the democratic procedures through election of officers, much use of class discussions, field trips, participation in community enterprises, and by getting the school involved with the community and the community with the school.

Because they attach great importance to the process of change, feeling that the world will be very different from what it is now by the time the children reach adulthood, they emphasize the problem-solving method. Figures, facts, procedures, and knowledge change but the problem-solving method is the one unchanging aspect of life. The ability to solve problems will be useful regardless of how much the world changes. Consequently, they do not demand that students acquire a storehouse of facts except as they might be useful in solving a specific problem the students may be working on.

Pragmatists believe that experience is not only private to the individual but is also what it is largely because of the social context in which it takes place. A person gains knowledge of himself through his knowledge of others and of others through his knowledge of himself. Since the breadth and depth of experience depend on the cultural context in which it occurs, preparing the individual to participate in that culture is the main objective of education. But this culture enters into experience only as it is experienced and lived and it can be lived only as the school enters into community activities, takes field trips, establishes miniature social groups, practices democratic procedures, holds elections, and gives students manifold opportunities to work and play together as members of social groups.

Pragmatists see the self as a social product; that is, personality is adequate and significant only in interaction with a social group. Selfhood is built and a sense of responsibility emerges through reciprocal and mutual relation of the self with others. There is a sociological as well as a biological component of intelligence, they believe, and for this reason it is important that the child be reared in a rich cultural matrix.

They feel the child learns what he lives. If it is a feeling which must be learned, the child must actually feel it. He will learn only to the extent that he does live it or feel it. One learns his responses only as he accepts them as his own. Consequently, pragmatists place great emphasis upon student interest and will expend considerable time and energy in motivating students and in eliciting their interest. Furthermore, they will study those things which interest students.

In physical education, they are much more interested in promoting total fitness than they are in promoting physical fitness alone. They see great potential in "educating through the physical" because of the social nature of games, contests, relays, and recreational activities. They would like a varied program of physical activities because such a program would provide a greater variety of experiences. Physical education should be an important part of the curriculum – for it contributes most to the formation of personality and to the socialization of the individual. They prefer *socializing* activities. For this reason, they prefer team sports to the individual and dual activities. While interscholastic and intercollegiate sports, when properly conducted, contribute much to achievement of educational objectives, they feel that physical education classes and intramural programs should have priority over athletic programs from the standpoint of money, staff, and facilities.

School health education, they believe, is an extremely important subject and should be a primary objective of education. Health education should help the child to lead a rich and full life. Health services are important but the child should also acquire the attitudes, dispositions, knowledges, and skills to practice lifelong habits of healthful living. School health education should begin with student interests and needs, make use of class discussions, visual aids, field trips, student groups, and student leadership, and it should involve the community, many members of the school faculty, and a variety of health specialists.

The pragmatists believe that education in worthy use of leisure is important to pupil growth since they believe that all people should have opportunities to use their leisure creatively and fruitfully. They believe play should be conducted so that desirable moral and ethical values will be developed.

Pragmatists believe that health education, physical education, and recreation education should be administered as a unified program since they have similar objectives and methods and often use the same facilities and personnel.

Like the idealist, the pragmatist physical educator prefers evaluation to measurement. He abhors standardization and norms which he believes tend to make all programs alike. He believes that growth and problem-solving ability can be evaluated but that they cannot be measured. Evaluation, he believes, should be continuous and persistent. The role of the teacher should be that of leader, not of director; that of resource person and counselor, not of commander; that of motivator and stimulator, not of dictator. Class control should be achieved through appeal to intrinsic motivations rather than through authoritarian methods since the pragmatist wants to develop self-discipline, initiative, and creativity.

REALISM

The Nature of the Universe

Like other philosophers of his time, Aristotle (384–322 B.C.) who was a pupil of Plato, was greatly concerned about the nature of the universe, man, God, and the soul and immortality. He believed that ideas or "forms," as he called them, were not separate from things or matter but were *in* them. Plato, it will be recalled, believed that ideas were separate from matter and that ideas impress matter into different forms. Aristotle believed that form or ideas and matter were always and eternally together and could not be separated. He believed that the world which we experience through our senses is the real world and not a mere copy of the real world as did Plato. Aristotle thought that the entire universe could be explained through the process by which matter continually seeks to assume different forms. An acorn has both form and matter and seeks to assume the form of a tree which has matter and a different form. The tree seeks to become an oak table which possesses matter and still another form. Matter is always striving to assume new forms. The form (idea) of an acorn, tree, or table is, however, constant and never changing. Form attempts to realize itself in matter and the more perfect the form (acorn, tree, or oak table) the more fully the form is realized.

Aristotle believed that every object in the universe has four causes. First, there is the form to be realized, which he called the "formal cause." Second, there is the matter which is to be formed, which he called the "material cause." Third, there are the tools, activities, or actions with which the matter is shaped into a form. This he called the "efficient cause" or "moving cause." Fourth, there is the purpose for which the matter was formed or the "final cause." Everything that occurs in life, Aristotle thought, could be analyzed in this way.

Man's Place in the Universe

Aristotle believed that man, like all objects in the universe, was matter striving to achieve a new form. Like plants, he has a function to perform. Like animals, he has the ability to imagine, to remember, and to experience pain, pleasure, and desire. However, unlike plants and animals, man possesses reason. He can think. He is creative. This makes man the greatest creation and gives him something of the divine.

Determination of Good and Evil

Aristotle believed that man acts with some goal in mind. He acts to obtain something in order to obtain something else, and so on. The aim is to realize his unique talents and abilities to the fullest. It is obvious that he believed that self-realization is the greatest good. He took into consideration man's feelings, desires and appetites when he taught that these must obey man's greatest faculty, his reason. When reason ruled, man would be happy. The reasonable or rational attitude Aristotle called the "golden mean." Happiness would result when a man steered the middle course between extremes. For example, courage lies midway between foolhardiness and cowardice. The good man is noble, just, honest, kind, and generous because he wants to be, not because he is forced to be.

The Nature of God

Aristotle believed that form, which is within matter, caused it to move, that is, to change its form. There is in the acorn the unrealized form of the oak tree toward which it is striving. It grows to become an oak tree. This is motion. The oak tree strives to become another form, and so on. Where does the process end or does it go on forever? Aristotle believed that it did end and at the end there was pure form without matter. This he called an eternal "unmoved mover" which he regarded as the ultimate cause of all motion, of all becoming in the universe. According to Aristotle, the "unmoved mover" moves men and draws matter but does not move itself because every object and living thing in the universe, and the universe itself, desires to realize itself because of its desire to satisfy the "unmoved mover" – God. God is the cause of all striving, is the unifying principle of the universe, and all forms are realized in Him.

The Soul and Immortality

Aristotle, as did most of his contemporaries, believed that everything which was alive possesses a soul. Plants' souls direct eating and digesting of food, growth, and reproduction. Animals' souls direct these functions and in addition receive and interpret sense impressions through their eyes, ears, nose, etc. The human soul does all things plant and animal souls do but in addition it has the power of reason. Reason he divided into two categories: passive reason which is "matter" and creative reason which is "form." Creative reason existed before either the body or the soul were created and will continue to live after the death of the body since it is a part of God. Passive reason, being matter, dies with the body. Personal immortality is impossible according to Aristotle since the only part which survives death is a part which was a part of God.

Man and the State

Aristotle, like his teacher Plato, believed that man is by nature a social animal and can fully realize himself only as a member of a social group. He argued that the state was prior to the individual members of the state in that the idea, "form," or drive toward formation of the state was in the individual. This idea was consistent with his beliefs concerning the nature of the universe. The goal of the state is to produce good citizens; consequently, it should be so organized and conducted as to enable each citizen to live a happy and virtuous life. The constitution should be so written as to satisfy the nature and needs of the citizens. It must also recognize the inequalities in men such as in abilities, wealth, birth and freedom, and confer rights accordingly. He believed that slavery was just but that only foreigners should be placed in the slave class since foreigners were inferior to the Greeks. He believed that a monarchy or an aristocracy were good forms of government while an oligarchy or a democracy were bad forms of government. Modern realists in the United States do not believe this, needless to say.

Man and Education

Aristotle believed that the aim of education should be to make people virtuous. We can find it easy to agree with this belief but we will find it difficult to agree with some of his other beliefs. He thought all education should be controlled by the state, that the state should determine which children should be permitted to live and which put to death because of physical defects; that the state should select a man's wife; and that the prime purpose of education was to develop citizens who could defend the state. He would have children turned over to the state at birth to be trained until the age of seven in physical activities. From seven until twenty-one years of age, they would be trained in music, literature, gymnastics, and sports.

Mind and Matter

Aristotle believed that mind was in all matter and caused it to take its form. While matter offers resistance to mind when it attempts to form it, it simultaneously seeks to be shaped. He held that neither mind nor matter could exist separately. Where there is one there is also always the other. He stated that everything in the universe has form and therefore must possess a mind.

Aristotle argued that true knowledge consists of understanding the real cause of things. He worked out the procedures for deductive logic, which process he called the "syllogism," so thoroughly that little has been added to this day. In this process man moves from a generally accepted principle to a particular. A well-known example of a syllogism is the following:

All men are mortal.
Socrates is a man.
Therefore Socrates is mortal.

Implications for Health, Physical Education, and Recreation

Since they believe in a real world outside ourselves and since man can live more effectively and happily by understanding that world, realists place greatest emphasis upon research and the scientific method. However, they have reservations concerning the applicability of the scientific method to the solution of problems in the area of ethics and morality.

Because they believe that man must conform to the conditions of reality, realists place greater emphasis upon conformity and discipline than do the pragmatists. They believe that equal weight should be placed upon freedom (which might lead to excesses) and upon the authority of socially tested experience. Although authority should be set as a counterweight to freedom, it should not contradict it but rather complement it.

With regard to the relationships between government and the schools, the realist takes a position midway between that of the idealist and that of the pragmatist. He would like to see the school influencing group culture, but not unduly.

The realist concurs with the pragmatist that the problem method of teaching is the one demanded by the nature of the situation. However, he believes the student should be more concerned with the question: "what is?" than with "what to do?" He believes that the content of knowledge (accumulation of facts) is of greater importance than that of doing, inquiry, or the problem-solving method though he would not completely omit the latter. To the realist the problem-solving method has value as a means to an end – the accumulation of knowledge and understanding of the world.

The realist rejects the concept of a dualism of mind and body. He regards both as belonging to the same continuum. Consequently, he places great emphasis upon physical fitness believing that a healthy and physically fit body enables one to be more efficient and more productive. Maintaining physical fitness is merely living in conformity with the laws of nature. He sees the student as a biological organism with a highly developed nervous system which interacts with the physical environment. Stimuli from within and without the student influence his behavior. As a result, he believes in rigorous, well-organized curricula and courses which place emphasis upon mastery of knowledge. He believes that the learning of as large a number of scientific facts and principles as possible is an important goal of education.

The realist's approach to teaching is objective. He prefers objective to subjective tests in evaluating students. His tests measure the quantity of learning and are likely to be thorough. He presents clear, distinct facts in an objective and logical manner and drills students in these facts until they are mastered. He has great faith in the scientific method and in research. He will carefully follow the criteria and recommended steps in curriculum construction, in writing course outlines and syllabi, in analyses of students, and in job analyses. He likes system, order, planning, and good organization. Prerequisites, students' records, catalog statements, and statements of objectives should be well formulated and neatly organized. He is likely to subscribe to the modern version of the conditioned reflex or modern behaviorism. Because of his objectivity, he is likely to be impersonal in his relations with his students. However, he is apt to display great enthusiasm when the student discovers something. This leads to good rapport with his students. He uses lectures, textbook and outside readings, and recitations to accomplish his teaching objectives. He likes the project method because there are definite, concrete, tangible, measurable, well-organized units of work – as in nature. He is open-minded, fair, objective, meticulous, and neat.

The realist would be likely to provide more time for drills than teachers of other philosophic beliefs. He would select activities on the basis of scientific evidence of their worth from kinesiology, anatomy, and physiology. He, like the idealist, endeavors to teach master values and sportsmanlike conduct, but unlike the idealist and like the pragmatist, he believes that what is moral and good changes with the time, place, and circumstances.

He regards physical fitness as valuable for itself. He prefers objective grading plans, likes norms, and is apt to grade on the curve. He dislikes subjective grading because of his strong belief in the scientific method and the reality of nature. He will not hesitate to use external discipline. He, like the pragmatist, believes the student should be brought into contact with the real world through field trips, demonstrations, experiments, and audio-visual aids. The pragmatist utilizes these devices principally to elicit student interest. The realist does so to bring the student into contact with the real world.

DEVELOPING A PHILOSOPHIC POINT OF VIEW

An individual's philosophy is dependent upon many factors. These include his knowledge of human anatomy, biology and sociology, his political beliefs, his economic status, his religious beliefs, his preferences, and the influences upon him of his family and various social groups with which he has come into contact. Since his knowledge should be continually growing and since the forces exerted upon him are continually changing, it is inevitable that his philosophic beliefs will not be static but will, to some measure, be modified and amended as time goes on. However, they should be relatively consistent and constant. A reasonably stable philosophy is necessary if there is to be a consistency between the physical educator's selection of content, method, techniques, evaluative procedures, and relative emphases.

A knowledge of the anatomic and physiologic bases of physical activity is essential to the formation of a philosophy regarding physical education. This would include an understanding of variations in body type, the influence of activity upon the various systems of the body, physical characteristics of children and adults of both sexes at various ages and the influence of exercise upon their bodies, kinesiologic principles, limitations of physical activity, and contraindications for specific types of activity.

The physical educator needs a knowledge of social groups, how social groups are controlled and educated toward acceptable objectives, how social groups of various kinds influence personality and behavior, and how social needs are best satisfied.

Political factors influence one's philosophic beliefs. The way in which a man is governed and the way that the state regards him influence his way of acting and thinking, his relationships with others, and his standard of living. An educational philosophy must be reasonably consistent with the form of government where the educational philosophy is being practiced. Pragmatism would have experienced considerable difficulty in Nazi Germany. Early physical education programs in this country did not succeed because they were brought here in their entirety from European countries. They were designed to conform to the political ideology, economy, and sociological forces of the countries from where they came. They were not designed to conform to those of this country. Differences in the philosophic beliefs of the people of the two continents account for the fact that while these physical education systems succeeded in Continental Europe, they did not succeed in the United States.

Economic factors determine the amount of leisure and the amount of money a person has to spend for recreational equipment and facilities. They determine the quality and the quantity of his education which in turn determines his recreational and cultural interests. If a man is chronically fatigued from grubbing out a living, he will have little energy left to participate in vigorous sports. If he works twelve or more hours each day, he will have little time left to participate in any kind of leisure activities. If all of his income must be expended in providing shelter, clothing, food, and other basic necessities, he will have no money left for expenditures upon recreational or leisure activities. The industrial revolution, automation, and cybernation have had — and are now having — profound influences upon the recreational habits and interests of people.

It can be seen from the preceding that physical education is an interdisciplinary field. It draws its principles, content, and method from many different disciplines. To become a good physical educator, a person must study all the disciplines. To develop a philosophy concerning physical education, he must correlate, integrate, and synthesize his knowledge from these different disciplines to select aims, goals, principles, content, and method. This is a task which will be at once frustrating and challenging. But it is challenge which physical educators enjoy. They manifest this in their enjoyment of the challenge of sports competition. Acceptance of intellectual and academic challenges can be equally enjoyable.

SUMMARY

This chapter has necessarily presented a very brief but concise introduction to three major philosophies (idealism, pragmatism, and realism). The reader should realize that there are several subgroups under each of these major categories, that individual members of the subgroups will have some differences of opinion in some areas with other members of the same subgroup and that there are other philosophic schools such as existentialism, aristotelianism, and naturalism. The major objectives of this chapter have been to stimulate some interest in philosophy, to encourage the reader to engage in the philosophic process, and to illustrate how basic philosophic beliefs influence selection of content and methods used by physical educators. When the physical educator understands that basic philosophic beliefs do influence relative emphasis given various physical activities, methods of teaching and counseling, emphasis given order and conformity, methods of discipline, and other aspects of teaching, he is more likely to be tolerant of opinions of other physical educators whose views are divergent from his own. He will also be less likely to argue emotionally and more likely to probe more deeply toward basic beliefs.

Taking the time to look at things from another person's philosophic base can be a very refreshing and enlightening experience. All of us should endeavor to see things from the other person's point of view. To do this we have to know what his points of view (philosophic beliefs) are.

We have presented the views of some Early Greek and of a few fairly recent philosophers regarding the nature of the universe, man's place in the universe, how they decide what is good and what is evil, the nature of God, the soul and immortality, man's relationship to the state, the function of education, and the relationship between mind and matter. Then we have shown the implications of these beliefs for physical education. We have shown that these different beliefs are likely to cause differences in relative emphasis given different activities, attitudes toward intercollegiate and interscholastic athletics, relationships with students, counseling procedures, attitudes toward the importance of physical fitness, methods of maintaining discipline, attitudes toward system and order, degree of reliance upon the scientific method, amount of reading assignments and lectures, amount of student participation in planning and selection of content, and grading procedures.

Finally, the reader was invited to develop his own philosophic stance. It was pointed out that knowledge gained from many disciplines (psychology, sociology, physiology, political science) would help one in developing a philosophy. It was also pointed out that religious and political beliefs, influences by one's family and friends, the form of government of his country, and his economic status all are related to and influence his philosophic beliefs.

QUESTIONS

1. Define (1) ethics, (2) metaphysics, (3) politics, (4) esthetics, (5) logic, (6) epistemology, and (7) philosophy.

2. What are the differences and similarities between science and philosophy?

3. Why is a physical educator who holds a relatively consistent and well thought out philosophy likely to do a better job than one who does not?

4. Compare and contrast the eight basic beliefs of idealism, pragmatism, and realism.

5. Compare and contrast the implications for physical education of idealism, pragmatism, and realism.

6. Write a 1000–2000 word statement of your own basic philosophic beliefs covering each of the eight areas (nature of the universe, man's place in the universe, etc.).

7. Write a 500–1000 word statement of the implications of your philosophic position for the conduct of physical education and/or athletic programs.

8. What is the relationship between philosophy, general objectives, specific objectives, principles, content, and teaching methods?

9. Which of the three philosophies discussed do you prefer? Why?

10. What do you believe should be the relationships between the individual and social groups? To what extent should the individual conform to the patterns of behavior of the group of which he is a member? What does the individual gain from being a member of social groups (the university, the city, state, nation, world)? How much freedom should an individual be permitted?

11. Debate the merits of the three philosophic schools discussed here.

12. What is authority? What are the restrictions and the responsibilities of leadership? From where does authority come?

13. What is the difference in the relationships between the individual and the state in democratic and communist countries?

14. To what extent, if any, should the schools endeavor to change society?

BIBLIOGRAPHY

1. Berlin, Isaiah, *The Age of Enlightenment.* Boston: Houghton Mifflin Company, 1956.

2. Davis, Craig Elwood, Ph.D., *Philosophies Fashion Physical Education.* Dubuque, Iowa: Wm. C. Brown Company, 1963.

3. Frost, S. E., Jr., Ph.D., *Basic Teachings of the Great Philosophers.* New York: Barnes and Noble, Inc., 1955.

4. Nash, Jay B., *Philosophy of Recreation and Leisure.* Dubuque, Iowa: Wm. C. Brown Company, 1953.

5. National Society for the Study of Education, *Modern Philosophies and Education.* Chicago: University of Chicago Press, 1955.

6. Van Dalen, D. B., "Philosophical Profiles for Physical Educators," *The Physical Educator*, October, 1964.

7. Zeigler, Earle F., "Philosophical Foundations and Educational Leadership," *The Physical Educator*, March, 1963.

8. Zeigler, Earle F., "The Implications of Experimentalism for Physical Education, Health, and Recreation Education," *The Physical Educator*, December, 1963.

9. Webster, Randolph W., *Philosophy of Physical Education*. Dubuque, Iowa: Wm. C. Brown Company, 1965.

Part IV

THE SCIENTIFIC
BASES OF
PHYSICAL
EDUCATION

12

The Physiologic and Anatomic Bases of Physical Education

IN THIS CHAPTER, we will introduce the reader to some of the physiologic and anatomic bases of physical education in order to help him better understand the nature and role of both the physical educator and physical education. He will review these facts and learn many more in courses such as physiology, anatomy, physiology of exercise, kinesiology, first aid, and athletic training.

THE UNITY OF MAN

In studies of and research about man it is usually necessary to compartmentalize and dicotomize. However, we should never do so in our teaching or coaching. The living human organism is not simply a collection of bones, muscles, blood vessels, nerves, brain, skin, and hair. It is the relationships and interdependence between the various parts of the organism which make it a living organism. When teaching adults and children, one must always take into consideration the milieu in which this living organism operates — its environment, both animate and inanimate. As the Gestalt psychologists say: "The whole is greater than and different from the sum of its parts."

If a watch is taken completely apart and the parts are laid on a table, we no longer have a watch. It is not only the parts but, more importantly, their interrelationships which enable the watch to perform. In studies of the

235

human, for the sake of order, convenience, and ease in understanding, knowledge is traditionally compartmentalized into separate areas such as biology, psychology, and sociology. While it is necessary to compartmentalize for purposes of study, this should never be done when teaching children. Children cannot be compartmentalized. We teach the whole child. When a child is taught how to do the cartwheel he also develops attitudes about his own body, toward his peers, and about physical fitness. He may also be learning basic principles of physics or kinesiology, conservation of equipment, healthful living, and social behavior. No matter what his subject area, a teacher can never deal exclusively with a student's mind or exclusively with his body. Some activities may be predominantly mental but always all aspects of a person's being are involved.

S. H. Bartley and Eloise Chute[1] made a comprehensive study of fatigue and impairment in man. They concluded that most fatigue which man experiences is not true physiologic fatigue but is psychologic in its origin and is caused principally by boredom. Every student has felt fatigue after hours of study and then has experienced the sudden disappearance of this feeling when a friend suggested doing something interesting such as bowling or dancing. For many people, what is needed to relieve the feeling of fatigue is not to lie or sit watching a dull television program but to do something which is interesting and challenging. These people need a consuming hobby or physical activity.

Dr. Stewart Wolf[2] conducted experiments in which peripheral resistance in the blood vessels decreased and output of the heart (stroke volume and heart rate) increased when the subject was told she was to exercise — even though she did no exercise. Peripheral resistance increased and stroke volume and pulse rate decreased when she was told that she would not exercise. The heart muscle and the muscles in the blood vessels, which are supposed to be involuntary muscles and therefore not subject to the will, did, in fact, respond to a mental stimulus. Apparently the involuntary systems are not as involuntary as had heretofore been supposed!

In another experiment, Dr. Wolf recorded elevation in blood pressure, increase in stroke volume and a fall in resistance to blood flow when a patient was engaged in a discussion of his problems and conflicts. However, this phenomenon did not occur when the patient was engaged in a pleasant discussion. In still another study, serum cholesterol (a mineral-like substance in the blood which contributes to hardening of the arteries and thereby to cerebral hemorrhage or to heart failure) was noted to fall during friendly, encouraging, and pleasant discussions but to rise significantly when personal conflicts were discussed.

The three studies cited illustrate the close relationship between the mind, the emotions, and physiologic processes.

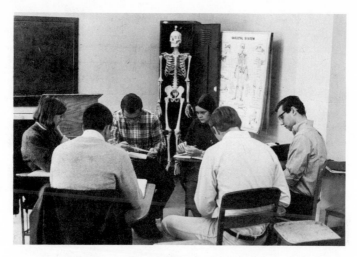

A buzz session in anatomy *(Courtesy: University of Connecticut)*

ADAPTABILITY OF MAN

All living things either adapt to stresses to which they are subjected or die. Animals adapt better than plants and of all the animals, man, principally because of his intelligence, can adapt most effectively. Man is found living in Alaska where temperatures have dropped to seventy degrees below zero and at the equator where temperatures soar to one hundred and ten degrees above zero. He has survived the arid climate of the Sahara Desert and the stifling humidity of the jungles of Africa. He lives at an altitude of 9000 feet above sea level in Mexico City and at or below sea level in Salt Lake City or next to the Dead Sea. He subsists on diets which vary greatly in content and in quantity. However, when the particular stress is great enough, man will die. He has frozen to death. He has died as a result of dehydration, as a result of eating poisonous plants, and as a result of malnutrition. Man's adaptive powers, when the stress does not come upon him too suddenly, are truly amazing.

Man adapts to the stress of most contagious diseases by developing immunity to them. If he had been brought up in a completely sterile environment, he would contract a multiplicity of diseases as soon as he was brought out of this sterile environment because he would not have had an opportunity to develop immunity – that is, he would not have adapted.

Man adapts to the stress called *physical activity* by increases in the elasticity of his blood vessels, the hemoglobin in his blood, the size of the alveoli of his lungs, the efficiency of his glandular system, the size and

Gas analysis in a physiology of
exercise class *(Courtesy:
University of Connecticut)*

strength of his muscle fibers, the elasticity of his tendons, and by developing a more muscular heart. These changes are brought about most effectively by increasing the dosage of physical activity progressively. To achieve maximal adaptation (conditioning) of the body as quickly as possible, the dosage of physical activity each day must be adequate to produce thorough fatigue. The absolute limits of human strength, power, speed, and endurance are still unknown. In each successive Olympic Games new records are established in many sports. This adaptability is illustrated by the following Olympic records.[3] (The first date after each event is the date of the first Olympics in which the event was contested.)

SWIMMING (MEN):

100 meter	*800 meter relay*
1896 – 1:22.2	1908 – 10:55.6
1968 – 52.2	1964 – 7:52.1
400 meter	*100 meter backstroke*
1904 – 6:16.2	1904 – 1:16.8
1968 – 4:09.0	1968 – 58.7
200 meter breastroke	*1500 meter*
1908 – 3:09.2	1908 – 22:48.4
1968 – 2:28.7	1968 – 16:38.9

SWIMMING (WOMEN):

100 meter

1912 – 1:22.2
1968 – 1:00.0

400 meter

1924 – 6:02.2
1968 – 4:31.8

200 meter backstroke

1924 – 3:33.2
1968 – 2:24.8

100 meter backstroke

1924 – 1:23.2
1968 – 1:06.2

400 meter relay

1912 – 5:52.8
1968 – 4:02.5

TRACK AND FIELD (MEN):

100 meter

1896 – 12.0
1968 – 9.9

400 meter hurdles

1900 – 57.6
1968 – 48.1

400 meter

1896 – 54.2
1968 – 43.8

800 meter

1896 – 2:11
1968 → 1:44.3

1500 meter

1896 – 4:33.2
1968 – 3:34.9

400 meter relay

1912 – 42.4
1968 – 38.2

1600 meter relay

1908 – 3:27.2
1968 – 2:56.1

500 meter

1912 – 14:36.6
1960 – 13:43.4

110 meter hurdles

1896 – 17.6
1968 – 13.3

Running Broad Jump (Long Jump)

1896 – 20 ft. 9-3/4 in.
1968 – 29 ft. 2-1/2 in.

Pole Vault

1896 – 10 ft. 9-3/4 in.
1968 – 17 ft. 8-1/2 in.

Running Hop Step and Jump (Triple Jump)

1896 – 45 ft.
1968 – 57 ft. 3/4 in.

Running High Jump

1896 – 5 ft. 11-1/4 in.
1968 – 7 ft. 4-1/4 in.

16 lb. Shot Put

1896 – 36 ft. 2 in.
1968 – 67 ft. 4-3/4 in.

Discus Throw

1896 – 95 ft. 7-1/2 in.
1968 – 212 ft. 6-1/2 in.

16 lb. Hammer Throw

1900 – 167 ft. 4 in.
1968 – 240 ft. 8 in.

TRACK AND FIELD (MEN) *(Cont.)*:

10,000 meter

1912 – 31:20.8
1964 – 28:24.4

Javelin Throw

1906 – 175 ft. 6 in.
1968 – 295 ft. 7-1/4 in.

TRACK AND FIELD (WOMEN):

100 meter

1928 – 12.2
1960 – 11.0

200 meter

1948 – 24.4
1968 – 22.5

80 meter hurdles

1932 – 11.7
1968 – 10.3

Shot Put

1948 – 45 ft. 1-1/2 in.
1968 – 64 ft. 4 in.

400 meter relay

1928 – 48.4
1968 – 42.8

Discuss Throw

1928 – 129 ft. 11-7/8 in.
1968 – 191 ft. 2-1/2 in.

Running Broad Jump (Long Jump)

1948 – 18 ft. 8-1/2 in.
1968 – 22 ft. 4-1/2 in.

Javelin Throw

1932 – 143 ft. 4 in.
1968 – 198 ft. 1/2 in.

Running High Jump

1928 – 5 ft. 3 in.
1960 – 6 ft. 3/4 in.

WEIGHT LIFTING:

Bantamweight

1948 – 677 1/2 lbs.
1968 – 808.5 lbs.

Middleweight

1920 – 540.12 lbs.
1968 – 1045 lbs.

Featherweight

1920 – 484 lbs.
1968 – 863.5 lbs.

Light Heavyweight

1920 – 639.334 lbs.
1968 – 1067 lbs.

Lightweight

1920 – 567.68
1968 – 962.5 lbs.

Heavyweight

1920 – 595.24 lbs.
1968 – 1259.5 lbs.

In most events performances in the 1968 Olympic Games exceeded those of the 1964 Games in spite of the predictions of many exercise physiologists that performances would not be as good due to the high altitude and consequent oxygen deprivation. The competitors improved upon previous performances principally because they *trained harder* and consequently *adapted* more fully to the stress of physical activity at altitude.

The improvements in performance pointed out above were made possible by improvements in many areas — techniques of performance, equipment and facilities, motivation, nutrition, coaching, and conditioning. However, it is likely that improved conditioning methods played a most important role. The distance our competitive swimmers cover in daily practice is at the present time two or three times as great as the swimmers covered in the 1940's. The same is true in track.

THE SKELETAL SYSTEM AND EFFECTS OF ACTIVITY UPON IT

The principal function of the skeletal system is to serve as the foundation or base of support for the human body. However, it also performs other necessary functions such as: (1) providing attachments for the tendons of muscles in order that they be enabled to move the body; (2) providing protection for vital but vulnerable organs such as the lungs and heart, the spinal cord, the brain, the eyes and ears, and the reproductive, urinary, and digestive systems; (3) manufacturing of blood cells; and (4) serving as a storeroom for calcium.

No engineer has designed a framework for a machine which can match that of the human body. Although bone consists largely of inorganic material (inorganic salts which are complex compounds of calcium and phosphorus), it can grow, develop, and repair itself. Furthermore, it is adaptable to environmental influences. It will atrophy when not used and hypertrophy as a result of increased use. For example, if a child is stricken by poliomyelitis and the innervation to one leg is lost, the affected leg will not grow apace with the unaffected leg and the bones of the leg will be shorter and thinner even though the virus has no direct effect upon bone, circulation, or muscle tissue. When teeth are lost, the alveolar process which supports the teeth will be absorbed. Steen and Montagu[4] point out two circumstances under which bone will hypertrophy: "habitual squatting with feet crossed produces 'squatters' facets' on the external malleoli of the tibia." They also indicate that when babies are habitually placed with the back of the head on a hard bed they usually develop a flat occiput. These are all manifestations of the body's adaptation to environmental forces.

The joints of the body permit a great variety of movements and the movements permitted at each joint are wonderfully adapted to the movement needs of the body. At the knee, movement is restricted laterally and anteriorly but there is full range of movement posteriorly. This makes walking, running, and leaping more efficient since flexion posteriorly only is needed while stability is needed anteriorly and laterally. The human thumb has a tremendous range of movement. Some anatomists and anthropologists believe that the great range in movement of man's thumb made possible the development and use of tools and thereby stimulated use of his brain. They believe that if he had not possessed this skeletal feature, he may have remained at the level of the apes and monkeys.

The skeleton provides pulleys (sesamoid bones such as the kneecap or patella, processes, trochanters, trochleas, and tubercles) over which muscle tendons pass before attaching to the bone. These enable the muscles to secure better leverage to move the body parts. Articular surfaces (where bone ends move over one another in joints) are smooth and are lubricated by synovial fluid retained and secreted by the synovial membrane which surrounds the joint. Tough but compressible, flexible, elastic cartilage is found between the articular surfaces of bones to cushion impacts and jars. The neck of the femur placed at an angle to the shaft of the femur, the longitudinal and transverse arch of the foot, and the cervical, thoracic, and lumbar curves of the vertibral column all act as efficient shock absorbers. These shock absorbers absorb the impact when a gymnast dismounts from the apparatus, when a broad jumper lands, and when a sprinter runs. Without these shock absorbers the jar would be intolerable and might shatter bones or damage the brain.

The vertebral column permits flexion, extension, hyperextension (arching of the back), lateral flexion, and rotation (twisting) and yet can support tremendous weight. Weight lifters clean and jerk 500 pounds to arms' length overhead. Understanders in balancing acts support four or more men on their shoulders. Professional strong men have lifted elephants. The vertebral column is truly an amazing piece of engineering. It permits a large variety of movements, many of which require exacting precision. Yet it has tremendous strength. This is made possible principally by the transverse and spinous processes of the vertebrae to which are attached a multitude of muscles and ligaments. When the muscles of the back become weak and atrophy as a result of continual sitting and little exercise, they can no longer provide the protection and stability to the vertebral column that they were designed to do. The result is that this responsibility then falls upon the ligaments. When the person with atrophied back muscles performs a quick movement or lifts a heavier weight than he is accustomed to, there is danger that he will tear ligaments, "subluxate" (move out of proper alignment) one of the vertebrae (usually a lumbar vertebrae), or "subluxate" his sacroiliac joint. These are painful injuries, are slow in healing, and can hospitalize a person for months. Strong back muscles will help to prevent these injuries.

In the same manner and for the same reason, the bones of the ankle or knee joint will be moved out of alignment momentarily with a sprain or a torn cartilage resulting when these joints are subjected to an unaccustomed

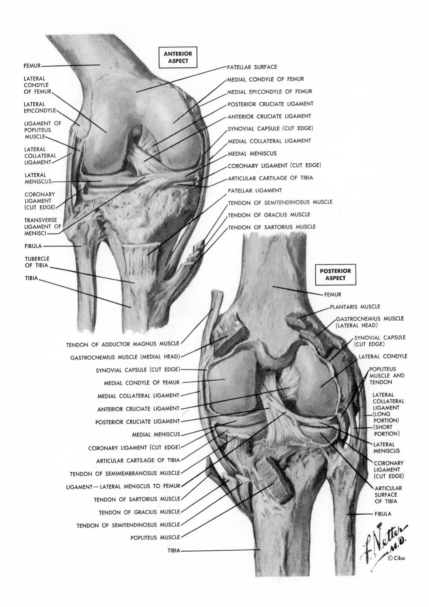

ANTERIOR ASPECT

FEMUR
LATERAL CONDYLE OF FEMUR
LATERAL EPICONDYLE
LIGAMENT OF POPLITEUS MUSCLE
LATERAL COLLATERAL LIGAMENT
LATERAL MENISCUS
CORONARY LIGAMENT (CUT EDGE)
TRANSVERSE LIGAMENT OF MENISCI
FIBULA
TUBERCLE OF TIBIA
TIBIA

PATELLAR SURFACE
MEDIAL CONDYLE OF FEMUR
MEDIAL EPICONDYLE OF FEMUR
POSTERIOR CRUCIATE LIGAMENT
ANTERIOR CRUCIATE LIGAMENT
SYNOVIAL CAPSULE (CUT EDGE)
MEDIAL COLLATERAL LIGAMENT
MEDIAL MENISCUS
CORONARY LIGAMENT (CUT EDGE)
ARTICULAR CARTILAGE OF TIBIA
PATELLAR LIGAMENT
TENDON OF SEMITENDINOSUS MUSCLE
TENDON OF GRACILIS MUSCLE
TENDON OF SARTORIUS MUSCLE

POSTERIOR ASPECT

FEMUR
PLANTARIS MUSCLE
GASTROCNEMIUS MUSCLE (LATERAL HEAD)
SYNOVIAL CAPSULE (CUT EDGE)
LATERAL CONDYLE
POPLITEUS MUSCLE AND TENDON
LATERAL COLLATERAL LIGAMENT (LONG PORTION) (SHORT PORTION)
LATERAL MENISCUS
CORONARY LIGAMENT (CUT EDGE)
ARTICULAR SURFACE OF TIBIA
FIBULA

TENDON OF ADDUCTOR MAGNUS MUSCLE
GASTROCNEMIUS MUSCLE (MEDIAL HEAD)
SYNOVIAL CAPSULE (CUT EDGE)
MEDIAL CONDYLE OF FEMUR
MEDIAL COLLATERAL LIGAMENT
ANTERIOR CRUCIATE LIGAMENT
POSTERIOR CRUCIATE LIGAMENT
MEDIAL MENISCUS
CORONARY LIGAMENT (CUT EDGE)
ARTICULAR CARTILAGE OF TIBIA
TENDON OF SEMIMEMBRANOSUS MUSCLE
LIGAMENT—LATERAL MENISCUS TO FEMUR
TENDON OF SARTORIUS MUSCLE
TENDON OF GRACILIS MUSCLE
TENDON OF SEMITENDINOSUS MUSCLE
POPLITEUS MUSCLE
TIBIA

F. Netter M.D.
© Ciba

Anatomy of the knee joint *(Copyright CIBA Clinical Symposia, published by CIBA Pharmaceutical Company, Summit, N.J.)*

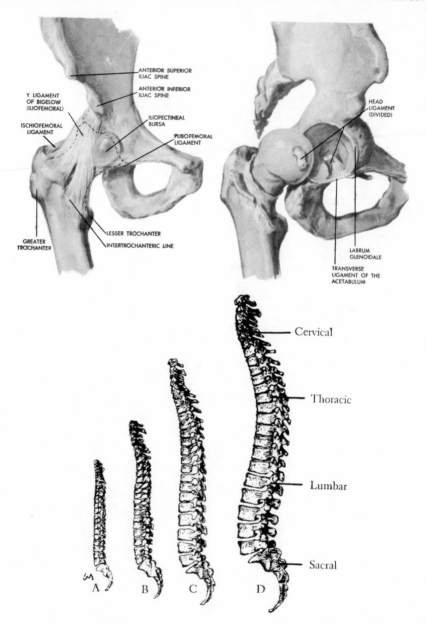

Top: The hip joint *(Copyright CIBA Clinical Symposia, published by CIBA Pharmaceutical Company, Summit, N.J.).* **Bottom: Vertebral column of A) new-born child; B) three-year-old child; C) ten-year-old child; D) adult** *(from Franz Frohse, Max Brödel, and Leon Schlossberg,* Atlas of Human Anatomy, *Fifth Ed.,* Barnes and Noble, Inc., *New York, 1959, p. 24)*

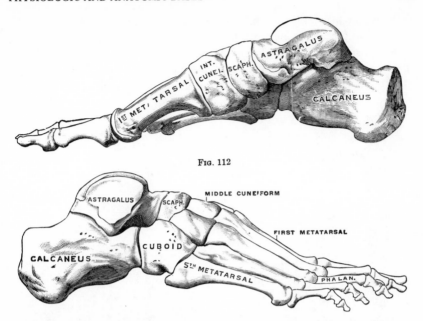

Fig. 112

Bones of the foot (Gray) *(from Wilbur P. Bowen,* Applied Anatomy and Kinesiology, *Fifth Ed., Revised, Lea and Febiger, Philadelphia, 1948, p. 192)*

force. When the muscles which flex and extend the knee joint are made stronger, they lend greater stability to this joint and decrease the probability of suffering a sprained knee (torn collateral ligaments) or a torn cartilage. When the muscles whose tendons pass over the ankle joint are made stronger, greater stability will be afforded the joint thereby making a sprained ankle less likely.

In contact sports, football in particular, the incidence of sprained ankles and knees and of torn semilunar cartilages of the knee joint is greatest in the early part of the season when muscular condition is still poor. The incidence of these injuries decreases as the season progresses even though the game is played harder. The reason for this is improved muscular condition.

The Skull and Concussion

The bones provide protection to a number of vital organs. The thirty-one bones of the skull include eight bones of the cranium, fourteen facial bones, two nasal bones, the hyoid, and the six ear ossicles. These bones serve to protect the organs of vision, hearing, smell, and taste as well as the brain. At birth, the cranial bones are separated by membrane-covered spaces to allow some compression of the skull during delivery. These soft spots, called fontanels, later disappear as the membranes turn into bone. While the hard, inflexible cranial bones of the adult provide protection for the brain, this feature also presents a problem. In the case of a rupture of a cerebral blood vessel, as in concussion and cerebral hemorrhage or stroke, blood fills the space between the brain and the cranial bones causing pressure on the brain. This results in loss of consciousness and damage to the brain.

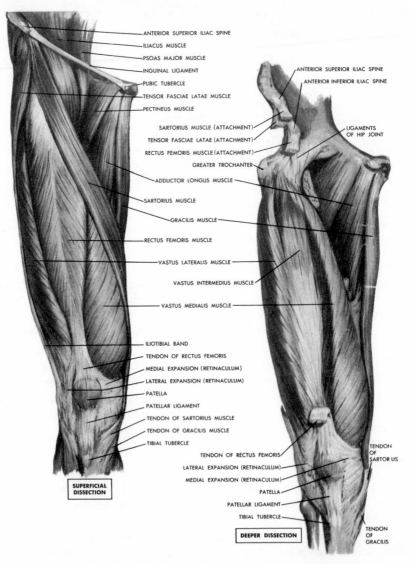

Muscles of the anterior aspect of the thigh, from: Disorders of the Knee *(Copyright CIBA Clinical Symposia, published by CIBA Pharmaceutical Company, Summit, N.J.)*

Whenever an athlete suffers a concussion (and any loss of consciousness, regardless of how brief, is regarded as a concussion), scar tissue is formed on the brain where the torn blood vessel nourishing that part of the brain healed. This damage is cumulative and for all practical purposes irreversible. The part

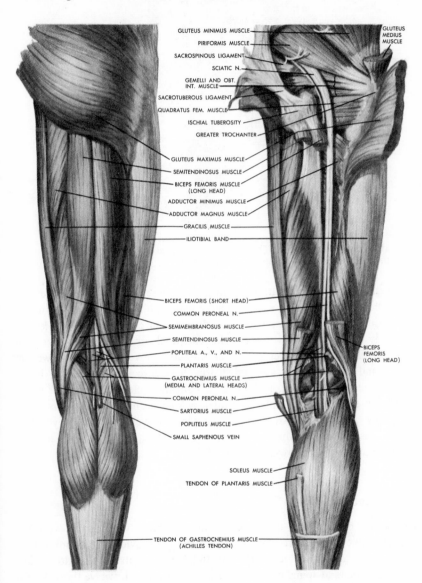

Muscles of the posterior aspect of the thigh, from: Disorders of the Knee *(Copyright CIBA Clinical Symposia, published by CIBA Pharmaceutical Company, Summit, N.J.)*

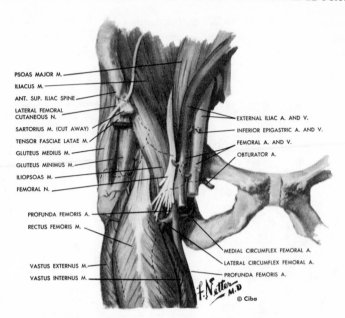

PSOAS MAJOR M.
ILIACUS M.
ANT. SUP. ILIAC SPINE
LATERAL FEMORAL CUTANEOUS N.
SARTORIUS M. (CUT AWAY)
TENSOR FASCIAE LATAE M.
GLUTEUS MEDIUS M.
GLUTEUS MINIMUS M.
ILIOPSOAS M.
FEMORAL N.
PROFUNDA FEMORIS A.
RECTUS FEMORIS M.
VASTUS EXTERNUS M.
VASTUS INTERNUS M.

EXTERNAL ILIAC A. AND V.
INFERIOR EPIGASTRIC A. AND V.
FEMORAL A. AND V.
OBTURATOR A.
MEDIAL CIRCUMFLEX FEMORAL A.
LATERAL CIRCUMFLEX FEMORAL A.
PROFUNDA FEMORIS A.

© Ciba

Muscles of the hip joint *(Copyright CIBA Clinical Symposia, published by CIBA Pharmaceutical Company, Summit, N.J.)*

of the brain with scar tissue loses its functional efficiency. Each successive concussion occurs more easily. The person who has had a history of concussions shows, to a more or less degree, the classic symptoms known popularly as "punch drunk" — the slurred speech, shuffling walk, dazed and stupid look, and sometimes poorly coordinated movements. This is why all but a handful of colleges and universities have discontinued boxing in the intercollegiate, intramural, and physical education class programs. It is also the reason any coach who plays a student who has a history of concussions is displaying a criminal disregard for the player's welfare. Any player who knows these facts and who continues to play after he has suffered a series of concussions can only be regarded as foolish.

The Vertebral Column

The spinal cord passes downward from the brain through the vertebral foramen (hole) of the vertebrae. This construction provides protection for the highly vulnerable spinal cord for the full length of its passage downward. Thirty-one pairs of spinal nerves, including eight cervical, twelve thoracic, five lumbar, five sacral, and one coccygeal, emanate from the spinal cord and pass through openings between the vertebrae.

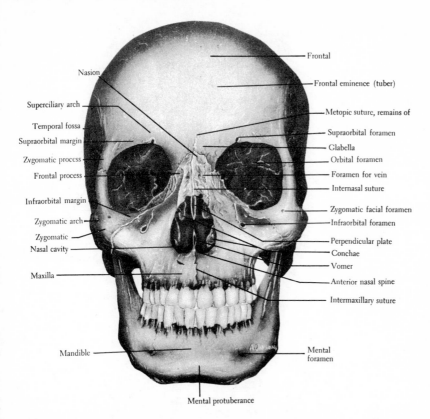

Nasion

Superciliary arch

Temporal fossa

Supraorbital margin

Zygomatic process

Frontal process

Infraorbital margin

Zygomatic arch

Zygomatic

Nasal cavity

Maxilla

Mandible

Frontal

Frontal eminence (tuber)

Metopic suture, remains of

Supraorbital foramen

Glabella

Orbital foramen

Foramen for vein

Internasal suture

Zygomatic facial foramen

Infraorbital foramen

Perpendicular plate

Conchae

Vomer

Anterior nasal spine

Intermaxillary suture

Mental foramen

Mental protuberance

Anterior view of skull *(from Edwin B. Steen and Ashley Montagu,* Anatomy and Physiology, *Vol. 2, Barnes and Noble, Inc., New York, 1959, p. 54)*

Back Injuries

In injuries where there is suspicion of a spinal injury, the patient should not be moved unless it is absolutely necessary and then only on a fairly rigid stretcher. The reason for this is that the sharp, jagged edges of the fractured vertebrae may sever the spinal cord or nerves leading from it and thereby cause paralysis.

When the muscles of the back are not strong enough to hold the vertebrae in proper alignment when a heavy weight is lifted or a vigorous movement is executed (particularly when there is a twisting of the spine) the displaced vertebrae may impinge (pinch) a nerve which passes between the vertebrae. This produces pain, restriction of movement, and may cause temporary paralysis. Sometimes the sensation of pain is felt at a site other than that of the injury. This is known as "referred pain." Because so many people today

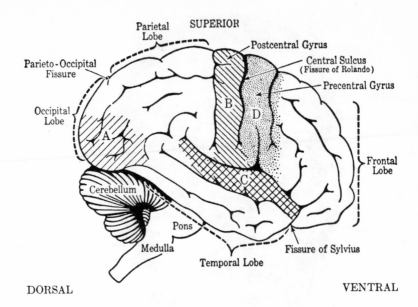

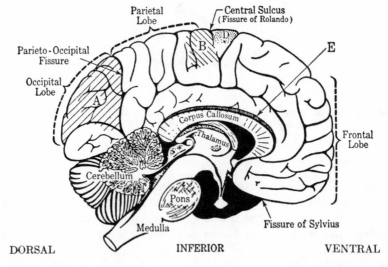

Top: Right cerebral hemisphere. Lateral view, showing important fissures, lobes, and projection centers of cortex, medulla and pons, and cerebellum. The dotted area (D) represents roughly the origin of main efferent tracts conducting impulses from the cortex to lower co-ordination centers; cross-hatched areas (A, B, and C) represent projection areas for vision, somesthesis, and audition, respectively. Bottom: Left cerebral hemisphere. Mesial view, showing thalamus, corpus callosum, and part of the projection area for olfaction and gustation (E) *(from Franz Frohse, Max Brödel, and Leon Schlossberg,* Atlas of Human Anatomy, *Fifth Ed., Barnes and Noble, Inc., New York, 1959, pp. 52 and 53)*

do little physical work and because so few indulge in vigorous physical activity, back injuries have increased in frequency during recent years. People sit at their desks all day, they sit while traveling from place to place, and they sit in the evening while being entertained. Then on a week-end they may engage in water skiing, skating, skiing, heavy yard work, or other equally vigorous activities. It is not surprising that the atrophied back muscles are not able to hold the vertebrae in alignment and that the vertebrae or the sacroiliac is displaced.

The Thorax

Twelve pairs of ribs attach on the posterior side to the thoracic vertebrae. The seven superior ribs (true or vertebrosternal ribs) attach on the anterior side directly to the sternum or breastbone by means of the costal cartilage. The next three lower pairs of ribs, the false or vertebrochandral ribs, are attached by costal cartilage to the cartilage above them. The two lowest pairs of ribs (11th and 12th pairs), or "floating" ribs, are not attached on their anterior ends. The heart lies not on the left side of the thorax, as commonly supposed, but in the center directly behind the sternum − being slightly tilted so that its upper part or apex projects slightly to the left of the sternum while the point projects slightly to the right. Here the heart muscle receives the greatest protection.

The ribs angle slightly downward from back to front on expiration. On inspiration, they assume almost a horizontal position being elevated by the intercostal (between ribs) muscles and the pectoral muscles of the upper thorax. When the ribs move to the horizontal position, the volume of the intrathoracic cavity is increased creating a partial vacuum in the lungs. Nature abhors a vacuum. Air moves in through the nose or mouth, down the trachea, and then into the two bronchi which branch off to the two lungs and which further divide into two bronchi in the left lung and three in the right lung. If it were not for the ribs and the relative firmness which they provide, it would be impossible to create a vacuum in the intrathoracic cavity since atmospheric pressure would cause soft tissue to collapse.

The Pelvic Girdle

The pelvic girdle protects the reproductive and urinary systems and a portion of the large intestine. It provides a base of support for all the vital organs. It also provides attachments for the largest muscles in the body and connects the bones of the legs to the vertebral column. All four of the abdominal muscles (external oblique, internal oblique, abdominus transversus, and abdominus rectus) attach on one end to the ribs or the zyphoid process of the

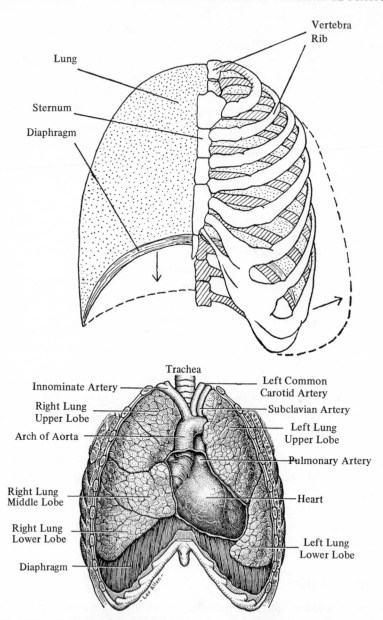

Top: The ribs, lungs, and diaphragm in their resting or expiratory positions; the dotted lines indicate the extent of movement of the ribs and diaphragm during inspiration and, consequently, the increase in capacity of the thoracic cavity *(from* Fundamentals of Physiology *(p. 90) by Elbert Tokay; Copyright 1944 by Doubleday & Company, Inc.; reprinted by permission of the publisher).* **Bottom: Organs of the thoracic cavity** *(from Zoethout and Tuttle,* Textbook of Physiology, *ed. 10, St. Louis, 1949, The C. V. Mosby Company)*

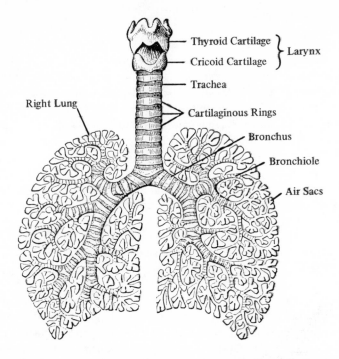

Respiratory tract (After Dalton) *(from Zoethout and Tuttle,* Textbook of Physiology, *ed. 10, St. Louis, 1949, The C. V. Mosby Company)*

sternum and at the other end to the bones of the pelvic girdle. When these muscles become weak as a result of lack of use, there are two principal undesirable effects. Both occur as a result of increased inclination or forward tilt of the pelvis (pubis moves downward and posterior surface of sacrum moves upward). When the abdominal muscles become weak they are stretched and are overpowered by the psoas and iliacus muscles and the muscles of the lower back. The result is an increased lumbar curve with probable low back pain. As a consequence of the tilting of the pelvis, the abdominal viscera are spilled forward creating considerable pressure against the inner surface of the abdominal wall thereby stretching the abdominal muscles still further. In addition, the vital capacity of the lungs is decreased as is the blood supply to the abdomen because of crowding of the sagging organs. Thus a vicious circle is set in motion. It is much easier to prevent this situation from occurring by maintaining a strong abdominal wall than it is to correct it after the condition has developed. The abdominal muscles perform other useful functions such as stabilizing the pelvic girdle or the thorax in different movements and aiding in expiration during strenuous activity,and during defecation, sneezing, or coughing.

Formation of Erythrocytes

It is in the red bone marrow, principally in the vertebrae, ribs, sternum, cranial bones, and the proximal ends of the humerus and femur, that the *erythrocytes* or red blood cells are formed by a process called *erythropoieses*. Red cells arise from stem cells called *proerythroblasts* which possess a nucleus but lack hemoglobin. Through mitosis these red cells become *erythroblasts* which acquire an increasing amount of hemoglobin until they become *normoblasts*. Degenerative changes cause the normoblasts to lose their nuclei at which time they become young erythrocytes which, when mature, enter the blood stream as erythrocytes.

There is an average of 35 billion red blood cells, or erythrocytes, in each person. The total number varies with age, time of day, altitude, and amount of physical activity. The number increases from birth to adulthood, is higher during activity than during sleep, is higher in people living at high altitudes than in people living at lower altitudes, and increases as people ascend to higher altitudes, during and after exercise, and with increases in environmental temperature.

The most important constituent of the red blood cells is hemoglobin. Hemoglobin unites readily with oxygen. As blood travels through the thin-walled capillaries in the alveoli of the lungs, oxygen is attracted to the hemoglobin of the erythrocytes in the blood, attaches to it, and is carried to the body cells where it is released. Carbon dioxide is then released from the cells and carried by the erythrocytes to the lungs where it is released and expelled. Athletes have a higher red blood count than do nonathletes. This enables them to transport more oxygen to the cells. Participation in vigorous physical activities will increase the red blood count and thereby the oxygen-carrying ability of the blood.

Inhalation of carbon monoxide gas is dangerous to life because this gas combines with hemoglobin 250 times more readily than does oxygen. Consequently, death can result in a few minutes since the blood is unable to transport oxygen to the cells. The cells of the brain are the first to be damaged.

THE MUSCULAR SYSTEM AND
THE EFFECTS OF MUSCULAR ACTIVITY

There are 656 skeletal muscles in the human body. They make up forty-two percent of the total weight in the male and thirty-six per cent in the female. Without muscles man would be unable to react to or act upon his environment. He would, in effect, be little more than a vegetable. Use and development of the muscular system has beneficial effects upon many other systems of the body. These will be pointed out in the following pages.

Influence of Muscular Activity upon Venous Return

Alternately contracting and relaxing muscles aid in the venous return of blood to the heart as a result of their "milking" action upon the veins. The heart pumps blood through the aorta and on into the arterial system with its branches to all parts of the body. From the branches the blood moves into the small arterioles, thence through the miles of tiny capillaries, to the larger venules, and then to even larger veins until it ultimately returns to the heart to be pumped to the lungs for oxygenation. By the time the blood has passed through the miles of tiny capillaries, it has lost most of the force which was provided by the pulsating heart. To enable the veins to carry blood back to the heart more effectively, they have been provided with valves which permit blood to flow toward the heart but prevent its flow away from the heart. When a muscle contracts, the circumference of the belly of the muscle increases and consequently presses the vein against adjacent bone or tissue. The vein is flattened and the blood is pushed toward the heart (since the valves prevent its flow away from the heart). In this way, physical activity aids in the venous return of blood.

This phenomenon explains why sitting or standing in one position for a long time can be so fatiguing and why activity can provide relief. A few

A personal health class *(Courtesy: University of Connecticut)*

soldiers during World War II, who disliked standing during lengthy reviews and parades, used the phenomenon to escape these reviews. By standing with the knees fully extended and without moving, they impeded the return flow of blood and fainted. They were then carried off the drill field on a stretcher to the dispensary and to the care of an attractive nurse. This was a foolish and dangerous practice and is not recommended by physicians.

Influence of Muscular Activity upon the Heart Rate and Volume

Muscular work produces lactic acid and carbon dioxide which must be carried away from the cells. Muscular work also creates a need for oxygen and nutrients. Carbon dioxide, lactic acid, oxygen and nutrients are all transported by the blood. During muscular activity, stress is placed upon the heart muscle since it must pump more rapidly to circulate a greater volume of blood per minute. The heart adapts to this stress by becoming stronger so that with each beat it contracts more forcefully and consequently sends out a greater volume of blood. One ultimate result of regular, vigorous muscular work is that the resting pulse (or heart) rate becomes considerably slower enabling the heart to rest for a greater proportion of the time. Seventy-two beats per minute is the average heart rate. Well-conditioned endurance athletes have heart rates as low as forty beats per minute. Their heart rates can accelerate to as high a rate as can those of nonathletes. However, athletes must do considerably more muscular work before their heart is sufficiently taxed to accelerate to this level. A nonathlete's heart rate may go to 120 beats per minute after running a mile in ten minutes. The athlete may have to run two miles at that speed or the mile in four and a half minutes to stress his heart sufficiently to accelerate the rate to 120 beats per minute.

Influence of Muscular Activity upon the Capillary Bed

Regular muscular work of progressively increasing dosages increases the capillary bed in the exercised area so that a greater volume of blood per minute can pass through the area. This makes possible more rapid removal of fatigue products and carbon dioxide from the muscle cells and more rapid transportation of oxygen and nutrients to the muscle cells so that the onset of physiologic fatigue does not occur as rapidly.

Influence of Muscular Activity upon Red Blood Cells

Another effect of regular muscular work upon organs other than the muscular system has been cited previously. This is the increased production of red blood cells by the red bone marrow. It will be recalled that the red blood cells carry oxygen to the tissues. The greater the number of red blood cells, everything else being equal, the more muscular work which can be accomplished before the onset of physiologic fatigue.

Influence of Muscular Activity upon the Respiratory System

Stressful muscular activity will positively affect the respiratory system in several ways. The walls of the air sacs, the alveolar septa of the lungs, will become thicker to permit a more effective exchange of oxygen and carbon dioxide. New alveoli or air sacs will be produced. There will be an increase in the elastic fibers. The diaphragm, the broad sheath-like muscle which lies at the base of the rib cage and which aids in breathing, will become stronger as will those skeletal muscles involved in respiration such as the pectorals, the intercostals, and the abdominals.

Influence of Muscular Activity upon Muscle Tissue

Of equal importance, but of greater drama, are the effects of muscular work upon the muscle itself; its size and structure, its strength, and its efficiency. Muscles that are not used atrophy (waste away). When a fractured limb is placed in a cast, the cast fits snugly. However, after two weeks there is considerable room between the cast and the limb — sometimes enough to insert the hand. This is owing to atrophy of the muscle. However, when the muscle is used, and particularly when it is stressed to its limits regularly, it hypertrophies or grows larger. Weight lifters have developed biceps which are twenty inches in circumference and thighs which are twenty-eight inches in circumference. Morehouse and Miller[5] point out that when all other factors are equal, the strength of a muscle is roughly proportionate to its circumference.

Muscle Fiber

The basic unit of the muscular system is the muscle fiber. Each muscle fiber is .03937 to 1.77165 inches in length and from .003937 to .03937 inches in diameter. Each fiber is enclosed by a thin elastic covering called the *sarcolema* inside of which is found a fluid called *sarcoplasm* and a large number of *fibrils* which are made up of 400 to 2000 tiny *filaments* which run parallel to one another down the length of the fiber. These filaments are made up of light and dark bands. The dark bands are called *anisotropic* (A bands) and the light bands are called *isotropic* (I bands). The anisotropic band is rich in calcium, magnesium, and potassium while the isotropic band is rich in phosphagen and adenine derivatives. Each filament or myofibril consists of parallel actin and myosin filaments. The actin filaments are only two-thirds the length of the myosin filaments. As a consequence of this overlap of the two types of filaments, a pattern of striations becomes visible in the microscope. The denser areas (where the filaments overlap) are called A bands and the lighter areas (where the filaments do not overlap) are called I bands. The myosin filaments are thicker and longer than the actin filaments. Muscular contraction is effected when these filaments slide past one another in a manner similar to a slide trombone.

The actin and myosin filaments are connected at regular intervals by tiny cross-bridges. At these cross-bridges, the proteins (actin and myosin) come in contact and one of them (probably myosin) acts as an enzyme to split a

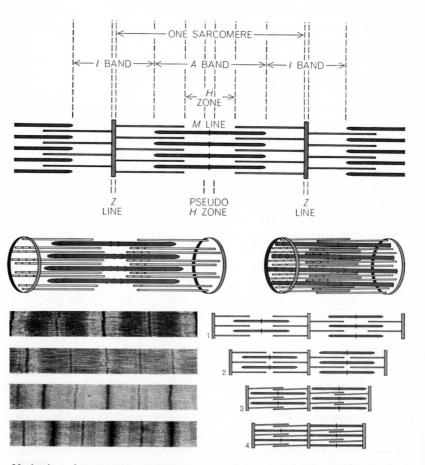

Mechanism of contraction of myofibril – the smallest structural unit in muscle *(from H. E. Huxley, "The Mechanism of Muscular Contraction," Scientific American, Dec., 1965, pp. 18 and 19. All rights reserved.)*

phosphate group from adenasine triphosphate (ATP) and thereby provides the energy for contraction. According to H. E. Huxley,[6] who was among the first to study the mechanism of muscular contraction under an electron microscope, the cross-bridges are the only mechanical linkage between the filaments and are responsible for the structural and mechanical continuity along the entire length of the muscle. It is the cross-bridges that must generate or sustain the tension developed by a muscle.

Muscle fibers are grouped together to form a *motor unit*. A motor unit may consist of as few as three muscle fibers (extrinsic muscles of the eyes) or as many as a hundred or more (muscles of the thighs). Each motor unit contracts as a unit since all its fibers are innervated simultaneously by one motor nerve. Where precise and delicate movements are needed such as in the fingers, tongue, lips, or eyes, a motor nerve will innervate only a few fibers but where gross movements are called for as in the thighs, back, or abdomen, a motor nerve innervates many muscle fibers. Some muscle fibers are very seldom used in routine daily activities, consequently they atrophy.

It is only during intensive muscular contraction that all the muscle fibers responsible for moving a part of the body are brought into play. The reason for this is that each motor unit requires a different minimal stimulus to produce contraction. This is known as the *threshold stimulus*. A minimal stimulus will bring into play only those motor units with the lowest threshold. Stronger stimuli will cause more and more motor units to contract. A maximal stimulus will excite all the motor units. The muscle fiber of each motor unit contract maximally if they contract at all but the whole muscle does not unless the effort is maximal. This explains why maximal contractions, as done in isometric exercises or in progressive resistance exercises, are so effective in increasing strength and muscle size. It also explains why light calisthenic movements or other activities done against little resistance will never be effective in producing great strength. However, if light exercises are sustained until thorough fatigue is produced they will lead to an improved blood supply to the exercised area and consequent greater muscular endurance.

Muscular Endurance

The principal reason for improved muscular endurance which results from physical conditioning is improved circulation. One or more arteries bring blood to each muscle. Numerous branches from the arteries supply a multitude of capillaries in the connective tissue of each individual muscle fiber. This arrangement makes for an easy exchange of materials between the blood and muscle fiber since the materials must pass only through the thin *endothelial cells* of the capillaries and the thin sarcolema of the muscle fiber.

There are about 4000 capillaries in a cross-section of muscle .16 of a square inch in area. Exercised animals have forty to forty-five percent more capillaries in muscle tissue than do sedentary animals. This increased blood supply to muscle tissue is in part responsible for the increase in muscle size (hypertrophy) which is an outcome of physical activity.

Development of Maximal Strength

Maximal strength, as has been stated, can only be developed through isometric exercises or through progressive resistance exercises utilizing springs or weights. It is the stress placed against muscular contraction rather than the number of foot-pounds of work accomplished which produces increases in strength. Modern Olympic and national weight-lifting champions have proven the effectiveness of placing maximal loads upon muscles in increasing strength. The 1968 Olympic Heavyweight Division Weightlifting Champion hoisted a total of 1259.5 pounds in the three competitive lifts – the press, snatch, and clean and jerk! If strength is to continue to increase, the resistance opposing the muscular contraction must be increased as strength increases.

Some people develop considerably more strength than others. The reason for this is not fully understood at the present time; however, it may be suspected that those with heavier bones can accommodate more muscle. Other reasons may be differences in willpower or motivation and length of the work arm of the anatomic levers relative to length of the resistance arm. Almost all levers in the human body are third-class levers. These levers have their fulcrum at one end and the resistance or weight at the other end while the force of power is applied between these two points. Obviously, in the human body the force point is almost always only a short distance from the fulcrum. This means that the work arm is considerably shorter than the resistance arm. These kinds of levers favor speed at the cost of force. They enable the body part to be moved very rapidly but also require the generation of a tremendous amount of force. For example, it has been found that three hundred pounds of force must be developed by the deltoid muscle to enable it to raise the arm and hand to an elevation of eighty degress while holding only ten pounds of weight.[7] Additionally, the muscle tendon inserts on the bone which it is moving at a very small angle so that at the beginning of flexion of the joint the major force of the muscles' contraction is used in stabilizing the joint (pulling the two bone ends toward one another) rather than in causing the joint to be flexed. It can be seen why strength is of great importance to success in athletics.

All other factors being equal, the greater the athlete's strength, the farther and faster a ball may be thrown; the faster the bat or racquet may be swung;

A kinesiology class *(Courtesy: University of Connecticut)*

the higher and farther he will jump or vault; and the faster he will propel himself over land or in the water. An athlete cannot increase the length of his anatomic levers or change the angle or point of insertion of his tendons but he can increase the force which he can generate by increasing his strength. Furthermore, strength may be improved more easily than any other factor which contributes to improved performance in athletics.

Strength and Age

Both men and women can effect increases in strength until the age of thirty. Consequently, men and women could continue to improve in most sports for a number of years after graduation from college. Strength in males increases rapidly from twelve to nineteen years of age and then more slowly until thirty years of age after which it declines very slowly until fifty or sixty years of age. After the age of fifty or sixty it declines more rapidly. Strength increases in girls and women follow the same pattern except that their period of rapid strength increases begin at nine instead of twelve years of age.

Physical Properties of Muscle

Muscle tissue possess four unique properties which enable it to perform its specialized function. These are contractibility, extensibility, elasticity, and irritability. Skeletal muscle fibers can contract or shorten to one-tenth of their resting length while the involuntary muscle fibers, such as those in the digestive tract, the trachea and bronchi, the urinary bladder and gall bladder, urinary and genital ducts, walls of blood vessels, capsule of the spleen, and the iris of the eye, can contract to one-sixth of their resting length.

Types of Muscular Contraction

Muscular contractions may be classified into three principal types: isometric or static; concentric, phasic or isotonic; and eccentric. In an isometric contraction, the force exerted by the muscle and the resistance applied to it are exactly equal and consequently there is neither shortening nor lengthening of the muscle fibers. In a concentric contraction, the angle at the joint being moved becomes smaller and the limb being moved approaches the one on which it is moving. In an eccentric contraction, the resistance is greater than the force being generated by the muscle and the muscle "gives" to the resistance. These three types of contraction could be illustrated in a wrist wrestling match. If "A" and "B" are equally matched and neither gives, they will both be undergoing an isometric contraction. If "A" wins the match, he will have undergone a concentric contraction while "B" will have undergone an eccentric contraction.

Qualities of Muscle Tissue

The application of a force to muscle tissue will cause it to stretch. When the flexor of the arm (bicep) contracts, the extensor (tricep) extends. Muscles of the heart, blood vessels, stomach, urinary bladder, and uterus can be stretched to a remarkable degree.

Muscle tissue will return to its original shape and size after it has been stretched. It is this elasticity that accounts for muscle tone. Muscle tone in skeletal muscles helps in maintaining posture and, in involuntary muscles, enables organs such as the urinary bladder and uterus to resume their normal size after they have been emptied. In standing, for example, when the head droops forward, the muscles at the back of the neck become stretched and consequently reflexly contract to bring the head erect.

Muscle tissue responds to a stimulus. The stimulus is usually a nerve impulse but other stimuli such as electric shock, irritating chemicals, and mechanical stimuli can bring about muscle contraction.

Muscular Fatigue

The feeling of fatigue may be caused by any one or a combination of several factors: (1) strenuous physical activity, (2) malnutrition, (3) circulatory disturbances, (4) respiratory disturbances, (5) infections, (6) endocrine disturbances, and (7) psychologic factors.

During physical activity certain chemicals are broken down when being converted into energy and lactic acid. Part of the lactic acid is oxidized and carbon dioxide and water are formed. However, if the activity is sufficiently vigorous and sufficiently prolonged, a point will be reached when the rate of production of lactic acid exceeds the rate of its removal by oxidation and diffusion into the blood stream. This excess lactic acid slows down the breaking up of glycogen and ultimately stops it. Recovery from this physiologic fatigue can be achieved by rest.

Muscle cells may be deprived of the chemicals necessary for contraction as a result of lack of essential food materials such as proteins, minerals, vitamins, and salt. An adequate and balanced diet will rectify this condition.

Circulatory disturbances, as in anemia, may prevent an adequate supply of oxygen and glucose from reaching the muscle fibers and also prevent the effective removal of carbon dioxide and lactic acid. In these cases, the red blood count must be increased.

Respiratory disturbances, as in pneumonia and tuberculosis, may prevent an adequate amount of oxygen from being taken up by the blood in the alveoli of the lungs.

The metabolic and toxic products of bacteria and viruses present during infections cause fatigue.

Endocrine disturbances which interfere with normal metabolism as in menopause, diabetes, and thyroid disorders also produce feelings of fatigue.

Grief, worry, anxiety, boredom, frustration, and other emotional states can cause a feeling of fatigue. Improved mental health can rectify this condition.

Physical education is accomplished when man moves. Muscles make movement possible. Undoubtedly, a thorough understanding of muscle physiology and anatomy is essential to every physical educator.

THE NERVOUS SYSTEM

Other animals are superior to man in size, strength, speed, endurance, power, agility, or tolerance of heat or cold. Other animals have more efficient cardiovascular-respiratory systems, stronger muscles, tougher hides, stronger skeletons, better vision, hearing, or sense of smell. However, no animal has a nervous system which is equal to that of man. Relative to body size, man has easily the largest brain of all animals. It is particularly the cerebral hemispheres which are responsible for the greater relative size of the human brain. While portions of the cerebral cortex control movement and sensory functions such as vision and hearing, the major portion is the *association area* which integrates sensory perceptions into concepts that give meaning to our perceptions. Here varied sensations are collected and unified. Here "thinking" takes place, ideas are born, and memories are stored. This area of the brain enabled man to survive against tremendous odds. It has enabled him to fly through space, explode thermonuclear bombs, design computers, write poetry, paint pictures, and build societies.

Divisions of the Nervous System

The nervous system consists of three major divisions, all influencing one another. These are the central nervous system, made up of the brain and spinal cord; the peripheral nervous system which consists of nervous structures outside the brain and the spinal cord; and the autonomic nervous system which consists of two parts – the sympathetic and the parasympathetic.

Central Nervous System

The central nervous system is the control center which regulates the activities of the body. The brain consists of three parts: the brain stem, the cerebellum, and the cerebrum. The *brain stem* consists of theee parts: the *medulla oblongata,* the *pons,* and the *mid-brain.* The medulla oblongata is a triangular enlargement of the spinal cord. Here are located the nerve centers for controlling the heart beat, the diameter of the arteries and veins, the rate of respiration, swallowing, and other reflex actions. Some of the nerve fibers, as they pass upward from the spinal cord to the brain or downward from the brain to the spinal cord, cross over in the medulla oblongata from one side to the other. This is why the right side of the brain controls the left side of the body and the left side of the brain controls the right side of the body. It explains why, when one side of the brain suffers damage, the opposite side of the body becomes paralyzed. This fact has implications for first aid work. The pons is an oval-shaped structure directly above the medulla oblongata which conducts nerve impulses between the medulla oblongata and the higher brain centers. The mid-brain lies above the pons. It is here that regulation of posture and equilibruim takes place. It also serves as a center for conduction of sound, touch, and visual reflexes.

Cerebellum: The cerebellum, which lies posterior to the medulla oblongata and the pons, is the second largest part of the brain. It serves to maintain equilibrium, posture, and muscle tone and coordinates muscular movements which have been initiated by the cerebrum. It has several parts.

Diencephalon: The diencephalon lies between the mid-brain and the cerebrum. Its parts are the *thalmus,* the *epithalmus,* the *subthalmus,* and the *hypothalmus.* These parts contain the olfactory (smell) centers, centers for control of body temperature, of emotions, of appetite, of sexual reflexes, and of fat metabolism.

A class in physiology

Cerebrum: The cerebrum with its five lobes (frontal, parietal, temporal, occipital, and central) covers all the other parts of the brain. It is the largest portion of the brain. Control of movement occurs principally in the *frontal lobe.* The *parietal lobe* contains the sensory areas which control sensations of touch, pressure, heat, cold, position, and pain. Visual sensations are controlled in the *occipital lobe.* Auditory and olfactory sensations are controlled in the *temporal lobe.* The most important area of the cerebrum and, in fact of the entire brain, is the *association* or central lobe area which coordinates the highest mental functions such as memory, learning, judgment, and understanding.

The Spinal Cord

The spinal cord, which is cylindrical in shape, passes downward through the vertebral foramen of each vertebra until it reaches the second lumbar vertebra (at the level of the small of the back) where it ends. It serves to conduct all nerve impulses having to do with sensation and movement both to the brain and from it to the muscles. Afferent nerve fibers conduct sensations of pain, touch, and temperature, for example, upward to the brain; efferent nerve fibers conduct impulses downward from the brain which cause muscles to contract or to relax.

Reflex Arc

Most of the activity of the nervous system is based upon reflex acts. The *reflex arc* is the anatomic unit which makes reflexes possible. The reflex arc possesses five essential parts which include the *receptor* (any sense organ), the *afferent neuron,* the *intermediate neuron* which is located in the spinal cord, the *efferent neuron,* and the *effector* (muscle).

The region of contact between two neurons, as between the afferent and intermediate neurons and the intermediate and the efferent neuron, is known as the *synapse.* The illustrated reflex arc is one of the most simple. Most reflex arcs are considerably more complex. Some involve several intermediate and efferent neurons, both sides of the spinal cord, and may include two or more levels of the cord. These result in a complicated pattern of muscular contraction. Nevertheless, the brain is not involved in even these more complex reflex arcs and all are unconscious responses to stimuli. The *knee jerk reflex* is illustrated when the doctor taps the patellar tendon just under the knee with a rubber hammer. The *flexion reflex* is illustrated when the flexor muscles contract to pull away the body part subjected to pain as when touching a hot surface. These are *inherited* reflexes.

Acquired reflexes are learned through repetition. Examples of these are typing or playing the piano. Highly skilled athletes develop a number of acquired reflexes. Reflexes may be triggered by *exteroceptors* (receptors on the surface of the body), *enteroceptors* (receptors in the viscera, blood vessels, heart or lungs), or *proprioceptors* (receptors located in muscles, tendons, joints, or the inner ear). Gymnasts, tumblers, divers, and acrobats depend greatly upon their proprioceptors to inform them of the body position with respect to the ground and of anatomic part to anatomic part. In all forms of athletics, participants depend to some extent upon all three kinds of acquired reflexes.

Effects of Oxygen Deprivation

Central nervous tissue has a greater need for oxygen than does the peripheral nervous tissue because of its higher metabolic rate. The highest centers of the brain, the cerebral and the cerebellar cortex, lose their ability to function if they do not receive blood for five minutes or more. The brain stem may withstand as much as thirty minutes of oxygen or blood deprivation, the spinal cord as much as sixty minutes, and peripheral nerves may recover after several hours of oxygen or blood deprivation. This explains why there may be permanent brain damage after recovery from drowning, other forms of asphyxia, or after a cerebrovascular accident.

Autonomic Nervous System

The autonomic nervous system controls the visceral organs. Its two divisions are known as the sympathetic and the parasympathetic systems. The afferent neurons of the autonomic system begin with receptors in the eyes, salivary glands, heart, trachea, bronchial tubes, esophagus, pancreas, stomach, small intestine, large intestine, and bladder. They pass to the brain or to the spinal cord where, directly, or through intermediate neurons, they make contact with efferent neurons which transmit impulses which stimulate the visceral organ. Some of the sympathetic impulses accelerate visceral activity while others inhibit visceral activity. Some parasympathetic (vagal) impulses accelerate visceral activity while others inhibit visceral activity. It was formerly believed that the autonomic system was independent of the central nervous system. It is now known that the two systems are closely interrelated. Emotional states brought on by the receiving of information which elicits an emotionalized reaction can cause visceral adaptations. For example, as has been pointed out, the anticipation of exercise or conversation about an irritating subject has been shown to accelerate the heart rate, to raise blood pressure, and to accelerate the respiratory rate.

Voluntary Movement

The impulses for all voluntary muscular acts originate in the cortex of the cerebrum. They are modified by the cerebellum so that the involved muscles contract in proper sequence. Proprioceptors in the labyrinths of the ears, the tendons, the muscles, the ligaments, and the joints send impulses to the brain which inform it of the body states and positions to enable it to modify or change the pattern of movement. It can be seen that in voluntary muscular movement the entire nervous system – central, peripheral, and autonomic – becomes involved.

Not only much practice but also much thought is required in the learning of any motor skill. The learning will proceed at a more rapid rate if the learner understands the movement – the movement pattern, the kinesiologic principles, the way it should feel, etc. This is why clear and concise verbal or written instructions; audiovisual aids such as sequence pictures and slow motion movies; skilled demonstrations; and guiding the learner manually speed up the learning process. Intense concentration is required in the learning of a new skill but after hundreds and perhaps thousands of efforts the skill may be performed almost unconsciously.

Grading Mechanism of Muscles

In the execution of all athletic skills, and for that matter all physical movement, the amount of tension developed by the muscle fibers must be directly proportional to the demands of the skill or the resistance offered. The amount of tension developed is controlled by the number of motor units activated. Each motor unit has its own minimal threshold of excitability. A weak nervous stimulus will activate only those motor units with low thresholds. As the nervous stimulus increases in intensity, a greater number of motor units become activated. All the muscle fibers in each motor unit contract according to the "all or none" law; that is, if they contract at all they contract maximally. Obviously, then, a stronger stimulus which will activate more motor units is required when picking up a large dictionary than when picking up a small piece of paper. The ability of muscles to adjust the intensity of their contraction to the resistance offered is known as the *grading mechanism* of muscle. In a maximal isometric contraction all, or nearly all, the motor units are involved. In lifting a peanut to the mouth only a few motor units are involved. In prolonged activities against little resistance as in maintaining posture, motor units take turns in doing the work. When an object of unknown weight is lifted there is a certain amount of stretching of the muscles and of the muscle spindles. Stretching of the muscle spindles stimulates the proprioceptive receptors and a reflex contraction of the flexors is initiated which is proportionate to the amount of stretching and adequate to relieve it.

Aids to Effort

Neural impulses can be increased in intensity to produce greater strength or endurance by such outside stimuli as whipping, "tongue lashing," encouraging words, cheering, music, hypnosis, suggestion, excitement, fear, or anger. Work animals and slaves have been driven to greater efforts by means of physical abuse. Studies have shown that oxygen consumption increases during calisthenic exercises when they are done with music. Soldiers have long sung during long marches to give themselves energy. Studies have shown that under hypnosis subjects show greater strength and endurance.

THE CARDIOVASCULAR SYSTEM AND EFFECTS OF ACTIVITY UPON IT

The average heart beats 72 times per minute; 4200 times per hour, 100,800 times per day; 36,792,000 times in a year; and 2,575,440,000 times during the average life span of seventy years without stopping. It varies its rate and intensity of contraction precisely to meet the demands of the body cells for oxygen, water, nutrients, and hormones. Many miles of blood vessels serve to transport blood to every part of the body. Some of these blood vessels are so small they can be seen only through a microscope. Some have their own muscle tissue to enable them to change their diameter. Some have valves.

Some have walls so thin that they permit the passage of oxygen and carbon dioxide molecules through their walls. When the volume of blood is lowered below the body's needs (four to six quarts in adults), new blood is made by the body. In addition to carrying needed substances to the cells, the blood serves to maintain a uniform temperature throughout the body; carries lactic acid, carbon dioxide, and urea from the cells; and transports defensive cells and immunogenic substances to the cells to defend against disease. It is the transportation system for cellular food, waste products, and other needs as well as a cellular cooling and heating system which man, in spite of his inventiveness, cannot duplicate. However, the physical educator with his tools – exercise, sports, and physical activity – can improve the performance of this marvelous system.

The circulatory system includes all structures involved in the transportation of body fluids. The blood-vascular and the lymphatic systems are its two main divisions. The blood-vascular system includes the blood, heart, arteries, arterioles, capillaries, venules, and veins.

Heart

The heart is a hollow muscular organ with four chambers. It is about the size of a man's fist. It lies behind the breast bone or sternum between the lungs. It is enclosed in a double-walled fibroserous sac called the *pericardium*. The space between the two walls of the pericardium is filled with a serous fluid called the *pericardial fluid*. The function of this serous fluid is to lubricate or to decrease the amount of friction during the heart's expansions and contractions. The wall of the heart is composed of three layers: the *epicardium*, the *myocardium*, and the *endocardium*. The epicardium is the inner layer of the pericardium and the outer layer of the heart wall. The endocardium is a thin, single layer of flat cells which covers the heart valves and lines the cavities.[8] The myocardium is made up of cardiac muscle fibers which run obliquely and are thicker where they pass over the ventricular area than they are over the atria. It is the myocardium that is particularly affected through physical activity vigorous enough to produce cardiorespiratory stress. The physical activity must be continued over a long period of time. Participation in endurance type activities such as middle distance or distance swimming or running, soccer, lacrosse, cross country, etc. cause the myocardium of the heart to obtain more complete emptying of the ventricles with each contraction which means that with each contraction *(systole)* a greater volume of blood is sent into the aorta and pulmonary artery. A result of a more muscular heart is that the heart need not beat as frequently when the body is at rest. It also means that a greater amount of work can be accomplished by the body before it becomes fatigued since during activity

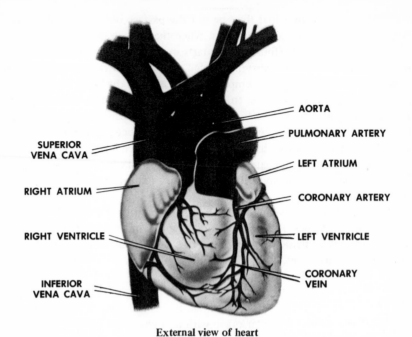

AORTA

PULMONARY ARTERY

SUPERIOR
VENA CAVA

LEFT ATRIUM

RIGHT ATRIUM

CORONARY ARTERY

RIGHT VENTRICLE

LEFT VENTRICLE

INFERIOR
VENA CAVA

CORONARY
VEIN

External view of heart

the blood can be circulated quickly enough to remove waste products from the muscle fibers and bring oxygen and nutrients to them.

Heart Rate

The pulse, or heart rate, varies greatly among different people and in the same person under different situations. The American Heart Association accepts as normal a range from 50 to 100 beats per minute. Some endurance athletes with very strong and efficient hearts have rates as low as 45 beats per minute. The average rate is 72 beats per minute. The rate can accelerate to 220 beats per minute. The rate in endurance athletes will go as high as it will in poorly conditioned people but a great deal more work must be done by the athlete than by the nonathlete to produce an equally accelerated rate. The nonathlete will tire much more quickly. Furthermore, the pulse rate in the well-conditioned or physically fit person returns to normal more quickly after an exercise session than does the rate in the unfit or poorly conditioned person. Experiments indicate that during exercise the blood flow through the muscles may be four to nine times greater in the well-conditioned person than it is at rest and three to six times greater in the nonathlete.

The pulse rate may be determined by means of digital (fingertip) pressure at any point where an artery lies near the surface, especially when the artery is located near a bone. The pulse may be felt at several points but is most easily and commonly felt at the wrist just outside the tendon and on the thumb side. The arterial pulse is due to the alternate expansion and contraction of the arterial walls owing to the contraction of the heart. When the blood is forcibly ejected from the heart into the aorta, its impact upon the elastic walls of the aorta sends up a pressure wave which travels along the arteries. This causes the pulse. The pulse is not caused by the passing of blood.

Heart Chambers

The heart has four chambers. At its upper right side is the *right atrium.* Into it empty the *superior* and the *inferior vena cava* and the *coronary sinus veins* which bring blood from all the body tissues except the lungs. On the upper left side of the heart is the *left atrium.* Into it empty the four *pulmonary veins* which bring oxygenated blood from the lungs. These are the only veins in the body which carry oxygenated blood. On the lower right side is the *right ventricle.* The *pulmonary artery* leads upward from its upper surface carrying blood to the lungs. On the lower left side is the *left ventricle.* The cardiac muscles are thickest and strongest in this region because they must force the blood through the aorta which carries blood to all parts of the body with the exception of the lungs.

Heart Valves

There are two types of valves in the heart. The *atrioventricular valves* (mitral or bicuspid valve and the tricuspid valve) are located between the atrium and the ventricle. Their pointed flaps open downward to permit blood to flow from the atrium into the ventricle when the atrium contracts. When the ventricle contracts, the flaps are pushed closed by the upward moving blood. The *semilunar valves* are located between the ventricles and the arteries which leave them. The *pulmonary semilunar valves* are located at the junction of the pulmonary artery and the right ventricle. The *aortic semilunar valves* are located at the junction of the aorta and the left ventricle.

Murmurs

Sometimes the valves become deformed or are partially destroyed as a result of faulty embryonic development or diseases such as rheumatic fever or septicemia. The result is *regurgitation* of blood past the valve when it is supposed to be closed. The abnormal heart sounds detected on a stethoscope in this condition have caused this condition to be called a *murmur.*

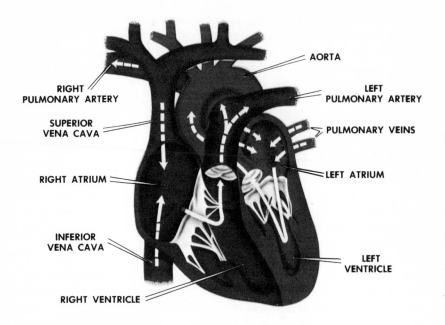

AORTA

RIGHT PULMONARY ARTERY

LEFT PULMONARY ARTERY

SUPERIOR VENA CAVA

PULMONARY VEINS

RIGHT ATRIUM

LEFT ATRIUM

INFERIOR VENA CAVA

LEFT VENTRICLE

RIGHT VENTRICLE

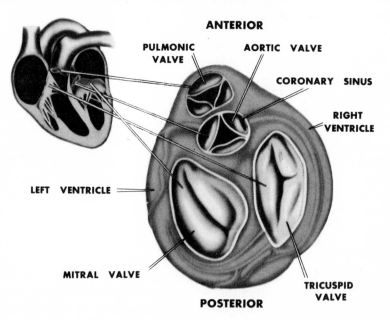

ANTERIOR

PULMONIC VALVE

AORTIC VALVE

CORONARY SINUS

RIGHT VENTRICLE

LEFT VENTRICLE

MITRAL VALVE

TRICUSPID VALVE

POSTERIOR

Top: Flow of blood through heart; Bottom: Valves of the heart

One of the effects of valvular malfunction is that the blood regurgitated into the atrium interferes with the return of blood into the atrium from the venae cavae and the pulmonary vein with resulting stagnation of blood in the capillaries *(passive congestion)*. The other effect is hypertrophy (muscular development) of the heart muscle as a result of having to work harder to meet the needs of the body. This condition is known as *cardiac compensation.* Some people's hearts compensate adequately to enable them to participate in fairly vigorous sports. Any person with this condition should obtain the advice of his physician before participating in physical activity of any kind. However, a healthy heart cannot be harmed by any physical activity regardless of how strenuous. An athlete whose heart and circulatory system has been declared healthy by a physician after a thorough examination need not worry about overextending himself. He may safely perform until complete exhaustion.

Muscle Fibers of the Heart

The muscle fibers of the heart lack a *sarcolema* (membraneous covering). They possess branches by which the protoplasm of adjoining cells forms a continuous mass. Consequently, the heart contracts as a unit instead of as separate motor units as do the skeletal muscles. This means that if the heart contracts at all, it contracts completely. However, the strength of its contractions may range from weak to strong. The strength of the contractions is determined principally by the amount of blood returned to the heart through the veins. The amount of blood being returned through the veins is determined by the amount of muscular activity as a result of the *"milking action"* of the muscles upon the veins. However, it is principally by varying the *rate* of the heart beat that the varying needs of the body are met. The rate of the heart beat may be influenced by body position, physical activity, altitude, digestive activities, emotions, body temperature (fever), hemorrhage, hyperthyroidism, drugs, and hormones. The rate is slower when lying down than when standing, when inactive than when exercising or immediately following exercise, at low than at high altitudes, and when calm than when emotionalized.

Arterial Circulation

The arterial system serves to transport blood from the heart to the capillaries. Arteries are elastic muscular tubes whose internal diameter increases when an increased volume of blood is sent through them and whose internal diameter is decreased by contraction of their circular muscles when they receive stimuli over the vasomotor nerves from the central nervous system. Arteries are of three types: (1) *conducting arteries* which are large in caliber, and predominate in elastic fiber; (2) *distributing arteries* which predominate in muscular fibers; and (3) *arterioles* which are tiny terminal branches of the muscular arteries.

The *vasomotor nerves* are of two types. The *vasoconstrictor* nerves cause contraction of the circular muscles of arterioles and consequently a decrease in the caliber of the arteriole. The *vasodilator nerves* relax these muscles thereby causing an increase in the caliber of the vessels. If a large number of arterioles are constricted, resistance to the flow of blood is increased and blood pressure rises. If the arterioles are dilated, resistance to the flow of blood is decreased and blood pressure falls. An increase in the carbon dioxide content of blood, such as occurs during muscular activity, causes the arterioles it comes in contact with to dilate by relaxing the smooth muscle in their walls.

The elasticity of the arteries is the principal factor responsible for the maintenance of blood pressure during diastole (the time between contractions of the ventricle of the heart). If the arteries were inelastic, the blood pressure would drop almost to zero and the blood would almost cease to flow during diastole. During systole (contraction of the ventricles) a quantity of blood is discharged into the aorta and its branches, stretching their walls. At the end of the contraction, the stretched arterial walls, because of their elasticity, recoil or decrease their diameter. This exerts pressure on the blood pushing it onward.

Blood Pressure

Normal adult blood pressure averages about 120 mm. of mercury for systolic pressure and 80 mm. for diastolic pressure. Strenuous physical activity may cause the systolic pressure to rise to 200 mm. and the diastolic to 110 mm. Age causes blood pressure to increase. At the age of sixty, the average systolic pressure is 135 mm. and the diastolic is 90 mm. Obesity also causes blood pressure to increase. Emotion can cause blood pressure to either increase or decrease. *Hypertension,* which may be caused by nervous factors or by kidney disease, will elevate blood pressure. In kidney diseases, the blood flow to the kidneys is restricted and they receive insufficient oxygen. When this happens, the kidneys produce a substance which causes increased contraction of smooth muscles in arteriolar walls. This mechanism is not completely understood at this time. Excessive amounts of hormones released by the adrenal cortex may cause hypertension. A reduction in ingestion of salt has been found to reduce the degree of hypertension.

The use of large amounts of salt throughout a lifetime will very likely lead to hypertension in middle age or beyond. For this reason, children should be discouraged from salting their food excessively. Atherosclerosis (hardening and loss of elasticity in the arteries) causes an increase in blood pressure. This disease is a major cause of cerebrovascular accidents (strokes or apoplexy) and also of coronary failure. These are the two top killers of man. Arteriosclerosis and atherosclerosis are caused by the deposition of cholesterol and ordinary fats of the blood between the inner and outer walls of the arteries. *Cholesterol* is a waxy substance resembling fat. It is found in every tissue of all living organisms. While its function is not completely understood, it is known that it: (1) serves as a transport vehicle for fatty acids; (2) is a structural unit of some tissues; and (3) serves as a lubricant for the skin. When it is deposited between the inner and outer walls of the arteries, it narrows the caliber of the arteries, thereby restricting the passage of blood and consequently increasing blood pressure; it causes the arteries to lose their elasticity thereby making them more brittle and more likely to rupture; and it causes the adjacent cells to become crowded and to become poorly nourished, resulting in their death and consequently producing ulcerated areas which, when healed, leave inelastic scar tissue. A number of studies have been performed to determine how best to decrease blood cholesterol. These have included studies to learn the effects of weight reduction, use of vegetable oils, use of chemicals and drugs, and exercise. The studies on the effects of exercise appear most promising.

R. H. Rochelle, Ph.D.[9] reports the results of an experiment to ascertain the effects of exercise upon blood cholesterol levels. Members of the experimental group, who ran two miles against time five days a week for a period of five weeks, decreased their average cholesterol count from 203 mg. percent before the five-week training period to 179 mg. percent after the training period. The cholesterol count of the control group remained the same. There was a temporary rise in the cholesterol count during exercise which the author believed was probably indicative of fat mobilization. Rochelle cites other studies which indicate that physical activity decreases the blood cholesterol level.

A study showing that the blood cholesterol levels of sedentary middle-aged subjects were higher than those of physically active subjects was done by Drs.. Chailley-Bert, Labignette, and Fabre-Chevalier.[10] Montoye[11] reported a decrease in cholesterol as a result of exercise but only when there was also a reduction in body weight. Groen's[12] studies lead to the conclusion that physical exercise reduces serum cholesterol levels. Myasnikov[13] fed rabbits cholesterol and had the experimental group exercise on a treadmill while the control group did no exercise. The blood cholesterol level of the exercised rabbits was lower than that of the nonexercised rabbits. The death certificates of 31,000 bus drivers (who sit at their job) and bus conductors (who stand and walk on their job) were compared by Dr. J. N. Morris and others.[14] They

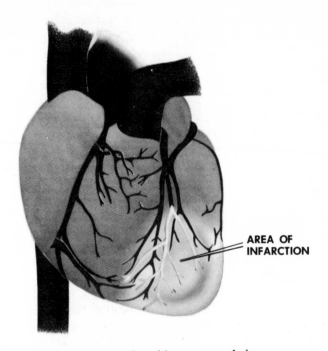

AREA OF
INFARCTION

Coronary circulation with coronary occlusion

found that fatal heart attacks were suffered by the drivers much more frequently than by the conductors. They obtained similar results when they compared physically active postmen with sedentary postal clerks. This evidence seems to indicate that a lifetime of fairly vigorous physical activity significantly decreases the rate of deposition of cholesterol in the arteries and thereby decreases the probability of an untimely death from coronary failure, cerebrovascular accident, or other circulatory failures.

Effects of Exercise upon Blood Pressure and Pulse Rate

Ernest D. Michael and Arthur J. Gallon [15] took periodic measurements of the pulse wave and blood pressure of members of the Santa Barbara basketball team throughout their sixteen-week season. They found that the resting and postexercise systolic blood pressures decreased significantly during training. While pulse rate and pressure-curve measurements changed significantly in three to six weeks, the systolic measurements took up to sixteen weeks to change significantly. The resting systolic blood pressure measurements and the recovery measurements after exercise decreased significantly during sixteen weeks of training. These studies prove that vigorous and regular physical activity will improve the efficiency of the cardiovascular system not only during physical stress but also when the body is at rest.

Venous Circulation

After the blood has been pumped by the heart into the arteries through the arterioles and finally to the capillaries, it begins the return trip to the heart by way of the venules to the veins and back to the right atrium. The blood flows rapidly through the aorta and the larger arteries but its velocity continues to decrease as it is dispersed through an increasing number of smaller vessels until by the time it is passing through the capillaries its velocity is very slow. The velocity of the blood flow is decreased in the smaller vessels because of their narrow caliber and their greater surface area, both of which increase resistance. The total cross-section area of the capillary bed is estimated to be 800 times that of the aorta. Increased resistance to blood flow is necessary to sustain blood pressure. With inadequate pressure the blood vessels would be in danger of collapsing.

Capillaries

The entire cardiovascular-respiratory system including the blood, heart, arteries, arterioles, veins, venules, and lungs, exists to make possible the work which is done in the capillaries. It is through the capillary walls that the exchange of substances between the blood and tissues takes place. Leucocytes, lymph, glucose, water, carbon dioxide, and oxygen move through the walls of the capillaries. Tissue fluid serves as the intermediary through which substances in the blood are transmitted to the cells. It occupies the spaces between cells and between the fibers of connective tissue. Tissue fluid resembles blood plasma except that it does not have red blood cells. It does possess proteins. It is because of the osmotic pressure exerted by the proteins, and also because of hydrostatic pressure, that the blood volume and consequently blood pressure is kept within necessary bounds. Hydrostatic pressure forces the plasma to be filtered through the thin walls of the capillaries. Osmotic pressure, exerted by the proteins, draws water from the tissues into the capillaries. At the arterial end of a capillary, hydrostatic pressure exceeds osmotic pressure and plasma is forced through the capillary walls into the tissues. Loss of fluid from the blood in the capillary increases the concentration of proteins and consequently osmotic pressure is increased while hydrostatic pressure decreases. The result is that, at the venous end of the capillary, fluid is drawn back from the tissues into the blood in the capillary. It is in this way that the tissues ultimately have their needs met.

Deep Breathing Exercises

The preceding discussion indicates the futility of deep breathing exercises. Oxygen brought into the lungs is simply expelled if a need for oxygen has not been created in the cells through vigorous physical activity. Need for oxygen must be created in the cells as a result of vigorous physical activity. The oxygen-depleted blood will then absorb the oxygen in the alveoli of the lungs to bring it to the cells. The respiratory rate and depth will be increased as a result of involuntary reflexes rather than through voluntary and willed movements. This aspect of the physiology of respiration has long been understood. Yet some physical educators persist in having their students inhale audibly with a powerful sucking noise and then exhale loudly and forcefully as they bend forward and wrap their arms around their belly or slap their chest repeatedly.

Venous Return

As the blood passes through the multitudinous capillaries, into the venules, and then into the veins, its velocity increases. However, the velocity of the blood in the venae cavea is never as great as it is in the aorta. Blood pressure is almost zero in the large veins. The pumping action of the heart is inadequate to return the blood to the heart without the aid of supplementary forces. Blood moving upward from the legs and lower body must overcome the force of gravity. Several mechanisms enable blood to be returned to the heart.

The valves in the veins, which permit blood to move toward the heart but prevent its movement away from the heart, help the blood to move upward against gravity. The "milking action" of alternately contracting and relaxing muscles, which periodically compress the veins as the belly of the muscle expands against them, also help to move the blood along. This "milking action" is one of the major factors causing an increased output of blood during exercise. It explains, in part, why sustained exercises done against light resistance many times, as in distance running or swimming, improve the cardiovascular-respiratory condition more effectively than do power activities such as gymnastics, weight lifting, and field events in which a maximal or near maximal contraction is done once or only a few times. Other mechanisms which aid in venous return are: (1) the sucking force of the atrium when it is expanding; (2) respiratory movements, and (3) movements of the visceral organs. During inspiration there is an increase in intrathoracic pressure which compresses the venae cavae. Also, the downward movement of the diaphragm increases the intraabdominal pressure which compresses the veins in the abdominal area. Peristaltic action of the intestines and vasoconstriction in the splanchnic area also aid in venous return from the visceral organs.

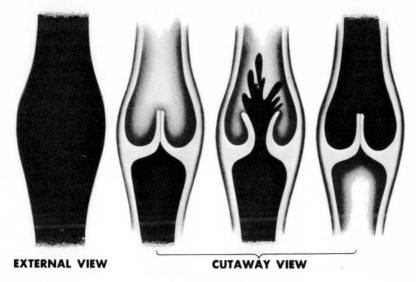

EXTERNAL VIEW   **CUTAWAY VIEW**

Valve of a vein

THE RESPIRATORY SYSTEM AND EFFECTS
OF ACTIVITY UPON IT

All forms of life must take in oxygen and release carbon dioxide. In one-celled animals, oxygen and carbon dioxide move through the cell membrane directly from the air surrounding the animal. In some worms respiratory gases pass through the skin into or out of blood in vessels just under the surface. Even in frogs some of the gas is exchanged through moist skin. In the higher forms of animals, air is sucked into lungs inside the body where the respiratory gases diffuse through the thin walls of the lungs into the blood.

Respiratory Mechanism

In the human, the intrathoracic volume is alternately increased and decreased. This is accomplished by the involuntary rhythmic contractions of the intercostal (between the ribs) muscles which elevate the ribs to increase the anterior-posterior diameter of the rib box. Also, the involuntary rhythmic contractions of the diaphragm which increase the vertical diameter of the rib box increases the intrathoracic volume. The diaphragm is a broad, sheath-like organ which lies horizontally across the lower end of the thorax. During relaxation it is dome-shaped. When it contracts, its center moves downward as it stretches across the rib cage. This increases the vertical diameter of the rib cage. Pressure is lowered within the thorax. Nature abhors a vacuum. Gases move from a place of higher pressure to one of lower pressure. The only opening to the outside is through the nose and mouth. Air then moves in through the nose or mouth where it is warmed and moistened. In the nose, ciliated tissues catch some of the larger impurities. The air moves into the *pharynx* and past the *epiglottic cartilage* which forms a lid over the *larynx* or "voice box." The epiglottic cartilage or epiglottis prevents food from entering the larynx since up to this point air and food have a common passageway in the pharynx. In drowning, the epiglottis often goes into spasm as a result of its efforts to prevent water from moving down into the trachea. When this happens, even though the person's mouth and nose are above the surface, he can bring no air into his lungs.

The air next moves into the *trachea* or windpipe, which is a tubular structure of smooth muscle located in front of the esophagus. The *esophagus* is the channel for food and liquids. In the thorax, the trachae divides into two branches — the right and left *bronchi* — which lead to the right and left lungs. Upon entering the lungs, the left bronchus divides into two bronchi and the right bronchus divides into three bronchi. These continue to subdivide into smaller and smaller bronchi until they become *bronchioles* or air tubes. These also continue to subdivide until they become the *alveolar ducts* which lead to the *alveolar sacs* or air sacs whose walls have numerous rounded elevations, which are the alveoli. There are millions of these alveoli. Their combined surface area is about 119 square yards — about half the area of a volleyball court. It is in the alveoli that the gas exchange occurs.

Bronchitis and bronchiectasis are caused by an infection of bronchi. Pleurisy is caused by an infection of the pleura. The *pleura* is a double-layered serous membrane which encloses the lungs and attaches to the lungs, the chest wall, and the diaphragm. A lubricating serum is found between the two pleural layers. The pleura is attached on one side to the lungs and on the other to the chest wall and diaphragm. This arrangement means that when the chest wall moves outward and the diaphragm moves downward they take the lungs with them with the result that an area of decreased atmospheric pressure is created not in the space between the lungs and the chest wall but within the lungs themselves in the alveolar sacs. In pleurisy there are adhesions between the two layers of the pleura. This accounts for the pain experienced during respiratory movements. Other major diseases of the lungs are pulmonary tuberculosis, pneumonia, and cancer.

The process of bringing air into the alveoli and the gas exchange in the blood taking place there is called *external respiration.* The process of gas exchange between the blood and the cells is called *internal respiration.*

During expiration there is a reversal of the processes which brought on inspiration. The respiratory muscles (the intercostals and the diaphragm) relax, the volume of the thoracic cage decreases, intrathoracic pressure increases, the lungs are compressed, and air is forced out of the lungs. During forced expiration, intercostal muscles which pull the ribs downward and backward and the abdominal muscles contract to decrease the intrathoracic volume further. Almost everyone has noticed the alternate contracting and relaxing of abdominal muscles (which aids in forced expiration) after an athletic event in which respiratory stress is produced. The elastic recoil of the lungs also aids in expiration. The diaphragm, in contracting during inspiration and moving downward from its dome-shaped position to a stretched position across the lower end of the rib cage, compressed the visceral organs. Now, during expiration, as the diaphragm relaxes, the visceral organs push upward against the diaphragm. This also aids in expelling air from the lungs.

Vital Capacity

Tidal air refers to the air inhaled during a normal inspiration. About 500 cc of air are inhaled by the average adult in a normal inspiration. *Complemental* air refers to the additional air which can be taken in during a maximal inhalation. In an adult, this amounts to about 1500 cc of air. After a normal expiration, an additional 1500 cc of air can be forcefully exhaled. This is called *supplemental* air. The sum of tidal, complemental, and supplemental air is called *vital capacity.*

Average vital capacity in an adult man is about 3500 cc. In women it is about 20 percent lower and in trained athletes it is an average of twenty percent higher. However, as we shall see, vital capacity contributes little to endurance. It is not so much a problem of getting an adequate amount of oxygen into the alveoli as it is of several other factors. Vital capacity has, in the past, been extensively used as a measure of physical fitness. Today tests of performance are principally used. Chest expansion is not a good measure of vital capacity since a well-muscled person can expand his chest to a greater extent than his lungs can fill.

All the air in the alveoli is not expelled with each expiration. Some remains in the alveoli to be mixed with the air brought in. Alveolar air contains about 14.5 percent oxygen, 5.5 percent carbon dioxide, and 80 percent nitrogen. Atmospheric air contains about 20 percent oxygen, .01 percent carbon dioxide, and 79 percent nitrogen. The remainder consists of water vapor and traces of rarer gases. If alveolar air were completely flushed out during each expiration and replaced by fresh air during each inspiration, the percentage of oxygen and carbon dioxide in the alveolar air would change radically during each breath. There would then be corresponding radical fluctuations in the gaseous composition of blood leaving the lungs with the result that the cells would not be provided with a uniform amount of oxygen in the blood.

Hemoglobin

The hemoglobin enables the blood to carry a hundred times more oxygen than it otherwise could. It is the hemoglobin in whole blood which is responsible for the oxygen-carrying ability of the blood. Hemoglobin is a constituent of erythrocytes or red blood cells. There is an average of about one and a half million erythrocytes in the blood of an adult male. People living at high altitudes have a higher red cell count than those living at low altitudes. On moving to high altitudes, the red cell count increases. Participation in athletic events increases the red cell count. After exercise, the red cell count has been noted to rise to 6,180,000. However, this increase is of short duration since within an hour or two the count returns to the preexercise level. Regular participation in athletics over a period of time will increase the normal count by about ten percent. An increase in the red cell count is probably a more important factor than is vital capacity in influencing endurance. Deep breathing exercises will increase vital capacity if they are done regularly over a long period of time while the child is growing but they will not contribute nearly as much to increased endurance as will activities which produce cardiovascular-respiratory stress and consequent total body adjustments. One of these adjustments is that the red bone marrow gets "in the habit" of producing a large number of red corpuscles.

Nervous Control of Respiration

Respiration can be adapted to the needs created by a wide variety of bodily activities. Two clusters of nerve cell bodies called the *respiratory center* are located in the medulla of the brain. These cell bodies rhythmically discharge nervous impulses which pass down to the spinal cord and there excite other nerve cells which in turn send impulses to the muscles of inspiration. The *respiratory center* appears to be influenced by all the nerves in the body. The *phrenic nerves* located in the spinal cord at the region of the neck innervate the diaphragm. *Intercostal nerves* located in the spinal cord at the region of the thorax innervate the intercostal muscles. Receptors in the walls of the alveoli are stimulated during inspiration and send impulses along the *vagus nerve* to the respiratory center which then inhibits respiration. This is known as the *Hering-Breur reflex*. By cutting short the period of inhalation, this reflex accelerates the rate of respiration. An increase in blood pressure inhibits respiration while a fall accelerates it. This is accomplished by efferent nerves located in the carotid sinus and the aortic arch. Receptors which are sensitive to the chemical composition of blood are also located in these two large blood vessels. When there has been a substantial lowering in the oxygen content of the blood or an increase in its carbon dioxide or acid concentration, these receptors send out impulses which accelerate respiration.

According to Karpovich,[16] several factors determine the rate at which oxygen is supplied to active tissue. These are: (1) ventilation of the lungs (or depth of the inhalation), (2) the oxygen capacity of the blood which is determined by its hemoglobin content, (3) the unloading of oxygen at the tissues or the amount of oxygen which can pass from the blood to the tissues, and (4) the "minute-volume" of the heart or the amount of blood the heart can pump per minute. There is obviously, then, a high degree of interrelationship between the respiratory, circulatory, nervous, skeletal, and muscular systems of the body.

Respiratory Rate

The average respiratory rate is about sixteen times per minute at rest. The range is four to twenty-four times per minute. Under physical stress the upper limit is about thirty per minute. However, a rate as high as seventy-five per minute has been noted in a subject while doing the crawl stroke. Emotion or excitement will accelerate the rate even before physical movement has been initiated. More air reaches the alveoli (where gas exchange takes place) in deep breathing than it does in shallow breathing. An excessive respiratory rate is fatiguing and inefficient. A fast rate demands more work of the respiratory muscles and decreases the depth of inspiration. Obviously, a slower respiratory rate while at rest is preferred.

Effects of Exercise upon Respiration

Regular and continued participation in vigorous physical activity will effect changes in the respiratory system. Chest expansion will be increased, rate of breathing will become slower, depth of breathing will become greater, a greater portion of the lungs will be used, and the diaphragm will be used more fully and its excursions will become greater. The physically fit person needs less air because he can utilize a greater portion of the oxygen he takes in than can a person who is not physically fit. In activities requiring a high degree of skill, the skilled person requires considerably less oxygen than does the unskilled simply because he can execute the movement with greater economy of energy.

The minute-volume of air taken in by an athlete during maximal physical stress is ten times that of the average person. Obviously, this is one reason that an athlete can withstand considerably more physical stress than can the nonathlete.

Inhalation of Pure Oxygen

Some coaches have attempted to improve their athletes' performances in athletic events by having them inhale pure oxygen previous to a contest. Research first showed this to be a worthwhile practice since performances were improved. However, exercise physiologists knew that oxygen cannot be stored in the body for later use. Consequently, they conducted further research in which they utilized the placebo idea. That is, an experimental group inhaled pure oxygen while a control group thought they were inhaling pure oxygen but were in fact inhaling atmospheric air. The control group showed improvements as great as the experimental group indicating that it was not the inhaling of pure oxygen which accounted for the improvements but rather the thought that they would or should improve.

SUMMARY

It is principally through moving of the human body that physical education accomplishes its objectives of intellectual and social development, promotes a favorable self-image, and provides experiences in the democratic process. Physical education is unique in that it is the only subject in the curriculum which concerns itself with improvement in the functioning of the body through physical activity. For these reasons, the physical educator should possess a thorough understanding of human physiology, anatomy, kinesiology, physiology of exercise, first aid and athletic training procedures, and maintenance of health.

The physical educator or athletic coach who does not possess these knowledges and understandings may require his students to do things which are hazardous. He is almost certain to fail to recognize hazardous situations. He is likely to ask his students to do things to achieve certain objectives which are unproductive or a complete waste of time.

A physical educator or an athletic coach who does possess these knowledges and understandings is likely to use class time more efficiently in developing fitness and in teaching athletic skills. He is more likely to conduct activities in a safe manner because he understands both the potential and the limitations of the human body. Furthermore, the teaching of physical activities is likely to be more satisfying to him because he has an understanding of the dramatic actions, reactions, and adjustments which take place within the human body during strenuous physical activity. Finally, a thorough understanding of the human body leads to an understanding of the unity of man — that social forces, for example, influence his mind which influences his emotions which influence his physiologic processes and thereby the quality and quantity of his movement patterns.

With this knowledge, the physical educator understands the role of physical stress, how much stress each student can safely accommodate, and when it is harmful as well as when it is helpful. He has a better understanding of how to proceed to develop endurance, power, strength, speed, or agility. He understands the relationships between these and knows something of the relative importance of each performance in different sports activities.

There are many other reasons for possessing knowledge of human anatomy and physiology. Physical educators with this knowledge will know the differences between boys and girls which dictate differences in the conduct of athletic activities. They will know how to improve posture. They will recognize evidences of ill health, of excessive stress, and of improving health. They will understand the biologic effects of the aging process. Through an understanding of the nervous system, they will have a little better understanding of the learning process, of fatigue, and of trauma.

Improvement in the physical fitness status of his students is the major biologic objective of the physical educator. Let us proceed now to a discussion of what physical fitness is, its importance to individuals and society today, the fitness status of American children today, and differences due to age, sex, and individual variations.

QUESTIONS

1. Present evidence that sometimes the fatigue which people experience is not true physiologic fatigue but is psychologic in origin.

2. Present evidence of the relationships between emotions and physiologic functions.

3. Present evidence of the adaptability of man.

4. List five functions of the skeletal system.

5. What are the engineering features of the human body which enable it to absorb shocks and impacts which occur when running, jumping, or vaulting?

6. What can a person do to prevent trauma to joints?

7. Why are hard blows to the head dangerous?

8. Why should one avoid moving a person suspected of having injured the vertebral column?

9. Describe the construction of the thorax.

10. List three undesirable results of weak abdominal muscles.

11. Discuss erythrocytes.

12. Why is a strong efficient muscular system desirable?

13. What is meant by "milking action" of the muscles upon veins? Describe the mechanism.

14. What are the influences of regular muscular activity upon: (1) heart rate and volume, (2) size of the capillary bed, (3) number of red blood cells, (4) the respiratory system, and (5) muscle tissue?

15. Describe the anatomy and physiology of the muscle fiber.

16. Explain why maximal contractions of muscles are necessary to involve all motor units and consequently to develop great strength.

17. Discuss development of muscular endurance.

18. Explain why strength is essential to success in athletics.

19. Explain the differences between isometric, isotonic, and eccentric contraction.

20. Discuss causes of muscular fatigue.

21. Discuss the three parts of the brain stem and their functions.

22. Discuss the parts and functions of the cerebellum.

23. Name the five lobes of the cerebrum and discuss their functions.

24. What is the reflex arc and how does it function?

25. What are the differences between inherited and acquired reflexes?

26. Discuss the functions of the two divisions of the autonomic nervous system.

27. What is the grading mechanism of muscle?

28. Discuss the anatomy of the heart.

29. Take your pulse while sitting and again after running in place for five minutes.

30. What is a heart murmur? What causes it? What are its effects?

31. Name the three types of arteries.

32. What are some of the causes of high blood pressure? What is the average blood pressure? What can a person do to prevent high blood pressure?

33. Describe the process which occurs in the capillaries which makes possible the exchange of substances between the blood and the tissues.

34. Why are deep breathing exercises largely a waste of time?

35. List four mechanisms which assist in venous return of blood.

36. Explain the respiratory mechanism.

37. Define the following: pharynx, larynx, epiglottis, trachea, esophagus, bronchi, bronchioles, alveolar ducts, alveolar sacs, alveoli, internal respiration, external respiration, tidal air, complemental air, supplemental air, vital capacity, hemoglobin.

38. Why is it important that a physical educator possess an understanding of human anatomy and physiology?

FOOTNOTES

1. Bartley, S. H., and E. Chute, *Fatigue and Impairment in Man,* First Ed. New York: McGraw-Hill, 1947.

2. Wolf, Stewart, M.D., "Psychosomatic Aspects of Competitive Sports," *Journal of Sports Medicine and Physical Fitness,* June and September, 1963.

3.. Grombach, John V., *The 1964 Olympic Guide.* New York: Avon Books, 1964.

4. Steen, Edwin B., Ph.D., and Ashley Montagu, *Anatomy and Physiology.* New York: Barnes and Noble, Inc., 1959, p. 51.

5. Morehouse, Lawrence E., and Augustus T. Miller, Jr., *Physiology of Exercise.* St. Louis: C. V. Mosby, 1959.

6. Huxley, H. E., "The Mechanism of Muscular Contraction," *Scientific American,* December, 1965, p. 19.

7. Rasch, Phillip J., and Roger K. Burke, *Kinesiology and Applied Anatomy.* Philadelphia: Lea and Febiger, 1963.

8. Frohse, Franz, Max Brödel and Leon Schlossberg, *Atlas of Human Anatomy.* New York: Barnes and Noble, Inc., 1959, p. 74.

9. Rochelle, R. H., "Blood Plasma Cholesterol Changes During a Physical Training Program," *The Journal of Sports Medicine,* January, 1961, p. 63.

10. Chailley-Bert, Paul, P. Labignette and Fabre-Chevalier (MME), "Contribution a l'etude des variations du cholesterol sanguin au cours des activities physiques," *Presse Med., 63,* 415, 1955.

11. Montoye, H.J., W.D. Van Huss, W.D. Brewer, E.M. Jones, M.A. Ohlson, E. Mahoney, and H. Olson, "The Effects of Exercise on Blood Cholesterol in Middle-Aged Men," *American Journal of Clinical Nutrition, 7,*139-145, 1959.

12. Groen, J., B. K. Tjoing, E. Manninga, and A. F. Willebrands, "The Influence of Nutrition, Individuality, and Some Other Factors Including Various Forms of Stress, on the Serum Cholesterol," *Voeding, 13,* 556, 1952.

13. Myasnikov, A. L., "Influence of Some Factors on Development of Experimental Cholesterol Atherosclerosis," *Circulation, 17,* 99-113, Jan., 1958.

14. Morris, J. N., P.A.B. Raffle, C. G. Roberts, and J. W. Parks, "Coronary Heart Disease and Physical Activity of Work," *Lancet, 265,*1053-57, 1111-20, 1953.

15. Michael, Ernest D., Jr., and Arthur J. Gallon, "Pulse Wave and Blood Pressure Changes Occurring During a Physical Training Program," *The Research Quarterly of American Association for Health, Physical Education, and Recreation,* Vol. 31, No. 1.

16. Karpovich, Peter V., *Physiology of Muscular Activity.* Philadelphia: W. B. Saunders, 1955, p. 61.

13

Physical Fitness

PHYSICAL EDUCATORS MUST constantly remind themselves that they are concerned with the total individual functioning as a member of society. While the major ultimate objective of physical education is improvement in physical fitness, it must be remembered that in striving to improve a child's physical fitness status physical educators are also influencing his attitudes toward himself and others; helping him to learn about his body — its limitations and its potentialities; and are teaching him to work cooperatively and productively with others. In reviewing the physiology and anatomy of the nervous system, the muscular system, the skeletal system, the respiratory system, and the circulatory system, the high degree of interdependence between all these systems has been seen. Maximal functional capacity of each is dependent upon all the others.

WHAT PHYSICAL FITNESS IS

Physical fitness is but one aspect of total fitness. The others are emotional fitness, mental fitness, and social fitness. All these are related to and influence one another. Emotional and social fitness are discussed elsewhere in this text.

One of the foremost students of physical fitness has been Dr. Thomas K. Cureton,[1] Professor of Physical Education and Director of the Physical Fitness Research Laboratory at the University of Illinois. He has presented the following charts which illustrate the relationships between organic condition, physique, motor fitness, sensory fitness, and sports skills.

Almost everyone is born with a fairly high level of organic fitness but with little in the way of physique, motor fitness, sensory fitness, or skills. He must develop the latter upon his organic base. Development of these will, in turn, contribute to the improvement of organic condition. *Organic condition* refers to the relative state of health and efficiency of the sense organs, glands of

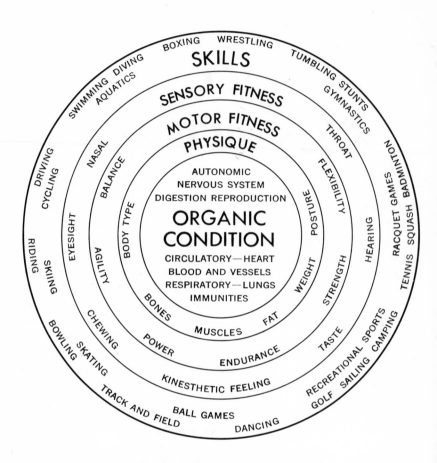

Aspects of physical fitness *(T.K. Cureton)*

internal accretion, and the digestive, skeletal, muscular, nervous, circulatory, and reproductive systems.

Physique refers to those aspects which are easily seen such as healthy appearance, muscular development, posture, and proper proportions between bone, muscle, fat, and size.

Motor fitness refers to those qualities which are subject to improvement, can be measured, and contribute to success in athletics. It is generally accepted that motor fitness includes six components: (1) endurance (cardiovascular-respiratory and muscular); (2) strength; (3) power; (4) agility; (5) flexibility; and (6) balance. These are the qualities which make for skill in running, jumping, dodging, climbing, swimming, lifting weights, carrying

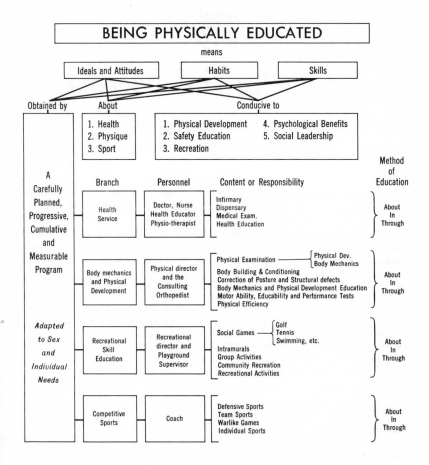

loads, and endurance in physical work. They are the primary concern of the physical educator. A number of tests have been devised to measure these qualities. Most of the tests have erroneously been called tests of physical fitness. They are, in reality, tests of motor fitness which is only one aspect of the still rather vague but comprehensive entity called physical fitness.

Strength is measured by the amount of resistance which a person's muscles can overcome. It is measured by means of dynamometers or by seeing how much weight can be lifted at one time. *Power* is the ability to expend energy in a short span of time as in the broad jump, vertical jump, or shot put. It is the explosive power of muscles. *Agility* is the ability to make quick, adaptive movements as in dodging around chairs or Indian clubs against time. *Endurance* may be of two types — muscular or cardiovascular. There is some

A Presidential Message

TO THE SCHOOLS
ON THE PHYSICAL FITNESS OF YOUTH

The strength of our democracy is no greater than the collective well-being of our people. The vigor of our country is no stronger than the vitality and will of all our countrymen. The level of physical, mental, moral and spiritual fitness of every American citizen must be our constant concern.

The need for increased attention to the physical fitness of our youth is clearly established. Although today's young people are fundamentally healthier than the youth of any previous generation, the majority have not developed strong, agile bodies. The softening process of our civilization continues to carry on its persistent erosion.

It is of great importance, then, that we take immediate steps to ensure that every American child be given the opportunity to make and keep himself physically fit—fit to learn, fit to understand, to grow in grace and stature, to fully live.

In answering this challenge, we look to our schools and colleges as the decisive force in a renewed national effort to strengthen the physical fitness of youth. Many of our schools have long been making strenuous efforts to assist our young people attain and maintain health and physical fitness. But we must do more. We must expand and improve our health services, health education and physical education. We must increase our facilities and the time devoted to physical activity. We must invigorate our curricula and give high priority to a crusade for excellence in health and fitness.

To members of school boards, school administrators, teachers and pupils themselves, I am directing this urgent call to strengthen all programs which contribute to the physical fitness of our youth. I strongly urge each school to adopt the three specific recommendations of my Council on Youth Fitness:

1. Identify the physically underdeveloped pupil and work with him to improve his physical capacity.

2. Provide a minimum of fifteen minutes of vigorous activity every day for all pupils.

3. Use valid fitness tests to determine pupils' physical abilities and evaluate their progress.

The adoption of these recommendations by our schools will ensure the beginning of a sound basic program of physical developmental activity.

In our total fitness efforts the schools, of course, will not stand alone. I urge that in all communities there be more coordination between the schools and the community, parents, educators and civic-minded citizens in carrying forward a resourceful, vigorous program for physical fitness—a program that will stir the imagination of our youth, calling on their toughest abilities, enlisting their greatest enthusiasm—a program which will enable them to build the energy and strength that is their American heritage.

JOHN F. KENNEDY

relationship between the two. *Muscular endurance* is usually measured by the number of chin-ups, push-ups, or sit-ups which a person can do. The movement is performed against relatively little resistance. *Cardiovascular endurance* is usually measured by the time required to run a distance of at least 400 yards. The distance should be great enough to produce cardiorespiratory stress. *Balance* may be either dynamic or static. It is not known at present if there is any relationship between the two types. *Dynamic balance*, maintaining balance while moving, is demonstrated by a gymnast performing on the side horse, or by a boxer. *Static balance* is the ability to hold a position such as standing on one foot. *Flexibility* is the range of motion possible in joints of the body and is measured in such ways as touching the floor with the fingertips while standing with knees straight.

All six qualities can be improved with the possible exception of balance. Research evidence indicates that when strength is improved, power, agility, and muscular endurance also improve. Research evidence further indicates that the most effective methods for improving strength are isometric exercises and progressive resistance exercises.

The qualities encompassed by sensory fitness include vision, hearing, taste, smell, and kinesthetic sense. The health and efficiency of these are probably determined principally by heredity but it is likely that healthful living will contribute to their improvement.

It is through teaching and coaching of movement skills that the physical educator makes his contribution to the improvement of physical fitness in his students. There are a great number of skills. The list presented by Dr. Cureton

Teamwork in football *(Courtesy: University of Connecticut)*

is merely illustrative. Any activity involving the larger muscles and which is fairly vigorous could be included. Physical educators often debate whether the less vigorous activities such as table tennis, archery, horseshoe pitching, and social dancing have a place in the physical education curriculum.

In discussions about physical fitness, two questions inevitably arise. These are: (1) How much fitness? and (2) Fit for what? It is implied in these questions that people no longer need a high level of physical fitness since they have machinery to do the physical work for them and that they need only enough physical fitness to perform duties involved in their job. Proponents of this point of view imply that if their job is to "push a pencil" all day long, they need only enough strength to push a pencil and only enough endurance to push it for eight hours a day. This premise is the result of a superficial view prevalent because of lack of knowledge of the nature of man or of the demands of his life.

WHY PHYSICAL FITNESS IS IMPORTANT

Man has been on this earth for over two million years. The industrial revolution began very recently — about A.D. 1750 with the invention of the flying shuttle for the hand loom. This speeded up the making of thread. Until the industrial revolution, man had to do all his work with muscle power. He did have tools such as hammers, saws, shovels, picks, and axes but to use these he had to provide muscle power. Before the industrial revolution, man had to carry heavy loads, chop wood, hoe the garden, carry water, and do many other physically demanding tasks. The hardy pioneers — only about three hundred years ago — had to erect log cabins, hunt, fish, clear land, and fight Indians if they were to survive. Medieval serfs pulled carts, broke up the soil with their hoes and picks, and lifted heavy boulders and timbers. Neanderthal man — thousands of years ago — depended upon his strength, power, agility, and endurance for survival.

For roughly 1,999,800 years of his time on earth, man has had to depend primarily upon his strength, power, agility, and endurance for survival. For only a little over 200 years has man had machines to help him with his physical labors. Today he can survive quite well with a minimum of physical activity. Elevators and escalators lift him to the desired floor. Automobiles, trains, airplanes, and motor bikes carry him to his destination whether it is on the other side of the world or just a block down the street. "Go-carts" even carry him around the golf course while he is "getting his exercise." Photo-electric light cells open his garage door. He has push buttons to eliminate the shifting of gears, power brakes and power steering to conserve his strength, windows which lower themselves when he pushes a button, and seats which move backward or forward when he presses another button. He moves almost not at all. Perhaps he can bend down, but if he does, he can't straighten up again! It is only for a microscopically short period of time during man's total span on the earth that he has not had to move and use his muscles to survive. We have pointed out that man has been on earth for 2,000,000 years and that he has had machinery to aid him with his work for only 200 years. To dramatize this, imagine a line 625 feet long (the length of two football fields placed end to end plus 25 feet) to represent 2,000,000 years. Two hundred years will be only 1/16 of one inch! Man was here a long time before he invented machinery.

During the great span of time when man did not have machinery to do his work, man's body made adaptations to enable him to move. He was designed to move, made adaptations to move, and consequently needs to move in order to develop and grow. Because evolutionary physiologic and anatomic changes require thousands of years, man is not likely to become adapted to a sedentary life in the near future!

Now, for the first time in his history, man can choose to move or not to move since he need not move to survive. It is unlikely that he will discard his labor-saving devices. It is only during his leisure hours that he can get needed physical activity. Will he be a spectator in front of his TV set and at athletic contests satisfying his ego needs vicariously or will he play tennis, badminton, handball or softball, swim, go for a hike or run, chop wood, or till his garden? It is principally the responsibility of the physical educators to convince him that he should choose to be physically active.

Speedball in a physical education class *(Courtesy: University of Connecticut)*

Man is better educated, better nourished, and receives better medical care than he ever has. The contagious diseases have been almost conquered. Infant and maternal mortality have declined sharply. Surgical procedures have been greatly improved. Length of life has increased. Man should no longer think of good health as merely freedom from disease. His goal *should* be to be fully and dynamically alive. One's state of health could be viewed as a continuum with death at one end, ill health a point arbitrarily drawn somewhere along the line, and the state of being fully and dynamically alive at the other end.

The greatest killers of man today are cardiovascular failures, cancer, and cerebrovascular accidents. The incidence of deaths from these diseases has increased simply because man is living longer. (He is escaping the diseases which, in the past, took his life when he was young.) A characteristic of these diseases, along with ulcers, hypertension and other chronic diseases, is that they take many years to develop. Their onset could be delayed, or perhaps they could be prevented altogether, if man practiced good habits of living throughout his lifetime – if he had sound habits of nutrition, rest, relaxation, and exercise, avoided smoking and excessive drinking, and if he practiced "the hygiene of the quiet mind." These habits, attitudes, and practices are the outcome, not of surgery or medicine, but of education. It is the function primarily of health educators and physical educators to encourage development of these habits, attitudes, and practices. Physical and health educators can make a most important contribution to our society in this area.

FITNESS OF AMERICAN CHILDREN, COMPARED TO FITNESS OF CHILDREN IN OTHER COUNTRIES

The level of physical fitness of American children is below that of children of most other countries. This is one of the penalties of greater material wealth, labor saving devices, luxuries, and abundant transportation. Namiko Ikada[2] utilized the Iowa Test of Motor Fitness to compare 395 Tokyo children with 355 Iowa children, nine to twelve years of age. The test battery included sit-ups, standing broad jump, shuttle run, forward bend, grasshopper, pull-ups for boys, bent arm hang for girls, and dash. Anthropometric (body dimensions) measurements were taken in height, weight, knee-finger length, and leg length. He found that Iowa children were heavier, taller, and had longer legs but Tokyo children scored better in all motor performance tests except sit-ups.

M. S. Kelliher[3] gave the Kraus-Weber Test for Minimum Muscular Fitness to 2325 Pakistani male and female school children and compared the results with those of the Kraus-Weber tests previously given children in Europe and the United States. European children scored highest, Pakistani children scored next, and children in the United States scored poorest. The Kraus-Weber Test includes six items which measure, on a simple pass or fail basis, abdominal and back strength and "hamstring" (hip and knee joint) flexibility. This test is by no means a complete test of physical fitness since it does not include measures of physique or organic condition. It is not even a test of motor fitness since there are no measures of agility, power, endurance, or balance included. It is, as its name states, a test of minimal muscular fitness needed to sustain satisfactory posture. This makes it nonetheless surprising that such a large proportion of children in the United States should fail a test as simple as this one. The inferior performance of children in the United States in the Kraus-Weber Tests is particularly surprising when it is known that failures can be practically eliminated in only a few weeks through a calisthenic, tumbling, and gymnastic program.

One of the authors [Baley] directed the Hattiesburg (Mississippi) Tumbling Tots and Teens between 1957 and 1960. The participants in this program were four to fifteen years old. In October, 36 percent of the new participants failed one or more items of the Kraus-Weber Tests. Ten weeks later, after having participated in tumbling and gymnastic activities for one hour on Tuesdays and another on Thursdays, only 4 percent failed one or more items.[4] A number of studies have shown an average of 55 percent failures on this test among children in the United States.

James Bosco[5] administered the Kraus-Weber Test to children 6 to 12 years old who had participated in a tumbling and gymnastics program for 12 weeks in Champaign, Illinois. The children attended the classes for one hour one to

Buoyancy *(Courtesy: University of Connecticut)*

three times per week. Only 9.5 percent of the children enrolled in this program failed one or more items of the test. Vigorous activities such as gymnastics, tumbling, wrestling, handball, soccer, speedball, and resistance exercises should have preference over the less vigorous activities such as archery, table tennis, and social dancing if improvement in physical fitness status is an objective of physical education programs.

ACTIVITY AND THE AGING PROCESS

Thanks to advances in medical science, public sanitation, and public health knowledge, length of life universally, and particularly in the United States, has been steadily increasing. We can expect to see increasing numbers of older people in our society. A large number of middle-aged and older men are prematurely disabled by the degenerative diseases such as arthritis, ulcers, or cerebral, peripheral, or coronary arteriosclerosis. A characteristic of these degenerative diseases is their slow but inevitable progression and long periods of disability before the victim actually succumbs to the disease. A man disabled by one of these degenerative diseases is a greater social loss and heavier burden upon his immediate family than one who dies immediately.

While the death rate from these diseases is high, their cost must be measured by more than the cost of hospitalization or through mortality tables. By the time some men reach their peak in knowledge, skill, and productive efficiency, they are on the way down in stamina, energy, and health. If they could sustain these qualities of youth, their productivity would be vastly increased. Most of the decrements in stamina, energy, and health, which are the result of having lived a number of years, could be significantly decelerated by the practice of healthful habits of living throughout life. Here again, health educators and physical educators have a socially significant contribution to make.

Biologic and chronologic age are not necessarily equal. Some people age more rapidly than do others but all can decelerate the rate of biologic aging through a program of physical activity. A number of psychologists and psychiatrists writing on the mental and psychological problems of older people point out that the tensions, conflicts, and emotional strains which are concomitants of a complex civilization can and do cause a number of physical ailments. These men point out that recreational habits play an important part in relieving tensions, emotional strains, and conflicts.

Baley,[6] for his doctoral dissertation, administered a questionnaire to 3000 men from various occupations who were between the ages of 20 and 60. Sixty-seven recreational activities were listed. The men were asked to indicate whether they liked, disliked, or felt indifferent to each activity; to indicate

the frequency of their participation in each activity; and finally to indicate
the reason if they did not participate as frequently as they would like in any
particular activity. Strangely, even in their fifties these men liked the vigorous
activities but did not participate in them. They listed "lack of time" as their
principal reason for not participating as frequently as they would like. This
was surprising in view of the fact they indicated they watched television every
day for two or more hours!

It was found that as men grow older they like fewer recreational activities,
feel indifferent toward an increasing number, and dislike an increasing
number. The three types of activities which showed the greatest decline in
amount of participation with increase in age were: (1) those which require
quick reaction time, (2) those which require physical stamina and endurance,
and (3) those which satisfy the romantic and erotic impulses. As men grow
older the proportion of the time which is spent on gardening, motoring,
hiking, metal-craft, bait-casting, still fishing, and checkers increases. The
recreational habits of younger men did not differ greatly from those of older
men. Participation in recreational activities of a sports type was meager at all
ages in comparison to participation in the more sedentary activities. Bowling,
still fishing, and bait casting were the only sports ranking among the twenty
leisure activities showing the greatest amount of participation for all four age
groups (20–29, 30–39, 40–49, and 50–59).

Throughout the European countries, excluding Great Britain, the emphasis
in school physical education programs has been primarily upon the physical
fitness outcomes rather than upon the development of leisure skills. Yet
considerably greater numbers of Europeans of all ages participate in hiking,

Swimming class *(Courtesy: University of Connecticut)*

hosteling, bicycling, mountain climbing, gymnastics, soccer, and mass calisthenics. Could it be that the development of an appreciation of physical fitness has greater carry-over value and gives greater assurance of continued participation in vigorous physical activity throughout one's life than does a recreational or sports program? This problem has never been studied. It may be that the subjective experience of being physically fit induces a person to lead a physically vigorous life more effectively than do pleasurable experiences in recreational activities while young.

DIFFERENCES BETWEEN MALES AND FEMALES

The physical and psychological differences between males and females are not as great as was formerly believed. Most people wish to maximize rather than to minimize these differences. After the age of puberty, girls in general become more feminine, while boys become more masculine in appearance, manners, and interests. Pelvic width relative to shoulder width is greater in girls than it is in boys. This enables girls to perform their later child-bearing function with greater efficiency. Girls have a narrower shoulder girdle. The narrower shoulder girdle and wider pelvic girdle of girls causes their center of gravity to be lower than that of boys. The bones of their shoulder girdle cannot accommodate as much muscle as can those of boys. All their bones, with the exception of the pelvis, are thinner and lighter than those of boys and cannot accommodate as much muscle. The respiratory and pulse rate of girls is slightly faster than that of boys. The stroke volume of the heart and the minute-volume of the lungs in girls is smaller, on the average. These cardiovascular-respiratory differences are probably due principally to difference in size rather than to other factors. Generally, smaller people have a smaller stroke volume of the heart and minute-volume of the lungs and faster pulse and respiratory rates than do larger people. These anatomic and physiologic differences do not, in and of themselves, rule out participation in any sports activities for girls, although they would make some sports such as football, boxing, pole vaulting, horizontal bar work, and others hazardous. These differences also make for unequal competition between boys and girls in most activities. Many of the differences between boys and girls are learned differences. These include attitudes, behaviors, values, and appreciations.

Boys and girls and young men and women in physical education classes, from kindergarten through college, should participate in many more coeducational activity classes than they now do. They date, they marry, they raise a family. They are with a member of the opposite sex probably more than they are with members of their own sex. Husband and wife should be able to enjoy one another's company in several different sports activities throughout their lifetime. The place to initiate the formation of these attitudes and skills is in the required physical education classes.

INDIVIDUAL DIFFERENCES

People differ in many ways — height, weight, density of bone and muscle, strength, power, agility, flexibility, length of arms and legs relative to trunk length, kinesthetic sense, balance, endurance, coordination, aggressiveness, competitiveness, and in many other respects. Different sports require different physical, mental, and emotional qualities for success. Success in football is more likely if a boy is aggressive, enjoys physical contact, is big-boned, and possesses strength and power relative to other boys. Success in swimming is more likely if the competitor is light-boned, buoyant, has long arms and legs, big feet and hands, and enjoys the feeling of fatigue. Success in basketball is more likely if the participant is tall, agile, and has good hand-eye coordination, has the ability to perceive spatial relationships quickly, and has good endurance. Success in gymnastics is more likely if the participant possesses strength and power relative to his own body weight, is agile, has good kinesthetic sense, possesses a good sense of balance, and has a type of physical courage different from that required in "contact" sports.

Every boy and girl wants — and needs — to succeed in something, and every boy and girl can succeed in something. The greater the diversity of sports offered in the required physical education, the intramural, and the

Isometrics for strength *(Courtesy: University of Connecticut)*

interscholastic or intercollegiate athletic programs, the greater the number who will be able to experience success. Some boys could never become outstanding ball players. Some boys and girls could never become outstanding in gymnastics. Some could never become outstanding in basketball. However, there is some sport in which each boy or girl could succeed and every boy and girl should experience success in some sport. This is one reason one of the best criteria for evaluating the quality of a physical education, intramural, interscholastic or intercollegiate athletic program is the number and diversity of offerings.

SOME CONTRIBUTIONS OF INTERCOLLEGIATE ATHLETICS

Interscholastic and intercollegiate athletic events should be utilized to enlarge the educational arena. Athletic events can be so conducted as to develop in spectators an appreciation of physical fitness and of skilled performance which, hopefully, will lead to increased participation by the spectators. Witnessing highly skilled performers, an appreciation of skilled performance, and a desire to emulate highly skilled performers is no guarantee that the spectator will begin participating — but it is a first step. Furthermore, there is benefit to the players themselves in having spectators at contests. Players will make greater efforts to achieve excellence when there is an audience present. As a result, they are more likely to observe the rules of hygienic living and expend greater efforts to achieve a higher level of physical fitness. If the

Speed and precision *(Courtesy: U. S. Marine Corps, Quantico, Va.)*

coaches and spectators appreciate ethical behavior, the players are also more likely to so behave.

It is the *striving* toward excellence and not the *being* excellent in athletics which is educationally worthwhile. There is little social value in a double flyaway off the horizontal bar, a 70-yard punt, or a 30-point game average. The value accrues to the participant during the time he is striving to become excellent. It is then that he develops determination, perseverance, patience, self-confidence, and improves his physical fitness.

Athletic events can provide a cultural experience for the spectators just as does the ballet, a musical concert, or a dramatic presentation. The performance of a highly skilled gymnast in the floor exercise is a poetry of motion. To watch a fielder run, leap into the air and catch a baseball is as much an esthetic experience as watching the ballet. This element is present in all sports.

SUMMARY

In previous chapters we have seen that throughout history, men and societies have used physical education as a media to improve physical fitness to achieve military objectives. When physical education and physical fitness are thus narrowly conceived it is almost certain that they will be deemphasized when the military objectives have been achieved.

When improved physical fitness is regarded as the sole objective of physical education, failure to recognize the unity of man has been demonstrated and the true potential of physical education can never be achieved. No matter what the physical educator does with, to, or for his students, there are always mental, emotional, and social, as well as physical aspects. There is always intellectual content; there are emotional reactions; and there are social interactions as well as learning of movement skills and physiologic reactions. Physical education makes (when well taught) contributions in intellectual, emotional, and social areas.

Nevertheless, the biologic outcomes must be primary because these are the unique concerns of physical education. No other course in the curriculum is concerned with them. Furthermore, as the amount of physical work required of people decreases owing to increased mechanization and transportation, the more important it becomes that people secure physical activity in activities other than at their work. Sports and other recreational activities can fill this void.

We have seen that, thanks to the abundance of labor-saving devices in the United States, children in this country do not possess as high a level of physical fitness as do the children of several other countries. The available evidence seems to indicate that we need to encourage our students to engage in more vigorous activities.

While it is meager, the available evidence seems to indicate that few men between the ages of 20 and 60 participate regularly and to an appreciable degree in sports activities even though they would like to do so. Though they state that they haven't time to participate in sports activities, they do spend two to three hours each day watching television. Their reason for failure to participate more frequently appears to be a rationalization. Physical educators must discover more effective means for achieving the "carry-over" objective.

It has been pointed out that there are physiologic, anatomic, psychologic, and sociologic differences between males and females and between individuals of the same sex. These differences have implications for the administration and teaching of physical education and for interscholastic and intercollegiate athletic programs.

In the next chapters we will see how mental, emotional, and social forces act upon this organic base.

QUESTIONS

1. Present a definition of total fitness, physical fitness, motor fitness.

2. Define each of the six components of motor fitness. How are they measured?

3. Present a justification for the inclusion of physical fitness as a major objective of physical education.

4. How much physical fitness do you want for yourself? Is this consistent with your other desires and goals?

5. Cite the evidence which seems to indicate that the level of physical fitness of American children is below that of children of other countries.

6. Discuss the recreational habits and interests of adult men ages 20–60.

7. What are some of the physiologic and anatomic differences between males and females and what are the implications for the teaching of physical education?

8. What activities should girls be discouraged from participation in? Why?

9. What are the implications of individual differences (anatomic and psychologic) for the administration of physical education and athletic programs?

10. Discuss the potential contribution of intercollegiate athletics to the objectives of physical education.

FOOTNOTES

1. Cureton, Thomas Kirk, Jr., *Physical Fitness Appraisal and Guidance*. St. Louis: C. V. Mosby Co., 1947.

2. Ikada, Namiko, "A Comparison of Physical Fitness of Children of Iowa, U.S.A., and Tokyo, Japan," *Research Quarterly*, Vol. 33, No. 4.

3. Kelliher, M.S., "A Report on the Kraus-Weber Test in East Pakistan," *Research Quarterly*, Vol. 31, No. 1.

4. Baley, James A., "Are Gymnastics and Tumbling Essential?" *Physical Educator*, May, 1961.

5. Bosco, James, "Let's Put Gymnastics Back into Our Physical Education Programs," *Physical Educator*, March, 1959, p. 5.

6. Baley, James A., "Recreation and the Aging Process," Ph.D. Thesis, The Ohio State University, 1952 (Available in microcard form from the Library of Congress and The Springfield Research Council and in microfilm form from University Microfilms, Ann Arbor, Mich.).

14

The Psychologic Bases of Physical Education

IN A PRECEDING chapter, the high degree of interrelatedness of all the body systems was pointed out. Each system influences and is influenced by the others. Physical activity affects the cardiovascular, respiratory, neural, muscular, and glandular systems and these systems, in turn, affect the quantity and the quality of the physical activity. In the present chapter, the influence of the external environment upon the organism shall be pointed out. The individual is aided in becoming a "human," or a social being, as a result of his interrelationships with other individuals. These interrelations influence the formation of his personality, his values, his motivations, his methods of striving toward satisfaction of his needs, and even his health.

PHYSICAL EDUCATION TEACHERS
STRONGLY INFLUENCE PERSONALITY DEVELOPMENT

Next to the family, teachers are among those aspects of a child's environment which most powerfully influence formation of his personality. Of all the teachers, it is probably the physical educator who most strongly influences the child in this area of his development. It is doubtful that teachers of other subjects can attain the highly motivated behavior of children secured by physical educators during closely contested athletic games. A high degree of motivation and even of emotion gives the teaching-learning process greater potential effectiveness. Whether this potential is realized depends upon whether the teacher has the necessary emotional control himself and whether he has a basic understanding of psychologic processes. In the classroom, as on the playing field, the emotionalized person is more alert and more likely to react. This point is illustrated in the counsel of an experienced professor who told a beginning teacher: "You will discover that in nearly every class there is a youngster eager to argue. Restrain the impulse to silence him. He may be the only one listening."

The physical educator can utilize the emotionally charged human relationships which occur in athletic events to direct the formation of children's personalities so that they meet the approval of society. It is necessary, however, that the teacher plan for and work toward these objectives. Such qualities as cooperativeness, team work, fair play, sportsmanship, and determination do not automatically accrue as a result of participation in athletics. Sports can be, and have been, used to educate men to brutality and clever deception (as they often are during war time), or they can be used to educate men to courageous adherance to sportsmanlike behavior in spite of overwhelming odds or great temptation. Can a football player be taught to refrain from "kneeing" an opponent during a pile-up when he is reasonably certain he will not be observed and he wishes to "even the score" for the elbow in the face he received during the previous play? Can such qualities as sympathy, honesty, courage, cooperativeness and initiative be taught? Psychologists, social-psychologists, anthropologists, and psychiatrists tell us that they *can* and are.

In this chapter, a cursory look will be taken at the procedures which make these learnings possible. Students in their general and educational psychology courses will study these processes in greater detail. Here the endeavor will be made to show the reader how to apply the principles arrived at through these learnings to the teaching of physical education. This should help the physical educator to utilize the expensive gymnasia, natatoria, stadia, and playing fields as laboratories and the athletic events and other physical activities as media for human development. It is hoped that future physical educators will utilize physical education not only to enhance the organic development of their students but also their emotional, intellectual, and personality development. It is hoped that as coaches they will not be *primarily* concerned with win-loss records, gate receipts, inches of newspaper publicity, or numbers of spectators but will be primarily concerned with utilizing athletics to develop integrated personalities. An understanding of personality development will help them to accomplish this.

ORGANIC BASES OF PERSONALITY

Every individual is first of all an organic system. His organic system is the core upon which personality is built. His body sets limits to the adaptations which he can make to the social and cultural environment. Furthermore, it is

Power plus showmanship, at Duke University

through his body that he reacts to and acts upon the environment. He is constantly adjusting to the environment at the physiochemical level through a series of internal changes. Examples of these physiochemical adjustments to environment are: (1) in the peristaltic movements and enzymatic actions of the digestive system, (2) the respiratory movements and gas exchange of the respiratory system, and (3) the pumping action of the heart and the exchange of waste products and nutrients between the blood and the tissues of the circulatory system. While the individual cells can tolerate very little change in the temperature, chemical composition or viscosity of their milieu (the fluid in which they are bathed), the entire organism can tolerate a considerable range in the temperature, humidity, viscosity, or chemical composition of its environment. On a hot day people perspire. This helps to cool the body to maintain the cellular environment at a constant temperature. At high altitudes the respiratory rate accelerates to help to maintain a constant cellular environment with respect to oxygen content. These adaptations of the total organism are initiated principally by the nervous and the endocrine systems.

Nervous System

The nervous system, from the standpoint of the biologic bases of physical education, was discussed in Chapter 12. It is now necessary that it be considered from the point of view of learning, socialization, and the development of the integrated personality.

The nervous system is the principal coordinating agency for all the body organs. It makes habit formation, learning, and reflective thought possible.

Through his exteroceptors in the eyes, the ears, the nose, the tongue, and the skin; the interoceptors in the viscera; and the proprioceptors in the muscles and in the semicircular canals, the human comes into contact with and adjusts to his environment. The affector or afferent neurons (which are located in the exteroceptors, interoceptors, or proprioceptors) synapse with the connector neurons which in turn synapse with the effector or motor neurons which activate the muscles or glands. The connector neurons for simple reflex actions are located in the lower brain and spinal cord but in more complex acts the connector neurons in the upper brain are used.

The synaptic connections which occur in the cerebral cortex are the most important from the standpoint of learning. Here, there are a multitude of connector neurons making possible a multitude of potential pathway choices among thousands of possible neural pathways, all of which are made in fractions of a second. Consider for a moment the possible alternate movements and the speed with which these decisions are made by a short stop in baseball, for example. At the crack of the bat he must decide in which of a number of directions he should begin to move or whether to move at all. He must decide whether to stoop or to leap, and if he decides to leap he must determine how high and in what direction. He must make the many body adjustments of the legs, arms, head, eyes, body, feet, and hands to catch the ball while at the same time he decides whether to run to second base, to put out the man at first, to throw to the second baseman for an attempted double play, or to throw to the first baseman. The throw must not be made too high, too low, or too wide. This is no simple reflex action but a highly complex one. Repetition of each of the alternate courses of action (practice) will facilitate the neural functions. Repetition is the physiologic basis of habit formation as well as of the development of skill.

It is the cerebral cortex with the great number of alternate responses, which its association or connector neurons make possible, that is responsible for man's superiority over other animals. The cerebral cortex makes possible extensive and long continued learning. Man has the same basic drives such as hunger, thirst, and sex, and the same basic emotional responses such as fear and anger as do animals. He also has the same fundamental reflexes. However, in man those fundamental reflexes and drives are modified and controlled by the cerebral cortex. The modifications and controls are brought about as a result of social-cultural influences. As the human grows toward adulthood, the social-cultural learnings exert an ever greater influence upon his behavior while the fundamental reflexes exert a decreasing influence. This aspect of human adaptation has important implications for physical education and athletics with regard to their potential for modifying behavior.

For the first month or two of its life, a baby is concerned only with satisfaction of its organic needs — food, water, warmth, and other physical aspects of its environment both internal and external. But as a result of his mother's repeated smiling at him, caresses, and other expressions of love, as she ministers to his organic needs, he becomes conditioned and associates these actions with satisfaction of his organic needs. He begins to smile at his mother and coo or "talk" to her. His socialization has begun! In fact, after a while he comes to desire these expressions of affection as much or more than he does satisfaction of his organic needs.

Autonomic System

It will be recalled that in Chapter 12 the autonomic nervous system was discussed. It was pointed out that it has two divisions – the sympathetic and the parasympathetic. These two divisions operate in opposition to one another. Where the sympathetic excites, the parasympathetic inhibits; and where the sympathetic inhibits, the parasympathetic excites. During the emotion of fear the sympathetic division causes the muscles controlling defecation and urination to relax and inhibits the digestive processes. The parasympathetic division causes the sphincter muscles of urination and defecation to contract, speeds up the digestive processes, inhibits cardiac action, increases activity of the salivary gland, and causes contraction of the iris. The sympathetic division causes relaxation of the sphincters, inhibits the digestive processes, accelerates the heart rate, decreases activity of the salivary glands, and causes the iris to dilate.

The parasympathetic division is related in functions to hunger, sex, and bodily eliminations; the sympathetic to the fundamental emotions of fear and rage. It must be remembered that the autonomic and central nervous systems function together. This is illustrated when a loud noise startles us and causes us to jump. As this occurs, the influences of the sympathetic system are seen and felt in the accelerated heart and respiratory rate, paleness, and inhibition of digestive processes. At a higher cortical level, similar reactions are seen and felt when the instructor tells us that we are doing failing work in the "Foundations of Physical Education" course. While there is much evidence that the autonomic functions may be modified and partially controlled by the action of the central nervous system, it is not certain that the central nervous system is dominant over the autonomic system. In other words, emotions, feelings, and fundamental drives (hunger, sex, and thirst) are the bases of human behavior upon which human personality is constructed. As Kimball Young[1] states: "Man is always a feeling and emotive being. Only secondarily is he an intellectual, rational, and deliberative individual." Participants in sports activities are usually emotionalized. Since emotions are primary, sports (which almost always elicit emotions) are a most effective educational media in the socializing process when they are effectively controlled.

Endocrine System

The human organism is made up of groups of highly specialized cells, each of which contribute in their own unique and specialized way to the total functioning of the organism. Life proceeds, not in the external environment, but in the internal milieu of the cells where they are bathed in the body fluids. The chemical composition of these fluids is controlled in several different manners. One of the most important of these is the control provided by the endocrine system. This system helps people to respond more effectively to their environment while at the same time providing controls for bodily functions. Most of the body cells give off chemical substances which aid in the hemeostatic process but the major responsibility for this function falls to the glands of internal secretion – the endocrine glands. Glands secrete hormones whose function is to set into motion certain bodily activities. These hormones are transported by the blood or lymph to the organs whose structure or function is to be modified. The hormones influence growth, metabolism, sex, mood, temperament, and initiate processes which prepare the body for fight or flight. Let's take a look at some of these endocrine glands.

The *parathyroids* are tiny organs imbedded in the tissue of the thyroid. It is believed that they influence metabolism, especially that of calcium. Removal of these glands results in hyperexcitability of the entire neural system, cramps, and in severe cases, convulsions.

The *pineal* glands are small organs located in the brain. While their precise function is not known, it is believed they influence the rate of growth. Physical educators in elementary and junior high schools will see great differences in the size of their students. These differences make mandatory certain adaptations in the program.

The *thymus* is located in the thorax. It is believed to guard against too early sexual development. Its size decreases after the age of thirteen. When it retains its size after this age, infantile physical characteristics persist. Physical educators must make allowances in program content and teaching methods for differences caused by the thymus. The amount of pubic hair is an accepted index of a child's physical maturity and is important for classification purposes in physical education activities.

The *islets of Langerhans* which lie embedded in the pancreatic tissue, give off a hormone called *insulin* which regulates the metabolism of sugar. When there is a deficiency in insulin the person suffers from diabetes mellitus (sugar diabetes). People suffering from diabetes mellitus often may participate in vigorous physical activity if they exercise caution in maintaining proper sugar balance in the blood.

The *thyroid* straddles the trachea. It secretes *thyroxine* which is made up of about fifteen percent iodine. The function of thyroxine is to: (1) stimulate body growth, (2) regulate energy discharge, (3) stimulate various internal organs such as the kidneys, sweat glands, liver, pancreas, pituitary, and adrenal glands, and (4) aid in controlling nervous tension. It is undoubtedly the most important regulator of the internal milieu of the cells. A student with a malfunctioning thyroid gland may lack the physical energy necessary to enjoyment of physical movement or he may be extremely nervous.

The *adrenals* are about the size of beans and lie near the kidneys. The inner core of the adrenal gland, called the medulla, produces adrenine. Adrenine causes pulse rate to increase, blood pressure to rise, increases the rate and depth of respiration, dilates the pupils of the eyes, aids in coagulation (clotting) of blood, stimulates release of blood from the spleen into the circulatory system, inhibits the digestive process, and causes contraction of the sphincter muscles. Adrenine supplements the effects of the sympathetic nerves in effecting rapid mobilization of energy. Under conditions of stress such as pain, exposure to cold, asphyxia, physical exercise, and under emotional stress such as anger and fear, both adrenine and the sympathetic division of the autonomic nervous system prepare the skeletal muscles and the involuntary processes for expenditure of energy. These mechanisms prepare man for fight or flight. They contributed to his survival during the two million years that he had to depend upon his strength, speed, power, agility, or endurance for survival. Today, however, social-cultural conditions cause a "feeling" of crises which sets up similar energizing by the adrenal cortex and the sympathetic system. Fear of an examination, "stage fright," fear of loss of status, anger with administrative decisions or with situations which may lead to loss of power or money result in physiologic effects which are similar or identical to those of primitive times which called for fight or flight. In stressful situations, the body is prepared for activity. Neolithic man (and TV cowboys) responded to anger or fear by fighting or fleeing; but in today's culture, a man may not strike his superior (or professor) when he is angry with him. He may not bolt from the examination room or off the stage when he feels fear. Consequently, he is denied the catharsis of physical activity to use up the adrenaline.

Dr. Hans Selya's theory that the chemical imbalance resulting from long continued and excessive stress and tensions is the cause of almost all diseases has received wide acceptance. He lists anger, fear, and anxiety among those stresses which may cause disease. When the body is subjected to these stresses, the adrenal and pituitary glands function to adapt the body to this stress by pouring out an excess of hormones which cause the blood pressure to rise, the arteries to constrict, the heart to pump faster, tbe blood sugar to increase, sensitivity to pain to decrease, the skin and scalp to tingle, and the blood to clot more quickly. For a while, the adrenal and pituitary glands succeed in keeping the body going, but if the stress is too great or of too long duration, the entire defensive mechanism breaks down. The manifestations of a breaking down of the hormonal-adaptation mechanism can take the form of heart disease, arteriosclerosis, high blood pressure, coronary thrombosis, ulcers, rheumatic fever, arthritis, kidney malfunction, diabetes, or almost any form.

When the adrenal and pituitary glands fail in their function as coordinators of bodily functions, the body ceases to function as an integrated unit. Illness follows.

When people are angry they feel like physically assaulting someone, throwing something, or just jumping up and down. These are indications that they are impelled to physical action. From the standpoint of health, it is unfortunate that social taboos prohibit giving physical expressions to these feelings. However, the adrenine can be worked off through socially acceptable physical activity such as punching the bag, chopping wood, smacking a handball, walloping a baseball, striking a tennis ball, or kicking a soccer ball. The famed psychiatrist, Dr. William Mennenger, has stated that participation in sports provides a socially acceptable form of relief for feelings of aggression.

From still another point of view, physical activity may help to decrease the likelihood of a person's suffering from the stress-caused diseases. Physiologists Morehouse and Miller suggest that exercise may increase the size and output of the adrenal glands, thereby resulting in a greater reserve of anti-stress steroids and a shorter time of response to stress.

While school children and college students are not likely to suffer from the stress-caused diseases previously listed, most of them will grow into adulthood, middle age and beyond. Dispositions and attitudes toward physical activity and habits and skills in athletics are formed and developed while people are students in school. If adults had participated in sports while they were in school, they would be more likely to continue participation throughout their adult lives. If they participate in fairly vigorous physical activities during the adult years, they will acquire a measure of protection (through the cathartic effect of physical activity) against the stress-caused diseases. However, the person's desire for excellence and for victory in the sport of his choice should not be so great that the almost certain frustrations produce a new source of stress and anxiety. That this happens to some golfers is well known.

The *adrenal cortex* secretes a hormone called *cortin.* Symptoms of cortin deficiency are fatigue, lethargy, loss of resistance to heat, and changes in basal metabolism. Apparently, cortin influences sexual development since tumors on the adrenal cortex are associated with unusual growth of the sexual organs, sexual precocity, and a tendency toward masculinity in females. It is obvious that a cortin deficiency would influence a student's behavior in a physical education class.

The *pituitary* gland lies at the base of the brain. It has four lobes and probably secretes eight or more different hormones. These influence growth, bodily temperature, basal metabolism, water retention, fat metabolism, blood pressure, and parturition (delivery during childbirth). Underactivity of the anterior lobe results in persistence of infantile features, failure of the sex organs to mature, and stunted growth. Overactivity of this lobe results in gigantism or acromegoly in which there is excessive growth of the fingers, hands, feet, and head and a thickening of the skin and muscles. Oversecretion by the anterior lobe also leads to personality changes such as loss of memory, decline in intellectual acuity, apathy, and drowsiness.

The *gonads* in the male produce *spermatozoa* which are necessary for reproduction. In addition, the gonads produce hormones which trigger bodily changes such as growth of pubic hair, voice changes, and increase in masculinity. The *ovaries* in the female produce *ova* which are the unfertilized eggs. The ovaries also secrete two hormones, *theelin* which acts as a general sex stimulant and *progestin* which prepares the uterus to receive the fertilized ovum. Female sex life is more complex than that of the male, since the female has the added problems of menstruation, gestation, childbirth, and lactation. Physical educators have been concerned that strenuous physical activity may be harmful to the more complex reproductive systems of females and have in the past urged a measure of caution. Recent evidence seems to indicate, however, that females can participate in most vigorous physical activities with safety.

THE RELATIONSHIPS BETWEEN THE ORGANIC BASE AND ENVIRONMENT

The pattern of growth and development followed by any living organism, including man, is the result of both the forces of heredity and the forces of environment. First, there are the forces within the organism such as genes, glands, nervous system, blood, etc. Second, there are the environmental forces such as altitude, humidity, temperature, nutrition, pressure, chemical agents, patterns of activity, light, sound, and social-cultural forces such as customs, mores, and values. At the very beginning of the life of a new organism, even within the uterus, there is an interplay of hereditary and environmental forces. This interplay was dramatically and unfortunately illustrated in the birth defects which resulted when pregnant women ingested the drug thalidomide. The resulting horrible birth anomalies were the result of environmental forces acting upon the unborn child. The fetus has no direct connection with the mother. However, the mother does provide its environment. Chemicals or drugs in her blood stream are part of the environment of the fetus.

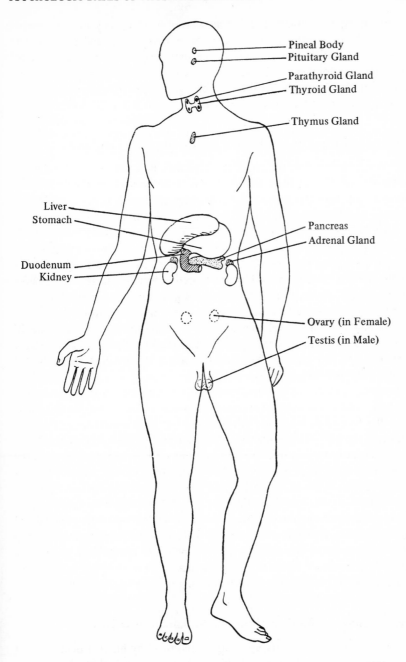

Diagram showing location of the endocrine organs and others which may be endocrine *(from* Fundamentals of Physiology *(p. 226) by Elbert Tokay; Copyright 1944 by Doubleday & Company, Inc.; reprinted by permission of the publisher)*

Man has experimentally produced all sorts of mutations by shooting X-rays or infrared rays at the fertilized eggs of various insects and animals. The evidence shows that the further on the path that the organism is toward completed development, the more difficult it is to affect changes in it. The earlier in its development that forces of change operate upon an organism, the more permanent are the changes effected.

Influence of Environment upon the Intelligence Quotient

That environment does influence the organism is borne out by studies on intelligence quotients. The coefficient of correlation between the intelligence quotients of identical twins is .9; between fraternal twins .7; between ordinary brothers and sisters .5; between children and their parents .3; between children and their grandparents .2. Yet, identical twins brought up in different families show low correlation in tests of intelligence. Furthermore, research has shown that the IQ scores of adopted children are influenced by the intellectual ability of their foster parents. Studies in which preschool children from an economically and culturally deprived community were paired in IQ scores with preschool children from communities with a high cultural and economic level showed that with the passage of years the IQ scores of the children from the intellectually stimulating community steadily increased at a faster rate than did the scores of children raised in the intellectually unchallenging environment.

However, it must not be concluded that the individual is only the *sum* of hereditary and environmental forces. As Kimball Young states, the individual is not the sum of heredity and environment but their *product*; i.e., heredity times environment. And to quote from Carmichael: "The so-called hereditary factors can only be acquired in response to an environment, and likewise the so-called acquired factors can only be secured by a modification of already existing structure, which in the last analysis is hereditary structure. Facts too obvious to bear citation show that the somatic structures that can develop out of a fertilized egg are in some measure dependent upon the physical and chemical structure of the given germ itself. The characteristics which develop out of such a germ, nevertheless, are not *predetermined.* They are on the contrary, *determined* by an environment acting upon the present nature of the individual at every stage of development from fertilization to death."[2]

Socially Induced Modification of Fundamental Drives

The individual reacts to, acts upon, and is modified by his environment. This environment is not only material. It also includes people with their habits, attitudes, traits, ideas, purposes, ideals and values. If the individual is to adapt successfully to his environment, he must adapt his pattern of living to that of the people in his social groups. While the individual possesses certain basic drives to provide satisfaction for such things as hunger, thirst, sex, rest, sleep, comfort, avoidance of pain, ego, power and mastery, recognition, etc., these drives are constantly being modified by pressures from his social groups. The pressures for modification may, in fact, be so powerful as to produce avoidant reactions to acts which, at the physiologic level, are pleasant and satisfying. Contrariwise, these social-cultural pressures may so modify the individual that he seeks out acts which at the physiologic level are unpleasant. The first phenomenon is illustrated in the behavior of people toward sex play outside marriage in social groups where there exist powerful taboos against such action. These taboos may be so great as to render a man impotent. The second phenomenon is illustrated in the behavior of people who at religious-magical rites dance on red hot coals or jab sharp instruments into their flesh and who do these acts with obvious pleasure and often with no serious organic after-effects.

The satisfaction of the basic drives is accompanied by pleasant feelings and emotions. Pleasant emotions or feelings accompany the release of tensions when drives are satisfied whether they have to do with hunger, thirst, ego needs, affection, or belonging. Conversely, when the drive toward satisfaction of a need is frustrated, unpleasant feelings or emotions are evoked. The consumatory experience of eating or drinking during hunger or thirst is satisfying and pleasant as is usually the satisfaction of the ego needs upon winning a game or earning an "A" in literature and composition.

When we lose the game or fail the course we experience unpleasant emotions such as disappointment, irritation, anger, or rage. However, these

Volleyball in a physical education class *(Courtesy: University of Connecticut)*

emotions are modified by the higher brain centers. The cerebral cortex acts to inhibit or to facilitate overt expression of these emotions. The emotions are really learned behaviors. This is why such wide variations in emotional expression by people belonging to different social classes, communities, and nationalities is seen. The American Indian boy was taught to manifest indifference to pleasure or pain. The people of some countries weep bitterly and long at the death of a loved one while in other countries they show little or no emotion.

The fans at high-school basketball games in some communities in Indiana and Illinois have given expression to terrifying rage and have physically attacked the game officals when their need for vicarious ego satisfaction was frustrated by these officials who had made decisions unfavorable to the home team. In South America, where people have learned to give vigorous expression to their emotions and where sectional rivalries in soccer are very intense, mobs have killed. At most soccer games in the United States, there is little expression given to emotional states; however, there is a great amount of emotional expression at football, basketball, and baseball games. At tennis matches, gymnastic, track, and swimming meets and at squash, handball, and badminton games in this country, the behavior of spectators is relatively decorous and calm. Furthermore, there are great differences in the behaviors of spectators at the same sport in different communities.

In some communities, where there is much public interest attested to by full bleachers and where it is obvious that the spectators greatly enjoy the game, the behavior of spectators is like that of people at the theater. They applaud skillful play whether the accomplishment was made by the home team or by the opponents. They never dispute the officials' decisions. They treat the visiting team as guests, who, by their presence, have made possible an interesting and enjoyable afternoon. In other communities, the spectators act like spoiled children having a mass tantrum. In basketball, they have been known to drop a hangman's noose from the girders of the gymnasium directly in the path of the game official running along the sideline. In baseball, they have thrown overripe fruit and bottles at the umpire. In football, officials have found it necessary to lock themselves in the locker room to escape angry "fans." The spectators at different sports possess different standards of behavior and the spectators at the same sport in different communities possess different standards of behavior. Yet, all people have the same basic physiologic and psychologic drives. It should be obvious that these are learned behaviors and that, as learned behaviors, they can be modified and changed. Teaching spectators desirable behaviors and emotional control is one of the important responsibilities of the physical educator and the coach. This is another reason they have an important and difficult job. They should and can influence the behavior of spectators as well as of participants.

Booing as a Catharsis

Permissiveness toward spectators at athletic contests in allowing them to give expression to feelings of anger may provide a catharsis for the neurotic or near-neurotic people who might otherwise give expression to these feelings in a less socially approved or perhaps illegal manner. Perhaps, if some people did not have the emotional safety valve of yelling, shouting, cursing, and hurling insults at athletic contests, they would give expression to their neurotic or psychotic needs in such overt acts as assault and battery, "muggings," mob disorders, or even in murder. It may be that some people are aware of their need for such a catharsis when they give expression to the thought that payment of the admission fee to an athletic contest entitles them to such behavior. It would be interesting to correlate the degree of neuroses with the degree of unsportsmanlike behavior displayed by each fan at an athletic contest.

The personality arises as a result of the interplay of society and culture upon the organism. Everyone becomes a member of a group which has a culture at the moment that he is born. The group and the culture are there before the individual. Consequently, in order to achieve satisfaction of his fundamental biologic and psychologic drives, the individual must learn to work through the rituals, customs and mores of his group to achieve satisfaction of these drives. However, he must also learn to modify or restrain some of the fundamental drives if he is to be integrated into the group.

Differences in What Is Accepted Social Behavior

An individual learns to make the most pleasurable and least uncomfortable response to his social as well as to his physical environment. "Normal" children and adults all over the world learn to make the socially accepted responses, to mask their failure to do so, or to suffer the penalties. Every group develops a system of rewards and punishments to inculcate children with its own mores, values, and customs. Gradually, the children learn to imitate culturally approved behavior and to repress that which is not approved.

There are vast differences in the kind of behavior which is socially approved in different cultures. What is culturally approved in one group may be shocking or revolting to another group. The Hopi Indians of America were taught never to compete or to give overt expression to hostility or anger. They never argued or fought. Among the Pilaga Indians of South America ". . . intercourse must not only be visible to the children, but carried on with little if any attempt to conceal the act from them. Absolutely no prohibition is placed on children's sexual activity by the adults. Children are at liberty to do as they please. The Pilaga child is articulate about his knowledge of sex at the age of three years."[3] If this seems shocking, it merely illustrates the degree to which cultural and social forces influence behavior and how much they vary.

DEVELOPING SKILL IN DEMOCRATIC PROCEDURES

While the school, as one of the more important secondary groups, contributes knowledge and skill, it also inevitably gives social and moral training which reflects the culture of which it is a part. Schools in the United States can no more prevent themselves from indoctrinating students in democratic ideals than schools in Russia can prevent themselves from indoctrinating students to communistic ideals. Nor should they − if the school's function is to prepare children to live in the society of which they are a part. A belief in the worth of the individual and a conviction that, to as great an extent as possible, all members of a group should participate in the making of decisions which affect the entire group are basic principles of democracy. If the school is to prepare children to live in a democratic society, it must teach them to value these principles and it must teach them how to utilize them in their daily living with others.

If physical educators are to instill a belief in the worth of the individual, they must teach children to respect everyone and to give everyone equal opportunities to become all they are capable of becoming regardless of color, race, religious affiliation, physical handicaps, deficiency in physical skills, mental insufficiencies, or other differences. They should teach children to feel empathy (not sympathy) for those with handicaps. A belief in the fundamental worth of the individual implies that the individual is of greater importance than gate receipts, being in the winning column, or building the prestige of the school or coach. It implies that students and players should be treated with respect and not shouted at, insulted, humiliated, or used as avenues of ego satisfaction for the teacher or the coach. It implies that the student's self-concept should be protected and nurtured; that he should be presented a diversity of activities in order that he can find one in which he can experience success; that progressions within a specific activity be gradual enough that even the most poorly coordinated can experience a modicum of success; and that those who cannot experience success in any form of athletic endeavor be encouraged in their efforts in other worthwhile leisure time activities such as music, dramatics, or the arts.

If students are to learn to utilize the democratic procedure of involving all members of a group in the reaching of decisions, they must be provided opportunities to do so. It is possible to provide many such opportunities in physical education and athletics. In demonstrations and exhibitions, students plan the theme, costumes, lighting, continuity, publicity, and ticket sales. Officers are elected and committees formed. In high school and college athletic contests, the players, with faculty guidance, formulate practice schedules and plays, plan publicity, organize ticket sales, and make other arrangements. This is not likely to happen soon in games such as football, basketball, and baseball where pressures exerted by the student body, alumni, fans, and booster clubs to win are so great. However, if we have confidence in the educability of people, there is no reason why this could not, in time and with persistent and courageous effort, be accomplished. In physical education classes, physical educators can help students learn leadership and followership by forming gym captains or leaders' clubs, by involving class members in decision and policy making, and by encouraging class discussion.

PSYCHOLOGIC NEEDS

In addition to their organic needs such as satisfaction of thirst, hunger, sex, hemeostasis or maintenance of balance of cellular environment, and physical comforts such as warmth, all people have psychologic needs. Both the biologic and psychologic needs create drives toward activity which will lead to the satisfaction of these needs. Satisfaction of needs results in feelings of well-being. Failure to satisfy needs leads to feelings of frustration and, in some cases, to anxiety, fear, or anger. The person who satisfies his needs reasonably well is said to have an integrated personality. A great discrepancy between needs and their satisfaction may lead to neurotic or psychotic behavior or to crime.

The physical educator who wishes to become fully effective in contributing to the emotional development of his students must possess a basic understanding of the psychologic needs, of how they may be modified, and of how they may be satisfied. We will discuss some of these psychologic needs.

Self-Acceptance

The mentally healthy person can live comfortably with himself and others. He can meet life's problems adequately, effectively, and constructively. As a result of this ability, he will feel emotionally secure. Everyone needs to feel he is normal, likable, able, and important. But at the same time, everyone must be capable of making a realistic self-appraisal of his limitations as well as his strengths — and he must be able to live comfortably with those limitations.

The formation of attitudes and feelings toward the self is begun during infancy. The infant is aware of the feelings of others toward himself and, in time, he comes to adopt these feelings toward himself. When a child does not receive genuine love and affection from his parents and those surrounding him, it is difficult for him to believe that he is likable and worthy for himself alone. He may conclude that he can become acceptable by achieving, by succeeding, or by accomplishing but that he is not acceptable for himself. He may be constantly seeking signs of affection from those around him but he is really expecting to be rejected. He may develop a feeling of failure and personal inadequacy and consequently not make efforts to succeed. He may become overly concerned with what people are saying or thinking about him. The result of a feeling of being unloved is a lack of self-respect and self-acceptance and a preoccupation with self which is wasteful of energy that could be used more productively. If the person is to be able to accept others, he must first accept himself.

While it is true that feelings of being unloved and unappreciated have their beginnings during infancy and in the home, and while it is true that the most productive time for developing feelings of being loved and appreciated is during the early years, physical educators can make contributions to the satisfaction of this need from kindergarten through college. As the individual grows older, it becomes increasingly difficult to make fundamental changes in personality structure. However, these changes can and have been made.

The physical educator can provide opportunities for the child to experience success by introducing him to activities in which he can find a

Communicating through movement *(Courtesy: University of Connecticut)*

modicum of success. He can protect and nourish the child's ego by treating him with respect and affection. He should avoid belittling, berating, and insulting the child. He should avoid making him feel inferior or guilty if he places second or second last in the contest. There are enough opportunities in physical education activities to provide every child with the feeling of satisfaction which comes with achievement. First, there is the great diversity of activities, each requiring different physical and psychologic characteristics for success. Certain combinations of characteristics are required for success in football. Other combinations of characteristics are required for success in basketball or swimming. Second, there are opportunities for each child to experience a modicum of success within the limits of a selected activity. There are different positions to be played and there is a need for referees, managers, and equipment men. If a teacher looks long and hard enough, he can find something commendable in any child, regardless of how inept he is.

Freedom

Forcefully restraining an infant causes him to react with anger and rage. The desire for freedom of action and of decision prevails in people of all ages and is universal. Reasonable independence of action is essential to emotional well-being. Furthermore, it is important from a societal, as well as a personal point of view, that children be given a measure of freedom (and of responsibility) commensurate with their abilities. This is a rapidly changing world. The automobile was first mass-produced in 1901. The first plane was flown in 1903 at Kitty Hawk. The first atom bomb was detonated in 1945. The first manned space flight occurred in 1961. New trades and professions have been, are, and will be formulated at an ever-increasing rate. Examples of these are electronics, cybernetics, and radar operation. People no longer live in one community all their lives. They must make adaptions to every new activity. They don't know what kind of work their children will be doing when they are adults and therefore can do little to prepare their children for their future occupation.

Because of these reasons, children must be prepared for a life of change. They must be educated for adaptability, creativity, and independence. The child who has been overprotected and whose decisions have been made for him may have experienced a temporary security but he will be little prepared for the independence and responsibility of adulthood. He needs practice during his growing and developmental years in making decisions — and in accepting the consequences of those decisions. However, the principles of progression apply here as they do in all learning. Preparation for the eventual freedom of adult life should be progressive. A child thrust on his own before he is ready may be made less, instead of more, secure. There should be a gradual assumption of freedom with increasing physical, mental, and emotional maturity.

The implication of the preceding for the conduct of physical education and athletic programs is that students be given increasing freedom as they mature. There are a number of ways in which this might be accomplished. Students can select or elect from among a number of activities. They could determine, with the counsel of the instructor, the amount of time to be spent in each of several activities. They could select their squad leaders and team captains. As members of interscholastic athletic teams, they could establish training rules, regulations, and penalties for violations. They could plan practice sessions, design plays, establish procedures for maintaining the cleanliness of locker rooms, and establish procedures for extending hospitality to their guests — the opponents. This list is by no means exhaustive. There are many other ways in which they could assume greater freedom and responsibility. These decisions should be made under the guidance of the physical educator or coach who can lend his knowledge, experience, and greater maturity to the deliberations. People enter into enterprises with greater enthusiasm and obey rules and regulations more willingly when the enterprise is their own or the rule is self-imposed than they do when the project or rule originates with others.

Belonging

Everyone needs to belong: to a family, to close friends, to a social group. In almost all of life's activities it is necessary to work with and for other people.

The physical education class, intramural program, and the interscholastic and intercollegiate teams provide opportunities to belong and to identify with a group. To avoid provincialism and to insure continued growth, an individual, as he matures, should feel that he belongs to ever-larger groups until ultimately he "belongs" to the world. During the formative years, physical education, and particularly that aspect of it called interscholastic athletics, can provide satisfaction for the need to belong.

New Experiences

An infant "tastes" his thumb, feels his blanket, chews on the sides of his crib, plays with new toys, and tries making different kinds of sounds. A toddler explores the kitchen cabinets, taking out all the pots and pans. He climbs over, under, and on top of everything in sight. He explores every corner of his home. A child "studies" the ant hill, the butterfly, or a stone. He wants to try skating, skiing, skin diving, horseback riding, and every new activity he sees. These are all evidences of the universal need in people for new experiences and for activity. It is unfortunate that in some people, as they grow older, the desire for new experiences wanes. It should be kept alive.

As people grow older, they need to accept new and progressively more complex tasks. The wider a person's interests, the broader will be his perspective and consequently the more stable will be his adjustment. A person with diversified interests is less likely to become disorganized after an unexpected event such as the loss of a loved one, loss of a job, or a handicapping injury or illness. The person with broad interests will have activities to interest him if he has to discontinue activities he is currently pursuing. It is not only unexpected events which make necessary that a person change his activities. The routine changes of life such as increasing maturity, marriage, the arrival of children, decrements in physical strength and stamina, retirement, and the death of one's spouse all necessitate changes in one's pattern of living – and particularly in the recreational area.

Physical education can provide new experiences for students by presenting a diversified program which includes as many different activities as possible. The program should include activities which children enjoy at their present stage of development and also activities from which they will derive increasing pleasure and satisfaction as they grow older. Elementary school children enjoy simple games such as tag, "capture-the-flag," relay races, drop-the-handkerchief, dodge ball, and hopscotch. However, during the elementary years they should be introduced, via simple lead-up games, to the more complex team games which they will enjoy during their high school and college years. In addition to being taught the team games such as basketball, baseball, and football, which will meet their present needs, senior high school and college students should be taught the individual and dual activities such as badminton, tennis, handball, swimming, and camping from which they will derive increasing satisfaction and pleasure after they leave school and grow older. The latter are the games of adulthood because as people grow older, they begin to care less for large groups. They feel the effects of loss in strength and stamina which they have not been able to sustain because of other commitments which have prevented them from maintaining a high level of fitness. Additionally, the inevitable decrements in physical fitness which are concomitants of the aging process cause the more vigorous and demanding games to be less enjoyable.

Since people like to do those things which they do well, the physical educator should make every effort to help his students develop a satisfactory level of skill. This will make more likely continued participation in the activity after the physical education requirement has been completed. If the physical educator is to offer both a variety of new experiences through the teaching of a large number of activities *and* help his students develop a satisfying enough level of skill to insure their continued participation in one or more activities after they have graduated, he is obligated to teach as effectively as possible. A thorough knowledge of the principles of physiology, anatomy, kinesiology, psychology, sociology, group dynamics, methods of teaching, use of audio-visual aids, and a knowledge of the latest research will enable him to serve both these objectives more effectively. Students majoring in physical education take courses in all these subjects. They should study them well.

Physical education and the physical educator can help the student to develop physical courage while keeping him relatively safe from injury. Physical courage is required to hurl one's body against an onrushing opponent, to rush the kicker, or to remain calm while kicking or passing when opponents are charging in. There is a possibility of injury but it has been minimized by the wearing of protective equipment such as helmets, shoulder pads, hip pads, and thigh pads in addition to a thorough training in how to fall and to give with an impact. A triple somersault on the trampoline is a hazardous stunt which requires courage to attempt. However, the trampolinist, before attempting this stunt, has mastered many stunts, each only slightly more difficult than the preceding stunt learned. The triple somersault is the present culmination of a series of learnings. Furthermore, the trampolinist mastered the stunt in a safety belt before attempting it without the belt. In addition, he has spotters stationed around the trampoline. During this process the football player and the gymnast have developed courage and a spirit of adventure which will make it more likely that they will be willing to attempt the learning of new skills.

Achievement and Recognition

Everyone needs to succeed and to be recognized for his success in order to feel emotionally secure. The need for recognition is a powerful motivating force which has driven people to many worthwhile accomplishments. However, where efforts to achieve recognition through socially approved manners has been frustrated or where education in culturally approved values has been faulty, the need for recognition has also led to undesirable behavior. The child who misbehaves, the student who cheats, the player who violates the rules, and the businessman who is dishonest are all striving to achieve recognition and attention. Those who are inadequate in knowledge, skill, or ability to achieve the level of success they aspire to in socially approved manners may seek short cuts. The child who cannot secure needed recognition through achievement in academic work or athletics misbehaves because he knows that by doing so he will receive the attention he covets.

Physical educators should and do harness this drive for recognition to motivate students to greater effort, improvement, and achievement. They give

Field hockey in a physical education class *(Courtesy: University of Connecticut)*

grades; place little gold stars after students' names on wall charts; hold contests and announce the winners; award emblems, numerals, letters, medals, and trophies; print programs with students' names on them; and announce their names in various publicity media such as newspapers, on radio and TV. It is not likely that students would subject themselves to the rigorous program and self-discipline that they do in interscholastic athletics if they did not receive this recognition and if there were no audience.

While a strong desire to win is a great motivator and usually increases the benefits accruing from sports participation, there are dangers in undue emphasis upon winning. The dangers arise principally as a result of efforts to achieve recognition by taking "short cuts." Athletic contests become socially unacceptable educational experiences when players endeavor to achieve recognition by taking unfair advantage by circumventing rules, when coaches endeavor to obtain recognition by securing unfair advantage by intimidating officials or by resorting to unfair practices in proselytizing or subsidizing, and when athletic directors and principals or college presidents permit or abet such practices. In these circumstances society, and the player especially, is being taught subterfuge, dishonesty, and brutality. Society will not long permit such teachings to go on in its schools when it recognizes what is being taught.

There is another undesirable effect of overemphasis upon winning. This effect is delayed until several years after graduation from school. During school years the student comes to believe that the game is not worth playing unless he can win most of the time or has assurance that he will win. After he leaves school, professional and work responsibilities and responsibilities to home, wife, and children prohibit him from maintaining his former level of physical fitness. In addition, the decrements in strength and stamina which are concomitants of aging become manifest. The adult now loses a great percentage of the athletic contests in which he engages. Since he was taught during his early years that it is disgraceful to lose and that the game is fun only when one wins, he is likely to decide that he will no longer participate.

Children enjoy physical activity, movement, and sports for their own sake — for the sheer joy of movement. Small children know the joy of movement. They skip, run, leap, and climb with no specific objective in mind. It just feels good. As they mature, they are taught to believe that this kind of behavior is foolish. They must have an objective — a reason for moving. By the time they are adults, the rituals surrounding participation in sports become more time consuming than the participation itself. They have to buy expensive uniforms and equipment, join clubs, make numerous telephone calls, and discuss plans in detail. It is unfortunate that they cannot capture and hold some of the spontaneity of children's play.

THE LEARNING PROCESS

Because human beings possess no recognizable instincts, as do animals, which help them to survive, man is dependent upon others for aid in survival during his first several years of life. During this time, he learns how to adjust to his environment and how to survive. Norman Munn points out the importance of learning when he invites us to imagine how a person would act if a drug were invented which could wipe out all traces of everything that had been learned. He states:

You would have all the normal reflexes and you might even creep or walk. You would have the same physiological needs, like hunger and thirst, that you now possess. But you would not know where to find the means of satisfying your needs. There would be no way of knowing, except possibly through taste and smell, which things were edible and which not. You would wear no clothes and even if they were given you, you would have no idea, except by observing others, what they were for. If you tried to put them on, you could not button or otherwise fix them. All the habits of buttoning, zipping, and tying that you learned so laboriously in childhood would have disappeared. If food and utensils were placed before you, you could not feed yourself with the latter. You would not even use your fingers, except, possibly, after finding others means inadequate. You would have no attitudes of cleanliness and, if you did, you could not perform the acts required to keep clean. You would have no knowledge of right and wrong, and no conscience. Your surroundings would be meaningless, your parents and your friends but strange creatures somewhat like yourself. You would even seem strange to yourself. If you had anything to communicate to others, which is doubtful, since all ideas are almost certainly learned, you could not communicate. Your vocalizations would be cries and strange sounds, not words. Your gestures would be of no avail because they would be mere reflexes; not the conventionalized motions which people understand. In other things, also, you would lack even the skill and knowledge of an infant. Only after many years of learning could you regain the attitudes, skills, and knowledge that you now possess.[4]

Conditioned Learning

The first learning is *unconditioned-response* learning in which babies learn to make simple responses to the environment such as sucking the nipple when hungry and withdrawing from painful stimuli. Then the baby begins to learn motor skills such as standing, walking, crawling, grasping, reaching out, and making gestures. This leads to the development of verbal skills. Some writers contend that speech and language difficulties are due to insufficient movement or motor experiences during infancy and early childhood. As children acquire the ability to verbalize they begin to develop the ability to solve problems.

Another simple form of learning is called *conditioned-response* learning. In this form, a stimulus other than the one which arouses the response is substituted. A newborn baby begins sucking movements when the nipple is placed in his mouth but not when he sees it. After a while the baby begins to suck when he sees the nipple. The visual stimulation has been substituted for the tactile one. A child is bitten by a dog. Later he experiences fear at the sight or even the mention of a dog. A child chokes while splashing around in the wading pool. Thereafter, he feels fear whenever he approaches the pool. We could offer thousands of examples such as the preceding of conditioned-response learning.

To return to the first example of the sucking reflex, the nipple in the mouth is called an *unconditioned stimulus* and the sucking an *unconditioned response*. The visual bottle is called the *conditioned stimulus* and the sucking aroused by sight of the bottle the *conditioned response*. The conditioned stimulus may be used as an "unconditioned" stimulus to elicit a response to a still different conditioned stimulus. This is illustrated in teaching children how to do rhythmic breathing in the water. The instructor first tells the students to exhale into the water while he counts from one to five and to turn the head and inhale on the count of six. He then counts to six repeatedly while clapping his hands on each count. Here, the word "six" becomes the unconditioned stimulus, the handclap the conditioned stimulus, and the head turn the conditioned response. Then the instructor stops counting verbally but continues to clap his hands rhythmically while the students count to themselves silently. The handclap then becomes the unconditioned stimulus while the silent self-count is the conditioned stimulus. The head turn continues to be the conditioned response. When the instructor stops clapping his hands while the students continue doing rhythmic breathing, the silent self-count becomes the conditioned stimulus. Utilization of this process can often be used to hasten the learning process. This is the simplest form of learning. A few psychologists believe that conditioned learning is the basis of all learning.

Research psychologists have shown that the efficiency of learning any motor or verbal skill is related to the level of motivation. Inducements such as food, drink, money, or recognition must be offered in order for learning to occur most effectively. When a person is satiated, satisfied, in balance with his environment, little or no learning occurs. A person needs a reason for learning or he stays in a rut. Hungry rats allowed to explore a maze with no food reward show inefficient performance. However, when they are given a food reward, their learning improves very rapidly — much more rapidly than does the learning of rewarded rats who are introduced to the maze for the first time. Obviously, the rats were learning something during their explorations. Students, too, will learn faster when they are rewarded for learning by being assisted to see the relevance of what they are learning to the satisfaction of their felt needs or drives.

Optimum Learning or Practice Periods

Research indicates that distributed learning is more productive than massed learning. In the learning of a specific skill by a particular person there is an optimum or best amount of time spent at practice. This optimum time varies for different people and for different skills. Learning becomes less productive if more than this amount of time is spent.

Learning approaches a *physiologic limit* beyond which performance cannot improve. However, a leveling-off of learning may be due to inadequate motivation, boredom, or fatigue, or it may be a manifestation of a period of integration of former learnings. This is called a *learning plateau.* Additional learning will occur with better motivation, rest, or completion of the integrative process. We can never be certain whether a cessation in learning is because of a reaching of the physiologic level or to a learning plateau. A physical education teacher, and especially a coach, must analyze the condition influencing the student to determine whether he is capable of additional learning. Is the student fatigued? Does he lack adequate motivation? Is he bored? Corrective measures must then be instituted.

Suggestions for Improving Teaching Efficiency

Sometimes the solution to a problem comes suddenly when the person "sees" the relationships between various aspects of the problem. This phenomenon occurs in the learning of motor skills as it does in the solving of puzzles or other problems. Psychologists call this *learning by insight*. Physical educators can give students the thrill of learning by insight by presenting good verbal descriptions, making good use of visual aids, and particularly by explaining the application of the elementary laws of physics to the accomplishment of the particular motor skill.

Research indicates that learning proceeds more efficiently when the learner verbalizes what he is learning and particularly when the teacher corrects the verbal descriptions. Munn[5] describes an experiment in which the task was to assemble a puzzle after watching a demonstration of the procedure. Of twenty-five children required to count while watching the demonstration, only three learned the task. In another group of twenty-five children who described what the demonstrator was doing, twenty-two learned the task in sixteen trials. When the demonstrator described what she was doing, all twenty-five learned the task in fourteen trials. In a fourth group of twenty-five children, all twenty-five learned the task in only twelve trials when they described what the demonstrator was doing and she corrected their descriptions. The implication for effective teaching of physical education skills is that the teacher demonstrate the skill and then have the students describe what she had done and that, additionally, she correct their descriptions. It would be helpful if the physical educator would ask the students, previous to the demonstration, to watch for specific things. For example, in teaching the head spring she might ask the students to tell her the angle of the back relative to the mat when the hips extend, the angle of the legs relative to the trunk when the hips extend, the position of the hands, etc.

The learning of one skill sometimes facilitates the learning of other skills. This is known as *transfer of training* or *transfer of learning*. Transfer of learning is most likely to occur when: (1) there is a similarity in the contents of activities (as in trampolining and diving), (2) there is a similarity in techniques (as in swimming the inverted breast stroke and the orthodox breast stroke), (3) there is a similarity in principles (as in the forward and backward somersaults), and (4) some or all of the preceding factors operate. The physical educator can produce a greater amount of learning if he will apply these laws of transfer of learning. He should point out the similarities in content, techniques, or principles between an activity or skill new to the students and activities or skills with which they are familiar. Handball, squash racquets, tennis, and badminton are similar in content as are basketball, lacrosse, and soccer. There are similarities in technique in the side stroke, inverted side stroke, single trudgeon, and double trudgeon crawl as there are in the elementary back stroke, breast stroke, inverted breast stroke, and the butterfly. There are similarities in the principles of throwing a softball, baseball, handball, and a javelin.

Research has shown that learning occurs more rapidly when the learner is praised for his efforts and encouraged to do better on the next effort than it does when no comment is made. Research also shows that learning proceeds more efficiently when there is a material reward given than when there is a verbal reward (praise) given. While reproof for errors made hastens learning, it is not as effective over longer periods as is praise. Physical educators and coaches should learn to use praise judiciously to improve the teaching-learning climate.

When students are made aware of the quality of their performance they learn more rapidly than they do when they are not aware of the quality of their performance. Awareness of the quality of performance causes the student to repeat actions which have been successful and to correct unsuccessful responses. In teaching the set-up in volleyball, for example, the physical educator should use such expressions as: "The ball should have been six inches closer to the net," "The height was just right," "Set it up in front of the spiker."

While intense rivalry may interfere with learning, competition and social recognition stimulate effort and thereby improve learning. There are many techniques for establishing competitive situations in physical education classes. Wall charts on which records of students' performances are kept which can be seen by all students, intraclass and interclass competition, races, and contests are effective teaching techniques if they are not overused. Interscholastic and intercollegiate athletic programs are based upon rivalry.

PHYSICAL EDUCATION AS AN INTEGRATING FORCE UPON HUMAN PERSONALITY

Kimball Young, in discussing the impulsions to activity, reminds his readers of the priority of internal stimuli over external stimuli; i.e., that the individual acts *on* his environment before he *reacts* to it. Fundamental activity begins within the individual. Although the exteroceptors are of importance, it must be remembered that responses set up by extrinsic factors are always greatly affected by the condition of the internal organism at the time the responses are initiated.

An infant acts upon his environment by crying when he feels uncomfortable or hungry, by kicking his legs and waving his arms when he feels the need for activity, and by cooing when he feels happy. He executes these acts as a result of internal stimuli. A child suddenly dashes across the field, climbs a tree, or rolls down a hill, not necessarily because he has an objective in mind, but simply because he feels impelled to do so by internal stimuli. However, as he matures, becomes conditioned by his society, and acquires self-discipline, he learns he must have a reason, an objective for action and, consequently, gives less and less expression to internal stimuli. His activities are initiated and conditioned more and more by extrinsic factors. It is probable that this dictation by external stimuli and the submission of the internal stimuli will contribute to personality disintegration. Play is a spontaneous and pleasurable expenditure of energy. It is characterized by a spontaneity of action which is not found in the imposed tasks of the regularized and restricted movements of work which are directed toward a more remote goal. Play presents an opportunity to give expression to internal stimuli and in so doing can contribute to integration of the personality.

Psychologists believe that much of the problem of maladjusted personality rests in the failure of the basic organic tensions to find release in socially acceptable manners. Athletics and other forms of physical activity can provide a socially acceptable form of release for feelings of aggression, for example. That they do so is indicated by some of the terms used such as "kill shot," "strike," "beat," "smash," "spike," "clobber," etc. Anger and irritation can be worked off by punching the bag, smacking the handball, chopping wood, and many other forms of activity.

Man is a psycho-social-physical entity. While, on the one hand, organic and functional disorders may exist independently, often psychic disturbances manifest themselves in physiologic malfunctions. On the other hand, organic malfunctions may be the cause of neurotic or psychotic behavior. It has been estimated that fifty percent of the people in physicians' offices are there with ailments whose basis is psychologic. Evidence has been accumulating that mental and emotional "stances" such as anxiety, anger, and irritability or discouragement can cause chronic ailments such as ulcers, hypertension, migraine, asthma, visual deficiencies, hemorrhoids, allergies, arteriosclerosis, and even a predisposition to tuberculosis.

Girls play too! *(Courtesy: University of Connecticut)*

SUMMARY

In this chapter further evidence of the unity of man has been presented — not only of the interrelationships between his psyche and his soma but also between himself and other people. The influence of other individuals and of social groups upon the formation of the individual's values and behaviors with specific reference to physical education and athletics has been pointed out. Procedures for inculcating sportsmanlike attitudes, for developing skill in democratic procedures, and for utilizing sports to delay or prevent the onset of the stress-caused or predominantly psychosomatic diseases have been presented.

The organic base of personality has been discussed from the point of view of the influences of the nervous and endocrine systems upon personality and the implications for consideration of individual differences in physical education classes. The powerful influence of the environment, both physical and human, in modifying the inherited organic base has also been discussed and implications for physical education and interscholastic athletics have been drawn out.

The nature of basic psychologic needs and suggestions for their satisfaction through physical education and athletic programs were discussed. Selected aspects of the learning process including conditioned learning, motivation, length of learning and practice periods, learning by insight (the cognitive dimension), the role of verbalization in learning physical skills, transfer of learning, reward and punishment, and rivalry and competition were discussed from the point of view of the physical educator.

Finally, the relevance and implications of the priority of internal stimuli over external stimuli for physical education were discussed. It was pointed out that people play when they are children primarily in response to internal stimuli but as they grow older, they more and more believe they must have a logical reason or excuse to play and increasingly surround their play with rituals and paraphernalia. This eliminates the spontaneity of their play. Needless to say, there is much more the physical educator must learn about the psychologic process. This chapter is intended as only a very brief introduction.

In the next chapter, we will look at personality formation from the point of view of the sociologist.

QUESTIONS

1. Present evidence of the influence of emotions upon physiologic processes.

2. Present evidence of the influence of emotions upon health.

3. Present evidence that athletic competition can provide experiences in emotional control and character development.

4. How would you teach, coach, and administer sports programs if your objective was to educate for brutality and deceptiveness?

5. How would you teach, coach, and administer sports programs if your objective was to educate for sportsmanship, ethical behavior, and citizenship?

6. Present evidence that the mind is involved in sports participation.

7. Present evidence of the modification of fundamental reflexes and drives by social-cultural influences.

8. Discuss the two divisions of the autonomic nervous system from the point of view of their functions and interrelationships.

9. What is the function and location of each of the following: parathyroids, pineal glands, thymus, islets of langerhans, thyroid, adrenals, adrenal cortex, pituitary, gonads, and ovaries?

10. Why has physical activity been advocated as a catharsis during continued emotional stress?

11. Discuss Dr. Hans Selye's theory on stress as a cause of disease and illness.

12. Present evidence of the influence of environmental forces upon the organism both before birth and afterward.

13. Present evidence that emotional behavior is learned.

14. What accounts for the difference in behavior of participants and spectators in different sports or in the same sport in different communities?

15. Is there any justification for a display of emotions by spectators at athletic contests?

16. How can the physical educator and coach help students to develop skill in democratic procedures?

17. Discuss the psychologic needs of self-acceptance, freedom, belonging, new experiences, achievement and recognition. What are they? How can the physical educator insure that they are being satisfied? Why is satisfaction of these needs more difficult and more important than it was in the 1800's?

18. What are the causes of a learning plateau and what corrective measures can the coach institute?

19. What are some devices and procedures which the physical educator or coach could utilize to increase the rate of learning?

20. Discuss the implications of psychologist Kimball Young's reminder that internal stimuli have priority over external stimuli.

FOOTNOTES

1. Young, Kimball, *Personality and Problems of Adjustment.* New York: F. S. Crofts, 1946, p. 24.

2. Carmichael, L., "Heredity and Environment: Are They Antithetical?" *Journal of American Society of Social Psychology, 20*:245–60.

3. Henry, Jules, and Zunia, "Doll Play of Pilaga Indian Children," in *Personality in Nature, Society, and Culture* (Kluckhohn, Clyde, and Henry A. Murray). New York: Alfred A. Knopf, 1949, p. 236.

4. Munn, Norman L., *Psychology, The Fundamentals of Human Adjustment* (Third Edition). Boston: Houghton Mifflin Company, 1946, p. 195.

5. Munn, Norman L., *op. cit.,* p. 221.

15

The Sociologic Bases of Physical Education

ONE OF WALT Whitman's poems summarizes nicely the major thesis of this chapter:

THERE WAS A CHILD WENT FORTH[1]

There was a child went forth every day,
And the first object he look'd upon, that object he became,
And that object became part of him for the day or a certain part of the day,
Or for many years or stretching cycles of years.

The early lilacs became part of this child,
And grass and white and red morning-glories, and white and red clover, and
    the song of the phoebe-bird,
And the Third-month lamb and the sow's pink-faint-litter, and the mare's
    foal and the cow's calf,
And the noisy brood of the barnyard or by the mire of the pond-side,
And the fish suspending themselves so curiously below there,
    and the beautiful curious liquid,
And the water-plants with their graceful flat heads, all became part of him.

The field-sprouts of Fourth-month and Fifth-month became part of him,
Winter-grain sprouts and those of the light-yellow corn, and the esculent
    roots of the garden,
And the apple-trees cover'd with blossoms and the fruit afterward,
    and woodberries, and the commonest weeds by the road,
And the old drunkard staggering home from the outhouse of the tavern
    whence he had lately risen.
And the schoolmistress that pass'd on her way to the school.
And the friendly boys that pass'd, and the quarrelsome boys,
And the tidy and fresh-cheek'd girls, and the barefoot Negro boy and girl,
And all the changes of city and country where ever he went.

INTERRELATIONSHIPS BETWEEN THE
INDIVIDUAL AND SOCIETY

The individual is born a psycho-physical being but with the passing of each day he becomes increasingly a psycho-social-physical being. If he is to be successfully integrated into his family, school, play, community, social and work groups, he must learn to modify, redirect, or to sublimate the drives for satisfaction of his basic organic and psychic needs. If he does not succeed in making these adaptations, he will not succeed in satisfying his needs – or, if he does satisfy them in socially unacceptable manners, the family or social group of which he is a member will punish him. The child (in most cultures) learns to use utensils when eating, to eat noiselessly and neatly, to have bowel movements and to urinate in the prescribed place, and to wear prescribed clothing in a prescribed manner. He learns to give expression to hostility, fear, anger, and affection in socially approved manners. He learns to compete in work and play according to accepted patterns. Those who learn, accept, and practice the mores, customs, and values of their social groups are likely to have the least personal and social conflict.

Physical education activities are society in miniature. Team and dual sports and the interrelationships between participants in individual sports provide opportunities for the participants to experiment and for the teacher to provide guidance in interpersonal relationships. Furthermore, the penalties for errors are not nearly as great as they are in the real world, which makes athletics a safer place in which to learn these interpersonal relationships than does the business and professional world.

Socialization of the Child

Evidence indicates that infants can be conditioned during their first two weeks of life and that the quality of social handling or mothering received by the infant influences such physiological functions as circulation, respiration, and digestion.[2] At about six weeks of age the "social smile" generally appears. With improving coordination – grasping, creeping, crawling, walking, babbling, and talking – the infant becomes increasingly able to give, receive, and react to social stimuli. During the child's second year his relations with each member of his family are of great importance in shaping his social personality. These relationships influence the qualities of dependence-independence, exhibitionism-shyness, aggressiveness-timidity, placidity-excitability, adaptability-rigidity, identity with his own sex group, and membership in his group.

At the age of two, most children prefer to play alone. After this age they begin to play with other children but without real social give and take. By the age of four, they play in pairs or small groups. At this age there is little difference between the play of boys and girls. By the age of five, boys reject feminine forms of play such as doll play and ironing clothes, and prefer the masculine forms of more aggressive games while girls become more interested in the feminine activities. This differentiation is seen even in the movement patterns of boys and girls at the age of five years. Beginning at approximately five years of age, girls' movements become increasingly feminine, delicate, and restrained. These are learned patterns. Physical education in the home and in the kindergarten or nursery school can facilitate these learnings.

At about the age of three, a child wishes to indicate he is no longer a baby and that he is his own boss and consequently resists adult direction. Nursery school children demonstrate aggressive and competitive behavior by fighting, bragging, and competing. A group directed by a tense, unsympathetic adult, or a group which is playing in a space too small or with an inadequate number of toys will demonstrate more aggressive behavior than a group led by a friendly adult or a group with more space and equipment. When the adult leader is sympathetic and the children feel secure they will behave with greater empathy and cooperativeness.

Beginning with his entrance into first grade, the child shows an increasing ability to sustain a defined role in a clearly structured game and to understand and appreciate his unique role in a more complex situation. During this age, the overt resistance to adults demonstrated at age three gives way to cooperativeness with adults and an acceptance of their authority. This change probably occurs because opportunities to give expression to feelings of aggression and rebellion have increased as a result of greater opportunities for bullying younger or weaker children, fighting with peers, and grumbling or complaining. Physical educators provide physical activities to channel these aggressive drives into socially acceptable patterns.

Participation in organized games forms the basis for effective membership in larger groups so that by the age of ten or twelve membership in large groups such as Boy or Girl Scouts is a part of every child's experience.

Warren Fraleigh[3] has pointed out that there is a definite and proven relationship between play and social-emotional adjustment. He reviewed several studies which show an unmistakable relationship between a high level of athletic skill and popularity and social acceptability by the peer group. There is high prestige value in physical skill among adolescent boys. His summary of the research literature in this area indicated that from early elementary grades through the early years of college, those who possessed greater physical skill ranked higher in social and emotional adjustment. He

Up and over! *(Courtesy: L.W. Ward and Nissen-Medart Co.)*

concluded that those with greater physical skills participate more in social and competitive play because they gain favorable self-evaluation and group status. This results in satisfaction which in turn leads to more participation which leads to greater skill in both the social and physical areas. However, when those with low physical skills participate in normal play activities they gain unfavorable self-evaluations and lose group status. This failure to experience success and satisfaction causes them to avoid further participation in normal play activities, they lose these opportunities for social and emotional development, and consequently fall farther behind in the development of physical skills. They then withdraw to less ego-threatening activities; that is, the less competitive and more individualized forms of play. The implication for physical educators is that they conduct physical education classes in such a manner that all students will be aided in experiencing success in physical education activities by:

1. Presenting a program which can be adapted to the unique abilities of each student.

2. Providing for homogeneous grouping of students on the bases of such criteria as: skill in the particular activity, physical fitness, motor ability, motor educability, or motor capacity.

3. Permitting and encouraging students to select activities in which they are likely to experience a modicum of success.

4. Improving teaching to facilitate learning which will lead to greater success.

5. Emphasizing progress made rather than errors and mistakes.

6. Allowing for more teacher-pupil planning in order to involve students in decisions reached.

7. Leading the students to understand that competition is interjected into the game situation to make it more interesting and enjoyable and that success or failure in athletics should not be taken too seriously.

Achieving Self-Realization

At the age of seven or so, the child becomes increasingly aware of himself and of how he measures up against his peers. Children of this age criticize the nonconformist, the deviant child, or the child who is a member of a physical, mental, economic, or national minority group. Children haze one another or invent names such as "Gimpy," "Blackie," and "Stupid." These early feelings of adequacy or inadequacy and of belonging or not belonging to the group influence the child with regard to the place he feels entitled to in the group. Unfortunately, these self-evaluations tend to persist. The physical educator should teach children to appreciate individual differences and should help them to realize that there are many activities in which certain deviations can become assets. Many cases can be cited where a handicap was turned into an advantage or where the handicap provided the motivation necessary to become a champion performer. Harry K., whose left leg was atrophied as a result of a bout with infantile paralysis when he was a child, became the National AAU and the NCAA champion on the side horse. Harold B., who had the same problem, established a world's record in the supine press. A young man whose right leg was amputated just below the hip won the national championship in platform diving. Another young man, who suffered a birth anomaly or defect which left him with useless hands, became the best table tennis player on his campus. Glenn Cunningham, who suffered such severe burns of his legs that his doctors told him he would never walk again, overcame his handicap so completely that he became an Olympic champion runner.

Adolescent Needs

Changes in social relationships accompany the physical and psychologic changes of adolescence. Adult authority must be challenged as the individual strives to wrench himself from a relationship of dependence to one of independence. Sex interests are activated. The student with outstanding athletic, social, or intellectual abilities will gain the respect of his peers. The adolescent may have many anxieties concerning his status with his peer group; academic achievement and acceptance by a college; independence, maturity and a job; marriage; and possible military service. Social groups utilize many of these anxieties to bring children and youth to conform to the prevailing mores, customs, and values.

On guard! *(Courtesy: University of Connecticut)*

It is during the years from earliest infancy through adolescence that the individual is being socialized and that his personality is being formed. Lois Murphy writes:

Basic capacities for rapport, love, and ease with people have their roots in earliest infancy. The character of adult relations with people, whether spontaneous or rigid, may have been shaped by the child's response to rigid or free training during the early years. The adult's ease in social groups of different kinds may be in part, at least, the result of the security or the anxiety developed in his relations with other children during the increasingly group-minded years of school. Attitudes toward other racial, religious, and economic groups will, at the adult level, have traces of early experiences of scape-goating, or of respect for individuals, fostered by the family, school, and neighborhood atmospheres. The capacity to participate in democratic government, as compared with the need to achieve power and wield it fascistically, will be the result of the whole complex of social experiences of the individual, of frustration or happiness in the family group, feeling of respected membership, or being excluded from school and neighborhood groups, as well as feelings of respect for the rights of others and sympathy for others which are experienced and fostered as the accepted mores of the group.[4]

Human social learning always takes place in relation to other personalities and consequently in an emotional context. All cultural behavior is learned behavior. Each new individual must learn it laboriously through the processes of imitation, identification, competition, and cooperation. This conditioning is achieved, in part, through providing a reward or hope of a reward and through punishment or the fear of punishment. Fear of punishment (which is not necessarily physical but may, for example, be loss of parental favor) creates anxiety. Anxiety produces striving for recognition, social status, or prestige and is, therefore, a most effective form of motivation toward social learning.

TEACHER VALUES VS. STUDENT VALUES

The social learnings among lower and upper classes are quite different from those of the middle class. Teachers often attempt to teach their middle class values to their students, the majority of whom belong to the lower class. Lower class culture organizes adolescent behavior with regard to aggression, sexual relations, and family roles into very different patterns from those of the middle class. Behaviors that are rewarding to a middle class adolescent are not at all rewarding to a lower class adolescent. For example, aggression in middle class society is expressed by "initiative" or "ambition" while in lower class society it is expressed directly by physical attack or by threats of physical attack. Aggressive or hostile action is, therefore, not necessarily a symptom of a neurotic personality among lower class children. In fact, failure to act in an overtly aggressive manner by a member of a lower-class society may be a symptom of failure to learn the accepted social behavior of his class. Behavior should always be viewed in relation to the social class of which the child is a member. The teacher of lower-class children has the difficult task of changing the values of children, which they have learned from their parents, to ones which are more productive in current society.

SOCIAL INFLUENCES UPON BEHAVIOR

Physical educators can learn much from social psychologists concerning the development and control of feelings of sympathy, hostility, aggressiveness, and fearfulness. An understanding of these human behaviors will not only make the physical educator's work more pleasant but it will enable him to be a more effective teacher. The physical educator who understands these mechanisms can provide a more effective teaching-learning environment and a more pleasant and happier classroom. He can circumvent or avoid conflicts between class members and he can guide children toward the formation of effective personalities.

Ambivalence of Aggressive Drives

That aggressive drives are fundamentally ambivalent is sometimes demonstrated in the sudden shift from a friendly or affectionate behavior to a sadistic one — or from a sadistic or aggressive behavior to an affectionate one. When an elementary school teacher gives the behavior-problem child who is constantly pushing, shoving, fighting, etc. a responsibility such as collecting papers, distributing books, cleaning blackboards, leading the apparatus class, or acting as team captain, the teacher is demonstrating that he recognizes this ambivalence. Sometimes when a child would be likely to demonstrate sympathetic responses, he is prevented from doing so by feelings of guilt or by threats to his ego. For example, a child who would normally demonstrate sympathetic behavior toward another child who had been struck with a flying baseball bat would probably not do so because of guilt feelings if he had been the one who released the bat after swinging at the ball — and particularly if his ego had been wounded as a result of striking out.

Frustration and Aggression

One of several products of frustration is aggression. If the instigation to aggression is stronger than the instigation to other behaviors, aggression will be the response. If the instigations to other responses are stronger, these responses will occur and acts of aggression will be held in abeyance. For example, if two children are building a snowman and a third child accidentally knocks it down, the two children are likely to attack the third child. If the playground leader points out that the snowballs are now in perfect position to initiate building a fort, the aggressive drives of the two children might be diverted to another response. If the football fans are angered with a decision rendered by the game officials, they might demonstrate aggressive feelings by booing, catcalls, or throwing items but if at that moment the half-time gun is fired and fifty very lovely girls in abbreviated drum majorette costumes parade onto the field, the boos will likely change to whistles and the aggressive drives to feelings of appreciation.

Substitution

Substitute responses may reduce frustration and thereby consequent aggression. Examples of this mechanism are: reading romantic stories when real romance is not available, producing amateur theatricals when a professional career in acting has been blocked, eating peach pie in a restaurant when there is no apple pie, receiving a compliment for doing a cartwheel instead of praise for doing a running front somersault. The physical educator can provide acceptable substitute responses. He can also help the student to establish reasonable and achievable goals.

The degree to which an act of aggression is inhibited varies directly with the strength of the punishment anticipated if the aggressive act is executed. The punishment, then, must be severe enough and certain enough to deter aggressive action. The greater the strength of the frustration, the more likely it is that the aggressive act will occur. Aggressive acts by fans at athletic contests are more likely to occur when the fans are taught that their team should win all or most of their games because then they will experience greater frustration when the team loses.

Individualized Interpretations of Frustrating Experiences

Of two people prevented in precisely the same manner from achieving identical goals, one may experience a great deal more frustration. Maslow[5] points out that a goal-object may have two meanings for an individual — an intrinsic meaning and a symbolic meaning. One child deprived of a candy bar may have lost only a candy bar. Another child may have been deprived not only of the sweet, chewy taste of the candy bar but also may feel deprived of his mother's love when she refuses his request. The candy bar for this child had psychologic values as well as intrinsic values. When the goal-object represents love, prestige, respect, or achievement, deprivation of the goal-object causes considerably more frustration. This is why coaches, players, and fans react so violently sometimes when they lose a game whose ideal purpose was to provide an interesting evening but whose actual purpose was to provide prestige and status.

Maslow states in the same section that: "When two monkeys are in a dominance-subordination relationship, a piece of food is: (1) an appeaser of hunger and also (2) a symbol of dominance status. Thus, if the subordinate animal attempts to pick up the food, he will at once be attacked by the dominant animal. If, however, he can deprive the food of its symbolic dominance value, then his dominator allows him to eat it. This he can do very easily by a gesture of obeisance as he approaches the food, as if to say: I want this food only to still hunger. I do not want to challenge your dominance. I readily concede your dominance." This has implications for the manner in which physical educators should approach their superior officers. That is, they should not appear to threaten the dominant position of their superior. Of course, they should not become obsequious.

When people are criticized by their friends, they normally feel threatened and attacked. However, if the friend tells them that he is offering this criticism because he likes and wants to help them, people usually accept the criticism and feel grateful for it. The "sandwich" technique — compliment-criticism-compliment — is an effective method for securing acceptance of a criticism. Use of this technique can enable physical educators and other teachers to become more effective by causing students to be more willing to accept and act upon the teachers' suggestions.

Learning situations should not be excessively frustrating since this reduces constructiveness, causes unhappiness and restlessness, and increases aggressiveness. Frustration also causes a rise in the amount of hostile action toward the person in charge and a decrease in the friendly approaches toward him.[6] Furthermore, there is a regression in the level of intellectual functioning. There are a number of implications for physical educators arising from these characteristics of people. One of the more important is that learnings should be presented progressively with the steps from one level to the next being as small as possible. This procedure will enable students to experience frequent evidences of their progress and success. Another implication is that teachers should facilitate the learning process by judicious use of audiovisual aids, wise use of other teaching aids, skilled demonstrations, and effective explanations. Still another implication is that teachers should compliment students who show progress, improvement, or good effort.

PHYSICAL EDUCATION AND DEMOCRACY

It would be extremely difficult to find a person in the United States who would say that he does not believe in democracy. Almost all people in the United States would insist that democracy is the best form of government. Yet, few would be able to give an accurate description of democracy or be able to indicate in what way it is basically different from other forms of government. Many assume that simply because they are born and raised in a democratic country they have skill in and will practice democratic procedures. Apparently, they assume that the knowledges, skills, and attitudes necessary for the practice of democratic procedures are acquired by magic or a process of osmosis. A little reflection should make it obvious that these procedures must be learned and developed through practice. The schools are in a most advantageous position to teach these procedures. Since the school is a social institution established to perpetuate and to improve social customs and since democracy is a most important social custom in the United States, it is the responsibility of schools in the United States to develop in children democratic attitudes and skills.

Democracy and Diversity

The essence of democracy is diversity. Democratic people cherish differences of opinion. The open forum of discussion enables all groups to give expression to their point of view. Utilization of democratic procedures usually insures that all aspects of a problem will be studied. The democratic method has confidence in the ultimate wisdom and justice of all the people in that they will select the best of many ideas which compete for their acceptance. The democratic method is not the easiest way for it demands that all people be educated concerning the issues and that after studying the issues they expend the energy necessary to make themselves heard and understood.

Willingness to study and to explore new ideas has been one of the principal reasons why the United States has become the most prosperous

Gliding over! *(Courtesy: U. S. Marine Corps)*

country in the world. Countries whose religious beliefs or customs encouraged the veneration of the old and which forbade the questioning, searching attitudes remained backward. This attitude serves as a deterrent to progress in this country. It is expressed in cliches such as: "The good old-fashioned way!", "Crazy new ideas!". These attitudes are chains which bind men to their past and prevent them from examining new and perhaps better ideas and methods.

Obviously, this is not to say that people should rush off and try every new idea. This would be wasteful of time, energy, and money. But minds should not be closed to an idea simply because it is new. Ideas must be evaluated. Facts, knowledge, and information must be accumulated. This illustrates, again, that the practice of democratic procedures is not for the slothful. Expenditure of energy and time is essential. It is not the most expeditious of processes. Monarchy, autocracy, dictatorship, and communism can arrive at decisions much more quickly. But democracy is the most just and the most accurate of the several methods of government simply because it considers different points of view.

Anarchy-Totalitarianism

Absolute freedom with no rules, regulations or laws, no discipline, no planning or order, and extreme individualism, can only lead to confusion, chaos, and anarchy. This end of the political scale must be rejected. The opposite end of the political scale, totalitarianism, in which the state is supreme, must also be rejected because even though it can be quite orderly and effect improvements quickly and efficiently, it is doomed to failure because it does not involve the people in the planning. History shows that the people will rise up and demand a voice in government. The Magna Charta, the Russian revolution, the Bill of Rights, and the "civil rights" marches are evidences of the strength of man's insistence upon governing himself.

Jay B. Nash[7] quotes Aristotle to illustrate a possible sequence in changing patterns of government which are the result of human greed and laziness:

A tribal chief or dictator with supreme authority.
The rise of nobility and its acceptance as natural.
Nobility declines through dissipation and debauchery.
Persecution of the people – rise in taxes and discontent grows.
The rise of the masses – revolution.
The wresting of peoples' rights from overlords – growth of democracy.
Democratic leaders prove unfaithful to their trust.
Rise of corruption and graft, selfishness, confusion, chaos, hate. The people become discontented and suspicious, demanding order, rallying behind a strong leader.
A tribal chief or dictator with absolute power.

This process, needless to say, may take hundreds or thousands of years to come full circle. Democracy must be protected and watched over by the people. A nation can be only as strong as are its individual members. Each individual must participate in the making of the rules and of the laws which protect the rights of *all* men.

Qualities Desired in People Living in a Democracy

1. Possess social morality and a social conscience to assure that the interests and welfare of all people will receive consideration.

2. Are educated in order that they will be capable of understanding the issues and able to express themselves and to vote intelligently.

3. Possess a spirit of peace and orderliness in order that they will not waste lives and materials in attempting to conquer the peoples of other nations and in order that they will live cooperatively with one another.

4. Possess the energy, resourcefulness, and creativity which enables people to achieve a high standard of living and a degree of material wealth which makes possible the pursuit of the cultural aspects of life which make for a full, rich, and satisfying life.

5. Possess a high level of health which will enable them to work productively and play with enjoyment not only during youth and middle years but also beyond middle age and into senescence.

6. Possess respect for the personality and rights of others for if they do not, democracy will move either toward totalitarianism or toward anarchy.

When students are taught and coached with the *objective* of developing attitudes and behaviors conducive to life in a democratic society and when *methods are utilized* which develop these attitudes and behaviors, then physical education classes, intramural programs, and interscholastic and intercollegiate athletics can make substantial contributions to life in a democracy. These learnings do not accrue automatically as a result of participation in sports. They must be planned for and striven toward. When the gymnasia, natatoria, and playing fields are regarded as laboratories for learnings in social behavior rather than as vehicles for the greater glory and fame of the school or coach, then athletics can begin to realize their great educational potential.

It is *because* of the highly emotionally charged situations which occur in sports; *because* many boys greatly desire the acceptance, respect, and admiration that comes with success in sports; and *because* the temptations to violate rules are great that athletics are a superior tool for teaching social and democratic behaviors.

Certainly, almost everyone will *say* that he believes in democracy, honesty, fair play, and sportsmanship. However, the test of the sincerity and depth of one's beliefs comes during moments of stress such as occur in athletic contests. Does the player call a "hinder" on himself in handball only when he's well ahead or does he do so consistently even when it is a hard fought and close contest? Does he call a foul on himself when he reaches over or touches the net in volleyball? If he is ineligible to receive a pass but instinctively catches the ball when it comes to him, does he tell the official

A mighty effort! *(Courtesy: University of Connecticut)*

that he was ineligible? If the official asks him whether he was eligible does he say "No"? Does he lie and say "Yes"? Does he say "You're the official. You should know."? What does he say if it's a sandlot game? A game with a rival school? A championship game? A professional game? Is honesty to be practiced only when the stakes are low? Is honesty a virtue or an expediency? It is easy to talk about honesty. It is quite another thing to practice it when it might mean the difference between success or failure in achieving a much desired goal such as winning an athletic contest. What kind of morality and social conscience should the coach teach?

These are very real and poignant questions which must be answered many times during the season of every sport. They point out why it is even more important that the coach be highly principled and a man of great character, than that he be a brilliant strategist, a champion performer, or possess a brilliant mind. Perhaps the coach, more than any man in the community, can influence the moral values of the community!

Cooperation

It is becoming increasingly important that people learn to work together cooperatively and in harmony for the benefit of all. People must develop knowledges, understandings, and insights to recognize that when they contribute to the common good they contribute to their own welfare in the long run — even though it may appear for the moment that they are doing themselves harm. They must, in addition to developing these knowledges, understandings, and insights, develop the disposition to behave for the common good. This is necessary because as the economy, the methods of production, the modes of transportation and communication improve, people become increasingly interdependent. When life was simpler and men produced their own food, built their own homes, made their own clothing, and provided their own entertainment, each family was relatively self-sufficient. It was not as important as it now is that men be able to work together toward a common goal. Today each person performs a very specialized function. A man working on an automobile assembly line may put one bolt on each car as it moves past him on the conveyor belt. Very few men completely produce a product from beginning to end on their job.

Each person is dependent upon others. Other people make his clothing; build his home; grow, make, and bring him his food. Millions of other people are involved in producing his car, his electric razor, his furniture, and his power mower. When people do not work together harmoniously, the lives of people thousands of miles away are influenced. When labor and management in the steel industry fail to reach agreement or compromise a crippling strike follows and people cannot buy a new car. When the transportation workers in New York City go on strike, millions of people have difficulty in getting to work or to shop and businesses fail. When a husband and wife fail to agree and a divorce follows, the couple's children may suffer emotional scars which persist throughout a lifetime. When the people of North and South Vietnam are unable to work together cooperatively, thousands of American young men must leave their jobs, colleges, homes, and communities to perform military service.

Undoubtedly, the development of morality and a social conscience is one of the most important tasks facing education today. This task will assume increasing importance as society becomes increasingly complex and interdependent until its achievement becomes imperative. When physical education is concerned with the whole man and utilizes the emotionally charged situations (with which it is pregnant) as tools for social learnings, it will make a contribution to society worth much more than any which can be made by other subject areas.

The Present Status of Sportsmanlike Attitudes in Athletics

How successful have the schools and colleges been to date in developing sportsmanlike attitudes? J. W. Kistler,[8] Professor Emeritus of Louisiana State University, has reported the results of a study which indicates that considerably greater efforts must be expended if sportsmanlike behaviors are to be demonstrated in athletics, let alone in transferring these attitudes to other areas of living. Following are some of Dr. Kistler's findings from the group he studied:

"Mine's in the gold!" *(Courtesy: Maine Dept. of Economic Development)*

1. Twenty-three percent of college men; thirty-six percent of college women, and fourteen percent of adult men did not consider booing of visiting team basketball players as they attempt to make a free throw, a sign of poor sportsmanship.

2. Fifty percent of college men; thirty-three percent of adults; and fifteen percent of college women approve of the practice of deliberately taking advantage of a situation in sports leaving it up to the official to catch players in the rules violation.

3. Forty-three percent of college women felt that a player should not tell the official when, in the player's opinion, a mistake had been made by the official which was harmful to the opponent.

4. Seventy-three percent of the women polled indicated that a player has no responsibility to report to the official that she touched the net on a play in volleyball when apparently the official did not see the action.

5. Approximately thirty-three percent of the men approved of "faking" an injury to gain a few more seconds of playing time.

6. Sixty percent of the college men and forty-five percent of the male adults approved of deliberately breaking rules when it appeared that something could be "salvaged" out of a bad situation by so doing. (These people approved of a guard in basketball deliberately fouling when he finds himself outnumbered three to one by offensive players when he is bringing the ball down the floor.)

7. Thirty-three percent of the men approved of "putting the pressure" on basketball and baseball officials by booing and razzing them in order to get them to make close calls in favor of the home team.

8. Seventy-five percent of college men; fifty percent of college women; and sixty-seven percent of adult males approve of tactics such as stalling which are designed to upset an opponent by making him nervous.

9. Sixty-one percent of the women taking part in this study did not think it evidence of a lack of loyalty if alumni watching a football game in which their team was being beaten by a large score should leave the game during the third quarter.

10. The study showed that college men and adult males who had "varsity" athletic experience had a poorer attitude about sportsmanship than those who had not participated in varsity athletics.

Dr. Kistler concluded that more emphasis must be placed upon a positive and planned approach to education in sportsmanship. He suggested that the "spirit" as well as the letter of the rules be taught and that students be taught that the game becomes a more interesting and thrilling contest when the opponent is at his best.

A Hartford, Connecticut, sportswriter quotes a pitcher's comments regarding his use of the illegal "spitball": "Why shouldn't I use the spitter? I was about through [age] when I decided to get me the pitch. If I get caught, they'd kick me out of baseball. If I don't, I'm through anyway, so how can I lose?"[9]

What effect do statements such as this have upon the moral values of the children who idolize this athletic hero? Does not this player have a responsibility to the community in addition to that of winning games? Business people who, as does the baseball pitcher, depend upon public recognition and acceptance, feel it their obligation to contribute to the welfare of the community through substantial gifts to charitable causes. Is it no less an obligation of the athletic hero to try to elevate standards of sportsmanship by exemplary behavior?

Values Held by Society and Sports

Play, games, sports, and athletics reflect the values of society and in turn influence the values of society. Bruce L. Melvin, professor of sociology at the University of Maryland, writes: "A value, as here defined objectively, is an act or accomplishment or the espousal of a belief by an individual or a group, any or all of which bring prestige, status, or reward from the society. To win at a game in baseball or football is a value in American society. To attain success financially or in the military carries values. Recognition by the society is symbolized in the movies by an 'Oscar,' a statue for a statesman, the presidency for a military man, or a high salary for a 'Babe Ruth.' Play in our society mirrors values of a people; the values of a people can be judged through this channel."[10]

As educators, we should be more concerned with *how play and sports can influence the values of our society* than with the mere fact that *they do reflect the values of society.* Mr. Melvin presented some clues as to how play and athletics can be utilized as a modality for influencing the values of society. Sportsmanlike behavior can be recognized by including an evaluation of this quality in the grading plans in physical education classes, by awarding medals or trophies to players and teams who demonstrate sportsmanship, and by publicly commending demonstrations of this quality in our writings and speeches. Physical educators, and coaches in particular, have a great deal more influence upon people than they commonly suppose.

Implementation of the Teaching of Social Behaviors

Physical educators could adopt an idea of Dr. Hartley Price of Florida State University, who directs the "Gymkana Troupe," an exhibition gymnastic group. At the Annual Home Show he presents the "Best Trouper Award" to the member of the troupe who has demonstrated throughout the school year the most sportsmanlike behavior by coaching, spotting, and helping other members of the troupe.

Baley[11] described a self-rating scale which is designed to make students aware of specific items of desirable social behavior which may or may not be manifested in an apparatus or tumbling class. Students are asked, at the end of the semester, to rate themselves on a zero to five-point basis on each of the items listed. The instructor then reviews this self-rating. Scores are revised upward as often as they are downward. It is extremely difficult for anyone to view himself objectively. Some of the items cannot be rated by the instructor. Only the student knows the true answer. The author used as a guide in the construction of this self-rating plan the NEA's statement of the objectives of a general education. A similar form could be constructed for any activity. A copy of this form can be found in the appendix. Use of this form, obviously, will not alone change students' social behaviors. This must be an all-out campaign.

Development of the following dispositions, attitudes, or points of view in the students and the community will help in accomplishing the goal of improved social behavior:

1. One of the major objectives in all games is to provide pleasure, enjoyment, and fun for the participants and the spectators. Hating one's opponent does not add to the amount of pleasure experienced nor does it add to one's effectiveness. Anger, in fact, detracts from both pleasure and effectiveness.

2. Another objective of all games is to find which participant or team is superior. The individuals or teams which violate or circumvent the rules have not proved they are superior even if they do win the contest.

3. Rules are designed to insure equality for all participants. In the final analysis, rules are made by the players and the coaches. It is foolish for players or the coach to complain about them during the contest.

4. Officials constantly study and discuss the rules. They are usually in the best possible position to see the play. They are nearer to the action than is any spectator or player on the bench. They are more impartial than any spectator or player. If they were partial, coaches would rate them low on the rating sheets usually used and the official would be unable to secure employment. It is a sign of immaturity to complain about officials' decisions. Complaining almost never causes an official to reverse his decision. "Booing" decisions may sometimes, even with an experienced official, result in upsetting his emotional equilibrium so that some close decisions may be called incorrectly.

5. A person who really appreciates and understands a sport will applaud excellent play by the opponents as readily as he will excellent play by the home team. The members of the visiting team are guests and as such they should be treated courteously and considerately. If they had not traveled to the home community, the enjoyable afternoon or evening playing or watching the game would not have been possible. It is the custom to thank a couple for an evening of competition in bridge or a friend for a handball game or tennis match. Why not thank a team for an interesting game!

6. Visiting teams should be made to feel at home by being met at the railroad station, airport, or college entrance by the team captain, manager, the lettermen's club, or a welcoming committee. They should be escorted to their rooms or the locker room, assigned towels and lockers, and their questions should be answered.

A technique for influencing the social behaviors of participants in the intramural program has been described by Baley[1][2] in *The Physical Educator*. A description of this technique is presented in the appendix.

It was the consensus among those involved in the program that the behaviors of the participants in this intramural program improved as a result of an increased awareness of social behavior and that this added to the enjoyment experienced.

Intramural handbooks can be utilized to draw the attention of students to sportsmanlike behavior and to interpret for them the specifics of sportsmanlike behavior. An illustration of this procedure is provided in the appendix.

Physical Education's Contributions to Individual Qualities Needed in a Democracy

It has been stated that democracy requires people who possess a spirit of peace and orderliness. An implication of this statement for the conduct of physical education and athletic programs is that the cooperative aspects of sports and games be emphasized as much as the competitive aspects. The satisfactions of working together cooperatively toward a common goal should be highlighted. It should be repeatedly pointed out that opponents in games and contests have made possible an interesting and enjoyable afternoon or evening. It is as foolish to "hate" opponents in basketball or football, or in any other game, as it would be to "hate" opponents in bridge or checkers. Coaches must stop making student players feel they are "supermen" when they win and absolutely worthless when they lose.

It has been said that democracy requires people who possess energy, resourcefulness, and creativity. A life of physical activity will make people more energetic. Resourcefulness and creativity can be developed through physical education and athletics if physical educators and coaches permit students to participate in the planning of conditioning programs and game strategies, in the designing of plays, in the selection of activities, and in as many different ways as possible. A democratic attitude on the part of the leader is most important. He should not utilize the students in his charge as avenues to his own ego satisfaction. He must constantly remind himself that skill in sports, physical fitness, and a favorable win-loss record are not the ultimate objectives of his program but are merely means to an end. That end is a happy, integrated, socially useful personality.

Democracy requires people who possess a high enough level of health that they will be enabled to work productively and play with enjoyment not only during their youth and middle years but also beyond middle age and into senescence. It is necessary that people be introduced to the activities which will give them enjoyment during their adult years while they are still students. It is much easier to pick up old interests when one is older than it is to initiate new ones. Teen-age boys enjoy tackle football and wrestling. These sports satisfy their current needs for the kinds of activities which give them an opportunity to develop physical courage and to prove their manhood. When they are thirty, forty, or fifty years old, they probably not only will not possess the physical strength and stamina to participate in these sports but would not enjoy them if they did. Consequently, during their high school years they must learn some of the individual and dual sports from which they will derive enjoyment during the last three-fourths of their lives.

Democracy requires people who have respect for the personality and rights of others. One implication of this statement for physical education and athletics is that students must be taught to feel empathy for those less skilled than they. They must be brought to the realization that each person is unique and that while he may be inferior in some qualities, he may be superior in others. They also need to be taught respect for people of all races, colors, creeds, social, or economic position.

Character

Character has been defined by Dewey as the "interpenetration of habits."[13] Habits are learned behaviors, attitudes, and emotional states. Interpenetration

The forearm should be horizontal *(Courtesy: University of Connecticut)*

means integration or interrelatedness. Various learnings become integrated or interrelated to produce manners of thinking, attitudes, emotional states, and behaviors which become typical for that person. These learnings, of course, come from many sources — the home, the neighborhood, the play groups, the community secondary groups, and the school. Unfortunately, some of the individuals, such as parents, and some of the groups which provide these learnings for the child are not concerned with the total social good. Parents, for example, may be primarily concerned with helping the child to achieve material success. Some groups which are supposed to be concerned with character education have often relied upon exhortation and preachments rather than upon learning by doing. Coaches and physical educators are in a favorable position to beneficially influence the development of character.

Application of the Laws of Learning

Learnings in character are subject to the same laws of learning as are learnings in other areas. The educator must *begin at the level of the student's comprehension.* If a student can do a neck spring, he should be challenged with a head spring. He need not be taught a forward roll! However, if a student has never tumbled before, he should first be taught a forward roll. He is taught mathematics before he is taught trigonometry, and plane geometry before he is taught solid geometry. The same is true of teaching social behavior. The range in ability to learn social behaviors is probably just as great as it is in ability to learn motor skills and in academic areas.

The more vivid an experience, the greater the learning. This law gives sports an advantage in serving as a modality for teaching social behaviors or character learnings because few experiences in education are as vivid as those experienced in the highly emotionalized situations common in sports. Obviously, *the laws of use, disuse, and recency* apply to character learnings as they do to other learnings. Knowledge and habits which are used become reinforced. The physical educator and the coach need to constantly encourage students to practice good sportsmanship.

The teacher must be aware of children's often limited understanding of the meaning of words. When teachers are endeavoring to teach various qualities of sportsmanship such as "teamwork," they must keep in mind that the meaning of the word is limited and unclear to a child. Consequently, the teacher must gradually enlarge the child's understanding of the word. An illustration of this process can be provided from the game of soccer. A boy may constantly endeavor to dribble the ball to the opposing team's goal in the hope of shooting a goal and consequently lose the ball to the opponents. The teacher tells him that it is not good "teamwork" to keep the ball but that he should pass the ball to a teammate. To the child "teamwork" now means "pass the ball." The next time he passes to a good friend who is covered by an opponent. The opponent gets the ball. The teacher then tells him that he should not pass to his friends if they are "covered" as this is not good teamwork but that he should pass to a teammate who is not "covered." The next time he has the ball, all his teammates are covered but he does not want to be accused of not practicing "teamwork" so he passes the ball even though he has a clear field ahead. The teacher tells him that there are times when the highest form of teamwork requires that a player keep the ball. Throughout this process the boy has developed an increasingly complete picture of the concept "teamwork" as it relates to soccer.

The teacher should create in the child a desire to be regarded as a good teamworker by commending or rewarding him for displays of teamwork. He should also endeavor to bring the child to react habitually in the desired manner. Finally, the teacher should endeavor to point out to the child the wider applications of teamwork and how it applies to family, community, work, and international relations.

Similar processes would be followed in teaching other character qualities such as integrity, initiative, thoroughness, dependability, loyalty, perseverance, courage (moral and physical), poise, self-sacrifice, modesty, consideration for others, resourcefulness, and honesty.

Evaluation of Sportsmanship

If the instructor includes development of these qualities in his statement of objectives of his course, he must make some effort to evaluate the degree to which the student has achieved them. While it is true that these qualities are extremely difficult to evaluate objectively, this is no reason for failing to make the effort. Their importance to an effective democratic society demands that every possible effort be made to achieve them. The instructor can utilize the evaluative device previously described. He can ask students to rate one another as to the degree to which they possess the various qualities being evaluated. He can keep a cumulative record in which he briefly cites examples of good or poor sportsmanship demonstrated by the student. He can place plus or minus signs in the roll book after the student's name whenever he observes the student demonstrate good or poor sportsmanship. However, the positive rather than the negative aspects of character should be emphasized. Performance is more appealing to youth than is restraint. Students should *help to decide* what acts constitute socially desirable behaviors. *All* the people in a democracy determine what is socially desirable behavior. *All* the people contribute to the formulation of rules, regulations, and laws. Rules, regulations, and laws free man. Without them there would be autocracy — rule by the strongest, most cunning, most selfish, and least moral. In sports, it is really the players who make the rules. When there is need for a new rule, modification of an existing rule, or discontinuance of an old rule, the players are usually the first to feel this need. They express their wishes to the coach or instructor, who makes known their wishes at the rules committee meetings. There the ideas are discussed and often a new rule is made or an old rule is modified or discontinued.

In Chapter 12 the interdependence of all the body cells was pointed out. The skeletal, muscular, nervous, circulatory, respiratory, digestive, and glandular systems are all dependent upon one another. All are needed. So it is with the individuals who together make up a society. When life began with a simple cell, the cell was independent of others. However, as cells combined and took on specialized functions they lost their independence but gained much more in security, survival, and efficiency. It is the same with society. As society becomes more complex, a measure of individual independence is lost but the individual gains in security, survival probabilities, comfort, and in leisure time. Physical education must emphasize the cooperative aspects of athletics as much as (or even more than) it does the competitive aspects.

Man is a psycho-physical-social entity. He begins life with predispositions to certain types of behavior determined by his genetic background. However, as he interacts with his physical environment, and particularly with his social environment, he is modified and changed or socialized. Physical educators play an important role in the socialization of the child in that they can direct and control his social environment in such manners that the child will become better adapted to life in a democratic society. The accomplishment of this task requires an understanding of the role of physical education in society, an understanding of society itself, and an understanding of man himself as a biologic and psychologic entity.

SUMMARY

When the baby is born, he is completely individualistic but the processes of socializing him begins immediately. Through the process known as conditioned response, he comes to value his mother's smile, caress, and cooing words. He learns to hold in abeyance, to modify, or substitute for certain fundamental drives because he seeks approval and the rewards that come with conformity and also to avoid the censure and punishment which result from failure to conform to the procedures and values of social groups of which he is a member. It is through contacts and interaction with others that he learns to smile, coo, talk, crawl, walk, write, love, standards of cleanliness, eating procedures, food preferences, emotional reactions, and almost everything he does and feels. The family and the school play the most important role in this process of socialization.

In the previous chapter, we quoted Norman Munn when he invited us to imagine how a person would act if a drug were invented which would wipe out all traces of everything that had been learned. Man would not know how to satisfy his most basic needs. He would not know, for example, what to eat, where to find food, where to sleep, or how to communicate. Almost everything an individual does, he has learned from someone else. This learning is socialization and it helps the individual to become a "human" — an acceptable member of society.

It is almost certain that society, through its various structures such as the family, communities, educational institutions, religious institutions, and political forms, and through its various communicative media, could develop people with ethical character — people who are tolerant, democratic, unselfish, honest, energetic, resourceful, creative, cooperative, practice good sportsmanship, possess a spirit of peace and orderliness, and who respect the rights and personalities of others. While physical education is only one aspect of one institution (the schools) of many institutions which influence the individual in this area, it can exert an influence, even though it may be relatively small, upon this important aspect of human behavior. Physical educators have an obligation to society to do as much as they can for the development of ethical character.

Suggestions have been made for facilitating social-emotional adjustment, aiding students to achieve self-realization, eliminating or reducing aggressive drives, developing democratic attitudes, values, and skills, and developing ethical character through athletics and physical education. While the processes for developing these qualities in people are still somewhat nebulous due to the need for more research in this area (and because research in this area is difficult), this is not sufficient reason for failure to make efforts in this direction. The development of ethical character is potentially a most important contribution of physical education.

QUESTIONS AND EXERCISES

1. How do parents affect socialization of a child?

2. How do elementary school teachers affect the socialization of a child?

3. How do physical education teachers and coaches affect the socialization of students?

4. According to Warren Fraleigh, why are adolescent boys with a high level of athletic skill more likely to rank higher in social adjustment than those with a low level of athletic skill?

5. How can physical educators facilitate social adjustment in adolescent

boys through helping them to experience as much success in athletics as possible?

6. Write up evidences from your own adolescent period of adjustments made between your adolescent needs and the requirements of other individuals or social groups (challenging of adult authority, reassuring yourself of your status with your peer group, and/or maturity and independence).

7. How can a physical educator use the ambivalence of aggressive drives to maintain class discipline?

8. Since frustration produces aggression and aggression reduces the effectiveness of the teaching-learning process, what can the physical educator do to reduce the level of frustration?

9. If the physical educator cannot reduce the level of frustration of a student or students, what else can he do to reduce aggressive drives?

10. What are the basic differences between a democratic and socialistic form of government? A totalitarian form of government?

11. Discuss the individual qualities required of people in a democracy and indicate how physical education can contribute to the development of these qualities.

12. Practices in sports reflect the values held by society but sports also influence the values of society. What can physical educators and athletic coaches do to influence society's values?

13. What are the implications of the laws of learning for the development of qualities of character?

14. Present some methods for evaluating social behaviors in physical education classes.

FOOTNOTES

1. Whitman, Walt, *Leaves of Grass.* New York: Doubleday, Doran, and Company, Inc., 1924.

2. Murphy, Lois Barclay, "Social Factors in Child Development," from *Readings in Social Psychology* by Theodore M. Newcomb, Eugene L. Hartley, and others. New York: Henry Holt, 1947.

3. Fraleigh, Warren P., "The Influence of Play upon Social and Emotional Adjustment, with Implications for Physical Education," *59th Annual Proceedings of the College Physical Education Association.* Washington, D.C.: AAHPER, 1956.

4. Murphy, *op. cit.*, p. 136.

5. Maslow, A. H., "Deprivation, Threat, and Frustration,"from *Readings in Social Psychology* by Theodore M. Newcomb, Eugene L. Hartley, and others. New York: Henry Holt, 1957.

6. Barker, Roger G., Tamera Dembo, Kurt Lewin, and M. Erik Wright, "Experimental Studies of Frustration in Young Children," from *Readings in Social Psychology* by Theodore M. Newcomb, Eugene L. Hartley, and others. New York: Henry Holt, 1957.

7. Nash, Jay B., Ph.D., *Physical Education: Interpretations and Objectives.* New York: A. S. Barnes, 1948.

8. Kistler, J. W., "Attitudes Expressed About Behavior Demonstrated in Certain Specific Situations Occurring in Sports," *60th Annual Proceedings of the College Physical Education Association.* Washington, D.C.: AAHPER, 1957.

9. Cassano, Joe, "In This Corner," *Hartford Times,* March 4, 1966.

10. Melvin, Bruce L., "Play, Recreation, and Leisure Time," *64th Annual Proceedings of the College Physical Education Association.* Washington, D.C.: AAHPER, 1960.

11. Baley, James A., "Practical Sportsmanship – A Unique Contribution of Physical Education and Athletics," *Physical Educator,* November, 1961.

12. , "An Intramural Sportsmanship Award," *Physical Educator,* December, 1965.

13. Dewey, John, *Human Nature and Conduct.* New York: Henry Holt, 1922.

Epilogue

THROUGH THE PAGES of this text, we have taken a look at physical education in a manner which should help those who are contemplating becoming a physical educator to reach a decision and which will give a preview of learnings, problems, and relationships which will be of concern throughout the lives of those who have reached a decision. It is, of course, impossible to develop a perfect understanding of a profession in one textbook. A tour through a campus can give a student only a limited idea as to whether or not he will enjoy attending that college. To know, he must live there. An introductory textbook serves somewhat the same purpose as does a tour.

First, we have looked at the edifice of physical education from the street to determine what it is and what it is trying to do. We have seen that it is a part of general education and has similar objectives and guiding principles. As a part of general education, its overall objective is to make contributions to personal and social effectiveness for life in a democracy. As in general education, principles have been established and generally accepted which serve as guides for the administration and teaching of physical education.

Next, we discussed the preparation of a physical educator for it is through the educational process that the physical educator becomes prepared to make efforts toward achieving the objectives of physical education according to established principles. The personal qualities desired in a physical educator have been discussed. The understandings, knowledges, skills, attitudes, and appreciations which should be in the possession of physical educators and which can be developed through the curriculum were presented. The competencies required by physical education teachers, health educators, athletic coaches, recreation education personnel, and athletic trainers were presented as they have been developed by the Professional Preparation Conference of the American Association for Health, Physical Education, and Recreation. Continuing professional growth through graduate education, professional organizations, research, writing, and attendance at conventions and clinics was also discussed.

363

Then we came into the building for a closer look at the physical educator at work in the gymnasium, on the playing field, in the natatorium, in his office, in the classroom, and in different settings such as in the several levels of public schools, in colleges and universities, in the YM and YWCA, the YM and YWHA, Boys' Clubs, in community recreation programs, industrial recreation programs, athletic clubs, in hospital recreation programs, summer camps, and in the armed services. Those of us in school physical education need to be reminded occasionally that physical education is conducted in many settings other than the schools and that sports is the most pervasive phenomenon on the social scene. This is attested to by the attention sports receive in the various publicity media, the salaries paid professional athletes, and the expenditures made on sports facilities, equipment, and attendance. We have looked at the diversity of duties of physical educators in teaching activities, coaching, directing intramural programs, in camping, dance, health education, adapted physical education, research, and administration of physical education and athletics.

In Chapter 5 we followed the physical educator out of his place of employment to his professional organizations and to some of the civic organizations with which he might participate.

In Part II we "looked through a telescope" at the distant and near past of physical education in order to develop an appreciation of the influences of geography, economy, climate, beliefs, values, industrialization, and scientific progress upon physical education. We have seen that, on the one hand, when survival is too difficult and demands all of man's time and energies, physical education does not prosper but that, on the other hand, when there is too much emphasis upon luxury, comfort, and enjoyment, physical education may become perverted, excessively commercialized, or sadistic. We have also seen that religious beliefs and beliefs concerning the nature of man may have either a detrimental or a beneficial effect upon physical education. Political movements, the development of transportation, electricity, the labor movement, the growth of cities, and television have influenced the nature of physical education.

In Part III we "rode in a helicopter" to get a broad look at physical education as it relates to the other activities of man, his institutions, and his values. We found this broad view through a study of philosophy.

Through a review of philosophy, we have been enabled to understand better the role of physical education in man's life and to understand how people's basic beliefs influence the administration, organization, and teaching of physical education. The student should develop an appreciation of the importance of developing a reasonably unified and consistent philosophy of his own (an eclectic philosophy) or of adopting those of an established philosophic school.

In Part IV we "looked at physical education through a microscope" to learn that its scientific bases rest upon the biologic, psychologic, and sociologic nature of man. The reading of these three chapters provides a preview of some of the courses the student majoring in physical education will take. In these areas he will likely take biology, zoology, physiology, anatomy, physiology of exercise, kinesiology, general psychology, educational psychology, and sociology. However, since most of these courses are taught by educators who have no background in physical education to students majoring in a diversity of areas, it is left up to the student to apply the learnings to his special field. Here we have drawn some of the implications for physical education, health, first aid, safety, and athletic coaching of specific facts from the three disciplines. An understanding of the anatomy of the cranial cavity should help the student to better understand the hazards of concussion. A discussion of the development of cardiovascular-respiratory endurance is more meaningful when it immediately follows or is tied in with a discussion of the anatomy and physiology of the cardiovascular-respiratory system. A discussion of emotions is more meaningful when it is part and parcel of a discussion of the nervous and endocrine systems.

Throughout this text, the unity of man, of physical education with health and recreation education, of these three areas with general education, and of education as a part of the total social scene has been stressed. Man cannot be split into separate parts. Physical education overlaps health and recreation education and shares many goals with them, as it does with general education. Education must serve the goals of the society of which it is a part. Each part has certain specialized functions but these facilitate accomplishment of the overall goals. An emphasis upon the unity and upon the commonality of objectives and goals will facilitate a greater degree of progress, it is felt, than will an emphasis upon the diversity and differences.

As a result of the tremendous increase in knowledge in all areas, it has become increasingly difficult to see and to understand the unity between different areas and in man also. Philosophy at one time encompassed all of the physical and social sciences but as man's knowledge increased, the separate disciplines of astronomy, chemistry, physics, medicine, dentistry, economics, psychology, sociology, and law were formed. Now, each of these has been further subdivided. In medicine, to mention only a few, we have pediatrics, surgery, geriatrics, eye, ear, nose and throat specialists, cardiologists. Further, medicine has those working in the paramedical services such as physical therapists, recreation therapists, X-ray technicians, and many others. The growth in knowledge has made specialization necessary, which makes it more difficult to maintain a unified point of view. Yet, it is important that the unified point of view be presented. In the undergraduate curriculum in physical education there are only two courses where this can be done — in the introductory or foundations course and in history and principles of physical education.

All learning proceeds from the general to the specific. If one were to learn about building space ships he would first see the general outline of the ship and then he would begin to learn the specifics of the construction of combustion chambers, instrument construction, communication systems, tubes, ingredients in the various metals used, and so forth. The process would take a long time and much study. So it is with physical education. This text has provided an over, under, side, and end view of physical education and has pointed out the road to be traveled by those who would become physical educators. Some samples of learnings as they apply to physical education have been presented to enable the reader to see what lies ahead and also to see the relevance of these learnings to physical education.

This trip will not always be easy — nor should it be if we believe that people become stronger as a result of adaptation to stress and if we believe that the role of physical education is important enough to require able and well qualified teachers of physical education. The space age makes as great demands for knowledge and intelligence as did primitive life for physical stamina and strength.

Now, at the conclusion of this course, is the time for the student to decide whether the problems to be solved, goals to be achieved, principles to be observed, and people to be served are challenging enough and worthy enough to warrant the dedicated efforts of his lifetime. The student should ask himself whether he can develop the maturity to identify with these problems and goals. We hope that he will because physical education needs able, energetic, selfless, and dedicated practitioners.

Appendix A

SELF-RATING OF SPORTSMANSHIP AND HEALTHMANSHIP (FOR APPARATUS I)

Health Habits: Score

    Showers   ———
    Dries Hair   ———
    Wears a clean and appropriate uniform   ———
    Always present   ———

Cooperation:

    Promptness – always on time   ———
    Coaches other class members   ———
    Offers to spot others   ———
    Assists in setting up and returning equipment   ———

Conservation:

    Handles equipment with care   ———

Tolerance:

    Appreciates abilities of those who are skilled and has empathy toward those who
    are unskilled (appreciation for individual differences)   ———

Courtesy:

    Observes the amenities of social behavior   ———

Personal Direction:

    Effort has been to the limit of strength and endurance   ———
    Has demonstrated self-confidence and courage   ———
    Has learned stunts in their progressive order   ———

Critical Judgment:

    Has had the courage to courteously discuss with the person in charge procedures
    which he sincerely feels could be improved upon   ———

367

TOTAL POINTS _____

NAME _____

COURSE, HOUR AND DAY _____

Note: Rate yourself as honestly as you are able, viewing your performance during the past semester objectively (as though you were someone else) on the following basis:

    5 pts. - always   2 pts. - seldom
    4 pts. - usually   1 pt. - almost never
    3 pts. - about half the time   0 pts. - never

This constructive self-analysis will help you to "know yourself" and in that way enable you to discover and to strengthen your weak areas to aid in character development.

Appendix B

THE PRIMARY PURPOSES of the University of Connecticut Intramural Sports program, as at colleges and universities throughout the country, are:

1. To provide for students opportunities for fun, enjoyment and fellowship through sports participation.
2. To give students opportunities to improve health and physical fitness status through participation in vigorous sports.
3. To provide students with opportunities to release tensions and feelings of aggression in socially acceptable manners; and to receive ego satisfaction and a feeling of achievement through sports participation in order to maintain mental and emotional health.

Medals, trophies, and all-sports points are awarded in order to provide incentive and motivation for greater effort, teamwork, fun, and satisfaction. They are symbols of excellence in these qualities. The awarding of these symbols is not the objective of this program. The great fun and satisfaction is in playing — not in receiving the symbols.

Participation in athletics is more enjoyable when players, coaches, and spectators conduct themselves in a spirit of good fellowship and good sportsmanship. For these reasons, the Intramural Council at the University of Connecticut has decided to:

1. Draw up a "Code of Sportsmanship."
2. Award a "Sportsmanship Trophy" to the Fraternity and Independent Living Unit demonstrating the highest quality of sportsmanship throughout each school year as determined by the scores given by the Intramural Representatives, Assistants, and the Supervisor of Intramurals.

CODE OF SPORTSMANSHIP

I. Conduct of Players:

A. Toward teammates:

  1. Demonstrate teamwork, cooperation, and subordination of the individual to the needs of the team by:

     a. avoiding criticism, sarcasm, and complaining.
     b. reporting to any and all practice sessions called.
     c. reporting on time for all contests.
     d. extending himself to the limits of his strength, endurance, and courage.

  2. Offer to coach and assist less skilled teammates and at the same time demonstrate respect for these players.

B. Toward opponents:

  1. Avoid making uncomplimentary remarks toward opponents and treat them with respect and consideration.
  2. Point out own rules violations while avoiding pointing out opponents' violations.
  3. Compliment skillful performance by opponents.
  4. Win without boasting and lose without excuses.

C. Toward officials:

  1. Never question officials' decisions which are of a judgment type. Example: In softball, was the pitch a strike or a ball? In volleyball, did the spiker touch the net?
  2. When the official misinterprets rules, avoid heckling or arguing with him but file a protest within twenty-four hours.
  3. Appreciate that the official is contributing his time, free of charge (in most cases), to do a needed but difficult and thankless job and that he is making every effort to be impartial.
  4. Realize that good officials never change a decision simply because players or spectators heckle or "pressure" them and that this kind of action will likely decrease the official's efficiency.

II. Conduct of Spectators:

A. Toward players:

  1. Avoid "razzing" or "riding" own or opponent players.
  2. Offer only constructive criticism.

B. Toward opponents:

  1. Demonstrate appreciation of excellent play by opponents as well as by own team.

2. Realize that "booing" is the weapon the coward uses when he cannot be identified as a result of being a member of a crowd.

C. Toward officials:

1. Never question officials' decisions which are of a judgment type. Examples: In softball, was the pitch a strike or a ball? In volleyball, did the spiker touch the net?
2. When the official misinterprets rules, avoid heckling or arguing with him.
3. Appreciate that the official is contributing his time, free of charge (in most cases), to do a needed but difficult and thankless job and that he is making every effort to be impartial.
4. Realize that good officials never change their decisions simply because players or spectators heckle or "pressure" them and that this kind of action will likely decrease the official's efficiency.

Good sportsmanship is simply a practical application of the Golden Rule to athletics. The practice of good sportsmanship makes greater — not lesser — demands upon strength, determination, and self-control. It is not the soft gentle way, but rather the "tougher" way because the good sportsman does not look for special favor or advantage but grants these to his opponent and then strives harder to win.

Appendix C

THE UNIVERSITY OF CONNECTICUT
SPORTSMANSHIP AWARD

The intramural program, as does the required physical education program and the intercollegiate or interscholastic athletic program, presents opportunities for utilizing sports as a tool to improve social behaviors. Admittedly, these qualities are very difficult to measure. This does not make them any less needed or less desirable. Beauty is difficult to measure but we know when it is or is not present; and we can secure a modicum of agreement as to the amount present. So it is with social behavior.

One of the first steps in a program to improve social behaviors should be to indicate specific instances of desirable and of undesirable social behaviors within the context of the particular activity or group of activities being studied. Obviously, no such list can completely cover all the possible situations which might arise. The list can be merely indicative – a starting point. People rating social behaviors can, and should, use many criteria. Furthermore, each rater should not, and likely will not, give each criterion the same weight.

House intramural representatives, intramural assistants, and the intramural supervisor will all see the social behaviors of members of the several houses from a different point of view. Therefore, a composite rating which would include the judgments of all three groups, it would seem, would have greater validity than a rating by only one of these three groups.

Recognition for Sportsmanlike Behavior

In order to focus students' attention upon sportsmanlike behavior and to motivate them to behave in a sportsmanlike manner, some sort of recognition should be given. Recognition can be given in many ways – through citation in publicity media, through the awarding of trophies, by recognition at a banquet, and in numerous other ways.

In the fall of 1960, the Intramural Department of the University of Connecticut instituted the Sportsmanship Award. This award is of the same size and status as is the coveted All-Sports Trophy. Winners are determined by means of the following procedures:

1. Intramural representatives, assistants, and the supervisor rank from first to fifth place the top five fraternities and the top five independent houses which, throughout the school year, had, in their opinion, demonstrated the greatest amount and quality of sportsmanship. Raters are told that they may utilize criteria which are not included in the "Code of Sportsmanship" or exclude some that are. It is believed that sportsmanship is a very complex and many-faceted quality which makes definition very difficult. However, if improvement is to be made, efforts to define this quality must be made. Obviously, the intramural representatives of fraternities rate only fraternities, while the representatives of independent houses rate only independent houses. Intramural assistants and the intramural supervisor rate both fraternities and independent houses. Each of these three groups see the house from a different point of view. The supervisor's contacts are principally with the intramural representatives in the office. The intramural assistants' contacts are with both the teams and the intramural representatives on the field and in the gymnasium. The intramural representatives' contacts are principally with the players in the game situations.

2. Ratings for all houses are tallied, and points awarded accordingly. Five points are given each time a house receives a first place rating, four points for the second place rating, three for third, two for fourth, and one for fifth. Points are then added to determine, in rank order, the first five choices of each of the three groups — the intramural representatives, the intramural assistants, and the supervisor.

3. Houses receiving a composite ranking of first place by intramural representatives receive ten points; second place, eight points; third place, six points; fourth place, four points; and fifth place, two points. Houses receiving a composite ranking from the four intramural assistants of first place receive five points; second place, four points; third place, three points; fourth place, two points; and fifth place, one point. The intramural supervisor's ranking brings five points to the team which he ranks first; four points to the team ranked second; three for third; two for fourth; and one for fifth. This technique weights the intramural representatives' evaluations at one-half of the total and the intramural assistants' and the supervisor's scores at one-fourth each of the total score.

4. The points earned through the rankings of the three groups of raters are then totaled to determine the final standings.

An example of this procedure follows: We will assume there are only five independent houses. From the representatives, Sherman House received two first place ratings (5 x 2 = 10 pts.), one second place (4 x 1 = 4pts.), one third place (3 x 1 = 3 pts.), and one fifth place rating (1 x 1 = 1 pt.). They had received, therefore, a total of 18 points. Trumbull House received one first place rating (5 x 1 = 5 pts.), two second place ratings (4 x 2 = 8 pts.), and two fifth place ratings (1 x 2 = 2 pts.). They therefore received a total of 15 points. Allen House received two first place ratings (5 x 2 = 10 pts.), two fourth place ratings (2 x 2 = 4 pts.), and two fifth place ratings (1 x 2 = 2 pts.),for a total of 16 points. New London Hall received a total of two second place ratings (4 x 2 = 8 pts.), one third place rating (3 x 1 = 3 pts.), and two fourth place ratings (2 x 2 = 4 pts.), making a total of 15 points. Tolland Hall received two first place ratings (5 x 2 = 10 pts.), and three fifth place ratings (1 x 3 = 3 pts.), making a total of 13 points. The intramural representatives therefore ranked Sherman House first with 18 points, Allen House second with 16 points, New London Hall and Trumbull House tied for third with 15 points, and Tolland fifth with 13 points.

The same procedure was followed to ascertain the composite judgments of the intramural assistants. The three intramural assistants rated the independent houses in the following way:

Intramural Assistants' Initials:	A.J.B.	J.L.L.	S.W.S.
First (5 points)	Sherman	N. London	N. London
Second (4 points)	Tolland	Tolland	Sherman
Third (3 points)	N. London	Sherman	Tolland
Fourth (2 points)	Allen	Allen	Trumbull
Fifth (1 point)	Trumbull	Trumbull	Allen

The tally of points will show that the intramural assistants have placed New London first with 13 points, Sherman House second with 12 points, Tolland House third with 11 points, Allen House fourth with 5 points, and Trumbull House fifth with 4 points.

The intramural supervisor ranked the houses in the following way:

First:	New London Hall	5 points
Second:	Sherman House	4 points
Third:	Tolland House	3 points
Fourth:	Allen House	2 points
Fifth:	Trumbull House	1 point

The house ranked first through composite scores of the intramural representatives received 10 points; second received 8 points; third, 6 points; fourth, 4 points; and fifth, 2 points. Composite rankings of the intramural assistants brought 5 points for first place, 4 points for second, 3 points for third, 2 points for fourth, and 1 point for fifth place. Ratings by the intramural supervisor brought the same number of points.

Now the final step. This procedure can best be illustrated by the following chart:

House	Ratings of IM Representatives 1/2 of total	Ratings of IM Assistants 1/4 of total	Ratings of IM Supervisor 1/4 of total	Total Points	Rank
Sherman	1st - 10 pts.	2nd - 4 pts.	2nd - 4 pts.	18	1st
Allen	2nd - 8 pts.	3rd - 3 pts.	4th - 2 pts.	13	2nd
New London	3rd tie-5 pts.	4th - 2 pts.	1st - 5 pts.	12	3rd
Tolland	5th - 2 pts.	1st - 5 pts.	3rd - 3 pts.	10	4th
Trumbull	3rd tie-5 pts.	5th - 1 pt.	5th - 1 pt.	7	5th

Though this procedure is obviously more complicated than a simple vote by the intramural representatives, it does present the great advantages of a weighted score which includes the judgments of the intramural assistants and the intramural supervisor in addition to that of the representatives. All three see the behaviors of the teams and their representatives from a different point of view and in different circumstances.

Index

Achievement and recognition, 326–328

Acquired reflexes, 266

Activities taught in physical education classes, 67–69

Adaptability of man, 237

Adapted physical education, 74–75

Adler, Mortimer J., 132

Adolescent needs, 341–342

Adrenal cortex, 313

Adrenals, 312

Africanus, Scipio, 160

Aggressive drives:
  ambivalence of, 343–344
  frustration, effects of, 344
  substitution for, 344

Aging and activity, 298–300

Amateur Athletic Union, 109–110, 193

American Academy of Physical Education, 109

American Association for Health, Physical Education, and Recreation, 15, 25, 56, 57–58, 102–105
  aims, 56
  budget, 103–104
  divisions of, 56
  organization of, 104
  services, 57–58

American College of Sports Medicine, 108–109

American Red Cross, 112

American Water Ski Association, 128

Amoras, Colonel Francisco, 184

Anarchy-Totalitarianism, 347–348

Anaximander, 211

Anaximines, 207, 209

Anderson, William G., 191

Anheuser-Busch Brewing Company, 94

Anisotropic bands, 257

Aristotle, 223

Armed services physical training, 97–98

Arnold College, 195

Arterial circulation, 273–274

Athenian Greeks, 156–159

Athletic clubs, 94–95

Athletic Institute, 197

Athletic and Recreation Federation of College Women, 105–106

Autonomic nervous system, 266–267, 310

Back injuries, 249

Bacon, Francis, 176

Baerwold School of Social Work, 90

Baker, Newton D., 196

Barnard, Henry, 189

Bartley, S. H., 236

Basedow's Philanthropinum, 178–179

Beck, Dr. Charles, 189

Beecher, Catherine E., 190

Behourd, 168

Belonging, 324

Berkeley, George, 218

Bernos, Dame Juliana, 172

Blood pressure, 274–276

Booing, 319

Bosco, James, 297–298

Boston Sand Garden, 136

Bouvé School of Physical Education, 195

Boy and Girl Scouts of America, 113

Boyle, Robert H., 128
Boys' Clubs, 91−92
Brace, David K., 14
Branam, Dean George C., 52
Brownell, Clifford Lee, 4

Caestus, 163
Campbell, Walter, 105
Camping and outdoor education, 73
Campus Martius, 161
Capillaries, 277
Capillary bed, influence of muscular activity upon, 256
Cardiovascular system, 268−278
Carry-over sports, 27−28
Central nervous system, 264
Cerebellum, 264
Cerebrum, 265
Chadbourne, Paul A., 130
Character, 356−357
Characteristics of the fit person, 25
Chase Manhatten Bank, 133
China, 149−150
Chivalry, 167−168
Cholesterol, 125, 275
Chute, Eloise, 236
Circulatory system, effects of activity upon, 124
Circus Maximus, 162
Civic responsibility, physical education's contribution to, 11−12
Clawson, Marion, 29
Clinics, 58−59
Coaching, 70−72
Colosseum, 162
Comenius, John Amos, 176
Communications, 50
Community Recreational Service Programs, 92−93
Competencies, 39−42
Concomitant learnings, 17
Cooperation, 350−351
Coronary heart disease and physical activity, 124
Coubertin, Baron Pierre de, 184−185
Counter-Reformation, 174−175

Courses recommended for majors in physical education:
    academic courses, 45−46
    activity courses, 46
    for athletic coaches, 47
Cozens, F. W., 4
Craft guilds, 168
Cunningham, Glenn, 341
Cureton, Dr. Thomas K., 289

Dance, 73−74
Deep breathing exercises, 278
Definition of physical education, 4−6
Delta Psi Kappa, 111
Demiurge, 214
Democracy and diversity, 346−347
Democracy and physical education, 346−359
Democratic procedures, 320−321
Democritus, 208, 210
Dewey, John, 194, 218−219, 356
Dialectic method, 170
Didascaleum, 157
Diencephalon, 264
Differences:
    between males and females, 300−301
    between individuals, 301−302
Disciplinarian education, 177
Division of Girls' and Women's Sports, 72, 197
Doctoral degree, 61−62
Donnelly, Rich, 132

Early settlers, 188−189
Eckstein, Richard W., 125
Eclectic philosophy, 203
Economic efficiency, physical education's contributions to, 11
Economics, 51−52
Education, Purposes of in American Democracy, 6−13
Educational Policies Commission, 6
Egypt, 148−149
Eliot, Charles W., 49
Emotional catharsis, 26−27
Emotional needs, 25−26
Empedocles, 209

Encyclopedia of Sports Medicine, 108
Endocrine system, 311–314
Eolithic age, 146
Epiglottic cartilage, 280
Epistemology, 205
Erythrocytes (*see also* Red blood cells):
  formation of, 254
  influence of muscular activity upon, 256–257
Esthetics, 205
Ethics, 204
Existentialism, 206

Fait, Hollis, 24
Fellowship of Christian Athletes, 111
Feudalism, 166–167
Follen, Dr. Charles, 189
Ford, Henry, 193
Fraleigh, Warren, 339–340
Freedom, 323–324

Gallon, Arthur J., 276
Garfield, President James A., 127
General education, 48–50, 130–133
Gestalt psychology, 206, 235
Gonads, 314
Gracchus, Tiberius, 160
Grades in physical education, 20
Groen, J., 275
Guilds, 168–169
Gulick, Dr. Luther H., 195
Gymkana, 353
Gymnasia, 157

Harper, William Rainey, 49
Hartwell, Dr. Edward M., 191
Heart:
  chambers, 271
  effects of muscular activity upon, 256
  murmers, 271–272
  muscle fibers, 273
  rate, 270–271
  valves, 271
Hemenway, Mary, 191

Hemoglobin, 282
Heraclitus, 208, 211
Hirschland, Ruth, 197
Hitchcock, Dr. Edward, 190, 191
Homans, Amy Morris, 191
Homer, 153
Homeric Greeks, 154–155
Hopi Indians, 319
Human relationships, 7, 9–11
Humanities, 52–53
Hume, David, 218
Huxley, H. E., 259

Idealism, 213–218
Ikada, Namiko, 296
Iliad, 154
India, 150–151
Individual humanism, 171
Inductive method, 176
Industrial recreational programs, 93–94
Intellectual development, 27
Intelligence quotient, 316
Intercollegiate athletics, contributions of, 302–303
International Council on Health, Physical Education, and Recreation, 106–107
Interscholastic athletics and physical education, 21
Interscholastic sports, numbers of participants, 120–121
Intramural programs, 69–70
Islets of Langerhans, 311
Isotropic bands, 257

Jackson, C. O., 28
Jackson's Mill National Conference, 39
Jahn, Frederick Ludwig, 179–180
James, William, 219
Jesuit schools, 175
Jewish Community Centers, 90–91
Johnson, M., 123
Johnson, President Lyndon B., 198
Judd, Leslie, 190

Karpovich, Peter, 283
Kelliher, M. S., 296

Kennedy, President John F., 197
Kistler, J. W., 351
Kraus, Dr. Hans, 197
Kraus-Weber Test, 296–297

Laboratory experiences, 42
Las Vegas, 136
Latin grammar schools, 174
Latium, 159
Learning process, 328–332
    conditioned learning, 329–330
    laws of learning, 357–358
    length of learning periods, 330
Lee, Joseph, 111, 126
Lerner, Max, 111
Lewis, Dio, 190
Ling, Per Henrik, 182
Locke, John, 177, 218
Logic, 205
Loyola, Ignatius de, 174
Luther, Martin, 173
Lyne, Russell, 129

MacCarthy, Dr. Shane, 198
Mann, B. V., 123
Mann, Horace, 189
Manorialism, 167
Maslow, A. H., 345
Master's degree, 60–61
Mayer, Jean, 122
McCurdy, James H., 196
McGrath, Earl J., 131
Melee, 168
Melvin, Bruce L., 353
Merchant guilds, 168
Metaphysics, 204
Michael, Ernest D., 276
Miller, Augustus T., 257
Milton, John, 175
Misconceptions about physical edu-
    cation, 17–22
Monasticism, 166
Montaigne, Michel de, 175–176
Montoye, Henry, 275
Moralism, 172–174
Morehouse, Lawrence E., 257
Morrill Land Grant Act, 189
Morris, Dr. J. N., 275
Morris, N. N., 124
Moses, Robert, 134

Motor fitness, 23–24
Motor skills, development of, 28
Motor unit, 259
Mulcaster, Richard, 176
Munn, Norman L., 331
Murphy, Lois, 342
Muscle fiber, 257
    contraction, types of, 262
    endurance, 259–260
    fatigue, 262–263
    grading mechanism, 267–268
    physical properties of, 261–262
    qualities, 262
    tissue, influence of activity up-
        on, 257
Myasnikov, A. L., 275

Nachtegall, Franz, 182–183
Naismith, Dr. James A., 192
Nash, Dr. Jay B., 4, 196, 348
Nationalism, 179–185
    in Denmark, 182–183
    in France, 183–185
    in Germany, 179–181
    in Sweden, 181–182
National Association for Physical
    Education of College Women,
    107-108
National Association of Basketball
    Players, 192
National Association of Intercol-
    legiate Athletics, 110–111
National College Physical Educa-
    tion Association for Men,
    107–108
National Collegiate Athletic Associ-
    ation, 81, 110, 193
National Council for Accreditation
    of Teacher Education, 197
National Education Association,
    101–102
National Education Association Re-
    search Bulletin, 58
National Federation of High School
    Athletics, 111
National Federation of State High
    School Athletic Associations,
    120
National Girls' Athletic Associa-
    tion, 105

National Parks, 29
National Parks and Recreation, 111
National Parks and Recreation Association, 111–112
National Recreation Association, 197
National Trainers Association, 111
Naturalism, 177–179
Nazi Party, 181
Neilson, Dr. Niels P., 196
Nervous system, 263–268
  and learning, 308–310
Neumeyer, Martin, 134
New experiences, 324–326
North American Gymnastic Union, 195

Oberteuffer, Delbert, 13
Objectives of physical education, 22–28
Objectives of professional preparation, 53–55
Octavian (Augustus), 160
Odysseus, 154
Olympic records, 238–240
Organic fitness, 23
Ovaries, 314
Oxygen deprivation, 266

Palaestra, 157
Paleolithic age, 146
Panhellenic games, 157–158
Parathyroids, 311
Parish schools, 174
Parmenides, 211
Pelvic girdle, 251–253
Persia, 151–152
Personal qualities desired, 37–38
Personality, organic bases of, 307–308
Phi Epsilon Kappa, 111
Phillips 66, 94
Philosophy, major concerns of, 206–213
Physical education environments:
  administration of athletics and physical education, 83–84
  colleges and universities, 80–82
  elementary schools, 76–77

Physical education environments: *(Cont.)*
  graduate teaching, 83
  junior high schools, 77–78
  senior high schools, 78–80
  teacher education, 82–83
Physical Educator, The, 355
Physical fitness, 22–24, 289–298
  of American children, 296–298
  definition of, 289–294
  why it is important, 294–296
Physical sciences, 52
Pilaga Indians, 319–320
Pineal glands, 311
Piper, Ralph, 190
Pituitary, 314
Platform (of AAHPER) for Physical Education, 15–17
Plato, 213
Political science, 51
Politics, 204
Pope Pius II (Picolomini), 171
Posse, Baron Nils, 191
Posse School of Physical Education, 195
Pragmatism, 218–223
President's Fitness Council, 30
Price, Dr. Hartley, 190, 353
Principles of physical education, 13–14
Problem solving, 221
Professional education:
  general, 43–44
  general objectives of, 41–42
  health education, 44–45
  specialized, 44
Professional organizations, 55–58
Professional Preparation Conference, 40
Progressive movement, 194
Protagoras, 208
Protestant moralism, 173
Psychologic needs, 321–328
Publishing, 59–60

Quintain, 167–168

Rabelais, François, 175
Raybestos Brake Lining Company, 94

Realism, 223–228
Red blood cells (*see also* Erythrocytes):
  formation of, 254
  influence of muscular activity upon, 256–257
Reflex arc, 265–266
Religious guilds, 168
Republic, The, 215
Research, 59, 75
Respiratory system, 279–284
  effects of exercise upon, 257, 283–284
  rate, 283
Rochelle, R. H., 275
Romans, 159–163
Romeo, Paul, 190
Roosevelt, Theodore, 100
Rousseau, Jacques, 178

Sargent, Dr. Dudley A., 191
Sargent School of Physical Education, 195
Savage School of Physical Education, 195
Scholasticism, 170
Self-acceptance, 321–323
Self-expression, 26
Self-realization, 6, 7–9, 341
Selya, Dr. Hans, 312
Sense realists, 176–177
Skeletal system, 241–254
Skull and concussion, 245–248
Social fitness, 27
Social humanism, 171–172
Social realism, 175–176
Social science, 50–51
Socialization, 338–341
Socratic method, 216–217
Sophists, 207
Spartan Greeks, 155–156
Spiess, Adolph, 180–181
Spinal cord, 265
Sports Illustrated, 133
Sportsmanship, 351–353
  evaluation of, 358
Strength:
  and age, 261
  development of, 260–261

Student teaching experiences, 47–48
Summer camps, 95–97

Taylor, Henry L., 124
Teacher vs. student values, 341
Teaching efficiency, suggestions for improving, 330–332
Thales, 207
Theobald, Robert, 50
Theodosius, Emperor, 166
Thermae, 163
Thompson, C. W., 123
Thorax, 251
Threshold stimuli, 259
Thymus, 311
Thyroid, 311–312
Transfer of learning, 331
Turnvereins, 189–190

Undergraduate preparation, 38–48

Values in physical education, 14–15
Van Dalen, Deobold B., 131
Vasomotor nerves, 274
Venous circulation, 255–256, 277, 278
  effect of muscular activity upon venous return, 255–256
  venous return, 278
Verbal realism, 175
Vernier, Elmon Louis, 4
Vertebral column, 248
Vital capacity, 281–282
Vives, Juan Luis, 175

Weight control, 122–124
Welser, Lyle, 190
Wettstone, Gene, 190
White, Dr. Paul Dudley, 126
Whitman, Walt, 337
Wilkinson, "Bud," 198
Williams, George, 193
Williams, Jesse F., 14
Wilson, Woodrow, 130

Wolf, Dr. Stewart, 236
Wood, Dr. Thomas D., 133, 195
World Confederation of Organizations of the Teaching Profession, 106

Xenophanes, 209

Young, Kimball, 316
Young Men's and Young Women's Christian Associations, 87–90, 113
Young Men's and Young Women's Hebrew Associations, 90–91

Zakerzewska, Dr. Maria, 193